The story of a top achiever who went from misfortune to multimillionaire while enjoying a high standard of living, the lifestyle of the rich and famous, which you too can enjoy in bad times or good times.

The financial and lifestyle book should be mandatory reading for those who wish to be successful in life and for many Canadians and Americans and others throughout the world, it is the only book they need to read.

Every week there is a new book published on how to manage money, how to be successful, how to enjoy life, travel and have a happy retirement with stories about noted individuals. This book is written by a person who has been there and done that.

This book is humorous, entertaining and is described in short form all the information one needs to be successful, rich, and enjoy a standard of living beyond belief.

It also tells you how to start from scratch, save and invest money to achieve the greatest financial rewards in ones life and getting the most, "bang for your buck" while allowing one complete independence, financially and otherwise through the life of Mattie McFinsky.

Misfortune to Millionaire

Marton Murphy

Library of Congress Control Number:		2012918828
ISBN:	Hardcover	978-1-4797-2980-7
	Softcover	978-1-4797-2979-1
	Ebook	978-1-4797-2981-4

This book was printed in the United States of America.

To order additional copies of this book, contact:
Xlibris Corporation
1-888-795-4274
www.Xlibris.com
Orders@Xlibris.com
119991

PREFACE

The best tips on how to be successful must be conveyed by someone who has succeeded beyond belief.

It is the intent of the author to write a book that is humorous, easy to understand and yet maintain one's interest throughout.

This is the first book in the world to be written about a self made entrepreneur, inventor, sportsman, builder, **traveler**, and philanthropist who was involved in many various work places in the early years gaining experience in business, politics, community, church and charitable endeavors.

Through the fictional life of Mattie McFinsky you will learn all you need to do to be successful in business while developing lifetime friendships that enable you to succeed and enjoy life.

Wishing you all the best in the future in whatever path you choose to be successful.

Marton Murphy

J.A.S. Bayer and Family in Model A Ford Car, Charlottetown Camera Club

Montague Hearse

Bill Nelson with horse and jaunting sleigh

Threshing at Tyron
Millie Gamble Fonds

School Busses at Macdonald Consolidated School, Mt. Herbert, 1910

Road Making in O'Leary
Jack Turner Fonds

Lifting Hay with Rope and Pulley

Ben Clow's Store

Early 20th Century Island Road

Digging Potatoes c. 1910

Cheese Factory

CHAPTER 1

Mattie McFinsky was the son of a Jewish father and an Irish mother. Two of the most persecuted races in the world. He was born in 1935, on a farm in Queen Charlotte Island in Eastern Canada.

For the first five years, which was the Depression, Mattie did not recollect too much of what went on; otherwise, it was a good household to be raised in. He swam in the brook when he was only five, which resulted in pneumonia.

He did not go to school until he was seven years old. He started out in grade 1 for a few months with a teacher called Mrs. Cameron, rapidly progressing into grade 2 as he had studied, or what is now called homeschooled, for the two years he was sick. He then progressed into grade 2, and within the year, he was in grade 3.

It was a ten-room school, two miles from the farm, with forty-four pupils and one teacher in ten grades. It was an interesting experience in the school as a brook flowed through the school property in the spring when the runoff was high. The students, particularly the boys, would jump across the small creek that passed through.

A chap called Jim Stoward, who was a couple of years older, was taunted to jump back and forth as was Mattie. Both waited, considering their chances of making it across the fast-flowing water, and at the same time they both decided to jump, meeting in the middle of the stream, and they both submerged in the water. They then had to sit by the potbellied stove until they dried out.

Times during the war were difficult as you had to have food stamps to buy gas, butter, sugar, etc. But on Queen Charlotte Island, there were lots of blueberries along the road, strawberries in the fields that were not being cultivated, raspberries in the woods, and cranberries so that there were lots of berries.

There were chickens, ducks, and various poultry, as well as pigs and cattle, so there was always lots of fresh meat. And being surrounded by water, there were a dozen different types of fish, so there was always a lot to eat. Unlike other parts of Canada, on the island there was a lot of wood, so there was a lot of fuel.

Since you could use horses for transportation and the horses would eat the food that was growing on the farm, and in the summer the horses could be raced as a form of entertainment.

Mattie's parents, Dan and Lena McFinsky, were excellent farmers and always had a hired man to help out with the farm chores, and Mattie's mother was an excellent cook, so there were always excellent meals.

It was normal to walk to and from school in the spring and fall, except for the month's holiday, to pick potatoes, which were the main source of income for the farmers on Queen Charlotte Island.

During the winter, Mattie and his brother James usually took a horse for the two miles to the schoolhouse. They stabled the horse at their cousin's, Walter Hues, which was about a hundred yards from the school. In the summertime, they would either walk or ride a bicycle.

A humorous incident occurred when Al Martin, one of the students who were two grades behind Mattie, put up his hand to ask the teacher to use the outdoor toilet. The teacher informed Al that the toilet was being used and he would have to wait. After a lengthy period, approximately ten minutes, the individual who had been using the facility returned to the classroom. At that time the teacher said, "Al, you may go to the facility now," and Al said, "Teacher, too late, I don't have to go now." The students sitting in the near vicinity could tell by the odor that it certainly was too late to go outdoors.

The days were long on the farm during the summer and shorter in the winter; but still there was snow to be shoveled, water to be hauled, cattle to be driven to the brook, and horses to be returned to their stalls and fed. There were also potatoes in the cellar of the house that had to be graded and shipped and hauled by sleigh to the railroad station where they were loaded on a railcar.

Hockey was played in an outdoor rink with the boards being about three feet high and the ice flooded with the barrels on sleigh, resulting in not too good of a surface. There were small shelters with a little woodstove in the interior for the players to keep warm. After the hockey match, the players would have to ride home in the sleigh or in the back of a closed-in truck box, which was commonly used to haul potatoes to market. The roads were usually filled in with several feet of snow during the winter months. There was only one main road in the area, and that would be plowed several days after a snowstorm. Cars were rarely used during the winter as the roads were covered with too much snow. There would be some excitement on the farm when there was a lightning storm as it would strike a house or barn in the vicinity of Mattie's farm, usually burning it to the ground. The farmers would all rally to the aid of the person who lost their property and have a building bee which would build a new building in very short order.

Wood was cut in the woods in eight- to ten-foot lengths, loaded on a sleigh, hauled to the farmyard, and piled in a large pile, ten to twenty cords for the kitchen stove and the furnace to heat the house. There was always somebody in the community who had a saw, and they would round up about six to eight people to carry the wood up to the saw— one to do the sawing and one to tow the blocks in a pile, one to push up the wood, and this was an excellent time to get together and work during the day and get the winter's wood sawed. Then while there was frost on it, it would be the chore of the hired man and the farm boys to split the wood into small pieces, where it could be piled in the woodhouse for use during the winter. The local sawyer, who went from farm to farm, had the habit of humming as he sawed, which made it a very interesting occasion; and after the days' work, numerous drinks would be served to all involved in the work during that day.

Also during the winter there would be sheaves stored in the barns, and these would be pitched down through a hole in the loft. And they would use either a gasoline engine or a farm tractor with a pulley on it to run the thrashing machine, and then the straw at the rear of the thrasher would have to be pitched back up onto the loft again, which was rather a very dusty job. If somebody disliked the feller who was pitching up the straw, they might urinate down on top of him, which would cause quite a problem.

During the winter, there would be card parties throughout the community and plays put on by the women's institute for entertainment. The younger people would play cards, numerous games such as Auction 45, fish, rummy, etc. The adults would play for money, perhaps a penny or a nickel per corner. And the evening would be ended with a large lunch, which was enjoyed by all.

A lot of women would spend the winter knitting socks, mittens, sweaters, etc., as well as baking, which kept them occupied through most of the winter.

There were large gardens grown with every type of vegetable, and during late summer, these vegetables would be harvested and bottled for the coming winter, as well as putting up all the various berries in the form of preserves, a much more difficult job than just flash freezing them, which is now the case.

It was two miles to the local church where Mattie went to serve Mass as an altar boy. This was quite a hike, particularly in inclement weather. Although there were some humorous incidents, such as the time he and another youth got in an argument over who would be the main assistant to the clergyman. They were jostling over the incense when it tipped on its side, and the charcoal landed on the floor, resulting in the carpet catching on fire. The clergyman had to do the Highland fling in front of the altar to put the fire out in the carpet.

On another occasion, Mattie had a long torch on the end of a stick which he was using to light the candles in the crib at Christmastime, but he got distracted by one of the other altar boys, resulting in the little Lord Jesus and family located in the crib, which was surrounded by white cotton batten meant to look like snow, catching on fire. One of the chaps, Albert Rowe, was sitting in the front row wearing his black overcoat, went up and put the coat over the crib, burning the lining out and putting out the fire, causing great humor and laughter in the church.

When Mattie turned fifteen, he finished grade 10 and was ready to go five miles away to the high school, which was run by the nuns. There were only four other boys and about twenty girls from various parts of the island. This was a young boy's dream with all these girls to pick from to go to movies, hockey matches, and dances with. In those years, you could take what was known as the Maritimes board. If you passed grade 11, the board examined for grade 12. Mattie took the exams, passed, and was ready for first year of college. When he wrote the exams, Mr. Jelly, the school inspector for the island, was standing at the rear of the hall. Mattie just put down what he knew, which did not take long; and as he was leaving the room, Mr. Jelly stopped and asked him if he was finished. He said he was and passed in his paper. Mr. Jelly informed him, "You either know an awful lot, or nothing at all, but hopefully you have passed." When the marks returned a month later, Mattie had passed both the eleventh and twelfth exams and was ready to head off to the capital city for college.

While at the capital, Mattie worked on the boats loading the potatoes, which was a union job and paid an excellent wage. Most of the hard work was done by Acadian fishermen, who spoke French, so Mattie made excellent money, learned French conversion talking to the Acadian people, and was introduced to their daughters, who provided excellent companionship.

One day Mattie was sitting in college talking to Donna McCourt, who was the daughter of a well-known Canadian band leader, making a date for Saturday night, when he heard the professor, Lt. Col. Willie McDougal, say, "Would the man who made nothing in math put up his hand?" When nobody put up their hand, Mr. McDougal said, "Mattie, I was talking to you. Why did you not put up your hand?" Mattie said, "Sir, there are a lot of other people surrounding me, who are better qualified than I to make nothing in math." Mr. McDougal replied, "Stay after class." He did so. Mr. McDougal informed him, "It costs a lot of money for your parents to send you to college. You also have a brother in the other university in town, so if you're not going to learn, there's not much point in you staying." He then inquired, "What are your plans for the future?" Mattie stated, "Well, Mr. McDougal, you're a very intelligent man, right?" Mr. McDougal agreed. He then said, "You are a number 1, Mr. McDougal." Mr. McDougal then inquired, "And what about the others in your class?" He said, "They are number 2s." "Oh, and," he said, "where do you fit, Mattie?" Mattie said, "I'm a number 3." Mr. McDougal asked, "What does a number 3 do in life?" Mattie answered, "I intend to go into business and hire all the number 2 guys who will become accountants, lawyers, engineers, etc., and I'll make money off each and every one resulting in my becoming a millionaire." "Well," Mr. McDougal said, "you might as well get started on that in the near future as you're not paying attention to me, only to the girls around you." With that, Mattie decided it was time that he started thinking about another way of life.

Mattie went back to the farm because the hired man, who had been with the family from when he was sixteen and was now forty-three, had cancer. He tried to negotiate better wages than he had been offered prior to college to no avail. He decided that he would leave the island and try his hand somewhere else. His father called up a businessman in a neighboring province, and Mattie went there to learn how to buy cattle and various livestock. The owner, Mr. Levine, told him that within a year, he'd have him back on the island buying all the livestock for the company, but within three months, he informed Mattie that he was well trained and now was the time to go back and start shipping railcars of livestock to the mainland. After doing that for one year, Mattie decided that he didn't want to work for somebody else, so he informed Mr. Levine what his intentions were. Mr. Levine said, "Well, if you plan to work somewhere else, it's best that you go to Calgary, Alberta, because that's where they have their mineral rights on the crown land, and there is a lot of oil in Alberta. So Mattie decided that he would leave in the very near future to become an oilman.

He had saved up some money, and he sold his 4-H calves to his father, who didn't pay a big price as he informed Mattie that he probably will have to return if he didn't find any work, and then he wouldn't have to pay as much to buy them back. So Mattie left with a few hundred dollars and took the train to get off the island to go to Halifax, where Donna Martin was going to nursing school. They were going to walk and hitchhike to Calgary, but Mattie found out that a lad he'd known from when he was five years old, Chuck Gulley, was working in construction with his first cousin. He managed to track the two of them down, and they were drinking a case of beer. There was no beer to be bought on the island, but you could do so in Halifax, Nova Scotia. They got into an argument, and Chuck's cousin, Billy, gave him a shove, and he fell backwards down the stairs, breaking his arm. Chuck came up and Billy said, "Somehow we'll have to get him to the doctor," but Mattie suggested he drink some more beer to kill the pain.

In the morning, when Mr. Flash Hollet, a noted hockey player, came to check the job site on behalf of his father, Chuck would take the wheelbarrow and with part of a load in it, push it a short distance and fall over on his arm. Mr. Hollet said, "Oh, oh, you have broken your arm. I'll have to rush you to the doctor." He did so, and the doctor set the arm. While he was doing it, Mattie asked, "Now, is there workman's compensation?" The doctor said, "Certainly." So he gave them the address, and Chuck and Mattie went to the workmen's compensation office where the guy said they would give him a monthly check. Mattie said, "How about a cash settlement?" To which the guy said, "Certainly. I'll take the particulars tomorrow, and I'll give you a cash settlement for the length of time that you'll be unable to use your arm." Now Mattie had a partner and companion who had money in his pocket, where he had none before. He had to inform Donna that he was going to take Chuck westward rather than her. She didn't want to be a nurse, so she left the hospital and ran away, but her mother coaxed her to come back. She didn't get married until her midthirties. Mattie regretted not taking her, but money talks.

After a couple of days, Chuck and Mattie started through Annapolis Valley heading for New Brunswick, Quebec, and Toronto, Ontario.

CHAPTER 2

Mattie, now in Halifax, left for the Annapolis Valley. Mattie walked through the countryside which was beautiful with the flowers all in bloom.

After one day, Mattie and Chuck made it to Digby and stayed there overnight in a little wooden cabin. They enjoyed all the scallops they could eat in the scallop capital of the world and then caught a boat early in the morning from Digby to Saint John, New Brunswick. Mattie and Chuck spent a few hours looking over the town, then continued walking west along the shore road, eventually catching a ride on a sardine truck. Unfortunately, there were already two in the front cab, so they had to sit in the back with a few dead sardines. They rode for a short distance, and when the truck turned off, they were back walking again. It was a cloudy day with a light rain falling. Mattie and Chuck got a ride in a car. Although the chap had informed them that he was going many miles, after smelling the sardines off their clothes, he cut the trip short and let them off. I guess he could no longer stand the stench!

Mattie and Chuck went back to walking and made it to Woodstock, New Brunswick. They planned to cross the border into Maine continuing on into New Hampshire and Vermont to the Quebec border, but they were turned back by the border-crossing gentlemen who told them they didn't have enough money to travel into the United States. He suggested the two of them head north and cross over the border into Quebec by following the old Highway 2 westward to Rimouski, Rivière-du-Loup, Trois-Rivières towards Quebec City. Since Mattie spoke a little French, they were able to follow the man's instructions and get by. However, due to the fact that a Catholic priest had recently been killed by two hitchhikers in Portage la Prairie, Manitoba, by cutting his throat from ear to ear and that 1955 was the year that electricity and TV covered most of Canada, Mattie and Chuck were ensured that it was almost impossible to get a ride as everyone in Canada knew about the tragedy.

They continued on. If they could find a cheap bed-and-breakfast for five dollars, then they would stay overnight. If not, Mattie and Chuck would just sleep on the side of the road. This allowed them to go from sunrise to sunset, thereby making many miles a day. If the two men walked at a steady clip, they could make three miles per hour plus. If they jogged, they could easily make five miles. They took turns doing both.

Mattie and chuck arrived in Quebec after about a week and a half on the road. They didn't know anyone there, so there wasn't much point in looking around the city as it was costing them time and money.

They started out again heading farther west on Highway 2 towards Trois-Rivières, a very pretty little town where three rivers join at the Saint Lawrence. Hence the name in French—Trois-Rivières. Mattie and Chuck continued on after spending the day there, westward towards Montreal. In Montreal, they stopped to see several cousins and spent a few days before leaving the city. Not used to a very large city, they tried on three occasions to get on the city bus. Each time they were pushed aside and wound up at the back of the pack as the city folks boarded the bus first. On the fourth try, they successfully elbowed their way through and got on the bus and headed towards the outskirts.

They found a ride in a milk truck which proved a rather slow form of transportation as the milkman still had some deliveries and was heading back to his dairy farm on the outskirts. For the last part of their trip in Montreal, they got a ride on the handlebars of a bicycle, and that's how they finally made it to the bus depot!

Mattie and Chuck paid the chap five dollars and boarded the bus. The driver told them, "Just go to the back of the bus and sit there." He would tell them when to get off. Fortunately, he had a heart of gold, and they rode all the way to Kingston. It was the end of the route, and Mattie and Chuck disembarked.

Mattie had a pen pal named Barbara Murphy, from the *China Messenger*, which was a religious publication that most people on Queen Charlotte Island subscribed to. Mattie was able to have pen pals and either write the letters or receive them in an attempt to pass away the storm-stead winters on the island.

From there, the two men travelled the Highway 2 westward along the Saint Lawrence Seaway to Toronto. Upon arriving in Toronto, they went to see two of Mattie's uncles. The first, Peter McFinsky, was head of maintenance at St. Michael's Hospital and had recently got married in his 50s. They spent a few days there. The second, Jack Duffs, allowed them to stay with him and his wife. Mattie and Chuck were also able to visit with their five cousins. That was most enjoyable as they didn't get back to the island very often on vacation.

During their visits to the kinfolk, they spent most of their time eating as they were very hungry. They put on considerable pounds in preparation for the trip south to St. Catharines to pick fruit in Southern Ontario.

Upon arriving in St. Catharines, they went straight to the employment office. The chap asked them where they were from and what they wanted. They told him they were from Queen Charlotte Island and that they wanted a job picking fruit. He said the strawberries were picked. The other fruit, cherries and peaches, were not ready yet. Therefore, when he heard they were from Queen Charlotte Island, he suggested that they would be best off to point their noses eastward and follow them.

Upon showing him their third pair of worn-out shoes with no soles and their socks sticking out through the hole in the bottom, Mattie and Chuck convinced him that they were desperately in need of a job since they only had pennies to their names. He suggested that they go to E. D. Smith where the foreman was a big Irish Catholic and would hopefully take pity on them.

They did as he instructed and went farther down the road south to the E. D. Smith farm. Upon arriving, Mattie and Chuck met the big man Charles O'Connor, who told them that he had no work at present. They convinced him that they were Irish Catholics and surely he could put them to doing something. He informed Mattie and Chuck they would be weeding strawberries. The ground was as hard as concrete, but since they were Catholics and used to praying, they would no doubt have no problem because they could pray and pick weeds at the same time. Mattie and Chuck thanked him graciously. As they had asked about sleeping quarters and what kind of benefits there were, he pointed to a house with no windows and said, "That will be your sleeping quarters and living area." Chuck asked him if there were any other benefits that they might enjoy, and he pointed to a house with windows in it and said that there were a dozen girls there from Quebec and that they could help themselves and he felt sure that Mattie and Chuck would enjoy their company.

They took him up on his suggestion, and for the next few weeks, Mattie and Chuck enjoyed the pleasures of some wonderful young ladies of a different culture, some who could speak English, and some who couldn't. With Mattie's smattering of French, they were right at home.

It was most enjoyable except for the hot dogs on Friday. Since they did not eat meat on Fridays, they had to make a decision— eat hot dogs or go hungry. Needless to say, the hot dogs won out. You were allowed one glass of milk, but Mattie always drank one glass and took a glass with the hot dog to the table. He was informed by another picker (by this time the cherries were ready to be harvested) that he could only have one glass. Mattie informed him that unless he could give Mattie a whipping, he would drink all the milk he wanted. The other picker and his friends declined and graciously allowed Mattie to fill up with milk which he enjoyed ever since he was a baby. He went picking the cherries, and after the cherries were finished, the peaches were on. The peaches were much easier to pick and much tastier to eat with the exception that within the first day everyone had gut-wrenching diarrhea. It was most entertaining to see the various pickers run for the outhouse, usually crapping their drawers before reaching their destination.

Upon the completion of picking the fruit, they'd been on the road since June 5. It was into beginning of July, and they decided to go and stook grain. They headed for the south of London to Ingersoll. At Ingersoll, they got on with two brothers, Grant and Cecil Proust. Mattie worked with Grant, and Chuck worked with Cecil. Cecil had pigs, and he called Mattie and Chuck nearly daily to go over and wrestle in the mud in the barnyard with the pigs. They had a lot of fun, but pretty soon they too smelled like the pigs. Mattie's employer, Grant, and his wife, Mary, had a very large dairy farm. The power went out while they were milking cows. At the rate they were going, they would have milked their few dozen cows in a week. Mattie asked Chuck to come over since his boss did not have very many cows, and between the two of them, they were used to milking a three-gallon pail in a matter of minutes. The cows were milked quite quickly to the happiness of Grant and Mary. They asked what they could do, and Mattie and Chuck, in turn, said, "Well, if we could have the forty-nine red maple leaf, GMC truck, and be introduced to some girls, that would be the greatest favor you could do us!"

They informed Mattie and Chuck that Dutch-Catholics lived across the road and had half a dozen blond beautiful girls. They took Mattie and Chuck over and made the introductions. The boys asked them to go out on Saturday night which the girls did. Mattie and Chuck had a most enjoyable time at a country dance, and the next day they went to an old gravel pit where they could swim and enjoy the very warm water as there was a little spring in the bottom of the pit.

They stayed there until the harvest was finished, and they started combining the rest. Then they left for Tillsonburg to pick tobacco. They got thirty-five cents an hour in Queen Charlotte, fifty cents an hour in Ingersoll, and they were paying a dollar an hour plus board in Tillsonburg! In Tillsonburg, Mattie and Chuck went to work for a family of Dutch heritage, but Mattie had the problem of sitting next to the little baby who kept crapping his drawers so the aroma of the food was counteracted by the smell of the crap in the baby's diapers! Mattie and Chuck decided that they would go into town and see what was going on. Chuck wanted some chewing tobacco, so they went to the tobacco shop. While he was in there, Mattie met a guy called Joe. They got to talking, and he mentioned that his daughter Bonnie and her husband Jack were sharecroppers for Les Alton down at Port Burrell on the shores of Lake Erie. So he said, "Give notice" and drove them back to the tobacco farm where they were sleeping in the garage, and Mattie and Chuck gave notice for a couple of days later so the farmer could get some extra help. Joe came, picked them up, and took them to Port Burrell. They had the pleasure of meeting a lovely couple and become part of a six-person priming crew, which is another phrase for tobacco pickers. They had to sleep in an old building. Two of the crew were very steady. Harry and Mel had picked for twenty years, so they showed them how to do it; and the two of them, plus Harry and Mel and one other guy stayed the full month until the crop was off, whereas the sixth guy was changed twenty-three times in that period of time!

It was so hot and damp that the mare pulled the stoneboat that hauled the tobacco leaves out to the end of the road. Then an old-timer with little tractor would load the leaves on a trailer and haul two or four at a time into the yard where the ladies would tie them together and the men would hand them into a building with rafters about three feet apart. It was called a tobacco kiln.

Mattie later got on, when the old man took sick, driving the tractor hauling the stoneboats into the yard, as the old chap had to quit. Mattie had tobacco poisoning which was a terrible rash and itch that was finally cured with calamine lotion. Mattie's partner had boils for which he had to go see a doctor to get treatment every few days.

Mattie missed the humour in the field. Harry had sinus problems, and the snot used to hang down about a foot; but when he would get to the end of the road, he'd give a gigantic sniff and then he could inhale right back up into his head again! This was most amusing because Mattie had never seen anyone who could perform a trick like that before.

Mattie would get up in the morning and get extra pay for taking out the kilns because they started at four o'clock in the morning, but because he had a really good picking crew, he'd be through at one or two o'clock when other crews in the area would work up to perhaps five or six o'clock. The old man got better and came back, and someone had to unload the boats and pass the leaves to the girls—two blond twins and a redheaded girl called Joan, who took an affection to Mattie, and he returned the favor. His buddy, who was blond and blue-eyed, loved to dance, but they didn't drink and smoke, so Mattie and his buddy fit right in with the three Mormon girls. They always had a spare, but it was a most enjoyable time. They went to many dances around the area and were invited to their houses where they were treated to excellent food, even though on the tobacco farm the food was top quality. However, the work was more made for slaves than it was for an ordinary folk. Since they had spent their young life picking potatoes bent over a basket in the wet weather, they decided to buy a car. They proceeded to McManus Motors in London, Ontario, where Mattie bought a 1947 Mercury which the salesmen informed was like brand-new having previously been owned by a priest and was only used to get groceries or to visit some ill person and give them the last rights.

As it was, the car turned out to be excellent. Mattie was now prepared to go get an Ontario driver's license and get it registered which they proceeded to do in Aylmer, then they could head out to Alberta.

CHAPTER 3

Mattie met the driver examiner who was to give him a driver's license. They proceeded to get in the '47 Mercury and go for a driver's test after Mattie had passed the written test. Mattie immediately drove through a stop sign, and the muffler fell off the car, resulting in the examiner informing Mattie that he'd be unable to give him a driver's license. Mattie said to the examiner, "Well, I have to leave tomorrow morning at six for Alberta. I'm not going to be able to go if I have no driver's license." So the examiner who had a heart of gold said, "If you promise me that you leave Ontario at daylight in the morning," this was late August of 1955. He said, "We'll drive right back to the office, and I will give you a driver's license so you can quickly get out of Ontario. And then let some other province worry about your driving capabilities." Mattie thanked him profusely. He immediately got his driver's license, and he and Chuck were all set to head for the oil fields of Alberta, with a stop in southern Alberta to pick sugar beets.

They left in the morning, heading for Sarnia, Ontario, and Port Huron, Michigan, which were cities on either side of the border. They crossed over into the United States with no problems and then headed up to Northern Michigan.

In a town called Flint, a tire was low, as it had a slow leak. So they stopped and bought a new tire for $11. Then Chuck decided they should have a smoke because most people around them were smoking. They bought a package of Lucky Strikes that cost them thirteen cents a pack. They filled up with gas, which was fifteen cents a gallon. They were very grateful that the prices were so reasonable. They headed north up over the straights of Mackinaw, over the longest suspension bridge in the world, turning westward as they followed Highway 2 to Wisconsin. They stopped in Wisconsin as there was a slight snowfall, and the hunting season was open. They asked the motel owner why there were so many people around the motels. He stated that they were all hunters from Detroit and the south. Mattie asked him if they were getting many animals. He said that they are hunting deer and he had only seen a few deer, but they did shoot one hunter yesterday. So he said they were managing to kill a few different species.

Then they left in the morning at daylight, driving to Minnesota and then into North Dakota where Mattie was familiar with a very rich farmer called Jeff Baldwin, who had a number of farms next door to Mattie's father in PEI. They visited with Mr. Baldwin, who was a good-looking big man who wore a ten-gallon Stetson and grew a lot of potatoes in North Dakota in the Devils Lake area, Treetown, Queen Charlotte Island, and in Jacksonville, Florida. They stayed overnight with him and then proceeded on through Montana.

They went into town where there was an oil crew from Texas looking for help yesterday. They proceeded into the little town of High River and were informed that the crew had filled up very quickly, as the harvest was over and people were looking for work for the winter. Then they went on to Calgary and were given directions to the Dominion Bridge site in southeast Calgary, where the American Oil Exploration Company had an office. They went to the office after checking in to the nearby Shamrock Hotel, where Mattie had to leave his watch because they had no luggage to speak of, just a small suitcase. At the oil office, they met the secretary who gave them each an application to fill out. Upon looking at the application, the first thing Mattie spotted at the top was your religion and nationality. He uttered, "Oh crap. This is just as bad a place at back at the island." So he decided after his experiences on the island, he would not fill out where it asked for his religion and nationality. But they filled out the rest and gave it to the secretary, who gave it to the boss, Mr. Walker.

The boss, upon looking at the application, called the secretary into the office and said, "Take this back out, and ask those two fellers to fill it out in full. If they do not, ask them why." Mattie informed the secretary if it was going to help him, he didn't think he needed it; and if it was going to hurt him, he'd be a darn fool. With that, the boss called out from the inner office, "Bring that feller in here." Mattie went into the office, and the boss asked where he was from. Mattie told him back the eastern part of Canada. The boss said he was from Dallas, Texas, and it's over two thousand miles. "That's a long piece. I bet you did not come that far." Mattie informed him he had come over three thousand miles, walking a good portion of it. The guy asked him how he traveled the rest of the way. Mattie told him he picked tobacco, a backbreaking job, and made enough to pay cash for a car. Mr. Walker said, "I'll hire you right now to start at seven tomorrow morning." Mattie informed him that as he only had $1.17 and Chuck had little more, he was going to keep looking for a job to start that same afternoon. "Well," Mr. Walker said, "it is two o'clock, and you will go on the payroll from 2:00 p.m. to 6:00 p.m. and then you'll start at 6:00 a.m."

Mattie asked, "What about my friend?" He said, "He's hired too. And you will get paid 191 hours at regular wages of eighty cents an hour. Then you'll get time and a half for everything over 191 hours, and you will probably come close to 400 hours per month. I will pay for all your meals and for your room. If you wish to take your car and three other people with you, I will give you five cents per mile." At fifty miles per hour was twenty-five cents an hour. And of course the oil company was supplying the gas.

Mattie figured that they had died and gone to heaven to get such a cushy job with such ridiculously high wages. The government was the biggest employer on Queen Charlotte Island and did not pay overtime, so nobody paid overtime. Mattie went back to the outer office and informed Chuck that they now had a job. As they were driving back to the hotel, Mattie gave Chuck the details of their job and the good luck. Chuck said, "That guy has to be the biggest liar in America. Imagine, he is going to pay for all our food. I'll eat two breakfasts. He'll never pay for that. And then pay for our room at night? And put gas in our car and pay for driving the car to work up north? I don't think he'll ever do what he promises." Mattie said, "Well, give it a try. It sounds pretty good, and it's worth taking the chance."

They went back to the hotel and charged their supper. The hotel was a common rooming place for oil workers and cowboys. Mattie and Chuck went into the bar after supper to see what was going on. Before too long, a fight started between the cowboys and the oil workers. Chairs were flying. Pretty soon a big cowboy hit Chuck in the side of the jaw, knocking him ass over teakettle. So Mattie decided it was time to get up and defend himself. They joined the side of the oil guys, and the free for all fight got in full swing. Finally after ten or fifteen minutes, everybody got kind of tired. They all sat down on the chairs that weren't broken and started drinking beer again, as if nothing ever happened.

The next morning, Chuck and Mattie went to work at the oil field yard at the Dominion Bridge Company. Mattie was put to work taking the windshields out of the Chevy trucks. These trucks had split windshields. So Mattie took a screwdriver and a hammer and drove it in the corner around the rubber band that sealed the moisture out and pry on it. Within an hour or so, he was going great guns! Mr. Walker walked up to him and asked, "How are you doing, son?" And he said, "I've got three windows out already." He said, "You are some worker." "Except," Mattie said, "I've broke all three." "Oh," he said. Never blinking an eye, he said, "That's fine, just you go get a mop and a scrub pail, and you start cleaning up the inside of the trucks. You can't get into any trouble doing that. We'll be leaving at the end of the week for a place called Grand Prairie, Alberta, up north, a two-day drive."

Mattie and Chuck worked in the yard the rest of the week and were informed by the foreman that they would have to get a chauffeur's driver's license and a box of tools. They went down and got an Alberta driver's license, which was easy as Chuck already had a Queen Charlotte driver's license and Mattie had an Ontario license. So they issued them another license. They had to go in and see Chief McGyver, a crusty old Irishman, who said, "If you get in any trouble, I'll lock you up in jail. Welcome to Alberta, and good luck in the oil fields." He was a very fine old policeman.

Then they proceeded over to a place called Ribtors. Old Mr. Ribtor came over and said, "Okay, I'll supply you a box of tools, to each of you, including toolbox. What will you give me for security if you have no money?" When Mattie passed grade 12 and got three of the nine prizes, his mother was very proud of him and bought him an Omega Seamaster watch, which was worth $130. Imagine how many hours anybody would have to work in Queen Charlotte at thirty-five cents an hour to get enough money to buy such an expensive watch. Mattie then pawned the watch with Mr. Ribtor. They already had a car, a tank full of gas, winter clothes which they bought at the Hudson Bay Company basement at very good prices, heavy parkas, and wool socks. Everything one needed to head for the cold, cold north.

The first of the next week, around the tenth of September, they started out on the old Highway 2, heading north to Grand Prairie. They got about halfway as the road was terrible in 1955 with bumps and holes. They could only do about thirty miles an hour. They stayed in a place called Faust, beside a native reservation. There they were introduced to the native Canadians, drinking a few beers and getting uproariously drunk.

Mattie and Chuck thought this was most entertaining. Of course the local farmers and lumberjacks were just as drunk. After all, that was the purpose of going in the bar. And especially, you could scrounge up some women as well, which was great for the single men. And if the locals were not happily married, well, they too were interested in the ladies. So the bar closed at eleven o'clock at night as the premier of Alberta, Reverend Manley, was a very religious man, who also had his own radio program.

In the morning, they had breakfast at 6:00 a.m. and proceeded at 7:00 a.m. northwestward to Grand Prairie, where they arrived early afternoon and checked into the York Hotel. This was the best hotel in town. Grand Prairie, which was a logging town, oil field town, farming town, was a very busy and prosperous place in September of 1955, with work for everyone. The weather was rather warm for the north, and the ground had not frozen over. The oil crew was going ninety miles south of Grand Prairie on mud roads. With the ground not frozen hard enough, they could not proceed to the job site, so they had to wait in the hotel for a few days, with everything paid in full of course, before they could proceed to the job site.

Mattie was sitting in the hotel lobby since he did not drink. An older man came over and said, "Are you not even having a beer?" Mattie said "No." He said, "You've got a bit of an accent. Where are you from?" He said, "Queen Charlotte Island." "Well, I'll be damned," the older man said. "That's where I'm from. What part of the island do you come from?" Mattie informed him, "Treetown." "Well, well," he said, "my name is Patty Croriley. I come from there a number of years ago. I owned a hotel five miles from Treetown, and it burned down. I knew some fellers who had come out on the harvest excursion, so I came to Alberta and then to Grand Prairie, and now I own this big fine hotel." He then proceeded to take Mattie inside the bar where Mattie had a tomato juice and Mr. Croriley had two ten-cent glasses of beer. Mattie had never seen this before. And again the bar was just hopping. Everybody was proceeding to get loaded for bear. So Mattie enjoyed a great conversation with his good friend, Mr. Croriley. Then Mr. Croriley treated him to supper that evening, and again they had another visit as Mr. Croriley was very anxious to hear news from the island and since they all knew everybody in Queen Charlotte Island, where they both came from.

As Mattie was sitting in the lobby that evening, watching the people come and go, a feller came and sat down beside him, asking him where he was from. And he told him, "Back east." "Oh," he said. "Well, we had an easterner come out here about a month ago. He was sitting in the pub, having a beer, and along came a few of us, saw him sitting by himself, and we invited him to join us at our table. He did so, and we asked him what he planned to do. He said he wanted to work in the oil field on the oil crews. So we told him it was a pretty tough job. He had to shoot himself a moose, number 1. Number 2, he had to swim across the Wapiti River, and then he had to make love to a native girl. We would be back in town in a couple of weeks on time off, twenty days to be exact, and if he had passed all three tests, we would see he got hired by the boss of our crew. Upon returning to town, our oil crew saw this easterner sitting at a table nursing his beer with his clothes torn and his face all scratched. So we went over and sat with him and asked him what happened. 'Well,' he said, 'I'll never do that again. Not for the best job in the world.' We asked him why, and he said, 'Well, you know, that part about shooting that native girl, I'm a crack shot, so there was nothing to that. The part about swimming across the Wapiti River, sure it was cold, but I swam in the North Atlantic on the East Coast, so that was easy. But that part about making love to the bear, boy that was the toughest thing I ever did.' he said. 'I was lucky to get away with my hide!' To which we all had a great laugh. Hired him immediately, and he went to work for the oil crew."

Upon hearing this, Mattie and the oil field workers laughed hilariously and spent another hour visiting with each other, telling stories of their various parts of the country where they grew up.

After a few days, the ground froze over, and it went down to twenty below zero. The crew headed out in the four-wheel drive Dodge power wagons and some normal trucks, a group of about thirty plus people for the camp down on Nose Mountain. It was a trip over rough, slippery, hilly roads, which were very difficult, getting stuck numerous times and having to use their wenches to hook on to trees to pull themselves out. The mud was up to their knees sometimes; other times they were driving over mostly frozen road, but at the end of a long, long day, they made the full ninety miles to camp, where it was warm and the cook had an excellent supper prepared. Since it was Friday, they all sat down at the table, and the cook asked them what they'd have to eat. They first asked a feller called Ted LaMonde, who was a surveyor assistant, if he was a Catholic. If so, they had whitefish. He said no, he was a Protestant. The cook said fine. Then he said to Patty Duffy, the drill push who was much, much older man, "Patty, what will you have? You're Catholic, so you'll have the whitefish." He said, "No, cookie, I was in the Second World War, and the pope gave us permission to eat meat. I've never got around to giving it back." So the cook served him up a big two-inch steak with onions and mushrooms on it.

Chuck and Mattie were used to Holstein steak back on the island, which was about a one-fourth -inch thick, almost like bacon. When they saw that delicious steak, Chuck nudged Mattie and said, "What will we do? We've eaten fish until we're starting to look like one. Are we still going to eat it?" Mattie said, "No way. If Patty can eat meat, so can we." So everybody dug into a big delicious steak and proceeded to eat pie for dessert. A tremendous meal, delicious, and lots of food.

With that, they went to bed in the camp, eight guys to a room with a stove. With four guys on one end of the trailer, four guys on the other end, stove in the middle, a chunk of wire hung up to hang their socks on, and some of them that smelled to the high heaven. Some of the older guys snored that you could almost hear them all the way to Grand Prairie, but nevertheless, they were extremely tired, and they slept like a log.

CHAPTER 4

Mattie got up with the rest of the crew at five o'clock in the morning, and they would go to the washroom facilities and after that, at six o'clock, have their breakfast, which was an excellent meal put on by the cook and assistant cook. Sometimes just the assistant cook would do the breakfast and lunch with the cook putting on supper and looking after laying out the food for the lunches at night.

The operation consisted of two to four caterpillar tractors which went ahead and, if need be, would cut down the trees to make a road, which was called a "cut line." The guys who operate the machine would be called cat skinners, and they would have their own camp separated from the rest of the crew. The cat operators were followed by the drill crew, consisting of three to five drills, which were a three-ton truck with a drill mounted on it operated by the driller and a second three-ton truck with a thousand-gallon water tank, which was driven by the driller's helper. These were followed by one-ton truck driven by a chap called the shooter or "dynamite man" who also had a helper to help him. This in turn was followed by the operator with his assistant, junior operator, and second assistant, which was Mattie on this particular oil crew.

In total this consisted of approximately thirty people in the crew, which was headed up by the party manager, who looked after the day-to-day operations, and the party chief, who had a degree and was the overall boss of the crew. There was also a supply truck driver who went back and forth to town, usually semiweekly, or sometimes every two days, depending on road conditions, etc.

Mattie stayed in that camp for approximately one month when the party chief came to him and said, "We're going to give you a raise from eighty cents to ninety-six cents an hour, and we're going to make you the junior operator, but you will have to take your car and go from Grand Prairie to Edson, Alberta," which was south by about three hundred to four hundred miles.

Mattie left the next day, driving by himself down a new road that had just been opened a week before, called the Valley View cutoff, which cut several hundred miles of the distance between Edmonton and Grand Prairie. Upon hitting the Yellowhead Highway or Highway 16, which was the northern Trans-Canada route, he travelled for another hundred miles to a small mining and lumber town called Edson. From there, he went another fifty miles into the bush. Since this was the first of November, he worked in Edson camp for November until just prior to Christmas. He then went into the town of Edson with the rest of the crew. Ted LaMonde, the surveyor's assistant, said his sister lived in Edmonton and her husband was in the air force and asked if Mattie and Chuck would like to go to Edmonton and spend Christmas. Mattie, having grown up on a farm mostly by himself, stated, "No, thanks, I would just as soon stay in the hotel,"—called the Victory in Edson— "and spend Christmas here by myself." He thanked Ted who left with Chuck Gilley for Edmonton, a couple of hundred miles to the east, which is the capital of Alberta, for the holiday season until the start of the New Year.

Mattie was sitting in the lobby of the Victory Hotel, and he saw everybody going into the bar and heard all the people laughing and enjoying themselves. So he went in and sat down at a table by himself. He ordered two ten-cent glasses of beer, just like Patty Croken had done in Grand Prairie. He just left them sit there as he watched the activities of the crowd in the pub, which was quite entertaining.

A chap came in and sat at the table next to him. He was probably around forty years old compared to Mattie's late teens. He asked Mattie how old he was, and Mattie told him he was twenty-five. You had to be twenty-one to get into a bar in 1955. The chap asked if he minded if he joined him. He introduced himself as Frank Lederer. Mattie introduced himself, and Mr. Lederer commenced, telling him that he had a wife and a son that was about Mattie's age, nearly twenty. He asked if Mattie would be interested to come and spend Christmas and the holidays with him and his family. Mattie said no, that he would be quite content to stay in the hotel. With that, Mr. Lederer said, "I also have a pretty eighteen-year-old daughter," and Mattie said, "Really?" He said, "Does that interest you, to have someone like that for company?" Mattie was all ears and said, "I'm ready whenever you are." So they got in Mattie's '47 Mercury and went to Mr. Lederer's house to meet his wonderful wife and family.

By this time, it was close to eleven o'clock, and Mr. Lederer was fairly well under the weather. When he opened the door, evidently he was not supposed to stay out so late nor get so drunk; his wife hit him over the head with a broom. Mattie realized she was not quite as nice as he had been informed. So he grabbed Mr. Lederer as he fell backwards and took him over to lean against the car. Then he informed Mr. Lederer he might as well come back to the hotel with Mattie. But Mr. Lederer said, "I've got two uncles who live about five miles outside town in a sod shack. Would you like to go out there and meet them?" Mattie, having read and heard about sod shacks, was very interested. They went to meet Mr. Lederer's uncles out in the country.

The uncles were in fine fettle from drinking their own home brew. They called it schnapps or dandelion wine. But since it was so potent, it was really moonshine. Soon Frank was into the keg of alcohol, and everybody was drinking. These three people from Austria were extremely musical, playing the accordion, the mouth organ, etc. One of the uncles, or two uncles together, would play instruments while one uncle and Mattie would dance, and then he would dance with the other uncle. Then Frank would be third in turn. So the uncles and nephew Frank drank the night away.

Mattie had a little nap and woke up in the morning at daylight. Frank decided it would be best for his health if he got home, but he was still pretty well hammered. So Mattie helped him into the car, and the uncles waved and shouted good-bye in German. Mattie drove out the laneway, right across the road into a ditch. The ditch was not very deep, but Mattie could not back the car out as the road was slippery. The uncles came out with two big horses and hooked them onto the rear bumper, pulling Mattie out. He and Frank motored slowly back to town as the road was more slippery than ever.

This time when they knocked on the door, Frank's wife welcomed them with open arms. She was worried to death that they might have slid off the road and gotten stuck and froze to death. She was extremely happy, as were her two children, to see Frank back in good health but pretty drunk. She quickly gave Frank a hot cup of coffee, which he drank down, sobering him slightly and then headed for bed on Christmas Day, and went soundly to sleep.

Mattie ate a delicious big breakfast and introduced himself to the mother and children, in particular to the beautiful young Austrian lass.

They talked for several hours as Mattie was as interested in Austria as they were in Eastern Canada and the farm life and the farm where Mattie grew up. After a thoroughly enjoyable discussion, Mattie headed for bed and slept right through till supper time.

Mattie got up to a delicious stuffed turkey with all the trimmings, lots of good sausage, Wienerschnitzel, and sauerkraut; but with the stomach protruding several inches over his belt, Mattie promptly headed back to bed again to sleep the whole night through.

Frank then took it upon himself to introduce Mattie to all his neighbors and friends. The son offered to take Mattie around his friends, but Mattie's interest was only in the daughter, so she introduced him to her friends. A great time was enjoyed by all over the Christmas and New Year's holidays.

The Lederers showed Mattie various Austrian games, and Mattie showed their family Irish and English card games.

Frank took Mattie to see a chap called a tool push, who ran the big rig. This, instead of having fifteen-foot stem on the drill rig, had a ninety-foot drill pipe, and they were looking for a lease hound. A lease hound is a fellow who goes around the lease and does all the dirty, difficult jobs. He was on a rig from Texas called Reading and Bates, rig number 4. Mattie asked about the pay as he'd heard it was dirty hard work, and he was told a dollar sixty five an hour. Mattie couldn't believe it. In three months his wages had more than doubled. At the rate he was going, he was going to be a millionaire before he knew it.

Then came the difficult part; the rig wasn't starting up for a week. South of Edson was a little coal town called Mercoal. Another friend took Mattie there and to get him a job where it's nice and warm in the mine underground. Mattie went down what seemed like miles in the underground, spent a day, and upon arriving at the top, the guy that was sick returned back to work, but they said, "We'll keep you on, Mattie, because you're a good worker." Mattie said, "No, thanks, that's two days I worked for you." And the pit boss said, "Two? You only worked one." "No," Mattie said, "that was two days, my first and my last." He thanked him profusely and walked at a fast clip away from the mine.

The days went quickly, and Mattie was ready to go to work on the big rig, a few miles outside town. Being in the mountains was a very deep hole, so they dug very slowly. You would only have to break pipe every day or so, at least once a shift, and there were three eight-hour shifts. So Mattie's job was to lug the pipe with others who are called roughnecks and cut wood and pile it, mostly piling and lugging it to an old guy who fired the boiler to keep up steam, so they had steam to thaw out all the drill pipes and keep the deck so it wasn't too slippery. This job was very undesirable because the old feller chewed plug tobacco, and whenever he spit, if you were within ten feet, he'd hit you bang on! So when Mattie was doing anything around the old-timer, who had to be seventy, he had to be very careful that he didn't get a splat of tobacco in his eye.

One of the roughnecks decided to quit, as the job was too cold, dirty, and dangerous. So Mattie was invited after a couple of weeks to go up on the drill floor as a roughneck. This was probably one of the dirtiest jobs on earth and hard like picking tobacco, plus it was extremely dangerous. And whenever they pulled out to change the stem, they'd break off the mud jacket, and you'd get covered from head to toe with a splash of mud, which froze within minutes. At least you were not wet, unless it was mild weather, and there was a Chinook blowing through.

Mattie did this for several weeks and then Big Austie, who stayed pretty well drunk because the shifts were three o'clock to eleven o'clock, or eleven o'clock to seven and seven to three, so if he was in the bar till eleven, closing time, by the time he got to the rig he'd be feeling pretty good.

On one of these occasions, he had a new '55 Packard Clipper, as he made big money; he promptly drove it into a tree on the side of the road. Now there was no way for Austie the driller, the derrick man who was ninety feet up in the sky when they were going into or coming out of the hole, and the two roughnecks and Mattie, which made five, the boiler man, would find his own way to work. He was strictly local. Because anybody could do his job, just sitting watching the gauge on the boiler.

Austie called Mattie over and informed him that he would now be driving his car to work. And everybody would pay a dollar, except Austie, the big driller. So Mattie took the four or five dollars per shift and chauffeured everybody back and forth to the rig each day.

Mattie stayed there until the middle of February, around Valentine's Day. The rig finished up and laid down the derrick and shut down for a few weeks until they moved to another hole. That meant there would be no pay, and Mattie was after all in the game to make money, as he travelled, by now thirty-five hundred miles. So he went back to town to stay with Frank and his family while looking for another job.

Again Frank came to the rescue. Being a very happy-go-lucky and jovial Austrian, everybody liked him, so he was informed by his friend that a chap called Norris Peyton was looking for a chain man. This would be the third man on the survey crew. It was ninety-six cents an hour, but he would get four hundred hours a month, where he was only getting two hundred forty hours at dollar sixty-five on the big rig, and the work would not be as dangerous and was only half as hard. Mattie met up with Mr. Payton, who was a very fine gentleman, and worked for a company Exploration International. When he heard that Mattie already had experience on the recording crew, and that it only took a matter of hours to learn how to be a chain man and all you did was walk around the line and keep warm, and keep an eye out for bears so that you didn't get attacked and usually followed by a trail of Whiskey Jacks, which were a pretty bird like a woodpecker, always looking for something to eat and pass the time by talking to them as they walked along the line. Pretty soon the Whiskey Jacks would crow at Mattie. Mattie would speak back to them about how was your day, and I'll be feeding you in about an hour, and we stop for lunch at noon.

Mattie had the best job in the world. Then came the twentieth of February, and the crew decided to go to town for ten days off, which seemed to be the ritual. The party manager, Mr. Payton, came to Mattie and said, "We need somebody to look after the camp, someone who is reliable and who doesn't drink. Your job would be to feed the cat skinners, and if there's a couple of drillers staying in camp, to get ahead of the recording crew, and you chain and lay out the line. Work will proceed as normal while the boys get the time off."

To the others, this seemed like a great deal, but to Mattie, they were losing all their overtime, which was time and a half, which was absolutely stupid.

Mattie said to Mr. Payton, "You bet your boots I'll stay. I'll do all that. I'll also take everybody's washing in. Just leave it behind, and I'll do the washing a dollar per head." Norris said, "That's fine, you'll get paid for doing the washing, for looking after the camp, for looking after the cat skinners and the drill crew. You'll be getting time and a half, and you'll also be paid for chaining." Mattie thought again he'd died and gone to heaven. He just couldn't believe the good Irish luck that was just coming upon him day after day. So he stayed on for the ten days, learned to play poker, quickly found out that with his good memory he could remember the cards; and even though the cat skinners were considerably older and the drillers, perhaps ten years older, he could clean their clocks at poker, hands down.

Mattie and a cat skinner were sharing the same trailer, and in the middle of the night, they heard a scratching on the door of the trailer. Charlie, the cat skinner, immediately jumped out of bed and started quickly putting on his clothes. Mattie asked Charlie, "What do we do now?" Charlie replied, "We jump out of bed and run like heck to get away from that darn bear." Mattie replied, "I do not think we can outrun the bear." To which Charlie said, "I'm not worried about outrunning the bear, just getting ahead of you, Mattie." The problem was solved when the bear gave up pawing on the door and went on his way into the bush.

By the time the crew came back on the first of March, Mattie was as fat as a hog, had hardly done any work at all, and had a pocket full of money that would choke a horse.

They continued on in March with the exploration, and towards the end of the month, it gradually started to thaw out being in hilly and mountainous country. The trucks would not climb the hills, so they started to pack up and head back to Calgary.

Mattie, having been gone since early September until April Fool's Day, was glad to be back in town. He didn't know anybody, but there was a chap called Bullet Bisonet who said, "I'm going to drive to Windsor, Ontario. Would you come along and help me drive and split the gas?" Mattie though it was a heck of a deal since his mother had a serious operation and his father had a heart attack while he was gone. The hired man's cancer had gotten worse, and he could no longer work. They had to hire a neighbor's boy who only did half the work that Mattie did. When he phoned them, they told him they looked forward to seeing him return. And he could almost see the tears in their eyes. He told them he'd be home as soon as possible.

They went into Edson. Again Frank came to the rescue and said a guy would buy his car, for which Mattie asked a thousand dollars. Frank said the man wants to pay six. Mattie, having learned from the Americans the art of making a buck, said, "I'll split the difference." Within a few hours, he had $800 in his pocket for a car that he paid $400 and drove to Calgary, Grand Prairie, and to Edson. Then he hopped in the surveyor's truck with the surveyor who was from England, who was hard to understand with such an accent. Of course he thought Mattie had an accent from Queen Charlotte. So it was actually the pot calling the frying pan black. Ted LaMonde was a very happy-go-lucky feller as they got to talking in camp over the winter they found out they had grown up only ten miles apart and their fathers were friends. Ted and Mattie became friends, a friendship which would last for over half a century. Chuck came along too. But Chuck decided he didn't want to go back east, so he and a feller called John Brown, who saved a lot of money, bought a year-old '55 Chevy, robin egg blue with white, and away they went to the west coast to work on the logging camps.

Ted decided he would stay in town as he had quite an appetite for young ladies, and being a handsome chap with a very pleasant personality, if he met a beautiful young girl, rest assured, that both would have a lovely time.

Mattie shook hands with John Brown, who also came from five miles away in the easterly direction, where Ted was in a northerly direction to Chuck and Mattie. He said good-bye to Chuck, Ted, and John, and he and Bullet Bisonet left the next morning at 5:00 a.m. for Windsor, Ontario.

It was not too long before Mattie found out, a matter of twenty miles, why they called his friend Bullet Bisonet. He put the gas pedal to the floor and tried to keep it there all day long. Unfortunately, on occasion he'd have to slow down. When Mattie got behind the wheel, Bullet said, "Give her snooze." Because Bullet quickly learned the western art of chewing snuff, he had his lower lip stuffed until it protruded with a big lump in it. He wanted Mattie to chew snuff, but Mattie rarely took a small dip. He didn't care for it too much with it being pretty bitter. Then Bullet swallowed the spit, which upset Mattie's stomach. Of course there was a spittoon on the seat between them so they could spit. Mattie left most of the snoozing up to Bullet, and they made it to Windsor in a little over two days, where Mattie bought a plane ticket and flew to Toronto to meet up with his uncle Jack Dugan and his six cousins, five in one family and one cousin in another family.

His other uncle Pete McFinsky had a heart attack and passed away at his job where he was head of the maintenance crew. He was a painter by trade on the island. He had a heart attack and dropped dead. He visited with the Dugans, and his cousin Ed looked around for a pickup. He decided he now wanted a bright red pickup to catch the eye of the people around him, and he wanted one about a year old. Of course, having had such good luck with the Mercury car, he was going to buy a Ford, or a Mercury, as in that day there was a dealership for Ford cars and trucks and Mercury cars and Meteor cars, with both no longer being made after the turn of the century.

CHAPTER 5

Mattie bought a 1955 red Mercury pickup. He then called his friend Pat Curley, who had worked in Toronto all winter in a clothing store, and who was looking for a drive back to the island. They started in mid-April driving through eastern Ontario, Quebec, New Brunswick, to Queen Charlotte.

It took them two days to drive the thousand miles, where Mattie dropped Pat at his parents in Treetown, and then stopped late in the day at his parents farm a mile away. Mattie's parents, Dan and Lena, were very glad to see him as the hired hand had not been as helpful as they had wished. This was the spring of 1956, the third week of April. Mattie went back to work as usual, grading the potatoes in the cellar under the house, milking the cows, and doing the chores around the farm.

In the middle of May 1956, Mattie started putting in the crop of potatoes and then harvesting the hay followed by the grain, followed by digging the potatoes.

It was customary to get potato pickers from the mainland in Nova Scotia in the coal mining areas, as there were large families and the economy was depressed in those areas. The potato pickers would look for Joe, the hired man's beer, which he kept in bottles in the brook to keep it cold, just below the house and barn. They proceeded to drink large quantities of beer at the noon lunch break. When they went to the field, they kept falling over their potato baskets. Work would then have to be stopped for the day, in midafternoon, as the potato pickers would be too drunk to continue on with their work. But eventually the potato harvest did finish. They graded up the potatoes and shipped them. Then Mattie went to work on the potato boats, loading potatoes, in the town of Summerside. He worked all winter on the farm in the year of 1956 and 1957.

Mattie got a new car coat, which was only three-quarter length. He took his neighbor Curly Joe Reed into town, where Joe got a quart and proceeded to drink it on the way back to the farm, adjacent to Mattie's father's place. Joe then proceeded to take his full-length overcoat out to a stump and took an axe and cut the bottom quarter off, making it a three-quarter-length coat just like Mattie's, which was in style. But you could see the axe marks all around where he chopped it off.

Joe had six boys, and during the summer, his wife, Hilda, put up eighteen hundred jars and cans of preserves—apples, chicken, etc. This was enough to make sandwiches for the whole winter. The neighbors got together and built Joe a new house, taking a matter of a couple of days to cut the wood and a day to haul it to be sawed. The next week they put up the house in a couple of days. The house was sufficient to hold a family of eight. Joe and Mattie became very good friends.

In the spring of 1957, Mattie bought a new big black Dodge car and traded off his red pickup. While Mattie and his mother were driving up the front road from the village, a policeman pulled up behind, whom Mattie knew, a chap called Linden Robb. He put on his flashing lights and came up to the car. Mattie asked him what was wrong. He told Mattie that he was doing 60 mph on a road that is only 50 mph. Mattie said he was only doing forty, but Linden said, "Well, you usually drive much faster, so I'll give you a ticket and we'll see what happens." A month later, on the appointed time, Mattie went to Summerside to court, where the judge was called Dick Mitt. Officer Robb got up and read the charge, and the judge said to Mattie, who he knew quite well, "What do you have to say for yourself?" Mattie replied, "I was only going forty, Your Honor." The judge stated, "I would take the word of one policeman over five ordinary individuals." So Mattie was fined. As soon as he went outside the court, the policeman stopped him and, as they were friends, said "Here's the money for your fine. I just wanted to show you that I could lie in court, and no matter what you said, you were going to get convicted. So don't ever do anything serious, or you'll wind up in jail for the rest of your life because most policemen lie." This was a lesson in injustice that Mattie never forgot.

Mattie continued on with the chores and again putting in the potato crop, harvesting the hay and the grain and the potatoes, while at the same time enjoying himself immensely as he was the only young guy on the island with a brand-new fancy car.

Mattie's father passed away from a heart attack in late June of 1957, resulting in Mattie and the hired man having to take over the operations of the farm business while living with his mother. Since he was very well-known, there was a very large Irish wake and an equally large funeral of hundreds.

There was a place called the Gordon Lodge, and it was about twenty minutes from the family farm. Mattie used to go there quite often as there were very good dances in the hall. Usually, on a Saturday night, a third of the young people would be outside, the boys fighting, and another third would be in their cars with their girlfriends enjoying a good time, while another third would be in dancing. Mattie heard them announce that this would be the last waltz, so he ran into the hall in order to see if he could meet a girl to ask to take home. He asked a girl to dance, who said, "Sure." When they finished the dance, he said he'd give her a ride home. She is "okay," and then he said, "Well, I guess we'll head for Kinkora, to your father's house, Bernice." To which the young lady said, "My name is Florence, and I live about ten or twenty minutes away in a place called Emyvale. " So Mattie proceeded there and made another friend with whom he went to dances most of the summer. There was also a neighbor's daughter, who was taking a secretarial course in the city, and her name was Jenny. Mattie used to drive her into the city, and they would go to a show or to a dance, which was not allowed because different nationalities and religions were not allowed to mix. None of the young people agreed with this; nevertheless, it was the rules and one of the reasons that Mattie left and went west in the first place.

Mattie, when he finished digging the potatoes in the fall of 1957, in late October, went to work on the potato boats in Summerside, loading seed potatoes, to be shipped all over the world. Again, this was the usual high-paying union job, so Mattie accumulated a fair bit of money.

Mattie then inquired if anybody wanted to go out to Alberta to work on the oil rigs. If so, he would charge them $50 each to pay for the gas. So Wilf Clark, Florence's brother, said he would go. Then Thane Bernard from Treetown and Alfred Trainer from Emerald. That made four, which was a carload, for the long trip west.

They started off for Alberta in early November, when a lot of the potatoes were shipped and there was no more work to do. Mattie got a hired man to take his place for the winter while he and the three friends left for the west.

They traveled all day from Queen Charlotte Island across the ferryboat to New Brunswick, and then across New Brunswick into Quebec. They crossed from New Brunswick into Maine, New Hampshire, and Vermont in the United States. And at almost midnight, Alfred Trainer said, "I'll drive for a while if you wish, Mattie." So they changed positions in the front seat, and Mattie went to sleep. They were only about two hours drive from the Quebec border. Mattie woke up after a couple of hours and said to Alfred, "I guess we are now in Quebec." Alfred said "No, not yet." They were driving about 70 to 80 mph on a good road. Mattie said "That's strange" as he looked out the window and saw signs saying New York City. He knew then that Alfred was making great time driving in the wrong direction. He then took over the wheel and turned the car around. They had gone four hours out of their way.

They drove back crossing the border at almost daylight, driving westward through Montreal and on into Ontario until they came to Ottawa. There they stopped overnight. There were a lot of people working in Ottawa from Queen Charlotte Island, as it was the capital of Canada. They met up with a couple of girls from their area on the island who then lined them up with two more girls from Ottawa.

They went to a dance across the border in Hull, Quebec. A good time was had by all. And the next day, by midmorning, they were back on the road, heading westward through northern Ontario.

The Dodge car had a problem with the engine hood popping up into the safety lock, so they had to use a piece of mechanic's wire to tie it down, but the same thing happened to the trunk, which they wired down as well. They then carried on westward across the prairies arriving in Alberta during the second week of November.

They turned north at Calgary and drove to Edmonton where Thane Bernard had a sister. Upon arriving at one of the main intersections in Edmonton, the light turned red as Mattie was about to drive through it. One of the guys said, "Stop! Back up." Upon which Mattie promptly backed into a Volkswagen. But the guy in the Volkswagen was by himself and in a state of shock after being hit, and four guys in the black car compared to him by himself in his, he said, "Never mind" and didn't even get out to look.

They then drove on to the address of Thane's sister, dropping Thane off by the side of the street. That was the last they saw of Thane, and they then proceeded to the hotel where they got rooms for the night.

Mattie quickly got a job back with the same Exploration Oil Company that he had worked for before and went to see his various friends to say good-bye.

Mattie was behind on his car payments, so he called Household Finance to inform them that he was now in Alberta and was going to be working in couple of days and would be able to pay them his back payments for November, December, and January by the end of December when he would get paid. They thanked him for calling, and the next morning a guy called Mr. Zak came to the hotel from Household Finance, asking if he could see the car. Mattie said of course. He then asked if he could drive it to make sure everything was working OK. Mattie passed him the keys. He then rolled down the window, telling Mattie that he'd have to take the car and impound it until he got November's payment.

Mattie's two friends Alfred and Wilf and another guy called Jock Sully were going to work on the big rigs. But there, you had to have your own transportation, as Mattie did several years prior to 1956.

Now they had to arrange for other transportation for the month of December.

Mattie went north with the Exploration Company, and they had new international trucks. But the heaters did not work very well, so they had to wear their winter clothes, which Mattie had mostly dress clothes as he did not bring enough of his heavy winter clothes out west. He then drove north with the new international truck stopping in Grand Prairie and then again in Fort St. John, on the way to Fort Nelson, British Columbia.

When they got to Fort St. John, about a dozen who were travelling in the convoy with Mattie went into the bar. Mattie had a top coat on and a derby hat. He looked very much like an office boss. A chap came over and asked if he could by the lads a drink. To which they said they'd certainly appreciate it since they did not have much money. After several hours of buying drinks, he asked them if he could supply the meat for their oil crew as it would be a fairly good contract. Mattie informed him that the boss, Gene Richardson, would be along shortly. They guy was a bit saddened to hear that he'd been buying beer for and talking to the wrong people. Nevertheless, Mr. Richardson arrived towards suppertime, and since he was the party manager, he arranged for the guy to supply them with his product.

They then drove north another nearly three hundred miles to Fort Nelson, where they turned eastward and went into the bush sixty miles to a place called Cocho Lake, where they set up camp on the job site where they were going to work in conjunction with Shell Oil. The boys still had some beer left, so the next day, they proceeded to set up camp and then build an outhouse out of the wood, packing boxes that the groceries and meat had come in. They were just finishing up and they tied some ribbon from the survey crew with a big bow around the toilet and were drinking beer, celebrating the end of their day, when Mr. Richardson arrived in the camp with the Shell client's representative, who asked the party manager what the guys were doing. "Well," he said, "it looks like they are celebrating by the outhouse." With that, they went into the camp cookhouse to have supper.

When they finished, Mattie was called into the party manager's office and warned that he would not have a job if that happened again.

The month went along fairly quick as work proceeded at a fairly rapid pace, except there was nothing to do but to play cards or watch movies that the company brought to camp once or twice a week.

The cook was a little different and the guy who slept on the top bunk above Mattie, as in this camp there was again two beds on either side of a partition where the stove sat. The beds were bunk beds, and on Mattie's side were two on lower bunks and two in upper bunks. Mattie would be awakened at night by the guy in the upper bunk having sex with himself. This was very disturbing, so Mattie would put his feet up where the spring had sunk under the lad above, giving it a giant heave, throwing the upper bunk guy out onto the floor, which was a drop of about six feet. Mattie would then roll over and go back to sleep. That ended anything of that nature from that guy in the bunk above while Mattie was in bed at least during the night.

After supper one night, Mattie went over to the cook and said you should come over to my trailer. There will be a guy lying on my bottom bunk, and I'd like you to go in and just yell, "I gotcha!" when you jump on top of him. The cook agreed. Mattie went back to his trailer and said to the guy in the top bunk, "I'm not going to be around here this evening, so since you are always asking me if you can use my bottom bunk if I'm not here, you are welcome to it." So Mattie invited a few of his friends over to the other end of the trailer, waiting for the cook to arrive. Shortly he came into the trailer, jumping on top of Wayne, who was lying facedown reading a book. Wayne, concerned about the sexual habits of the cook, nearly jumped out of his clothes, yelling and screaming. Throwing the cook off his back onto the floor, this was enjoyed by Mattie and all his friends.

It was getting close to Christmas, and Mattie and the crew were preparing to head back to Edmonton. They left several days before Christmas, arriving in Edmonton on Christmas Eve.

Gene Sully invited Mattie to stay with him at his sister's place. Since this would be free room and board, Mattie gladly took up the offer. Unfortunately, several of the young children in the household had the mumps, which Mattie promptly caught, with his right side of his face swelling up for a week over the Christmas holidays. He then moved to a hotel back in the city. On the first of the New Year of 1958, Mattie took the mumps on the left-hand side for two weeks, along with the Asiatic flu. He lost a considerable amount of weight, but by the middle of the month, he was able to get back to work.

He was able to get a temporary job with Kenyon Oil Field Services, on a service rig, which was again a very cold, wet, and dirty job. When servicing the oil wells, the oil would soak your clothes, turning your skin brown. He worked there for a week until the chap, whose place he was taking on the rig, got better from the flu and returned to work. During the first three days on the job, Mattie did not have any money, so he did not eat. Bill Peyton said, "Why are you not eating, lad?" He said he had no money. Bill said, "What a fool you are. Why didn't you tell me?" He then called the lady over who was serving the meals and also owned the restaurant and told her that whatever this lad wants to eat, to just put it on the company bill.

Mattie was very thankful for such a kind guy to advance him the money for the food, as the room was already being paid for by the company as they were staying in a hotel.

With the sick rig hand returning, Mattie then caught the bus to Calgary, and there he got a job with the oil exploration well-logging division, working for a superintendant called Bill Smith. He mentioned to Bill Smith that they had no money and would appreciate it if they could get an advance, as he knew him from 1956 and December of '57. Mr. Smith said, "Sure" and advanced Mattie enough money to pay the November, December, and January car payments.

Mattie quickly paid Household Finance and recovered his car from the impound lot and gave it to Gene, Wilf, and Austin, so they could go to work on the rigs with their own transportation. Before, they had to pay to ride in December with someone else.

Mattie then called up his friend Ted LaMonde and asked him what he was doing. Ted informed him that he had gotten married even though he was only twenty and had gotten a job with Air Canada, the national government airline. Ted then asked Mattie where he was staying, and Mattie said he was staying in a hotel. Ted invited Mattie to come and stay with him and his new wife in their apartment.

Mattie was sleeping the chesterfield, and he awoke in the night to the sound of voices coming from the bedroom. It was Ted's wife saying, "No, no, no, Ted, I will not." Mattie rolled over and went back to sleep. In the morning, Ted and Mattie were having toast for breakfast, and Mattie asked Ted, "I hate to inquire into your business, but why was your wife saying no, no, no?" "Well," he said, "I married a girl from Saskatchewan, and those girls do not make love." Whereas Mattie offered his regrets that he had married into such an unfortunate affair. Then Ted left for work. When Ted's wife got up, she suggested they play a game of cards as she worked the afternoon shift, running a restaurant. Mattie kept getting more curious by the minute and asked, "Tell me why you were saying no, no, no. Ted informed me that you did not care to make love." She promptly replied, "That jerk. He told me that whenever an islander came to stay overnight, that you people were like Eskimos and he had to share me with you, and that's why I was telling him no, no, absolutely not."

Mattie then waited a couple of days until his new truck was ready and then he could head out of town well-logging crew.

CHAPTER 6

In the middle of January 1978, Mattie picked up his new truck and headed out with the well-logging crew. This consisted of the supervisor and an assistant who was his foreman. They travelled in one truck, Ken and his brother George Samchuk. Mattie was in charge of the dynamite, which they used to put down into the holes, and he also had a helper with him, making it a four-man crew.

They proceeded up to Peace River, and there Mattie checked in to the hotel along with the three other chaps and waited for their first well-logging job in the area. They would travel south of Peace River, which was the center of an oil field, and to the northwest territory border and into the territories on occasion and then over to Grand Prairie and north to Forth Nelson. They had a lot of driving to do their job.

While they waited to go out to the rigs, they would go in the bar. By this time Mattie was twenty-one, and Ken and George loved to have a few drinks, and they would play a game called BS Poker, on the back of dollar bills against one another and anybody who was interested in playing a game of chance for money.

Mattie had been used to milking cows, lifting potato bags and drill stem, so he was tough as nails. The Samchuk boys would suggest to anyone sitting around at neighboring tables, "How would you like to twist Mattie's arm?" And they would bet $10.00. They would twist with the right hand first since most people are right-handed. Even if Mattie lost, along with his two backers George and Ken, they would say, "Well, we'll twist with the left arm, which will make even more money, but we'll double the bet." If it was $5, it would go to $10, and if it was $10, it would go to $20. Of course, since Mattie was left-handed, he'd twist them down in the flash of an eye. So the boys would pocket their money, and at twenty cents for two glasses of beer, they could drink comfortably for the evening.

When they headed out to a well, the well would be just finishing up, and companies would be there running tools and well tests. A drill would already have preceded the four-man crew of Exploration Oil to the site. They usually loaded the holes with dynamite, and if they didn't, then that was Mattie's job. Otherwise, if they were already loaded with the dynamite, he would just sit in the truck and set off the charges. If they had to reload the holes, then the helper would do that. So it was about as soft and easy and warm job in the thirty- to forty-degree weather that you could possibly get. And then upon completion of a job, there might be one on their way back or a little farther north. If not, they'd stay in Peace River until another job came up. The winter went by very quick from mid-January to the first week in April of 1958.

Mattie then proceeded back to Calgary with the crew. Since it was very slow that spring, 90 percent of the people in the oil industry got laid off. This is rather traditional for a couple of years. In Mattie's case, they offered him a job around the shop where he would empty the waste paper baskets, pick up pints of whiskey for the happy hour for the supervisors and bosses, visit with the secretaries, etc.

Mattie considered staying on, but since his mother was back east, he decided that he should probably return to the island. He then spent a few days in Calgary, leaving in mid-April to head to Toronto, and then on to Queen Charlotte Island.

Leaving Calgary about five or six in the morning, he got fifteen miles east of town, and a chap was hitchhiking. Mattie stopped and picked him up. The hiker asked him how far he was going. Mattie said, "A lot farther than you are going unless you can swim." "Well," the hitchhiker said, "I'm going to Oshawa, Ontario, thirty miles east of Toronto, to pick up a truck. And I've got a week to get down there." Mattie informed him that he would get a lot faster trip than he had planned. Mattie had no plans to stop. After driving for about fifteen hours, he let the hiker drive for a few hours, but he wasn't that good a driver; and since it was after dark, Mattie had a short nap and got behind the wheel again. In forty-eight and a half hours, Mattie and his passenger were in Oshawa, Ontario, where the lad was going to pick up a new truck. The fellow phoned his boss in Calgary to tell him everything was going good, and his boss asked him if he made five hundred miles yet. He said, "Yes, not only did I make five hundred miles, I've made 2,237 miles." Naturally his boss didn't believe him, but there he was, at the gates of General Motors, to pick up his truck. With that, Mattie shook his hand and accepted his thanks, turned around, and drove the thirty miles back to Toronto to visit the Duggan family and his cousins, including the sixth cousin, Helen Hagen.

His cousin Ed, who worked at the Kraft Dairy, asked if he would like to join him and his wife at the spring Easter party. Mattie said he would be quite interested as he loved to dance, but he needed a girl to dance with. His cousin Ed said, "Four doors down the street is my father's friend PJ Kelly, and he has a nice-looking redheaded daughter." So Mattie promptly headed down the street and asked her if she'd like to go to the dance. She quickly agreed, and on Saturday night, they all headed to the hall where they had a big supper and a full night of dancing.

Mattie then visited a friend called Bill Mallett, his cousin Helen and her husband Jim, who drove a bus for the Toronto transit, and their family, including many other islanders who were working in Toronto. Since Mattie now took a drink, there were many parties; and islanders were always looking for a reason to celebrate, so they would have a party to meet Mattie and hear all about the far distant west, to which they planned to go to someday, but few ever did.

Mattie then drove to Montreal to visit his cousins Mary McFinski and Doris Cook. After spending a couple of days in Montreal, he proceeded on to the island, driving by himself. Upon arriving at the island, he decided to go into the potato business in a big way. In order to make enough money to fund his potato-growing efforts, he bought a truck and hauled all of the number 2 cull potatoes that couldn't be sold by railcar to Toronto on the open market. He would haul these potatoes to the mainland. He paid twenty-five cents, bag and all, sold them to the small stores, the restaurants, etc. He'd haul two hundred bags a trip, and at $2.25 a bag, it was $450. Then he would go to the Sussex and Studholm cattle sale in Sussex, New Brunswick, about a hundred miles west of Moncton, and Moncton was a hundred miles west of the island. There he would buy calves for $10 each, load up thirty in the back of the truck, take them back to Prince Edward Island, and sell them for $30 each for a total of $900 and another $600 profit. Now he had a total, for one day's work per week, of $800 profit. If you figured it out, the ordinary wage earner was getting about fifty cents an hour, $5.00 a day and twenty-five days a month would be $125 a month. Mattie was getting six times that in a week. So now having learned to make money quickly and how to save 100 percent of it by staying in the bush for four months, Mattie found a way to quickly pile up the money.

It was an election year, so Mattie started working politics for the federal election. Jack Baker was running for the conservatives. The liberals had been in for years. Naturally, Mattie joined up with the locals, Alec Duggan, who was the head, along with Lee Cook. Mattie's job was to drive a car, and he'd be given two cases, one of black rum, the cheapest kind available, and one case of cheap golden wedding whiskey. On Election Day, it was up to him to drive around the polls, taking people to vote, and to give them a pint of whichever rum or whiskey they preferred. If they happened to be temperance people and did not take a drink, then he would offer them two dollars, which was four hours' work. If there was a family, then the stake would be up to five dollars. Everybody was bought and paid for when they went to the polls on the island, except those who did not drink and refused to take the money. The money was then given to Mattie and his associates, and they then could spend the next month or two living high on the hog with the political funds.

The rule on the island was that if you voted for the party in power and nearly everybody knew what your political allegiance was, then you would get a job as everybody with the government would be fired as soon as the election was over, providing a new party got into power, either the liberals or the conservatives. The federal government was the better job because there you could hold your job. Since there was very little other work on the island, government jobs were prized far above anything else. They did not pay a lot of money in those days, probably $75 to $100 a month, whether it was working on a boat or joining the Mounties, working on highway crews, or in the government offices, etc., but at least it was guaranteed. But there was no overtime, which Mattie did not care for at all, so he decided that he would never work on the island as the west was far more superior.

Mattie then decided to put in a big crop as he was one of the biggest potato growers on the island. But he needed more funding. During the election, he talked to a feller called Doug Weir, who was a very good friend of the family. Doug was a handsome big guy. He said, "Well, I went up to Maine, USA, and they're going from one row potato planters and potato diggers to two rows, and you can buy ones very cheap."

Mattie then decided that this was the other way to get quick money, so he hired his friend Lloyd Mayhew, who joined him, and together they headed for Maine to buy potato diggers and planters at towns called Presque Isle and Mars Hill and various other towns throughout the area. They paid $50 each for the potato planters, loading up the equipment on the back of the truck, taking it to Queen Charlotte Island and selling it to the farmers for $300 per piece of equipment, making $200 per machine. If the farmer didn't have any money, then Mattie would take six hundred bags of potatoes, allowing a dollar per bag. This was a total of $600 and after paying $50 for the equipment and $50 to haul them down, which was very reasonable because they had already hauled a load of number 2 potatoes over and made money on them. So they now had $200, and they'd hauled a half dozen pieces of equipment and would make an average of about $300. So that would be a couple thousand dollars for a few days' work. Mattie was doing extremely well. He had more money than he knew what to do with.

He then planted potatoes in the spring and bailed hay for all the farmers within miles, which made more money. Unfortunately that year, 1958, he planted potatoes for his cousin Gloria Martin and her husband Leo Scott from

Newfoundland and got a disease in his potatoes called ring rot. Therefore he was known as a ring rot contact, and he had seed potatoes sold at $3 per bag, but now they were reduced to the cost of seventy-five cents for eating potatoes, not making any money in 1958.

He continued on with the calves and number 2 potatoes through the winter of '58 and '59, and the following year he put in even more potatoes. That was a terrible year, the worst in the history of the Maritimes. Mattie's crop got Fusarium rot, and a lot of the potatoes were rotten when he dug them and the ones he put in storage during the winter, resulting in his crop being about 80 percent lost, losing him thousands of dollars.

Well, he thought, things can't go bad three years in a row, and after all, he could make money during the winter out of the potatoes and calves. And he was loading cattle for Victory Meat Packers in Fredericton, New Brunswick. He got enough money to put in even more potatoes, figuring to keep increasing and sooner or later you'll win. In the spring of 1960, he put in potatoes on a half dozen farms scattered all around. He was the biggest potato grower on the island and one of the biggest in the Maritimes, after McCain Foods. Unfortunately, things were bad three years in a row. The price was worth nothing, just thirty-six cents for a seventy-five-pound bag, which was just 50 percent of the cost to grow them. By this time, Mattie was broke, owing thousands of dollars. He went back on the boats, stevedoring; and when they were all loaded, in early November, he decided he would head for Toronto, taking his hired man, Cal McNeal from Glace Bay, Nova Scotia. He got a ride with a distant acquaintance over to the mainland, and Cal and Mattie were separated in Amherst, Nova Scotia, with Cal going to Cape Breton Island. A guy lifted the suitcase out of the car and said, "That's the lightest suitcase I've ever lifted." Mattie informed him that it was full of oats for Cal's mother's chickens. The chap then decided he and his girlfriend would head on to Toronto, so Mattie caught a ride all the way up to Toronto, Ontario, at no charge. Sure beat walking as they did in the spring of '55.

Mattie spent about a week in Toronto visiting his friends, and then decided he would head to Alberta via the Canadian CP train, this was quite an experience as there were a number of military personnel going from the east to Alberta and the west coast, both army and navy as well as a number of women, girls actually, who were traveling westward in the fall of 1960.

When happy hour rolled around about four o'clock, the porter would come around with small bottles of various liquor; it was eighty cents for a double shot of whatever brand you wished. There was a group of about a dozen that joined Mattie in happy hour from around four o'clock until after midnight. There was one little guy who kept walking through asking if he could have a drink of pop, so one hefty sailor poured a good portion of one of the little bottles into a quarter of a 7Up bottle and gave it to the little guy to drink. It took quite a while before the conductor figured out that it wasn't the swaying of the train, but the little guy was pretty well hammered.

The train had a dome car, so they could go up to the second level and watch the lights of the cities pass by. After they were through partying, they would then go to their compartments, particularly the ones who the government was paying their way west and were so fortunate; but in the case of Mattie, he was going to sleep in his seat, but one of the girls who was going out to British Columbia invited Mattie to share her bunk. Upon getting settled away for the evening, the lady in the opposite bunk said, "Are you two young people united in the holy bonds of matrimony?" Mattie informed her not to worry because bunks were for sleeping, nothing else. With that, she rolled over and started to snore.

The trip lasted a little over two days to Calgary, and upon arriving in the station in downtown Calgary and the Palliser Hotel, which was owned by the Canadian Pacific Railroad (CPR), Mattie grabbed his gear and jumped off followed by several of his newly made friends. As they were shaking hands and hugging each other good-bye, the train started to pull out of the station. Some of the fellows were feeling pretty good, so the conductor had to get a helper and pull them on one by one with Mattie pushing with everybody waving both from the station house platform as well as from the interior of the train.

Mattie's brother had come west in a new Volkswagen to work as a geologist, after hearing Mattie write about all the money that could be made in the oil fields in the west. Brother Jim was a geologist, and he went to work up north in the oil fields being part of a group that found a large oil field. During the summer of 1960, Jim had drove back east in his new Chevrolet Corvair a brand-new product which looked good, but was a bit of a lemon; and he agreed to take their mother, Lena, across Canada to the west, and Mattie would rent out the farm to a neighbor at no charge. Jim spent a couple of months till Christmas in the north quickly deciding that after spending a year in northern Quebec working for the Krupp empire from Germany and finding a large iron ore mine that the oil fields in the northern Alberta and British Columbia were not any better environment in which to work.

He then returned to Calgary to go to the University of Calgary and further his education degree where he promptly got a teaching position, and he stayed for several years.

Mattie went to work again with Exploration Oil. This would be his fifth season working for the company. By this time, he had progressed to a full-fledged driller with top pay working twelve to fifteen hours a day, seven days a week, thirty days a month with a vehicle to drive and all expenses paid. It was a virtual gold mine. As Mattie lay in his bed at night, he got to thinking. He was now in his early twenties and had accomplished nothing, had failed to get an education, had worked three hard long years saving his money only to lose it all in three years of investing into potatoes, plus losing all the money he made out of the equipment sales, the cattle sales, and the buying and selling of potatoes. Plus selling fertilizer, potato spray, etc., some of which he never got paid for; but Mattie always said, "I'll never be broke as long as I have people owing me."

As he thought back of the years he had worked on Queen Charlotte Island, he was taught by his mother, a nurse, who had graduated with her RN in 1921 and who had worked in Boston for the very rich during the twenties. She had saved every cent and was left money by the very rich that passed on and thanked her by giving her large amounts of cash for her kindness to them. This resulted in all through the years of the Depression. Whenever money was needed, Lena only had to go to the big steamer trunk and take out a wad of bills to carry the farm through the hard times and enabled them to keep Joe Peters, who came to work at sixteen back during the First World War as a hired man to help plus many others during the busy harvest season. During the war years, Mattie would accompany his mother throughout the community helping deliver babies, setting broken legs, sewing up cuts, etc. He learned during that period to see how the people thanked his mother profusely for her good work, and he realized that if you help others, they will respect you and help you in turn, and that set Mattie on a path of doing good for others that stuck with him all through his life. Further, he learned from his father that being the happy-go-lucky Irishman, always with a smile on his face and a joke to tell, everybody loved to share time with him and enjoy his company whether they were having a drink or just a sociable visit. Mattie's father also taught him during those formative years to "let your word be your bond, don't burn your bridges, because you might have to cross them on your return." He also made Mattie promise three things on his deathbed. One, to keep the farm that no one ever felt that he as a young man, long before the First World War, would be able to hold on during the war and the Depression that followed. Two, since he did not feel that Mattie would stay on the island, he told Mattie to take his mother wherever he went. And three, that he would have a boy and call him Daniel after his own father. Mattie agreed to all three, and as he spent the winter of 1961, he thought about all he had learned from his father who had died when he was just a late teenager.

Mattie had always heard about the Gill Lumber Company that had gone broke and paid one hundred cents on the dollar. He decided in the fall of 1960 that he would save every cent and pay what he owed in full, even though he had declared bankruptcy; he was advised by a lawyer who was a noted alcoholic to declare bankruptcy with the promise that he would pay back in full when he got the money, but afterward informing Mattie that he no longer had any liabilities that he could do as he felt. Nevertheless, Mattie worked the oil fields in the winter and most summers, but if there was a shortage of oil field work in the spring, he would drive a taxi in the spring and fall, which proved to be very lucrative. If there was a shortage of work during the summer as the oil companies had a habit of slowing down in the summer while the ones who worked in the head offices and were higher up took holidays. Mattie would go on the construction crews, working in the city as an equipment operator during the day and either driving taxi or working for a freight loading company loading tractor trailers with freight, most of which was done by hand in those days. At the end of three to four years, Mattie had saved up a considerable amount of money, which he saved by putting his checks in a tobacco tin; and when accountants would call him from head office and ask where his checks were after not seeing them cashed, Mattie would inform them that since he did not have to spend any money out of pocket and all his expenses were paid for by the company, he was saving every last cent, except for a little bit he used to play poker which always resulted in making money rather than losing any.

In the spring of 1961 on the first of April, Mattie and Big Bob Hull went to work for the Waldron Ranch, which was halfway between Calgary and Pincher Creek in southern Alberta. The ranch was owned by a very wealthy man who Mattie had done some oil field work as he owned a company called Canadian Exploration. Mattie and Big Bob went down to the ranch, and this was quite an experience for Mattie as the cowboys all carried six guns for shooting gophers and rifles in their saddle scabbard. A few days after they arrived, the boss left his big stallion tied up to the hitch rail and went to town about an hour's drive to the south, and the guys all said to Mattie, "You say you've ridden horses for years, let's see you ride that one." So Mattie untied the reins and jumped up on the saddle, not realizing that when cowboys get off their horse, they loosen up the cinch strap so the horse can breathe easily. So the horse started to buck a little as Mattie was a strange rider, and the saddle started to slide sideways around his belly; and as everyone cheered and clapped, the horse got even more scared, so Mattie jumped off as the saddle swung sideways and luckily saved himself from being trampled by the horse to the enjoyment of all the cowboys who were watching.

Mattie's job was to drive a pickup loaded with grain, and they would go out in the pasture and feed sixty-plus bulls, and there was this other young fellow who was his assistant, Big Bob. Mattie would drive, and he and Wayne would dump the grain out in a row for the animals to feed on. Mattie would stop to let the animals catch up, and then start back with a jerk with Wayne falling off the back of the truck; then he would drive faster, and Wayne couldn't catch up, and the bulls would be running as fast as they could behind. Well, Big Bob thought this was the best of entertainment, but poor Wayne would practically ruin his shorts when this happened.

In another few weeks, towards the end of the month, they had over a thousand one-year-old animals. These animals would be shipped to Colorado in big cattle liners, so the boss picked Mattie and Big Bob to go to town and take feed in for the animals in the corrals at Lundbreck. The herd arrived a day later, upon getting everything all ready to go for the cattle and rooms for the men for a couple of days while they were loading the trucks. Mattie and Big Bob met up with several native people, and they paid for the whiskey that Mattie bought at the nearest liquor store for some serious drinking. After talk of fighting and whatnot, the natives decided that the two islanders were too rough characters for them to mingle with, and they decided to go alone, with Mattie and Bob going to the bar. There they met a chap who was playing a guitar and singing "Have Another Cup of Coffee and then I'll Go," a song the chap had written the previous year. Three ladies were attracted to the singer, and Mattie and Bob joined up; but after an hour or so of drinking, they decided they better go back and check on the storage area to make sure everything was okay for the cattle. Upon returning to the bar, the singer informed them that two oil field people had taken their two girls and gone to the motel by the Texaco service station. Mattie and Bob headed over, and Bob asked Mattie to knock on the door and demand the ladies come with them. After knocking on the door, Mattie was standing, waiting patiently for one of the guys to open the door, which he did, punching Mattie between the eyes and breaking his black plastic rimmed glasses, which were all the rage at the time and had been introduced by Buddy Holly, the country western singer. Mattie turned around and said to Big Bob, "Look what that guy did." Bob said, "That was not very friendly of him." He then proceeded to kick down the door, and he and Mattie entered the room. Big Bob picked up one of the guys and threw him through the picture window while Mattie wrapped a pole lamp around the head of the other guy. By this time, the girls had left, and the guys were after them as fast as their feet would carry them. Mattie and Bob sat down to drink their whiskey and stated that westerners don't last long against islanders. In a very short time, the Royal Canadian Mountain Police (RCMP) arrived and said, "We're going to take you guys into custody for breaking the furniture." Bob promptly stated, "You'll need to get another half-dozen guys if you want to take us." They immediately left, and Mattie and Bob continued on drinking, toasting to how they had scared off the RCMP. Big Bob would sooner fight than eat, and he was always hungry.

Soon the two Mounties arrived back, one around forty, the other in his early twenties, and they had with them very large German shepherd that looked like he was a cross between a wolf and a pony. The senior officer then said to the boys, "Would you like to come peacefully, or do we have to turn the dog loose?" Mattie informed the police that they would be glad to go along with them. The police took them to a place called Blairmore west on Highway 3 and locked them up in cells overnight. Adjacent to their cells was a fellow who sang all night; he was entertaining, but he kept them awake until the wee hours.

In the morning, the jailer came about nine o'clock and took Mattie and Bob to the magistrate's court, where an ex-miner, now retired, was the magistrate, and they proceeded with the trial. The magistrate informed the boys that there were hundreds of dollars of damage, and he wanted to know how much money they had. Mattie told him he had nearly a hundred dollars where Bob only had a couple of dollars. The magistrate said, "Well, that won't pay for the damage. I will turn you loose if your boss will take you back and pay the money for the damage you did."

The magistrate then looked at the two police officers and said to the younger one, "Where are you from?" To which he replied, "From Queen Charlotte Island." The magistrate looked at him and said, "Well, these are your buddies then, from the same area." So he told the Mountie, "Take them back where you got them, meet their boss, and make sure he'll pay their wages for the damages, and they're a lot better off working and making money. There will be no charges as these boys are a couple of kids and sowing their wild oats. Also, I want you Mounties to collect from the other two involved for half the damages because they threw the first punch."

That's exactly what happened, and upon meeting the foreman, who immediately hired them back and knowing that they were probably in jail overnight, he put them to work loading cattle to go to the United States. They then went back to the ranch afterwards and went back helping an old cowboy from Denmark to calve the cows where they lived in line shacks back in the foothills. When calving was through, they decided they would leave and would go back to Calgary to go to work in the oil field as the ground had dried out and the work would start up again; and if they weren't successful, they would go to work on the construction crews.

Mattie was staying with his friend Jock Gillie at a motel on the Trans-Canada Highway during late spring/early summer of 1965 when a knock came on the door; it was Bonnie Hagan, stopping by to say hello to Mattie and Jock. She inquired of Mattie if he would like to go to Queen Charlotte as her father had bought her a new white Sunbeam Alpine convertible, and she would like to go to the East Coast in early summer with a stop along the way in New York to see the world's fair. Bonnie was drop-dead good looking with raven black hair a model's figure. Mattie felt as if he had died and gone to heaven.

Mattie stated that he was planning on going to Libya in Africa, but in the morning, he would call Jack Clark who was head of the personnel for Exploration Oil and see if he could go to Halifax with the crew that was going to the Grand Banks in the North Atlantic up the coast of Newfoundland to explore for oil by ship. Bonnie said she would stop by the next evening and see how he made out. On Monday morning, Mattie called Mr. Clark and asked if he could go to Halifax, Nova Scotia, for the summer rather than go to Libya with his friend Jock. Jack Clark said he would phone back by noon, which he did, letting Mattie know that it was fine with the company if he wished to go to the East Coast rather than Africa. Jock was somewhat dismayed that the two friends weren't going to be together for another couple of years; he then called his friend Jim, who also worked for the same oil company, and Jim went in Mattie's place. Bonnie stopped by that evening to see Mattie, and they agreed to leave that week for the world's fair in New York, then on to Queen Charlotte to spend a few weeks together; and then Bonnie would drive Mattie to Halifax, Nova Scotia, where he would go to work on the oil ship. After a few months when the crew finished up, Mattie would return to Queen Charlotte Island, and he and Bonnie would spend a few weeks together again on the island, and then drive back to Alberta. Bonnie then drove Mattie to Halifax; he joined up with the oil crew where they spent several weeks learning the ropes about the boat. Most of the oil company workers were from Texas with a few from Western Canada, but they all worked on the main boat, which was from Norway. The oil company had rented two boats, one for the senior personnel and one for the dynamite boat, of which Mattie was in charge of. It was an excellent job as Mattie slept in the middle of the ship in a cabin in the same area as the captain and the chief engineer, which was the best area on a boat to sleep. Nevertheless, the seas would get so rough that they had to tie a rope from the front of the ship to the back in order to get around the ship without being swept overboard by the waves. They made a trip back to Bridgewater to get more dynamite and then to get some repairs in the port in Halifax. While in port, Mattie and another chap named Doug Newman from Three Hills, Alberta, would go to the horse races and the Sea Gull Club where dances were held. There they would meet girls, and Doug would invite them down to the ship. He would first prepare the crew before they arrived for the girls and have them line up, and as Mattie and Doug came aboard, the crew, which were mostly Cape Bretoners and other Nova Scotians, would all salute when the western guys came aboard. The girls thought that Mattie and Doug were rather important as they had never seen that happen except for the military.

Mattie and Doug would go to the Sea Gull Club where there was an excellent bar and dance hall. While sitting at the bar one night, there was an old chap, an ex-sailor who said, "Would you buy another sea-faring buddy a drink or two?" Mattie assured him that he would; he then said, "I'll tell you a couple of rhymes." And with that, he said, "In Halifax, the city by the sea a lady's ass and a whiskey glass made a jackass out of me." Then he asked if he told a longer one, would Mattie remember it, and Mattie assured him he would try. This was midsummer of 1965, and he promptly quoted, "I was standing on the street corner not doing any harm when along come the chief of the police Peter White and he took me by the arm. He led me to the jailhouse, and there he rang a bell, along come Jervas Tanton and led me to a cell. When I woke up in the morning the bedbugs and the chief were playing a game of ball. The bedbugs were ahead, but the chief he hit a home run, and he knocked me out of bed."

In late summer, Mattie went back to the island and spent a couple of weeks on holiday. Afterwards, Mattie and Bonnie started to drive the three thousand miles back to Calgary, Alberta. It was an excellent trip, going east and returning west. As Bonnie and Mattie had been friends since they were teenagers, Bonnie suggested to Mattie that if she worked and Mattie went to college in British Columbia year-round, she would help him go through college to be a lawyer, but it would take a few years to get a degree and three more to become a lawyer. Mattie figured that was too long of a time, so he thanked her profusely and decided he would try and get into business for himself as he did not look forward to traveling the world with the oil company, which was what one had to do in order to get ahead in the oil business.

The years went quickly by, until the fall of 1965. Mattie was sent by the oil company, who he had now worked for ten years, to Texas to take further courses in electronics. While there, one of the senior people asked if they knew anybody who could speak French as there was a fellow in Louisiana who had invented a new type of drill rig which was mounted on Ford tractors, on half tracks, for the swamps of Louisiana, and which the oil company executive felt would work in northern Alberta as the Rainbow oil field had just been discovered, and there was a great shortage of drill rigs.

It was suggested to the boss that Mattie could speak French, having learned it while stevedoring the boats. The next day, Mattie was driven to the airport where he met the pilot of the company plane, which took him from Texas to Baton Rouge, Louisiana. There he and the pilot got a hotel, and Mattie inquired where there was a dance because he knew it would be just like on the island, with the good old Acadian fiddles and accordion. He went to a dance, met a nice girl, and they had the most enjoyable evening; and since the following day was Sunday, she went with Mattie and the pilot to see the fellow with the drill rigs. Mattie looked them over and saw that he had a new type called a top drive, which would drill three times as fast as the existing rigs, at about a third the cost.

He then phoned Decker Sims and Jack Ryan, the two men who headed up Canada, and said he had found what the chap in Dallas had wanted, and he could buy the half-dozen rigs that the guy had and could easily build more. While he was talking to them, the pilot said, "Don't let them buy the rigs. Buy the drills yourself and let them put up the money." Mattie suggested this to the two vice presidents, and they brought Jack Clark on the line, the accountant for northern United States and Canada, and stated that they were agreeable to putting up the money to buy the drill rigs for Mattie's company called Murfinksy Drilling. The pilot then suggested that Mattie made sure that they would supply him men, credit for parts, a shop, the works, in order to create a drilling company. They quickly agreed to this as well. Then the pilot came again with a further suggestion since he had just pensioned out of the US Air Force in Alaska and was now in his early forties, and he really enjoyed the native girls, so how about asking them to buy a plane and the pilot would fly it up to Canada and stay with Mattie as a friend and as an airplane pilot. He informed Mattie that he felt that he was going to go places now. He had saved his money—he had gotten experience from Mr. Levine in Fredericton, New Brunswick, on how to make a dollar, from his mother on how to save a dollar, and from his father on how to conduct a good business. The bosses in Canada quickly agreed that they could lease a plane, and they would also have the use of the plane and pilot, but Mattie would be in charge. Mattie went from just an employee to owning his own drilling company, including having a plane, so he immediately started to hire US experienced drillers and asked if the people in Calgary, Alberta, high up, would see that he had sufficient support staff. They assured him he would as well as bring in a camp from Alaska to get him started and set up more camps as soon as he could build more drilling rigs.

Mattie was overjoyed; he and the pilot went back to the hotel and celebrated with bourbon till midnight, both happier than a pig in you-know-what.

The rigs were shipped back to Calgary immediately, and Mattie flew back to Dallas with the pilot, informing the Texan that the vice presidents for the northern United States and Canada had asked Mattie to return with the rigs and start building more. The pilot agreed to follow with the twin-engine Beechcraft Baron, a beautiful plane that would seat six people.

Mattie got back to Calgary and rented at the Trans Canada Motel situated on Thirty-Sixth Street NE and the Trans-Canada Highway. Then he leased pickups, put together his full crew, took them all down to the Hudson's Bay Company where his cousin Hal Smith was manager and outfitted them in good heavy winter clothes.

He was now ready to head north, so they loaded all the rigs up on tractor trailers and headed for their first job at High Level, Alberta, which was about eight hundred miles north of Calgary up near the Northwest Territories border. Mattie had drove a hard deal, with work seven days a week for the drill rigs, night and day, a guaranteed rate per hour as well as a footage bonus, a real sweetheart deal. Unfortunately, when he got into the bush at Rainbow Lake, it went very cold, forty below. And since the tractors only had canvas heat houses to keep the fellows warm, although they did most of their work outside, they found it too cold to carry on, and then the tractors could only travel about fifteen miles per hour, although that was about the maximum you could travel on the cut line, Mattie could see he needed to do better. He promptly loaded up the trucks, hit the sixty miles from Rainbow Lake oil field into High Level, where all his friends when they stopped for supper said, "Well, that was a short winter, Mattie. Maybe you go back to the southern states, give her a try down there. This is a bit too cold for your drilling company." Mattie assured them that this was not the last they would see of him. They drove night and day to Calgary, arriving at the motel, and Mattie went to work immediately the next morning renting Jack's welding down by the CPR railroad tracks and started to build water tanks to put on the back of big GM and Ford trucks that he had rented. He then pulled the four wheels off the tractors, put a water tank in front of each one, and mounted the drill rigs on the big trucks behind the water tanks. Now he had brand-new trucks with diesel-powered rigs, and he just needed water trucks to haul water to his equipment. He immediately hired a bunch of gravel trucks and went to his friend Maxie Schuler of Ace Salvage and got the thousand-gallon tanks that airplane engines come in to the Calgary airport. After bolting them down and chaining them securely in the boxes, he rented a second welding shop, and he could get two water trucks ready per day. This gave him new trucks with diesel-powered drill rigs mounted on the back of them, including several water trucks he bought to haul camp water and help other contractors, if there were any on the crew in need of water.

The winter went by quickly, and Mattie cleaned up financially, arriving back in Calgary on the first of April, but there was not a lot of work for the drill rigs for the summer. Not enough to keep his men employed at least. When he went to settle up with the Trans Canada Motel, Reverend Olson, who was a Baptist minister from Saskatchewan, asked him what he was going to do for the summer. He said he wasn't too sure, but that he'd sure like to come up with something to keep his equipment going. Mr. Olson said to Mattie, "Why don't you take your drills off the trucks and put gravel boxes on them so you can haul topsoil around Calgary for the gardeners and landscapers?" To which Mattie replied, "That'll only last a month." The reverend responded with, "Then try this. We at the motel are hiring a company to pave the potholes, another one to fill the cracks, another one to paint the lines, another to move the snow, another to sand the parking lot, another to sweep it up. Why not just put that together, and you'll get enough work to keep you going, at least partway through the summer."

Mattie thought this was one heck of an idea, and he promptly went to the Catholic Church on Elbow Drive and filled all the cracks, the potholes, swept it, painted the lines, and asked the reverend if he would announce from the pulpit that Ace Pavement and Parking Lot Maintenance had done the work for free, and if they liked the job, then send him some work. He got around a dozen new customers to give him a start, so he moved on down Elbow Drive to the north and went to the next church, repeating the process and getting more customers. When the reverend was thanking him for doing the work, he said, "You should go another three blocks north, turn left for three blocks, and there you'll find the synagogue. The people that go there, own most of the property in Calgary. You have got a last name of Jewish heritage, so you should fit right in." Mattie did so, and while he was checking the cracks and the potholes and seeing how many lines he had to paint, a chap came out with a little black beanie on his head and said, "What are you doing?" Mattie said, "Reverend, I'm measuring your lines, checking your cracks, and am going to fill them in and sweep your lot and make it look like new." He said he was called a rabbi. Mattie had not known this as there were no synagogues on the island, so he then asked, "What's the charge?" Mattie said, "I'd like you to announce, Rabbi, on Sunday during service that I did the work for you." The rabbi said, "But our service is on Saturday." Mattie said, "This is Thursday, so be it. I'll have everything done by tomorrow, and if your congregation likes my work, then call me next week, and I'll be glad to give them good service and a very reasonable price." By Saturday evening at seven o'clock, Mattie's phone was ringing off the hook, and within the week, he had booked up solid for the summer of 1961 and the following summer as well, and it had cost him next to nothing for advertising. With each new customer, Mattie would always ask them that if they were happy, tell others, and if they were unhappy, tell him. Most of his customers would want a discount of at least 10 percent, so Mattie quickly figured out that if he added on 20 percent, then he had 10 percent to give as a discount and 10 percent to come and go on. Or if he had to go back and do touch-ups, then he was still ahead of the game.

Mattie then quickly realized that there was a fortune to be made in this business. A pothole two- to four-feet wide and three inches deep could be paved over to a width of twenty feet by twenty feet with a nice square patch. With the center being three inches deep and the rest a quarter-of-inch-thick asphalt, then if you got just the right amount of thinner mixed in with your paint, then you would wind up painting the lines every year. They'd be nice and fresh, and the parking lots would look like a million bucks. Further, if you took a load of sand, stretch it out, and get double the mileage, and if any shopping center owner asked you if they were getting enough sand, then you could inform them that if you put down too much, they would have to pay you to sweep it up, load it up, haul it away, and dispose of it. Only putting down the bare essentials then Mattie could keep their cost down for them while at the same time protecting them against insurance claims, and he would assure them that there would be no liability whatsoever while getting paid for a full load every time.

Within the year, Mattie had the complete city sewed up for all the maintenance, including the railroads, oil companies, shopping centers, apartment buildings, warehouses. You name it, Mattie had them all in his pocket.

He quickly learned to get hockey tickets, football tickets, and take his customers out to lunch. If there was a trade show in the United States, send them down to a warmer climate, particularly Las Vegas, jackets, knives, pens, anything you could possibly think of, he would give away. So much so that he ended up forming his own promotional products company and always using the name ACE, which stood for A Calgary Entrepreneur.

Now he had the world by the tail. He would go north in the fall, drill for six months up north, haul water, and he quickly learned to put trailers behind his water trucks to move the track equipment for the oil companies. Whenever they needed to hire, no questions asked, Murfinsky Drilling got the job. In the spring he would go back hauling topsoil. He got the soil for nothing, fluff it up with a shredder, and then sell it for an exorbitant price. He also started acquiring a fleet of street sweepers in the sixties, working for the city of Calgary, night and day, and sweeping throughout the city. Then as soon as it got warm enough around mid-May, the asphalt plants would open, and Mattie would go back to his paving, crack filling, and painting lines. He would make hundreds of thousands per year while a schoolteacher or nurse would probably make seventeen thousand a year and a policeman or firefighter would get fifteen.

Mattie began to think he was a genius. He was back with a bulging bank account and money in his pockets galore, new vehicles, and purchasing new equipment for his drilling, maintenance, and pavement companies.

CHAPTER 7

That summer, Mattie's mother passed away from a stroke, and Mattie had gone back to Prince Edward Island as his mother would have liked to make one last trip back there while she was still alive. Unfortunately, this was not to be as she was only in the hospital for one day before passing away. Mattie's brother James and his mother traveled by train back to Prince Edward Island for the funeral and wake. Again, the church was full as she had done so much in her lifetime to help others as a nurse and a respected and valued member of their local community in the Treetown area.

After the funeral, Mattie's brother went to get his birth certificate from the reverend, and when he returned, Mattie inquired what he needed it for. James said that now that their mother had passed on, they were free to marry any religion, nationality, or culture of their choosing, and Mattie promptly agreed. Mattie inquired who his brother was going to marry, and he mentioned a lady of a different religion. Mattie stated that his mother would not have agreed, and James agreed but said that she was no longer with them and that he would like Mattie to do two things. Mattie asked what they were. James then asked him to be the best man at the wedding, to which Mattie agreed to; then James asked Mattie to keep his nose out of his business for the rest of their lives, to which Mattie agreed to as well. They then proceeded to the gentleman's club in the little town of Kingslow to celebrate the life of their mother, who they both deeply loved.

In the fall of 1966, Mattie went back up north with the drill rigs. He worked through the winter and came back in the spring and again did his spring maintenance and pavement during the summer, repeating the process over again to the fall of 1967, and again in the oil field for the winter.

The cook was doing a very poor job in camp in midwinter of 1967, so Mattie threw him out in a snowbank, which resulted in the cook doing a much poorer job; so in order to make him happy, Mattie asked him what he liked to drink to which the cook answered with, "Hennessey cognac." So Mattie sent his cousin Joe, who was working with him on time off, with the request that he bring back several bottles of the cognac. Upon Joe's return, Mattie gave the bottles to the cook whereupon the cook promptly invited Mattie over to his quarters to play crib and drink at five cents per point. Since Mattie loved to play cards or crib for money, he readily agreed. The camp attendant always brings the mail to the cook, who then distributes it to all the workers in the camp. As they played cribbage, the cook mentioned that Mattie got a lot of letters, four or five, all with different writing on them. Mattie stated that this was true because when he was out, he loved to dance and party. And since he drove taxi on the weekends, he would always go to the various dance halls in Edmonton. And since many of the ladies didn't have their own cars, then he would be dressed up in a black suit with a white shirt and tie, and being a good dancer, he would invite them to ride home with him, which they readily agreed as in Edmonton the weather is cold and snowy even in the spring. Therefore, Mattie made a lot of friends plus he had two existing lady friends that he had known as a teenager in Prince Edward Island who had also now come to Alberta, giving Mattie something to look forward to when he went to the city.

The cook said to Mattie, "You should get married because you must be getting old." Mattie informed him that he was either thirty or thirty-one, and he wasn't sure because he didn't pay much attention to age. Whereupon the cook said, "I will read your letters and then tell you who you should marry." As the cook was doing so, Phil Hurd, the Canadian head of the Rocky Mountain Oil Company, came into the cook's quarters and said that he was going to the head office in Calgary for Canada, then he'll be flying on to Denver, Colorado, where the head office was, and if there was anything the cook needed, to just write it down. Then he told Mattie that he was doing a great job of drilling, and if there was anything he could do for him, he would only be too glad to do so. The cook promptly said, "Mattie is going to get married, so I've decided on who he should marry, a girl from Saskatchewan. Whereupon Mr. Hurd said, "Why do you think you're qualified to give Mattie directions on who to marry?" The cook said, "I should know since I was married seven times, and they all failed because of my drinking." Mr. Hurd promptly agreed and asked what the cook wanted him to do, so the cook said he wanted Mr. Hurd to get a dozen roses and send them to a lady by the name of Bonnie, with a note saying, "Come to Calgary and I'll make it worth your while. I've got something to tell you during the stampede the first week of July." Mr. Hurd agreed to do as asked and promptly left for the head office. Mattie finished the winter drilling and then headed to the south. He and his cousin Joe then decided that they would move from Edmonton to Calgary as the weather was better. It was closer to the mountains and a more lively city although not as many dances. Upon arriving in Calgary, they went to work repairing the drill rigs and working for Mattie's business during the day while they did the repairs on nights and weekends. Spring went quickly by, and Calgary Stampede started up, and Mattie's friend Bonnie came to town, where Mattie promptly took her out thirteen of fourteen days and informed her that he would marry her. She replied with "You usually ask a girl to marry you?" Mattie stated, "Well, when I hire people for the oil fields, I usually ask them if they'd like to work with me. And if they think I'd be somebody they'd enjoy, so I feel when you're getting married you should inform them in the same manner." Bonnie replied that she would love to get married, and Mattie informed her that he was leaving for the States with rigs, but he would be back in early fall. She stated that she was going to be teaching in Calgary, and it would start up the first of September and that a good time to get married would probably be October or November. Mattie agreed, and in late August, Mattie and Bonnie drove to Montreal, Quebec, to attend the world's expo. They had a most enjoyable time, and upon their return, Bonnie started teaching school, and Mattie went back to his construction and paving work. He shared an apartment with two Americans and a chap from Scotland who also worked in the oil field. Within a few weeks, his friend of over twenty years Jock Gillies returned from Libya, and as he and Mattie were having a few drinks, he asked Mattie what his plans for the future were. Mattie told him he was going to get married, and Jock asked if he was kidding, but Mattie reassured him that he was really going to get married. Jock, who was a good-looking guy with bright blue eyes, always full of music, and a blonde wavy hair, said, "Well, I guess in that case I'm going to have to get married too. Do you mind if I use your phone?" He picked up the phone, and he called Yvonne in Queen Charlotte Island and said, "My friend Mattie is getting married, so I should too. Will you marry me?" She answered with a yes, so he told her to come to Calgary so they could get married right away. Within a week, Yvonne arrived in Calgary, and Jock asked Mattie to help him arrange for a hotel for the wedding reception and if he would be the best man, to which Mattie readily agreed. Then the next day, they headed downtown to buy furniture for the two apartments that they had rented on Elbow Drive in Calgary, Mattie on the third floor and Jock on the second floor. Upon arriving at the furniture dealer, Mattie said, "I'll have a dinette suite for the kitchen." Jock said that he would have one too, and Mattie said, "I would like a chesterfield, a chair, a coffee table, etc." Jock said that he would take the same. Mattie said, "I will have a bedroom set with a dresser and a set of drawers, etc." Then the owner said to Jock, "Well then, of course you will have the same." Jock said that that was correct, so he said that he would give a discount of 30 percent off and free delivery, which pleased the islanders, and now they were all ready to get married and set up housekeeping.

Mattie and his bride-to-be Bonnie agreed to get married in mid-November. They held the wedding at the Sheraton Hotel that was newly built, and since the owner was a friend of Mattie's, who drove him in the taxi around downtown, he agreed to put on a tremendous affair. His name was Mr. Sheftel, and Mattie also knew him from the synagogue. The hotel was built round, which was very distinctive architecture, and Mattie's uncle Dave who was also of Jewish heritage and a great joker said that it was an ideal place to hold the wedding reception and on the wedding night because there will be no corners for the bride to hide from Mattie in a round hotel. A great time was had by all, and Mattie and Bonnie set up housekeeping, and Mattie immediately headed out with his oil field equipment for the far and distant north.

Mattie now had completed a large part of his journey in life. He had three excellent businesses with the maintenance business in the spring, the paving and construction business in the summer, and the oil field work in the winter. Now being married to a tall beautiful woman, he had completed everything he had wished for. During the first ninety-one days, Mattie was only home for a few hours. In one of those few days, the phone rang, and it was the expediter Homer Brant calling to say that they needed Mattie back up north where Mattie had drills, and one of their crews need more drill power as they get into tougher digging, and the guy who can do it is Mattie. So Mattie said that he would take a taxi to the hangar where the private plane is. "Not to worry," Homer said. "I dispatched the taxi ten minutes ago. He should be there within the hour." So Mattie realized then that the client is always right and that the oil companies were good to work for. They paid promptly, and you were assured your money.

The winter quickly went by, and Mattie now looked forward to getting back to the city where he could rejoin his wife. The years went quickly by, and everything went just as well as planned for Mattie and his new bride. In 1969, half an hour east of Calgary, lots came up for lease for a thousand dollars right beside a lovely lake where Mattie always water-skied during the summer as it was so close to the city; and Mattie always had a boat as he loved to barbeque, party, and water-ski. On the new lot which he only owned for a few months and then Western Irrigation decided to sell the lot to Mattie for a thousand dollars, Mattie was overjoyed, promptly buying the lot and building a new cedar log house. But during the following winter, evidently the fireplace was not put in properly by the contractor, and the house burned down, and Mattie flew home to see his first building in ashes. In the spring, he went back to paving after the spring maintenance work was done. A guy called Anjie Narod was building the nicest apartments and high-rise towers in Canada, and underneath the towers and the apartments were parking, and Mr. Narod wanted someone to pave it. But because of the smoke, it would be a very difficult job that nobody seemed to want. Mattie agreed to do it, and upon completion, Mr. Narod flew in and said to Mattie, "You're living in a rented apartment, these are the best in the world. I will give you a ten year lease for one hundred and fifty-five dollars a month." They had indoor and outdoor pools, a miniature golf course, a free suite a few doors away that for ten dollars a night Mattie's friends could stay and park their car in underground parking. It was a dream place to live, and the rent was cheap, which Mattie really appreciated. He thanked Mr. Narod profusely, and immediately they moved to their new apartment on the ground floor by the swimming pool. It was only a couple minutes or a few blocks from where Bonnie taught school, and only about ten blocks from Mattie's office and shop, so it was an ideal location.

Mattie then decided—he was driving a Mercury as he had done since 1955, his sixth Ford and a big black luxurious car—that he would sell it to his friend, and he and Bonnie would fly to Toronto and buy a new station wagon. Again, Mattie went up with his cousin Ed and cousin Al Laffan, and they went looking at cars as Al knew a salesman where he bought his vehicles. The salesman showed Mattie a 1970 Ford Country Squire with wood paneling on the side, and it was a beauty with a big V8; whereupon Mattie promptly shook his hand and bought the vehicle. Bonnie suggested that she did not want to move back to the lake as it had bad memories because it had burned everything they had accumulated as mementoes up until that time. Mattie agreed and phoned Alberta to sell the lot to an Irish friend. The lot was double the width but half as deep as others for sale, and so Mattie had hauled clay in and got all the dirt from the new road that was built in front of their house and made it twice as deep and got paid five dollars an hour to haul all the stone from a school that was being demolished. Those were beautiful limestone rock used to build the breakwater and a dock for his boats as by now he had both a sailboat and a powerboat. The lot sold within hours only to be resold again thirty years later for a million dollars. It was subdivided into two by a lady who was the third owner, and she got five hundred thousand for each lot. Mattie often regretted selling the lot because even at that time, he realized they weren't making any more land; therefore lots would go up in price, not realizing if it was by the water the price of the land would skyrocket. Mattie and Bonnie then left to drive to Prince Edward Island since Mattie was used to driving fifteen to twenty hours a day to job sites or across Canada to go back and visit the islands. He knew the motels would be full, so they just slept in a sleeping bag in the back of the station wagon in a school parking lot, church lot, or even on the edge of a graveyard. Upon arriving on Queen Charlotte Island, Mattie promptly went to pay his bills; it had now been ten years. And remembering the Gill Lumber Company, he went first to the Esso Bulk Oil Dealer who he met on the road and paid him in full plus 5 percent, a dollar and five cents, although he didn't pay 5 percent for every year. However, Art Clark thanked Mattie profusely and said he never expected to get the money. Mattie said he knew Mr. Clark told everyone around that he too would never be broke as Mattie would always owe him. He then went in to see Keith Stiewart, who was head of the co-op feed store and paid him in full. Keith was an excellent friend of the family and a good friend of Mattie, so he gave Mattie a hug and said with tears in his eyes, "You've made my day." Mattie thanked him for never saying anything over the years and not asking for the money whereupon he took his leave and proceeded towards the town of Summerside. At the edge of the city, he stopped at Peter's brothers who sold tombstones, and he paid them the balance on his father and mother's beautiful tombstone with the request that the brothers would tell the people who they had informed that Mattie never paid them the bill in full, particularly Don Gillies, Jock's father, who had asked Mattie when he was going to pay his bills. They said many thanks for the money, and they would inform everybody that Mattie had paid his bills. And while it had taken a little while, it was better late than not at all. He then proceeded into the city where he met up with Les Simkins, who was one of the three multimillionaires on the island and also came from Treetown and went to school with Mattie's father, Dan, as they were very close friends. When he paid Les, Les said to his wife Daisy, "I told you, Mattie Murfinsky would always pay his bill." With tears in his eyes, he gave Mattie a hug and wished him well because at this time he was in his eighties, and as he had been a friend of the family for generations, this meant the world to Mattie. Mattie continued on and paid all his bills even the bootlegger. After he paid Frankie Jones, Frankie got out the mouth organ and guitar and started singing as well as jigging with his feet, keeping time with the music, and he made up a little song from memory about Mattie. He said, "Mattie, it's so good to see you after all these years." When he finished playing a tune for Mattie, he called all his friends and said drinks are on the house. Needless to say, the house was packed within the hour, and Mattie drank to all their success as well as his own. They wished him all "Godspeed and God bless, and may you live forever." And they also toast for Frankie, saying, "May your given hand never fail." An old Irish saying for when you're drinking. Since Bonnie was off school for the summer, Mattie and Bonnie spent a month touring the island. And having drove down through Quebec, Nova Scotia, etc., they decided they would drive back through the United States, promptly heading down through Maine where Mattie's mother had nursed in her youth and then on to Boston, Massachusetts, where she had also nursed for the very rich and made a lot of money. They stopped to visit Mattie's Aunt Lily in Cambridge, Massachusetts. When Mattie knocked on the door, a very large woman answered and said, "What's a character like you coming around here begging for? Get out of my sight before I call the police." Mattie was rather shocked and started back to the car. At that, he heard this woman's voice saying, "Who was that, Kate? My nephew should be arriving soon." Mattie then realized that was his Aunt Lily, who had done the same thing as his mother and went to Boston to nurse the very old, sick, and very rich, also inheriting large amounts of money when they passed away. Lily was so glad to see Mattie. It was terribly hot and humid that she went out and bought a new air conditioner and then cooked up a big scoff of Maine lobster, potatoes, everything Mattie loved, including clams and oysters. It was a wonderful feast to behold. He and Bonnie stayed for several days before deciding to carry on westward, stopping in Toronto to visit the kinfolk and revisit all of Mattie's cousins as well as his aunt and uncle.

Mattie and Bonnie left Toronto, Ontario, in their new Ford station wagon and headed westward back to Alberta. On the first of September, Bonnie will be going back to teach school not far from their beautiful apartment in southwest Calgary in a brand-new luxurious area. Mattie will go back to his construction work for the rest of the summer, where the times are very good in Calgary and there are lots of works. Although it was a bit slow in the midsummer of 1970 as people go on holidays in July and August and therefore do not do a lot of work on their properties, which is why Mattie and his wife decided to go back east to travel through Eastern Canada and return back via the United States, which is a very beautiful country through Maine, New Hampshire, Vermont, Southern Quebec, Southern Ontario, and then westward through Michigan, Wisconsin, Minnesota, North Dakota, Montana, and then northward to Calgary, Alberta.

Work had piled up, and Mattie was very busy in the fall of 1970 during the months of September and October; and it was the late fall, so he was able to work up to Remembrance Day, which is in mid-November. It was time to get the drill rigs and water trucks ready to go north.

Mattie went north with his crews to work for his main client Gulf Oil plus Mobil Oil, Esso Oil, Texaco, and numerous other oil companies. He also worked for many contract exploration companies such as Century Exploration, Teledyne Exploration, Compagnie Générale de Géophysique a company from France for whom Mattie did a considerable amount of work as he spoke French and a lot of their employees came right from Europe. Most of the oil companies that he worked direct for and the contracting exploration companies that he drilled and hauled water with were out of the United States with very few Canadian companies. One was Norcana owned by his friend Dick Bayley. There was another company called Quest owned by two of his friends Ed Rutledge and Joe Little. He had crews with other companies as being the only drilling contractor with his own twin-engine plane and pilot, plus all brand-new equipment on late-model trucks with state-of-the-art drilling equipment and with very large water trucks. He only had one competitor, Jim Bennett, who was known in the oil field as Bull Bennett because he was about six foot six and around three hundred pounds and tougher than cement nails. Mattie had worked with Jim in the potato warehouse on Prince Edward Island for a company from Montreal, Quebec, with Jim being one of the strongest men on Queen Charlotte Island. Jim came west just a year or so ahead of Mattie, and he wrote a letter back to his brother who read it aloud to a bunch of young fellows at the Gordon Lodge dance hall, stating that he was making eighty cents an hour where Mattie was only making thirty-five working part-time in the warehouse and that Premier Monroe in Alberta was paying overtime and all expenses, a much better deal than in Queen Charlotte Island, which was the reason that Mattie went to Alberta in 1955. Bennet Drilling became one of the largest drilling companies in the world, as Jim had went with Jock Gillie only with a different crew in Africa where he made substantial wages and paid no income tax as that was the rules when you're overseas. With all the money he made overseas, he was able to buy a number of drill rigs and start up in the sixties, rapidly growing into the giant outfit that he now owned in the seventies.

Year after year Mattie kept up the same work effort—working in the oil fields all winter, doing the maintenance on the roads and streets, etc. in the spring, and running the asphalt crew all summer. He made friends with the Jones family who owned a concrete and asphalt plant, and they sold Mattie products for five dollars per ton, which was much cheaper than the other manufacturers. At that time, there were only a large family of Italian heritage and Jim Boone who owned Pioneer Paving and a company Mattie used to work for General Paving, which was still owned by his good friend Red Dunn and one other contractor Ted Lambert, who was also a close friend of Mattie's. The three big companies did all the streets and roads, and knowing that they could not compete with Mattie and Lambert Paving, they were quite content to let them do all the small- and medium-sized jobs while they did the very large ones. Mattie had a distinct advantage over his friend Ted Lambert as Ted went to Florida or Mexico over the winter and spent what he made during the summer while Mattie just kept piling up the maintenance and sweeping revenue on top of the paving revenue. And then he added the oil field money to the first two, so that in 1972 Mattie made four hundred and twenty-two thousand dollars net profit, which was a horrific sum of money. People who worked for the government would be lucky to get twenty thousand per year. Mattie was making the equivalent of forty salaries, and he then realized it was time to start thinking of something else. In the fall of 1967, he opened up six tree lots in major shopping centers in four quadrants of the city of Calgary, which by the fall of 1972 cleared in three weeks twenty-four thousand dollars, which was 20 percent more money than the ordinary worker made in a year. This Christmas tree money, he donated to Camp Horizon which was run by the Easter Seals, a nationwide charity that was formed to assist the handicapped. In the fall of 1967, Camp Horizon was built just outside Calgary at Bragg Creek, the largest and best equipped camp located in the best surroundings in Canada. The driving force behind the camp was the Kinsmen Club that was noted for their good works. Mattie did not have any children, and it looked like a family was not in the future. Even though he tried to adopt, it was almost impossible, although he regretted that he did not adopt a half a dozen children and hire a nanny; but this was in the days before the Filipino nannies, so one had to get a lady from the United Kingdom, which were fairly expensive. Mattie's wife loved to work and was a career woman, so Mattie realized there was no family in their future.

In 1972, Mattie's wife had worked with the first female principal in Calgary, and after that an overly religious chap, both of whom she did not get along after having worked for a number of years with a chap called Bill Fair, who was one of the nicest gentlemen and a very professional teacher as principal.

Mattie and Bonnie took a trip to Europe to ski, and she was given time off by the principal who, upon the return, notified Bonnie that she was called down to the head office; and the chiefs downtown Calgary informed her that if she took another holiday even with the principal's permission, the school district, only having to pay half rate for a substitute, would lay her off. There was little snow in Europe, so they returned back to London, England, and went to Ireland for the Easter break, where they tried to rent a car but were unsuccessful except at the last place they tried to rent from. There was an Irish lady who had come from England to get married in Dublin. She informed Mattie that since his name was Murfinsky, he could have her and her husband-to-be's car, and they would borrow one from a friend, so Mattie was in luck. He checked into the hotel, where the car rental agency was, and he mentioned to the manager of the hotel if he could get a drink. The manager said unfortunately no since the bar was closed. After checking into his room, Mattie heard a knock on the door; and upon opening it, he found a chap with a little commode with all the various mixes on the top where the wash basin usually sat and in the little compartment where the chamber pot usually resided, and it was full of whiskey. Everything you'd like to drink, beer, etc. He told Mattie to help himself and they would bill him in the morning, so Mattie proceeded a toast to an excellent holiday and enjoyed the company of several newlyweds who would run down to fetch alcohol or mix sometimes with no clothes on. This when combined with the drinks made for an excellent and interesting evening. In the morning, they took their rental car and left for the south of Ireland to Cork by the water. There they checked into a bed-and-breakfast, which was run by an elderly Irish lady. She immediately provided the best of whiskey, stating that she was so proud to entertain an American. Mattie tried to tell her that he was a Canadian, but she persisted in asking if he knew her cousin in Boston, to which Mattie informed her that Boston was thousands of miles to the east of him. She then wanted to know that he must be closer to her cousin in Los Angeles, California, so he told her that was fifteen hundred miles to the south. With Ireland being so small, she could not realize the large body of land that was America.

She informed Mattie that he should attend the dog races, so Mattie and Bonnie agreed to go. Mattie went down to the rail and placed his bet with the "bookie a wee" man with a big salt-and-pepper cap on his head. The dog he bet on came in about ten lengths ahead, paying a tremendous wager. The Irish chap sitting beside Mattie asked how he knew, what with Mattie being a stranger and all, that that dog was going to win. Upon which, Mattie asked, "Did you not notice that dog relieving himself at the rail before they started off after the rabbit? That means he was much lighter and faster, a sure sign." His newly found friends immediately produced pints, insisting that he'd have a drink with each and every one, so a great night was had by all.

Mattie then proceeded around the west coast of Ireland through Kerry, Tralee, and northwards to Galway Bay then turning east and heading back to Dublin, stopping at the halfway point in the Connemara hills to attend a dance. The music was so good you could hardly hold your feet still, with Mattie and Bonnie hitting the dance floor and dancing the foxtrot, the waltz, jiving. You name it, they danced it and were having a tremendous time until they found they were the only ones on the dance floor, and everyone else was standing on the sidelines clapping and cheering them on. They then proceeded to Dublin and flew from there to Alicante, Spain, which was on the water. There they spent a week eating mussels and other various seafoods, drinking whiskey, lying on the beach, and swimming in the water. At one dance, Mattie asked one German girl to dance, not realizing that her boyfriend had no sense of humor and took exception to anybody fiddling around with his girlfriend. Mattie was lucky to get away with his hide. At the end of the week, they were leaving from the airport when Mattie was hit with frequent bathroom trips, so he spent over an hour in the bathroom in a cubicle beside a clergyman, who took turns with Mattie running out to see if the plane was running on time, and then running back in to the bathroom again. They finally returned back to Dublin and then flew on to London, then finally back to Calgary with a company called Ward Air, which was run by a friend Max Ward, who Mattie had met when he was up in the North Country, when Max had owned a small flying service. His airline was one of the best in the world—fine linen, beautiful stewardesses, and have all the free drinks you wanted. It was better than flying first-class in other airlines. It was a trip to remember forever as it was Mattie's first trip back to the old country in 1972.

CHAPTER 8

Mattie now realized that it was now the fall of 1972, and he'd had the good luck of meeting Doug Weir, who put him on to buying the used equipment and tripling his money, buying the calves and again tripling his money, and then buying the potatoes and quadrupling his money. In addition, he had met the Texas oilman who told him about the drill rigs and put him on to his second big hit, which really made a bundle of money. He had then met Reverend Olson, who had suggested putting the seven or eight services together in the maintenance and contracting business just like Safeway had put together meat, drugs, vegetables, etc. And as he had suggested to Mattie, "You bring the milk in during the morning and the butter and meat, and you sell all the products in the afternoon and during the week." So it took little or no money to get into any of those businesses. It was exactly the same with the Christmas trees. You brought them during the end of November, you sold them over the next couple of weeks, and then you paid for them out of the profits. So it took no money to make thousands of dollars in profit, and you didn't have to donate any money out of your main business as the Christmas trees would raise enough money to donate more to good causes than any other person in Alberta.

Mattie kept wondering when his fourth big hit would come. For this, he had to wait several years until 1974 at a convention in the fall in Las Vegas where he met by chance a fellow called Ed Johnson, who was president of Bitucote Products of America. Mr. Johnson suggested to Mattie that his company who was from France would give Mattie a franchise for all of Canada, providing he was willing to build plants from coast to coast, a distance of almost five thousand miles. Mattie agreed, and Mr. Johnson flew up from the States, and Mattie picked a site thirty miles north of Calgary to build a plant. So he applied for a building permit, but before it could come through, he started stripping the land and preparing to pour concrete. Immediately, a lady who was administrator of the town came over and told Mattie that even though he had paid for the land, he had to wait for her to issue a permit. Mattie said that he would continue on since he had already paid for the ground. Within hours, the RCMP showed up on the site and told Mattie they would arrest him if he did not quit construction. Mattie knew that there were filling him full of baloney, but Mr. Johnson suggested that it was not wise to fool with the law; so Mattie informed the Mountie to shove the land up their ass, and he and Mr. Johnson headed back for Calgary. This was in January, but there was not much snow on the ground due to the mild winter. Mattie had done a lot of work for a very rich man named Ed Parlee, and it was January the sixth, Ukrainian old Christmas, so he went over to see Mr. Parlee to say that he had an opportunity to get in business, but he had no land and acquired the rights to make asphalt emulsion. After seeing the balance sheets of the company from France in the United States, Mattie knew a gold mine when he saw it, and he had the money in the bank and the cash and credit to build an empire across Canada.

Mr. Parlee had just bought two new Mercedes, one for his wife and one for himself, and said, "Mattie, before we talk business, this is old Christmas, and we have to celebrate." So he proceeded to a globe on a stand, pressed his foot, and there were a dozen bottles of various alcoholic drinks. He asked Mattie what he would like, and Mattie responded with, "Whatever you've got the most of." So they sat down and proceeded to drink half glasses of whiskey and vodka. Mattie explained his problem to Mr. Parlee, who stated, "You don't have a problem, Mattie. You just don't understand business." Mattie replied, "Oh, I think I do." Mr. Parlee told Mattie that he was still wet behind the ears and pointed out that he wasn't even forty yet. He then informed Mattie how to get land quick and asked him where he wanted to buy. Mattie told him he wanted to be in Foothills Industrial and that there were only twenty-two lots with two left. There were twenty-eight people interested, and he knew that a fellow from Sweden was in the running for one, so that left him against twenty plus others competing for the other lot. He explained to Mr. Parlee his predicament in detail and what he was going to build. Mr. Parlee promptly picked up the phone and called the Canadian Pacific Railroad and said to them, "I've got a guy in my office who wants to get one of those parcels of land in the new industrial area." The chap on the other end asked what Mattie was going to haul on the railroad. Mattie replied to Mr. Parlee that it was trainloads of asphalt; whereupon the man said, "Send him to me immediately. Can he be here within the hour 'cause I've got a meeting to attend to." Mr. Parlee said that Mattie could and called upon one of Mattie's old friends who worked for him named Ray Rudiak and told him that he had one more call to make and that Ray should take Mattie down to CPR, and he would try to set up a meeting with the city of Calgary. He then talked to a high official in the city of Calgary and told him that his friend Mattie Murfinsky needs to get land in the Foothills Industrial that they own, and he's already got approval from the CP Railroad. The guy said that he was leaving for Hawaii tomorrow morning, so he'll have to come to see me this afternoon.

With that, Mattie and Ray headed down to the top of the Palliser Tower which was owned by CPR and where their head offices for Western Canada were located. Upon arrival, Mattie was escorted in to see the head officer for Western Canada, where the guy said, "Ed Parlee says you're going to rail asphalt, so the last lot goes to you. Sign here, then take this to the gentleman at the city of Calgary and tell him I've approved it, and they'll give you the last lot." Mattie and Ray went across the street to the city hall and met the chap who was in charge of land development for the city of Calgary. He took one look at the paper that was already stamped and said that the land would cost him forty thousand an acre, and the parcel is two acres. Mattie immediately wrote a check for eighty thousand dollars, and the city of Calgary employee immediately stamped the paper. Where a few hours ago it was a long shot for Mattie to get land; he now had land right in the best part of Calgary in the fastest-growing city in Canada to build his asphalt emulsion plant. He thanked him profusely, and remembering that he did not thank the man at CP Railroad, he phoned him from the city office and thanked him and told both gentlemen that he would always owe them a favor. They thanked him back, and that was the end of a major deal, as this land in years to come would be worth a million dollars an acre, not a bad profit.

Mattie and Ray then drove back to meet Mr. Parlee, whereupon Mattie shook his hand until his arm nearly fell off and gave him a hug and was on the point of kissing him on both cheeks since he was still pretty well loaded, but Ray pulled him back by the collar and said, "That's thanks enough, Mattie, he likes you, and is only too glad to do you a favor." Whereupon Mr. Parlee poured another glass a whiskey and said, "Now we've celebrated old Christmas, we've celebrated my new Mercedes, we must celebrate your deal because you'll go on to make so much money that you'll be unable to count that high, just like I did." Ed Parlee sold his company a few years later for eighty-one million dollars to the Teachers Pension Fund. Mattie then bought land at every opportunity. As dark was coming, Mattie took his leave and went home to Bonnie to tell her about all his good fortune and to take Mr. Johnson back to the Palliser Hotel where they dined in fine style as it was the best hotel and the best restaurant in Western Canada.

Mattie now realized he was on to his fourth pot of gold; he could not believe his good luck. That a potato picker and an oil field roughneck could now be on to another gold mine, knowing that Bitucote Products were making a fortune in the States, and he could see his life improving by the week. Mattie then went to Gulf Oil and Esso Oil, who were tearing down their refineries;

and there he got all the tanks, pumps, motors, everything he needed to build a miniature refinery for five cents on the dollar. He couldn't believe his good luck. The head of the Esso refinery lived just a couple of doors away from Mattie at Mr. Narod's beautiful complex, and on many occasions, they swam in their outdoor pool at their back door or their indoor pool during the winter months. He was retiring with the demolition of the plant and had started at the refinery as a young engineer in the same year 1935 as Mattie was born, so they always had lots to talk about and had enjoyed many a drink together. Now he was only too glad to give Mattie all this equipment for next to nothing, as there was not much of a market for a used refinery, particularly all of the tanks, motors, pumps, etc. Mattie then wondered who would build the plant; he then phoned Mr. Johnson in St. Louis, Missouri, the geographic center of the United States, and the headquarters of Bitucote Products from France. Mr. Johnson informed him that he knew a man named Mr. Hunt, one of the best in the world who was now retired from a major oil company, and he was living in Alabama. He offered to call him and thought that he would be glad to go to Canada on the first of April to build Mattie a plant. Within the day, Mr. Johnson had phoned Mattie back to tell him that Mr. Hunt was on his way by plane, so Mattie should get him a hotel room. He was going to show Mattie how to build the plant and how to operate it from start to finish.

By this time, Mattie had one hundred employees, and one of his mechanics was a young teenager by the name of Ron Mullen; he was very young but very smart and hardworking. So he and Mattie sat down over drinks, and Mattie asked him if he thought if he could put up the plant under the supervision of Mr. Hunt, the American engineer. Ron said that he would give it a try, and Mattie knew from the couple of years Ron had been with him that he was a crackerjack at getting things done; but now he needed a first-class welder, so he asked Ron if he knew anybody. Ron said, "Blaine Hope is probably one of the best welders I've ever seen and a terrific hard worker, and that's the two things you need in a welder—someone who will stick with it and who knows what they're doing and can get along with other guys." So they invited Blaine to join them for drinks after work the next day and asked him if he was up to the task to build a perfect manufacturing plant in a very short order. Blaine assured him that he could and would be willing to start as soon as the frost was out of the ground.

Mattie then started to hire a contractor to strip the land of topsoil, grade it, gravel it, and fence it while Mattie hired an engineer to build the first quarter of a building to hold the manufacturing plant and a large bay next door to store chemicals and do fabricating. The building went up within weeks. The engineer who was hired unfortunately was not up to the mark and set the building grade too low, and it was lucky that Mattie was in the grading and paving business and was able to drain the water away with very little clearance. So Mattie took over the rest of the building construction.

The tank farm was commenced at the same time as the building doing the two projects consecutively, with Mr. Mullen and Mr. Hope working sixteen hours a day alongside Mattie. The plant went up, and building so fast that Mr. Hunt said it had to be a world record. He couldn't believe that anybody could get work done that quickly. On weekends, Mattie would take Mr. Hunt up to Banff and get the largest suite with the best view of the river, valley, woods, and the mountains. There they would drink and dine like kings. Mr. Hunt had always worked with the heads of oil companies, so he was impressed that Mattie was a down to earth ordinary laborer who had never forgotten his roots and who believed in treating his employees royally.

Mattie then prepared a bid for a county who was tendering a million gallons of emulsion and the trucking of the product. He then went with his main competitor Chevron Oil who was Neil Boon. He and Neil had steak sandwiches at the Eagles Club, and over a few beers, Mattie asked Neil what he was going to bid on the biggest job of any county or municipal district in Canada. Neil said he was going with thirty-six cents a gallon, whereupon Mattie said, "Neil, you'll never get the job because I'm bidding thirty-five!" At that, Neil laughed and said, "So what, you don't have a manufacturing plant, and it takes a year to build one." Mattie told him to wait and see what happens. Upon the day that the tenders were opened, Mattie knew that there would be a third bidder, Alberta Asphalt, and that was the unknown quantity as the president would not tell Mattie what he was going to bid. The day of the tender opening, Mattie went an hour north of Calgary to a town called Didsbury, where the county had its headquarters, presented his tender, had his lunch, and then went to sit in the gallery to wait for the tenders to be opened. He was so nervous that his teeth were rattling and his knees were shaking like he was an epileptic because this was an extremely valuable tender, and it was all Mattie needed to make his year of 1975. Mattie knew that he had done a lot of work for Gulf, and they were planning to tear their plant down; but they were going to run it for a couple more years, and he had an excellent working relationship in the oil field as a contractor to Gulf, so he would have a dependable supply of asphalt and hopefully at a good price.

The hour arrived for the tender to be opened. The secretary took out two letters, and Mattie was thunderstruck because there was no tender from Alberta Asphalt on such a giant contract with a profit of two hundred and fifty thousand dollars in six months. They read the first tender, and it was Mattie's ACE Asphalt and Maintenance Products as he had changed his name. Mattie knew that his tender would be at thirty-five cents. The secretary then slowly opened the second tender from Chevron, looking up at Mattie in the gallery as he did so and read out thirty-six cents per gallon, just as the Chevron salesman had told him. Mattie just about passed out stone-cold, only to be awoken by the reeve, who was Mr. Bagloe, saying, "Mr. Murfinsky, come down and have a seat at the table." He did so, and since there was nobody there from Alberta Asphalt or Chevron as Mr. Boon figured, he would get the job for sure. Mr. Bagloe said, "Do you have a plant ready to produce this?" Mattie assured him that he would have one when they were ready to start up on the first of June, which was in several months' time. He then asked, "What about the trucking?" Mattie told him that he had some trucks but was willing to buy four brand-new ones. Mr. Bagloe looked around at the other six councilors and said, "Gentlemen, what do you think?" At the other end of the table was a young man, a little older than Mattie, a good-looking fellow with short hair called Sid Vollman, who spoke up and said, "Everybody needs to get a chance, and I say we give Mr. Murfinsky the contract for both the product and the hauling as he seems to be a very eloquent and efficient individual." The chairman then asked the councilors to give a show of hands. All the men around the table were farmers, and they knew that everyone had to start from the bottom and work their way up; and although they did not know Mattie personally, they were willing to give him a chance. They all voted in favor, and Mattie all of the sudden in a matter of minutes knew he was going to make a quarter of a million dollars just like that.

Mattie immediately drove at high speed down to Calgary where he passed on the good word to Mr. Hunt, Ron, and Blaine. Time went on and the plant progressed at an unbelievable rate. The weather was good, and as all the work on the plant was outside, if there did come a shower, they would work under a tarp. They worked two shifts of night and day, but Chevron Oil got to the secretary of the county and got him to convince the road superintendent to order product two weeks early. This posed a problem as Mattie's plant was several weeks away from being completed and with good luck would probably be done by the first of June. Now if he could not supply their demand, he would lose the contract.

Mattie had met Parnell Hagen at his shop on the main road in Macleod Trail Calgary, and he was accompanied by his partner Jock Mackinnon. Mattie was accompanied by Ron Mullen, and they were having a few drinks at the Eagles Club a block away and, after having lunch, went down. Their two competitors were looking over some of their highway equipment. Alberta Asphalt did highway work as well as having a manufacturing plant 150 miles to the south, and there was another emulsion plant, the Hounder Asphalt in Edmonton, two hundred miles to the north as well as Mattie's competitor Chevron Oil, one of the seven biggest companies in the world in Calgary. They had a few words about Mattie's company's work on the highways as Alberta

Asphalt had been in the business for decades where Mattie and Ron had just gotten into it, so their work was no doubt better; but nevertheless, Mattie took exception to being criticized and rather rudely started to argue with his two competitors, with Mr. Hagen expressing his opinion of what he thought of Mattie with his partner Jock not saying anything.

Now several weeks later, the shoe was on the other foot. Mattie had to see where he could get product. It was hopeless to ask either his competitor the big oil company who had plants all across Canada and Hounder Asphalt who were seven partners and had a few plants but were known to be mean and aggressive just like a German shepherd. That left Mattie with no other source than Alberta Asphalt, so Mattie informed Ron Mullen that they were going to head to Lethbridge and meet up with the two partners. Ron, who had one close fight and that was when he beat three other guys in Dunvegan, Manitoba, when he was pretty well-set with whiskey. Ron was about six feet tall, two hundred fifty pounds, and the only equal Mattie had ever seen in fighting ability was Big Bob Holland. Mattie and Ron left for Lethbridge to meet with Alberta Asphalts' two owners to see if he could interest them in a deal to supply asphalt until his plant could get going. Mr. Hagen told him absolutely no way. Mattie then looked at Jock, who was probably ten years older than he was and twenty years older than his partner Mr. Hagen and said, "What do you say, Jock, you had a chance to get the contract with a bid of thirty-four cents, but your partner had a flat tire and didn't get his bid in. Now he's saying no even though he knows how much money can be made because he says it's going to take us until fall to get the plant going and then the road building season will be over. Now you're getting a second kick at the cat, a chance to make all the money instead of Hounder Asphalt, Chevron Oil, or Ace Asphalt." Jock said, "It makes sense to me," then he turned to his friend Parnell Hagen and said, "You missed the boat on this tender, and now we've got a chance to get back in. I own half this company, so either you buy me out or I'm going for the deal because you say they're not going to get the plant going, so we're going to make all that money. And I never turn down a deal like that."

They went for drinks and toasted the new deal, shook hands all around, and several days later Alberta Asphalt supplied the product. Hounder Asphalt and Chevron were in a state of shock. Mattie had done it again, pulling off the deal of a lifetime. Mattie, Ron, and Blaine worked night and day with all three sleeping right on the job with Mr. Hunt staying in a hotel nearby and coming at midnight to see how work was progressing. In two weeks time, by the first of June the plant was up and running with the tanks full of product, all material on spec. Mattie phoned up Jock MacKenzie, thanking him profusely for his help, and Jock stated, "Good luck to you. Nobody ever thought you would pull the deal off, but you deserve it. We made tens of thousands in those short weeks, and if you're ever stuck again, I will come to your rescue." Mattie thanked him from the bottom of his heart, knowing that only another true Gaelic guy with a heart of gold and a sense of fairness would have done what Jock did. And for the rest of his life, he never forgot Jock MacKenzie with the heart of gold.

The summer of 1975 came and went, and Mattie fulfilled the contract, made his quarter million, and built the rest of the addition onto the plant. Now having thousands of square feet of facilities for his maintenance, construction, oil field, and now a manufacturing facility second to none. On top of it all, the building and plant were paid for in full with money to spare, the Toronto Dominion Bank having come out with a new deal of two hundred thousand over five years with a low rate of interest. Six months after Mattie got the loan, he and one of the vice presidents from Toronto, Ontario, sat down with the manager of the main branch in Calgary, Bill Brooks, and toasted Mattie's good season. With that, Mattie pulled out a check for two hundred grand and thanked them for their assistance. They couldn't believe it, they said, "You were the first guy in Canada to get that type of a loan and to pay it back in six months when you had five years in. Unbelievable." Mattie thanked them, and they thanked him, and Mattie was now on the road to creating an asphalt empire across the nation. Mattie then asked Ron and Blaine if they would go to the neighboring province of Saskatchewan and build a plant in a little town called Wolseley. There they got another complete set of equipment from Esso Oil that was tearing down a plant in Regina, Saskatchewan. They started that plant early in the new year and had it all ready to go by mid-April. The province of Saskatchewan had the largest asphalt emulsion tender in North America, but Mattie could not get a bid. The party in power, the NDP, had a jerk for a purchase agent, and he absolutely refused. Mattie tried every politician he knew the name of until he got a chap in Moose Jaw, Saskatchewan, a small city to the west of Regina. A guy named Hy MacDonald had been a former member of the previous government. He went to friends he knew in the new government and told them that Mattie deserved a chance. That night Mattie received a call from Mr. MacDonald, saying that Mattie's tender would be ready to be picked up tomorrow first thing in the morning, and it would close at four in the afternoon. Mattie picked up the tender and sat down in the hotel room to make his bid. They made copies of the tender and filled it out three times the last time he was at the purchasing office, but instead of depositing his tender, he went back and redid it for the fourth and last time and lowered his price by half a cent per gallon.

God was with Mattie again, and he was low bid on the southern half of the province, and with his friends at Gulf Oil having their refinery at Moose Jaw, Mattie had a good source of asphalt at a good price he hoped because now he was talking over a million dollars which was a lot of money in the midseventies. Mattie won by a cent, so he went back to his hotel, phoned up his friend Brian Power, and said that he got the tender. Brian said, "I'll be at your hotel in fifteen minutes, and we can have a drink. I'll bring a quart with me." So they sat down to talk and have a few drinks before they went for supper. Brian was an excellent chap, probably one of the finest people in all of the whole province. As it was now four thirty, Mattie made a quick call back to Alberta to Gulf's head office to Bob McIntyre. Bob was another Gaelic guy, and Mattie had been dealing with him for nigh on fifteen years, and he knew him to be one of the finest businesspeople in North America. When he informed Bob that he had this contract which would take a tremendous amount of asphalt because asphalt emulsions were two-thirds straight asphalt and one-third water and chemicals, whereas hot-mix asphalt only took 3 to 8 percent in the mix, so Mattie now was becoming one of Bob's biggest customers and probably the biggest for Gulf Oil in Canada. Bob said, "Fly back immediately after you check your plant tomorrow in Calgary, and we'll meet for lunch. Take the first flight so we can meet and go at eleven o'clock." Mattie spent the evening with his friend Brian Power and at six the next morning made sure the plant was 100 percent, but knowing the quality of work put into the plant, he knew there would be no problems. His two superintendants introduced him to Ryan Kinsman, who was only a late teenager a little younger than they were, and Mattie asked Ron and Blaine if they thought he could do it. They said, "Well, you trusted us, and we would trust Ryan Kinsman with any job that a person could give him." Mattie knew they were a good judge of character, so he raced the sixty miles to catch the plane at eight o'clock to take the hour-and-half flight back to Calgary. As soon as he got off, he called Bob McIntyre and arranged to lunch at eleven o'clock at the Glenmore Inn hotel where Mattie always had a table reserved in front of the fireplace and a waitress who waited continuously with drinks and food at his request. Rod toasted Mattie on his good luck. Mattie toasted Rod on his good luck in getting one of the largest contracts in Alberta, Saskatchewan. When you consider that now, Mattie had the lion's share of the work in Alberta; now he was a big-time player in the neighboring province. They finally finished their drinks at four o'clock in the afternoon, and after fifteen years of doing business together and cementing one of the biggest deals in Canada, they each went their own way.

The next year, 1977, Mattie built with Ron and Blaine another plant in Moose Jaw, Saskatchewan, getting the balance of the tanks from the refinery in Regina. They had moved them there during the summer, so they were all ready to go. Again, they built another new building and at the same time started a plant to the north in a town called Edmonton, two hundred miles north in the capital city. During October until April, Ron and Blaine and their group of welders, pipe fitters, etc., put up two more plants now in the space of less than three years. Mattie now had four plants and could supply all of southern Alberta from Calgary and all of southern British Columbia; and from Edmonton, he could supply into central British Columbia and all of northern Alberta. Now he was also in position to supply the southern half of Saskatchewan, Manitoba. Not only that but he was situated within a few hundred yards of the Gulf refinery, one of the best companies in the world to deal with, and his gold mine had expanded to the point where he was now the largest purchaser of asphalt from any oil company in Canada, including Gulf and being one of Gulf Oil's best customers during the summertime where in the winter he was a preferred contractor to move equipment, haul water, and drill for Gulf during the fall and winter months. Mattie now knew there was no stopping the avalanche. He was on the road to make millions, and in his first year in Saskatchewan, he made half a million dollars. Couple that with Alberta, and he was heading for million dollar years which was unheard-of for a small businessman in the mid to late seventies.

He then moved in the fall of 1980 to build in Taylor, British Columbia, right across from the Pacific Petroleum refinery where a friend gave him the number of Mr. Sunstrand, the president of Sun Oil for Canada. He phoned Mr. Sunstrand who told him that if he added certain chemicals from Germany to the asphalt from the British Columbia refinery, he could make emulsions out of it as it had a fair bit of wax in it, a first. Mattie tested it and found it worked perfectly. Now he could supply the far north of British Columbia, the far north of Alberta, the Northwest Territories, and the Yukon Territory; so now he was the major player in Western Canada. At the same time, he was building in Fort St. John, British Columbia, he was also building in Lloydminster, on the border of Saskatchewan and Alberta to give him his third plant in Saskatchewan. This now put him up to six plants in four years, and he wound up taking 66 percent of the asphalt that was made at the Pacific refinery, resulting in terrific prices from both Gulf Oil and Pacific Petroleum; and in Edmonton, Alberta, he was a major purchaser from Esso Oil, who supplied Edmonton and Lloydminster. In the spring of 1981, after he finished the winter working in the oil fields and just before he started doing the maintenance, he and Bonnie went to Las Vegas where Mattie loved to play blackjack and stud poker in the back rooms. He got a free trip from his friend Hyme Hashman who was big in travel junkets all over the world. While playing at the table, he met a fellow called Mr. Lorenzo; and as Mattie drank lots of free whiskey, he and Mr. Lorenzo talked between hands of poker. Eventually Mr. Lorenzo said, "Mattie, you've drank too much whiskey to play poker. You should stop because you're only losing money, and there's no point in playing the game. Why don't you come up to my room and have a drink, and I will give you the formula on how to make crack filler as I sold my company called Blackline Products for ten million dollars, and now I work for DuPont. If you buy the synthetic rubber from us by the truckload, we will tell you how to make the best crack filler in the world." Mattie couldn't believe his ears; he was now hitting a jackpot, all thanks to a total stranger. They went up to the room, and Mr. Lorenzo gave Mattie a sixty-dollar gold-plated pen. Mattie couldn't believe it; he was giving away pens worth sixty cents. Mattie immediately called Bonnie and said, "Take my cousin Reverend John E. Cash and go see *Hello, Dolly* the musical because I'm going to stay here and do business deal."

Mr. Lorenzo said, "Here's how to make it, and since you're already in the emulsion business, it's easy to start up. You just mix up a few barrels of synthetic rubber with your emulsion, and then the highway crews no longer have to heat up a tar kettle with hard asphalt to get it liquid to four hundred degrees and waste their time. You can produce your product for a third the price and get the whole market across Western Canada." Mattie was so excited that he asked Mr. Lorenzo what he could do for him. Mr. Lorenzo responded by telling Mattie to call him whenever he had some free time, and he would come up and go fishing; and if Mattie's friends could take him hunting, he would be grateful.

Mattie said he would and immediately left the next day for Calgary where he and his cousin Father Cash and Bonnie could go skiing in the Rocky Mountains in Alberta and in British Columbia. Within weeks, he had his plant making rubberized asphalt; he raised the price from fifty cents a gallon to a dollar fifty per gallon and put it mostly in forty-five-gallon drums. In the first month, he supplied eighteen barrels on the back of a dump truck to the governments of Alberta and Saskatchewan. Before the end of the month, he was supplying truckloads, with eighty-plus barrels to the load, and he started making the product in Edmonton and Saskatchewan as well; and the government shifted from the Hooters Oil Company with their roofing asphalt to Mattie's product throughout Western Canada. Mattie had now found a sixth pot of gold, all by good luck, this time just a tip from an acquaintance, and Mattie could not believe it. The profit from making crack filler was beyond belief, and Mattie had 100 percent of the market. He would in that summer do highway surfacing, city paving in both Calgary and Edmonton, running six manufacturing plants supplying hundreds of crews across the west at fabulous prices, and gearing up for another busy season because the oil boom was still on in the seventies. Although there were signs of a new national energy policy in 1981, which would slow down the oil field work, but Mattie didn't care a rat's rump because he was already making so much money and working in so many fields. At the Las Vegas show, he had picked up fourteen dozen lines of construction equipment as well as manufacturing his drill rigs. Now Murphy's International was a major equipment manufacturer and distributor of equipment. He'd added a fifth line of work to his business plus he had dozens of trucks that during the winter hauled water and had drills mounted on them, and during the summer they hauled asphalt and asphalt emulsions, along with other contracting and was now up to nearly a thousand employees. He started work on a plant in the Yukon Territory as they used calcium chloride, which if it was dry lasted a few weeks. He supplied the emulsion and the equipment to put it down on the road which he also operated, and then sold them the equipment to spread the gravel, roll it, etc., to make a finished product. Mattie now had seven plants. In the Yukon, it was only a three-month season, but he always cleared one hundred thousand plus a month, a third of a million dollars in three months. It was a long haul, three hundred miles to haul the asphalt in, plus another three hundred miles to haul the emulsion out in the Yukon Territory, but Mattie had the market 100 percent to himself, so there was nothing he could do but make a bundle of money.

CHAPTER 9

Mattie now was at the top of his game; he was one of the biggest businessmen in Canada in his field. All of his trucks and buildings were painted green and white, the colors of the old country, and by now Mattie had hired so many good and honest, intelligent people that he could afford to take a holiday in the winter for the first time to Hawaii. In the winter of 1980, he and Bonnie went to Hawaii to tour all the islands, and it was there he met a chap called Hank Hana who used to be a five-star general in the United States Air Force, the only full-blooded Hawaiian to become a general. Mattie was lying on the beach when Mr. Hana came along and lay down beside him and started up a conversation. He asked Mattie where he was from and what he did, etc. He had along with him playing in the sand a beautiful little preschooler, and Mattie remarked about how she was a wonderful little grandchild. Mr. Hana said, "That girl there is my daughter. I have a very young wife." Then along came a beautiful blonde, and Mr. Hana introduced her as his wife, stating, "We should go to the top of one of the towers to one of the best restaurants in Honolulu, and I'll give you a tip on what I do now. And it's a chance for you to make a fortune in the travel business and to travel first-class for twenty-five cents on the dollar, take cruises for 35 percent of normal rates, and stay in hotels, rent cars, and take tours for half price." Mattie could not believe his ears because now that he had turned forty, he thought it was time to see the world. He thanked Mr. Hana and said they could meet at four for drinks, and they could spend the evening talking the travel business and how Mr. Hana was going to make Mattie another bundle of money.

Mattie and Mr. Hana and their wives met at the top of one of the towers in one of the best restaurants in Honolulu. Mr. Hana informed Mattie that when he retired as the first five-star general of Hawaiian heritage in the US military, he was looking for something to do. And upon inquiring into different businesses, he settled on selling travel throughout the United States through people who worked direct from their homes, the first to market travel in this manner in the world.

Mr. Hana informed Mattie that he could go to Pan American or Eastern and get the software from these airlines, which was what he had done, and Mr. Hana would help Mattie set up a business in Canada.

When Mattie returned to Calgary, he inquired of Pan American and Eastern regarding the software but found out they were in financial distress and would be closing down in the not-too-distant future. Mattie then inquired further afield and found out that American Airlines had what was known as Sabre computer software for the travel industry; they had two types, the expensive mainframe which could be set up in your office, plus a system called EasySabre, which any competent person could learn to run in anywhere from one hour to one day. Mattie ordered the expensive setup for his main office and then several dozens of the simple systems to operate, EasySabre.

Mattie then hired a young college student who was not only very presentable but had a terrific personality and was intelligent as all get out. The girl promptly started out on the road selling to various insurance agencies the program, where if you were to buy a franchise from a large travel company nationwide, it would cost tens of thousands of dollars; but Mattie decided that since insurance companies always had free staff, a free office desk, and thousands of clients, that would be a far better way to proceed rather than selling through home-based agents.

The young lady sold the franchises at five thousand a pop, where the software and training only cost Mattie a thousand, which let him make a profit. Immediately he had a large number of agents well established in all parts of the city, and he then sent the young lady throughout Alberta setting up people from the north down south to the Montana border, and Mattie himself traveled to Saskatchewan and British Columbia approaching insurance agents in those two provinces.

It was a slow time in the industry, and one of the largest US travel agencies and financial companies had closed down several dozen branches in that year while at the same time Mattie was opening up dozens. The money did not matter to Mattie as he was already running all of his other companies, but it was the perks that Mattie was really interested in. Now he could fly anywhere in the world in business class for 75 percent off, with 65 percent off cruises, and hotels and rental cars for half price, a great deal for him and Bonnie. Also, since he was traveling on business throughout the world, he could also write off over a third of his expenses as a tax deduction.

In the years that followed throughout the eighties and nineties, Mattie saw the world at very little cost while all the while traveling in high style, with first-class seats, luxury cars, and the best hotels. Mr. Hana never did get to make a trip to Canada; unfortunately, he was like Mr. Lorenzo and had health problems that stopped him from doing the traveling on which he had planned for himself and his wife.

As the years went by in the early eighties, Mattie was again thinking about what he could add to his already-growing list of companies and various businesses, as he was already buying property across Canada at every opportunity and, in most cases, building facilities to represent his existing companies. This meant he didn't have to worry about tenants as each and every location was profitable in their own right. If one company did not make money, then he had no worries because the others would be making a healthy profit.

Mattie then proceeded to build his first plant in the United States by buying up a United Farmers oil terminal as they were cutting back due to financial difficulties. Mattie as usual bid lower than his only competitor, who was outside the state, and he had his excellent price on asphalt which was just across the border in Saskatchewan and had his own trucks to haul the asphalt into the States as well as haul the product to the various counties and contractors.

Mattie then started selling asphalt for the Gulf Oil refinery to the contractors throughout the state, which was very lucrative but a concern to Mattie because contractors had a habit of going broke, and to sue a company internationally is a very difficult proposition. After some serious thought, he called up his friend Bob McIntyre and said, "Bob, I've developed the market, now all you have to do is take the orders."

Bob met with Mattie, and they celebrated this new market that Gulf Oil now had acquired, and all they had to do was take orders as the dollar was lower in Canada than in the United States; so not only would they make their usual profit, but they would also make money on the difference between the Canadian and US dollar. All went well for a few years. When the present government was in power, they were only too glad to buy product more cheaply and have a competitor in the business; but unfortunately for Mattie, the government changed, and one of the largest companies and also one of the richest families in the United States gave a larger donation to both parties than ACE Asphalt, which was now called ACE Industries International because it was in so many different businesses and now was operating internationally.

Mattie was low bid, but when he did not get any orders, he phoned the commissioner in the capital in Bismarck, North Dakota, and was informed that since he was low bidder but not high donor politically, he was out of luck. Mattie then, after reading about numerous companies who tried to do business in the United States but lost their shirt, realized that when he was up against one of the richest families in the United States, one of the biggest companies in the United States, and a system that did not play fair, that the wise move was to sell and get out of the United States. So Mattie sold all his equipment to the small oil companies, getting rid of his portable office and manufacturing facilities, even the land back to the farmer who originally sold it to the United Farmers many decades ago. Within weeks, Mattie was out of the business in the United States and had turned a very large profit over the few years and had sold the facilities for much more than he had paid for them. Again like the growing of potatoes, he had learned another lesson, which was just part of the cost of doing business.

Mattie then opened up a tank farm on CPR land in Winnipeg, Manitoba, and since his plant in Wolseley was located only a couple miles from the western side of Manitoba and had access to reasonably priced asphalt a short distance away as there was no refinery in Manitoba as it had been closed down, he was in an excellent position to capture the Manitoba market. Mattie did, as well as securing the transportation and selling all of the equipment to the government of Manitoba as they operated their own crews.

Over the years, Mattie found the government of Manitoba to be one of the fairest groups of people in North America. Alberta was also under Harv Alton, the deputy minister, who was an extremely fair guy and proved it in one instance when the Alberta lab informed Mattie that his product did not meet the specifications. Mattie immediately drove to Calgary where his competitor Chevron was shipping product to a government highway job. He took a sample from their tank, and having Bonnie take pictures of him doing so, he then drove to Edmonton to meet with the deputy minister. Mattie passed him the sample and told him that he had tested the sample in his own lab and that it had failed, and his own sample had passed and had also passed at EBA Engineering firm, a company Mattie had hired to test it as backup. Mr. Alton, a great engineer, phoned Mattie and said, "Your competitor's sample has failed, and since you're low bid, who cares if they both failed, you're going to get the job." He then canceled Mattie's competitor's purchase order and awarded the work to Mattie. This taught Chevron a lesson in business. It was quite common for the sales people of his competitors to travel throughout the west, saying, "You know, you have to give Mattie credit. That lad is the sharpest and most successful businessman in the west. Unfortunately, his product is not up to spec, and even though we think the world of him, we think it's only fair to warn you that in a year or two his product will fail on the roads." This was all BS, as the product would last for years such as the case of the original county where Mattie had gotten his first business. He used to go and have lunch with that young man called Sid Vollman, who, in a few years, rose up to be the reeve of the county. And he and Mattie became friends for the rest of his life, and they would go out to the roads that had been done in 1975 and years later. And even with the heavy traffic, they were still as good as new, but this was in part because Mr. Vollman was a very intelligent person who had built roads for the oil companies and knew that if you put down a foot of gravel that cost next to nothing and packed it well using water, with the water being free and then put two layers of asphalt over the top, the road would last almost forever. It was very rare to strike an individual such as Mr. Vollman who had the intellect, the sense of fair play, and the knowledge of road building as well as running schools, keeping taxes low, etc. Mr. Vollman along with Harv Alton in Edmonton, Jack Sutherland in Saskatchewan, and the various premiers of Manitoba were all 100 percent intelligent, fair, and hardworking, with a strong sense of fair play.

The Hounder Oil Company, which had been taken over by an international group of companies used a very simple way to rig the market. They would approach an executive with the government offering them a job at the head office in Alberta, close to skiing, fishing, boating, and at much higher pay with double the holidays. The government worker would jump at this job, resulting in the employees left behind waiting in the wings for a job for them which no doubt was promised. In return, they would pick up Mattie's samples on an almost daily basis, but they would only pick up monthly the samples from Mattie's competitors. The government laboratory was of inferior quality, resulting in that they would quite often fail Mattie's product; nevertheless, they would use it and while it worked perfectly on the road, they refused to pay as this was a clause that was in their tender. Mattie approached Jack Sutherland, and he said, "Well, to go to court is a long and costly process for both of us, so we'll set up an arbitration, hire a mediator, and then we'll go to mediation." So they did.

Mattie by this time had an excellent chemist, a guy named Dr. John Lerner who used to teach in Pennsylvania in the United States and at McGill University in Quebec; he was a brilliant man. They went to arbitration, and the arbitrator awarded 100 percent to ACE Industries International, but nevertheless, it was still difficult as some Saskatchewan government employees were still waiting on the possibility of getting a prime job with one of the major competitors that Mattie was in business against. About this time, Mattie and Dr. Lerner came up with a formula where they could mix in crude oil, and since heavy crude oil is about 95 percent asphalt and about 5 percent diesel fuel, Mattie did not have to buy any diesel to mix in with his product to soften it. That saved about ten cents per gallon depending on the product, plus the crude oil was much cheaper than the asphalt as it did not have to be refined. Mattie was now making way more money than his competitors, enabling him to bid lower and make a far greater profit.

Mattie then continued moving eastward into Ontario where he had a plant in the west end of Toronto and was rapidly gathering large percentage of the market in Ontario until one day there was a tender closing at the government purchasing agency, and again Mattie was low bid since he was located across the road from the Gulf refinery. He got great prices from them as he was their largest purchaser of asphalt and diesel products in Canada as well as the biggest purchaser of these type of products ahead of anybody else in Canada. Upon reading out the bid, they asked Ron Mullen, "Is your plant all ready to supply? If so, we'll award you the contract." At that time, one of his competitors spoke up and said, "ACE Asphalt International's plant burned down last night." This was a shock to Mr. Mullen as he had not been to the plant yet that day as he had been out calling on various clients. Mattie as well had not realized that his plant had burned down. Ron then immediately phoned Mattie and informed him what had happened and mentioned that their competitors all left, patting each other on the back and smiling. Little did they realize that one of the competitors had bought a piece of land where a family of Italians had an asphalt plant located, so in order to eliminate the competition, they kicked them off from the newly acquired land. The family was very aggressive, and they immediately bought another piece of land and set up the plant within a matter of days. Mattie phoned all the hot-mix asphalt producers, but since they were all in league together, none would even listen to his plan to pay very high rent. If he could acquire a plant within a week, he would get a very large contract. They simply told him that they weren't interested, except for the Cosmos family, who when Mattie phoned them, said, "Sure, we'll even help you move your plant and get it back in order on our land, and we'll work night and day. We want to get back at the company who hosed us."

Mattie then mounted all his tanks on trailers that he bought from his friend Bud McCaig who had a very large trucking company across Canada and had done millions of dollars of work for Mattie and was also a valued friend. Within a few days, the plant was moved into a fenced yard with watchmen and German shepherds patrolling the perimeter. Mattie then notified the purchasing agency of Ontario along with his other contracts that his plant was all ready to go. One particular engineer for the county of Oxford, Roy Blakely, even drove the hundred and fifty miles to Toronto to see Mattie's plant and to meet Ron Mullen. He phoned from the site and said, "Well, your plant is not as fancy as your competitors, but then they've probably had the price rigged here for decades, but nevertheless, I will buy from you." He too was one of the honest, intelligent and nicest man Mattie had ever met. His office was located in Woodstock, Ontario, in the county of Oxford. Mattie then put up another plant in the far north and then immediately moved by the mideighties to build plants in the geographic center of New Brunswick in a town called Oromocto. In the same year, he built in the yard of Ultramar Oil just outside St. John's, Newfoundland, not realizing that the government there owned an emulsion plant of their own in conjunction with the New Brunswick firm Atlantic Asphalts.

Mattie was competing in New Brunswick with the Igloo Oil company who owned nearly everything in Maritime Canada. They also made a product called cutback, which was diesel fuel mixed with asphalt, which was not nearly as environmentally friendly, polluting the air, and much more costly. Mattie got a quote from them on asphalt, and it was a third higher per ton; so Mattie phoned them from Calgary and asked why the prices were so high, to which they replied, "Well, we're the only ones in the province with a refinery, so if you don't like it, you can do without." Mattie had supported the liberal party, and the premier was a distant cousin on his mother's side of the family. He immediately went to the premier's right-hand man who asked him if he could get asphalt elsewhere. Mattie told him he could get it from Quebec, and the premier's office said they had never before allowed someone to buy asphalt from outside the province. But in Mattie's case, he could buy where he wished. Mattie had asphalt trucked in from Quebec City to the center of New Brunswick at a much cheaper price than buying from the Igloo Oil company. He then found that his competitor controlled dozens of businesses and was trying to give Mattie a hard time. Whereupon, Mattie phoned his cousin George Monaghan in Queen Charlotte Island who was a lawyer but now highways minister, and when one of the sons from Igloo went as usual to get the contract at a very high price, they were informed by Mattie's cousin that the island would not be buying any asphalt from their company as Mattie had already agreed to set up a terminal on the water in Georgetown on the island, and Ultramar would be using a tank farm to supply the asphalt throughout the island. This resulted in the family that owned the Igloo Oil company pulling in their horns and realized that Mattie was a power that was hard to defeat.

Mattie then quickly completed his plant in Newfoundland, got the contract for ten cents a gallon cheaper, and was making a dollar a gallon profit where elsewhere the norm would be ten cents after competition entered the market. Mattie was making a ninety-cent-per-gallon profit instead of a dime—a license to print money. Unfortunately, he had not figured that the province was rather corrupt and was run by a man called Premier Peckerhead. When Mattie got his check, it was forty-two thousand dollars short, and he was informed by various people who were on his side in the province that the contractor who was doing the roadwork was the first cousin of one of the high-up engineers in the province. Mattie again realized that he was up against a brick wall; he immediately loaded the plant and moved it to the center of Nova Scotia in a place called Debert. There he quickly set it up, as it was portable, and within a few weeks, was all ready to manufacture asphalt for the Nova Scotia government. Little did he realize that he had gotten out of the frying pan only to step into the fire. The Nova Scotia engineers made the Newfoundlanders look like Sunday school teachers. They refused to buy product at all as they wanted a roof over the tanks, a first in the history of the world. You name it, they wanted it done. If Mattie had hung in there, they probably would have made him do the Highland fling in front of the parliament building, in the nude. They were the most ridiculous, corrupt group of people that he had ever encountered; and by now after North Dakota, Newfoundland, and Nova Scotia, he was beginning to see that there was more stupid, corrupt, and lazy people in government than he had ever believed. This was especially true when compared with the west, with the exception of British Columbia, where you had to wear night-vision goggles to watch the government employees in that province. One of the highest people in the province was brought on the carpet for various forms of dishonesty, and rather than go to jail, the prime minister of Canada made him a senator.

Mattie knew with that, again he was in deep water with cement blocks tied around his waist, so he closed down the plant and operated only the one in Maritime, Canada. Within a few months, one of the richest families in North America with a number of the largest business in the United States offered for one division of Mattie's company, ten million dollars, in the mideighties. This was a large sum of money even to Mattie, but they had a condition that he would have to work with them for five years. Mattie and his accountant met with them one week and the following week met with a group of former Esso Oil companies, and in each case, his answer was the same. Not interested. He had left working for an excellent company where he had been for ten years to work for himself, and he would never, even for a hundred million dollars, work for a foreign company resulting in selling his soul. A true-blue Irishman, Mattie put his way of life ahead of a large quantity of money.

Now it was the mideighties, and Mattie had been getting a lesson in politics over the years as highway work is, in a large number of cases, very corrupt then and in decades before and would be in the years to come all over the world. In fact in most of the world, bribery was perfectly legal and a tax write-off. Mattie then decided as he'd worked in the elections in 1957 as a late teenager and again in the sixties with Paul Lougheed, who would later become premier of Alberta. He was one of the most intelligent, honest, and most personable individuals you could ever meet, who was elected premier from 1971 until 1985. Mattie had worked with Mr. Taylor, the oldest parliamentarian in the British Commonwealth, and he was also president of Mr. Taylor's Riding, which was one of the largest in Canada, stretching from central Alberta to the US border from British Columbia to the Saskatchewan border. Mr. Taylor informed Mattie that in 1956, when he was public works minister in charge of all the highways, Mattie's old friend from General Contracting had a job west of Edmonton and had driven to Edmonton and met with Premier Monroe, where both gentlemen arrived in Mr. Taylor's office asking if he could give more money for a road they were building west of Edmonton called the Yellowhead Highway. Mr. Taylor told them absolutely not, that they had bid the job; and if they had run into some tough goings, then it was up to them to know how to run their business, whereupon both men left in a bit of a huff.

Fifteen years later in 1971, Mr. Taylor was far ahead in the nomination for the Social Credit Party of Canada, but Mr. Monroe, not one to forget a slight, refused to back Mr. Taylor as he was a single man and instead backed a farmer named Harry Storm, resulting in the Social Credit Party's going down to defeat at the hands of Paul Lougheed's Progressive Conservative Party. Meanwhile, Mr. Monroe was an excellent premier and had an excellent government and was a friend of Mattie's since 1955.

Mr. Taylor promptly quit the Social Credit Party and ran as a federal member of parliament, getting elected by a large majority with Mattie's help and took up residence in the capital in Ottawa, Ontario. One evening, Mr. Taylor was sitting at a table for four when Mr. Monroe approached him, who by this time had been appointed senator by the prime minister. He walked over to Mr. Taylor offering to shake hands and saying, "Let bygones be bygones, and let us sit and have supper together." Mr. Taylor, not one to forgive easily, told him that all the chairs were taken and did not even stand up. Mr. Monroe looked at him in amazement that a decade later he still never forgot what the leader of the party had done to him.

In 1976, Mattie backed a fellow called Joe Clark, who was only in his thirties and unknown against some of the best known and wealthiest people in Canada for the leader of the conservative party, which were in opposition at that time. No one expected Mr. Clark to be in the running, with a little hard work and conniving, Mattie and a few guys put together a group which defeated the other powerful candidates, resulting in Mr. Clark at thirty-nine becoming the youngest political leader in Canada and later on in 1979, to be the youngest prime minister of Canada.

Mattie was beginning to find that politics played a big part in business, and now having worked to elect the prime minister of Canada in 1957 and helping to elect various premiers across Canada in the past thirty years as well as a prime minister in 1979 in the form of Mr. Clark, who only lasted a matter of months and lost a vote of confidence in parliament. And then with the conservatives losing, the liberals took over again with Mr. Trudow as the leader. Mr. Trudow was a very nationalistic individual, and he kept the country in the hands of Canadians to some extent.

In 1984, Mattie was president of the Big Bow River Riding and campaign manager for Mr. Taylor, one of the finest gentlemen in politics in all of Canada, a very rare individual indeed. Mattie won one of the largest majorities in Canada, and the conservatives won a big plurality in Canada overall under Prime Minister Baloney. Shortly after the conservatives got in, the prime minister put Canada up for sale. He was attempting to make a free trade agreement with the United States, and in order to win their approval, he offered anything and everything to the Americans and any other foreign company to the detriment of the Canadians, because once you sell your country, the foreign companies take most of the profits back home to where their head offices are located and your country becomes just a colony just like the European countries did in Africa.

Mattie realized that now in order to be a success in the manufacturing of asphalt products, he had to have his own refinery; and Gulf sold the Moose Jaw refinery, which was located in the center of the west, to his competitor Chevron which was a disaster for Mattie. Fortunately, they were so unhappy competing against ACE Asphalt International that they put the refinery up for sale, and it was in turn bought by Petro Canada, which was Canada's national oil company. But Mr. Baloney immediately put Petro Canada up for sale, and just a few years prior to somebody buying it, he put the Moose Jaw refinery on the market. Mattie went to two of his billionaire friends who were big in manufacturing asphalt products all over the world like he was, but with only a third the branches across Canada; but nevertheless, they could see that it would be good to have their own secure asphalt supply, so Mattie and Malosky brothers put in a bid of six million. Unfortunately, seven prominent conservatives in Saskatchewan had put in a bid for four million, and even though Mattie was a prominent conservative, it was one against seven. Mattie and his partners lost the refinery even though his offer was much higher, and the prime minister even threw in a free cracker for producing diesel, which was worth about a million dollars, so Mattie's price was nearly double. Mattie was shocked that a guy who had Irish blood like himself would do such a thing, only to find out later that the prime minster was caught doing underhanded deals for substantial sums of money.

Without the refinery and secure sources of asphalt and having forced Chevron to sell their emulsion business, which was bought by a family from the United States that had made such a big offer for Mattie's plants. The Hooter Oil Company from overseas was bought by international buyers, who were well versed in how to do business under the table. Also, the Cock Oil company did not stay in the business very long; they sold out to Esso. Mattie was then faced with the Igloo Oil company in the Maritimes who had their own refineries in Central Canada, Esso, one of the largest oil companies in the world with their own refineries, and the Potters Emulsion was now owned by an international oil company that also had one of the biggest refineries in Canada. Mattie could now see the writing on the wall, so he started to consider that it might be wise to sell.

He had been hiring engineering firms over the years and paying double for his engineering services. He then decided to form his own engineering company specializing in oil field surveying and building roads for the oil companies in the winter while in the summer he would do work for the sixty-plus counties and municipalities throughout Alberta. Within months he saw the need for recycling concrete and asphalt, which was being dumped in the landfills and of course would not decompose, he saw the Cosmos family in Toronto doing this and getting paid to bring the material into the yard and then getting paid to resell it. As the oldest brother said, "We're making a killing, Mattie, and you should be doing this out in the west." So he started a firm up with two partners, but Mattie was never much for partners, and he operated this firm for a few years and then sold it out to two chaps who were in the construction business making a good dollar on the deal and getting clear of his two unsavory partners at the same time.

Mattie then formed another engineering and environmental company as the environment was becoming a big thing across the country. He then decided that one of his senior engineers, Mo Walsh, wanted to buy the oil field and municipal engineering company, so within a month, he sold the recycling company and sold the engineering company to Mo who went on to make millions with it, as he had branched out into cranes across the west, which were probably one of the best investments that an individual could get in to. He well deserved the success as Mattie found him to be an asset as an employee, and he felt he deserved to own his own company. The recycling company, Sierra Engineering, also did extremely well; but Mattie now was finding that between all his companies, politics, charities, church, and community work, he was working fifteen hours a day seven days a week and had been doing so for over thirty years. And when one considers that in the military, in the police, or as a fireman you only work twenty years and then pension off and then get more pay going back to work for the government in a new job and putting in a few days a week in order to receive your paycheck. It was then that he realized that he was paying for a lot of people to get their education, a lot of people to provide services for the government, and they were reaping the benefits while he was getting all the hard work.

Mattie was then in his fifties, and in the early eighties, he'd had six heart attacks in a row in a matter of an hour and was legally dead for four minutes. The doctors informed him that he probably only had two hours to live, whereupon he hired a helicopter and flew the eighty miles in a half an hour to Calgary. There he met Dr. Young who saved his life, and within four days, two in intensive care and two more in cardiac recovery, and he was back on the road running his businesses. It was then that he decided to offer his companies to employees; but because he had so much land, buildings, and equipment, it was impossible to sell it to a few individuals. Oil had dropped from $42.00 a barrel to $9.90 a barrel in 1986, the west was in a Depression with tens of thousands of businesses going broke, a large number of people unemployed, and naturally the banks would not lend any money. If you don't need money, go see the banks; if you need money in hard times, then Mattie told people that that's what pawnshops are for. Mattie would also inform his employees as well as anyone who came asking for advice that you could make more money, saying "I do" in fifteen minutes by marrying a man or a woman whose parents had money than you could make working all your life. Now Mattie decided it was time to semi-retired since he had no family, and none of his nine nieces or nephews were interested in carrying on the business as it required so much travel, long hours, hard work, a lot of investment, and a lot of responsibility—something very few people wanted to do. It was only then that Mattie realized that it was because he had worked so hard with such long hours and secured such great employees by giving away Rolex watches to them for five years' work, upon which on the back he'd inscribe, "Thanks for a job well done, Mattie." Rolex said he was the only company in the world that gave away Rolex watches after a short period as a company associate, as it was common to get a watch worth a few hundred dollars after you had worked twenty-five years.

Mattie then realized that he had eight or nine good tips and was financially secure for the rest of his life even though he was giving away a lot of money to various good causes. Working with the seniors and the handicapped and supporting four churches, he still had far more money than he knew what to do with, and he was rapidly traveling to most parts of the world and saw that in the near future, he would no longer be wanting to travel.

About this time the owner of Microsoft got into the travel business creating a company called Expedia. At that time, a guy called Bill Bates had billions of dollars, and Mattie saw no future going up against a hard-nosed guy who was only concerned with money rather than anything else. One who, when the partner who had made him so wealthy took cancer, was overheard asking another employee, "How can we get a hold of Pete's shares because if he has cancer we need to secure them before he gives them away or dies," never realizing that his partner would live on for many years. Perhaps as long as he did himself.

Mattie now having learned how to be a failure and how to have many successes and make a lot of money had also gotten a lesson in how corrupt the government could be, how greedy big business was with few scruples, and how politics was such a dirty game. As a good friend told him when you encounter politicians remember, a quarter are lazy, a quarter are stupid, a quarter are crooked; so every time there's a vote, it's three to one against the honest, intelligent, and hardworking politician.

In the 1950s, the prime minister of Canada decided he'd like to have a senator for the first time of Jewish heritage, and he asked his executive assistant over breakfast to give a call to Nate Philsosky, who was a prominent politician in the largest province in Canada. The executive assistant said he would call after breakfast and see if Mr. Philsosky would be interested in taking up a senator position. The next morning, when the prime minister and his assistant met for breakfast, the prime minister asked the assistant if he had gotten a hold of Mr. Philsosky, and the young assistant answered that he had. The prime minister asked what Mr. Philsosky had said. The assistant replied, "Oh, he was very interested and enthusiastic." With that, the prime minister asked, "Where did you locate him as he travels a lot?"

"I got him at his riding in Nova Scotia." In return, the prime minister said, "Well, he lives in Ontario. What was he doing in Nova Scotia?" The assistant said he was in his riding, and Mr. Philsosky is a member of Parliament for Nova Scotia, and he was really amazed that you would pick someone like him."

"Young?" the prime minister said. "He's got to be sixty." The young assistant said, "No, he's only a little over thirty." With that, the prime minister realized that he had called the wrong Philsosky. Calling the young assistant a complete idiot, he said, "What am I going to tell my friends and supporters now that you've picked the wrong guy?" With that, the assistant just shrugged his shoulders and said, "Well, accidents and mistakes do happen."

Another rare political election occurred on Queen Charlotte Island where a young fellow only in his twenties was working in the capital, and he went back to the island to run for the nomination of the liberal party. His name was Moe Whiz, and he had one opponent, a gentlemen in his sixties who was very well-off and very well-respected who had worked for the party for forty years and was also an elected MLA or member of the legislative assembly in the present government. When Election Day rolled around, the young aspiring politician from Ottawa who was born on the island invited every high school student from every school in the province, bussing them in to a big hotel where he treated them all to hamburgers, hotdogs, and pop, as you have to be eighteen years old to vote in an election but only fourteen to get a membership in a provincial party. The election started, and it was a sure thing that the older politician would get elected by about a ten-to-one majority, not realizing that young Mr. Whiz had sold more memberships than his opponent. When the vote was counted, the young fellow from the mainland had defeated his surefire opponent by a good margin, proving that in politics, it's the person with the smarts, not the person who has been around the most, who deserves to be elected loses, and the shrewd guy who had learned politics at the hands of major liberal leaders won.

In one of the Northern Territories, they had trouble getting a candidate who could run for leader as the leader of one party had been caught selling drugs. Another had been caught in a scandal with contractors while the third had stepped in one of his own traps on his trap line and was badly crippled. Nevertheless, they held the election, and the worst man won, which goes to show that rarely does the best candidate win. In one of the prairie provinces, after the election, they caught two-thirds of the elected politicians in one party involved in corruption of one sort or the other with some going to jail and others just being fined. The result was so negative that the party in power had to change its name and run under an alias in the coming years.

In a province in the mideast, a group was demonstrating against the provincial premier, and as they were outside the premier's office chanting and waving signs, the curtains opened and the premier's assistant opened the window, dropped his drawers, and mooned all of the protesters. Needless to say, he easily lost the next election.

Mattie was coaxed by a fellow islander to again start growing potatoes in Queen Charlotte Island. He only did this for one year as the chap he was financing did not seem to have the ability to make money.

Mattie got a phone call from the guy he was backing on the island that he and Mattie were being sued by a large oil company, one of the biggest in Eastern Canada, for the failure to pay for gas that Mattie's partner claimed was not delivered, but the oil company claimed the tanks were filled.

Mattie flew to the island, hiring a guy named Lou MacCool. Lou had a reputation as a very smart and shrewd lawyer, but Mattie was not informed that Lou was also an alcoholic. Upon going to court at the appointed time, Mattie appeared on behalf of him and his partner while the major oil company bought several lawyers from the mainland, as they were taking no chances as they had never lost a court case before in their life.

The oil company being the plaintiff went first in the court hearing, stating that Mattie and his partner had received oil products that totally filled their tanks; and if Mattie's partner checked the tanks and found that they were only half-full, then their employees stole it. It was now time for Mattie's lawyer Lou to get up and speak on Mattie and his partner's behalf. Unfortunately, he had been drunk the night before and was now snoring loudly and farting at the same time. Between the noise from the snoring and the smell of the farts, the judge had to ask Mattie's lawyer to leave the courtroom. This left Mattie with no lawyer. The judge then called both the big oil company and Mattie up in front of the bench where he informed Mattie that the case would have to be adjourned because since Mattie had no lawyer, it was against the law to allow a company to go ahead with a case without representation from the legal community.

Mattie told the judge that he was backing his partner, and as a partnership,

Mattie was within his rights to represent the partnership himself. Mattie then stated that the agent who delivered the fuel had never filled the tanks in the first place, as this was a very common practice all across Canada. Ninety-nine percent of the people who used product from the oil companies were not aware that you could run a meter and get a meter ticket while pumping no product through the pump and meter, just air, and it would still produce a ticket. The judge, after hearing both sides, said, "If I was King Solomon, I could not decide whether the big oil company delivered the oil or shortchanged you, Mattie, or perhaps you got the oil and gas and your employees stole it before your partner got to check the tanks. Therefore my decision will be that it will be a saw off with no verdict for either side and that you will each have to pay your own court costs." He then instructed Mattie that he would be foolish to pay his lawyer Mr. MacCool anything because snoring and farting were not counted as representing a client. In fact, the best that you could say about Mr. MacCool was that he was providing some sort of entertainment for the court.

The large oil company had never been defeated, winning court cases for hundreds of millions of dollars, and with one of the very senior people in the courtroom as well as the two highest-priced lawyers in the Maritimes, they were very upset that they were unable to win their case, with the judge saying to Mattie, "You know, when you represented yourself, there's an old saying that says he who represents himself in court has a fool for a lawyer, but I must congratulate you on how you presented your case and made such a eloquent statement on behalf of you and your partner. And even though it was a draw, I would call it a win for you." With that, he wished Mattie, "Bon voyage and Godspeed back to Western Canada, and all the best in the future."

Mattie had been offered the chance to run in many elections as a conservative, and in Alberta, it would be very easy to win. You could practically run the family dog, and it would win the election. He was also offered if he ran federally a cabinet post, as he was one of the two main federal conservatives in Alberta as well as one of the leading provincial conservatives. He refused and then twice was offered the chance to become a senator. This meant moving to Ottawa in the east from where Mattie had left many years before because of the politics and the way they did business, and this was firmly impressed on his mind after he went back in business in the Maritimes. He realized that in order to get a fair deal, you would practically have to carry gun, and he often wondered if the politicians and the civil servants slept in grain augers. He turned down the senate seats, even though it would be nice to have senator before his name, because he would be away from his beloved west, and he did not like the winters down east. And besides, he would be only making less than a quarter of the money. He thanked each prime minister who offered him the position and suggested a Calgary lawyer who was also of Jewish heritage to take the position he was offered, which the individual gladly accepted. Then when the liberals came to power, the prime minister was one of the top businessman in Canada, so in order to be fair, he wanted to pick an individual who was a conservative. So he chose Mattie who had to again recommend someone else. This lady was a former provincial cabinet member and would just love to have this job. The prime minister picked her at Mattie's suggestion, and the lady thoroughly enjoyed her post. The conservative lawyer only stayed for a few years; then he got tired of the east and tired of the senate and moved back to Alberta where he resumed his law practice.

Paul Lougheed decided in the spring of 1985 that since oil had dropped in price so much that he would retire. Ron Getty, one of the top athletes in Canada, plus one of the best-looking couples in the country as well as the nicest individual in Canada decided to run for the position. He held a meeting with three ridings in Edmonton only to gather a few dozen people. He called up his friend Mattie and told him that the people he had running his campaign weren't up to snuff and asked for Mattie's help. Mattie told him he would help and to come to Calgary in the next few days where he arranged a room downtown, and he packed it with people waiting to get in. The next night, they went to a little town of seventy-five people, and they had over one hundred people in the hall, a number of whom came from the surrounding farming area.

Mr. Getty's opponents were an excellent chap who had been a cabinet minister in Mr. Lougheed's government and the ex-senator. Mattie would attend various meetings to send delegates to the convention in Edmonton, and in his own ridings around the country town of Ajax thirty miles north of Calgary where he kept his race horses and riding horses and had one of the biggest houses on the prairies with indoor and outdoor pools, saunas, Jacuzzis, for a total of seven thousand square feet over three floors. He ran Ron Getty's campaign as well as his own businesses. His own MLA who was number 2 in the conservative party to Paul Lougheed did not mention who she was going to vote for, so Mattie phoned her one weekend, and she said she didn't really care who got elected to be premier. Upon which, he told her he was going to back Ron Getty, and he lobbied everybody in his riding and all the ridings across Alberta to vote for Mr. Getty resulting in Mr. Getty winning by a big majority on the first ballot. The sitting MLA in his riding then notified the press that she had backed the former senator who was also of Jewish heritage, and that Mattie used devious tactics along with a Pastor Weber in northern Alberta to get Mr. Getty elected and that Mattie was anti-Semitic. This caused an uproar since Mattie had hundreds of people of Jewish heritage as his friends and clients. Upon the bad news appearing in the paper, Mr. Getty, who was now premier, phoned Mattie asking what he should do. Mattie suggested that he throw her out of the cabinet on her butt. Within forty-eight hours, there was a picture in the paper of her being ejected from the cabinet sitting in a rocking chair and being given the boot out the door, and seeing justice prevail like this made Mattie happy.

Mattie had a very large multimillion-dollar job up north on the Alaska Highway for the federal government. The engineers and supervisory staff on the job were sent in from the outside, and a lot of them had the IQ of a demented goat, resulting in the federal government owing Mattie millions. One of Mattie's trucks had hit a bridge, and the federal government hired local natives with buckets to clean up the river which cost a fortune and refused to settle up for the damages, wanting Mattie to have lengthy liabilities. Mattie phoned the prime minister and told him his problem and also Mr. Taylor his friend and member of Parliament. The prime minister told him to fly to Ottawa the next day, and they would settle the matter. Mattie arrived in Ottawa and was met by Mr. Taylor's assistant, who whisked him to the office of the deputy minister of public works. Upon arriving at the office, he met the assistant deputy minister, and when he asked where was Mr. McPhee, the deputy minister, he was told that the deputy minister had been fired an hour before. This caused some concern with Mattie, and he asked what was going to happen with his case. The gentleman who was now in charge said that everything would be settled in full, that he had already drawn up a letter and there would be no claims. This meant Mattie didn't have to worry about his credit being tied up in such a large deal. Mattie then found out very quickly that when you can get one of the top civil servants fired on a day's notice, it pays to be in politics.

One more important concern bothered Mattie, and that was that they still owed a very large sum of money from the job on the Alaska Highway. Within a few days, the public works minister Stew McGinn, a lawyer from the east, was in Calgary to speak to a large group, and Mattie was called to introduce Mr. McGinn as they were both Maritime born, fellow Irishmen, and friends. After Mr. McGinn finished speaking, Mattie was asked to thank him, and they both adjourned to the Mewata Armouries headquarters in Calgary for drinks. Mattie explained his problem to Mr. McGinn, that he was owed the money, and to fight the federal government, it would take years to win his case. Mr. McGinn said, "I would set up a tribunal to hear your case. You pick who you want for a mediator, and we'll hold it in Vancouver on the west coast of British Columbia. The government will pay for someone to represent you, another businessman, and the government will have their own senior bureaucrat there. Lawyers could be involved but only as advisors. They couldn't participate." Mattie couldn't believe his ears as now he was having a brand-new form of settling claims, which the federal government set up at his request. Within a few weeks, Mattie received a phone call from a senior bureaucrat asking what dates would suit him to come to Vancouver, so Mattie suggested several and they agreed. He suggested Mr. Norman Reed a very senior engineer and the same gentleman who was the mediator in Saskatchewan. The bureaucrat promised that he would check out Mr. Reed and get back to Mattie within twenty-four hours. He did so, and Mr. Reed was appointed as the mediator. Mattie picked John Vanderhook, a well-known and respected businessman from Calgary to represent his company.

They then went to the court of arbitration, and after two days of hearings, Mattie won 90 percent of his case while living in one of the most luxurious hotels in Canada, eating the best of food, with everything paid for by the federal government. Mattie could not believe what could be accomplished politically if you were on the right side. He then had one other problem in the late eighties. He had supplied several shifty contractors from British Columbia with products and equipment. These individuals were in the habit of doing a job and then only paying half for the services they received, whereby they would make a large profit at other people's expense. They did not figure on Mattie who took them to court, first having hired a lawyer by the name of Ron Bedfellow. He asked Mr. Bedfellow what it would cost to have him do the case, and not trusting lawyers, he had him put it in writing. Mr. Bedfellow wrote down seventy-five thousand and then with a felt pen drew a stroke through it and wrote down fifty thousand.

With the money agreed upon, they shook hands and went to court. Unfortunately halfway through the case, Mr. Bedfellow arrived at Mattie's office stating that he wanted more money, so Mattie called his own accountant into the office and asked how much they had paid Mr. Bedfellow on the fifty-thousand-dollar account. The accountant informed Mattie that they had paid one hundred thousand. Mattie was flabbergasted that Mr. Bedfellow was already double-paid and only halfway through the case. When he asked him how much more he wanted, Mr. Bedfellow told him he wanted another ninety thousand; whereupon Mattie picked him up by the scruff of the neck and ass of the pants and threw him out the door, then instructed one of his secretaries to write to every lawyer in British Columbia. They got a number of replies back, and Mattie settled on a guy called Bruce McCain, another Gaelic chap who was a Rhodes scholar and whose father and uncles had been judges. So they went to the center of British Columbia to a town called Kelowna, and Mr. Bedfellow arrived with the future president of the Alberta Bar Association as his lawyer plus two more. Mattie also had a guy named Mr. Summers from British Columbia, the town mayor and also a lawyer.

At the end of about nine days in court, there were three judges—one from Vancouver, one from Kamloops, and one from Kelowna all from British Columbia. They informed the people in court that the following day they would render judgment and told both sides to be prepared with final arguments. Mr.

McGinn and Mr. Summers went to the bar and had a few drinks returning back after 10:00 p.m. to the hotel whereupon Mattie went to the desk and asked for a bathing suit as every night before bed he liked to have a swim. The night attendant informed Mattie that the pool was closed for swimming at ten o'clock, but Mattie was not to be denied his swim, so he stripped down naked and jumped into the pool. Upon climbing out, another lawyer who had been the number 3 man to Mr. Clark when he was prime minister in Canada and when the conservative government got defeated came to work for Mattie named Mr. Jennings, stopped by to see where Mattie was and advised him that he should get out of the pool and if there was anything else about the case they should talk about it further. As Mattie climbed out onto the cement deck, there was a loud cheer and a generous applause. It was the ladies' curling club of Kelowna who were sitting in a balcony out over the atrium in the center of the hotel complex. Mattie took a deep bow, quickly took the towel from Mr. Jennings, and made his way to the elevator so he could get back to his room.

Mr. Jennings went down to Mr. McGinn's room and got all the files, and he and Mattie went through box after box. But it was not as difficult as they had assumed as Mr. Bedfellow had only had boxes a quarter full, and even though there was a pickup with a camper on it stacked to the top, there was only a few files in each box, and it was all for effect when they lugged them into the courtroom. So they rapidly went through all the files, and by the wee hours of the morning, they came across the piece of paper where Mr. Bedfellow had written the original price for his services. Mattie put it in his shirt pocket, had another drink to celebrate, and both went to bed. In the morning, they went to court, and by now this case was catching the attention of lawyers across Western Canada. Never before had anyone taxed an account such as Mattie did. When they were all seated, the head judge inquired if there was anything further they wished to say or if there were any documents they wished to present. Mr. Bedfellow's lawyers said they were prepared to rest their case, but Mr. McGinn stood up and said, "Your Honor, during the past two weeks we've debated day after day of what the original quote was. Mr. Bedfellow has said that he got whiplash in an accident when he was a young college student, and his memory was so good he won the lawsuit and has been blessed with a photographic memory. You've heard Mr. Murfinsky, my client, speak in great detail to tell the court exactly what happened, so this case is completely about credibility—whether or not Mr. Murfinsky is telling truth or Mr. Bedfellow is lying—and I now have a piece of paper that will settle the argument once and for all." With that, he passed it forward to the clerk of court. You could hear a pin drop in the silence. Mr. Bunting, who was the head lawyer for Mr. Bedfellow, grabbed the paper out of the hand of the clerk of court and took a look at it, then turned to his client and stared as much as saying, "You stupid jerk." As he did so, the clerk grabbed it back out of his hand and passed it back to the judge, who took one look and asked the clerk of court to make copies for himself and all parties and said, "Normally I would take a week to render judgment, but in this case, I'm going to award 100 percent along with all costs to Ace Asphalt International Inc." All three judges got up totally upset at the way that Mr. Bedfellow had tried to con Mattie and his company as well as the court.

The word was spread about to people and written up in the law review, with the consequences that Mr. Bedfellow and his partner split up and the building that they owned which was worth millions was lost to the mortgage company. The last time Mattie saw Mr. Bedfellow, he was having a hot dog at a street vendor rather than his usual filet mignon. This was yet another major court victory for Mattie, his third in a row in under a year, and he began to feel good as he had purchased a complete set of law books as his father wanted him to be a lawyer. He had decided that with those law books, as well as his political acumen along with hiring good lawyers and firing the bad ones, he could win any case he wanted. With that, Mattie decided he'd had a hundred years in business even though it was only twenty five, a quarter of a century, and it was time now to hang up the gloves and semi-retire as he had memories of people coming in the office to see Mr. Walsh of the engineering company, and Mr. Walsh had pushed them off onto Mattie. When they entered Mattie's office, the chap told Mattie what a jerk he was, and Mattie told him, he would check with the engineer and see if there was bad feelings, and if so he would see that they got the fellow a good deal. Mattie warned him that to fool with him, he would be better to pick up a piece of hot steel. The chap said to Mattie, "You're twice my age, and I would clean your clock in minutes." Mattie didn't answer, just grabbed him and threw him out ten feet across the parking lot. The next day, the police arrived, a young chap in his twenties and an older chap in his forties. The young fellow pulled out his notebook and started writing down the details. The older guys told him to put it away and said, "All Mr. Murfinsky is doing is giving those guys a little smartening up and doing our job for us." And said to Mattie, "Mattie, we've been called in a dozen times when you throw people out on the street. It's time to hang up your gloves." Mattie had a pair of monkey face gloves, so he took a lace out of his shoe and the knife out of his pocket, punched a hole in each glove, and put the shoelace through each glove and walked over to a picture hanging on the wall and hung up his gloves. The senior officer said, "Muhammad Ali has hung up his gloves, and now you've done the wise thing to hang up yours." Mattie now decided that along with fighting, excessive drinking, gambling, smoking, working day and night seven days a week, it was time to turn over a new leaf. So he completely quit playing cards, using tobacco, drinking alcohol, fighting, working so hard and long, and the next day became a new man. He never did smoke or use tobacco in any form or ever gamble again in his life. Although he did have the odd sociable drink, he severely curtailed his fighting, slowed down while driving, and turned over a new page and a new future for the nineties.

Chapter 10

Lawyers and Politicians

In business it's very important that you enter the political field if it's only delivering fliers at a very young age. Mattie started as a teenager. This allows you to make the necessary friends, acquaintances, and connections to help you with your business and the personal problems of your associates throughout your life.

Mattie started out with his neighbors on Queen Charlotte Island with his job being to pick up voters and drive them to the polls on Queen Charlotte Island and throughout Maritime Canada. It was common in the mid '50s to give either two dollars or a pint of whiskey or rum to the voters in appreciation of their vote. It was very important to be on the right side, politically, as after every election in Maritime Canada, all government employees and contractors got laid off; therefore this would pose very serious problems to businesspeople and families who were suddenly out of work and was one of the reasons why Mattie left the Maritimes to go to Western Canada where the government was not as political.

It was customary for lawyers, large farmers, businessmen, or other professionals to run as candidates. By supporting these candidates, if elected you had friends in high places, but you had acquaintances in the various ways of life, which could be very important to your own success in business or in your own way of life. You would also be in position to provide jobs for your friends and relatives through the various elected politicians, who would help you in return for your support in their campaigns.

Mattie, when he went west, also participated in all elections, both for mayor and councilor of the city he was living in and for the MLA in his riding plus supporting a candidate for premier. He would also be on the boards of the provincial and federal candidate in his riding, which resulted in him attending all provincial and federal leadership conventions and campaigns.

In the '50s and '60s, it was Mr. Manning who was an excellent premier of Alberta, resulting in Mattie being a very strong supporter of the conservative Social Credit Party and Premier Manning and his caucus. Federally he started out in the campaigns of John Diefenbaker. The liberals had been in power since the midthirties when Prime Minister Mackenzie King got elected and changed Canada for the better as the liberal leader in Canada. In 1957, Mr. Diefenbaker, a lawyer from northern Saskatchewan, who previously ran for different political offices unsuccessfully on a number of occasions, but in his first attempt to become prime minister, he was extremely successful. He was a great orator, and it was always a pleasure to hear him speak. He loved to tell the joke of Prime Minister MacDonald, who when coming to Queen Charlotte Island to debate the opposition leader Mr. Mackenzie, he joined a group of his supporters the night prior to giving his speech the next day. Many toasts were drunk to the good health of Mr. Macdonald's party by one and all. Upon getting up to speak, Mr. Macdonald looked about to see if there was a drop to drink, but there was nothing available. He asked a supporter if he would be kind enough to put a pail not too far from the speaker's podium. The two politicians flipped a coin, and Mr. Mackenzie won, thereby going first to speak. Upon conclusion of his speech, it became Mr. Macdonald's turn. Shortly into Mr. Macdonald's speech, his stomach took a turn for the worst, so he then stepped quickly to the pail adjacent and barfed into it. He quickly returned to the podium, stating, "I hope that the previous speaker's speech did not affect your stomach in the same way it did mine."

Mr. Diefenbaker was followed by a liberal prime minister who had been a diplomat. A gentleman called Mr. Pearson who was a very quiet, ordinary individual who was in turn followed federally by a very charismatic chap called Pierre Trudeau. Mattie greatly appreciated Mr. Trudeau as he was a great nationalist and was strongly against big foreign business taking over Canada. Mr. Trudeau was followed by a chap called Joe Clark, a very plain individual who won a surprise nomination against a number of big-name individuals. Mattie was a strong supporter of Mr. Clark and helped engineer his come-from-behind win. Unfortunately, Mr. Clark unwisely went to a vote over a budget in parliament and got defeated resulting in Mr. Trudeau returning to power. Mr. Trudeau was followed in the early '80s by a man called Mr. Muloney, a lawyer for big business and a very charismatic individual much like his predecessor. He was noted for reducing the federal sales tax on small business and for introducing free trade between Canada and the United States.

In 1984, Mattie was president of one of the largest ridings in Canada, from Central Alberta down to the US border and from the Saskatchewan border to the British Columbia border. He supported a gentleman named Mr. Taylor who was one of the oldest parliamentarians in the British Commonwealth who had never lost an election since he was a late teenager, and he was now in his seventies. A schoolteacher by profession, Mr. Taylor was a very down to earth, hard working, and honest person and probably one of the best politicians that Canada ever had. On election night, Mr. Muloney and the conservative party won one of the biggest majorities in the history of Canada. Mr. Taylor, who had won the nomination against three of the most prominent people in Western Canada on the first ballot by a large majority, went on to win the election in one of the largest ridings in Canada with one of the biggest majorities in the history of Canada.

On the mayoralty scene, Mattie supported various mayors from the mid-1950s until the early 1980s either as a chief coordinator of an area in the city of Calgary or as co-campaign manager, winning every election for twenty-five years, which was not only very interesting and challenging but as he was involved in dealing with the city sometimes, it paid off to know the mayor and councilor in your area.

In 1968, Peter Lougheed became the leader of the conservative party and in 1968 led the Progressive Conservatives to a substantial win over the conservative Social Credit Party, which had been in power for thirty-six years. These were tremendous years for Mattie's business as he had done a lot of work for the provincial government; and since he knew almost all of the cabinet ministers on a first-name basis, it helped when you were in equipment sales, road construction, engineering, and transportation.

In 1985, Mr. Lougheed retired provincially, and Mattie's friend Mr. Getty, who Mattie supported in his election campaign, won as leader of the conservatives and became premier. He was a fine-looking gentleman, extremely honest, and an excellent athlete in his day. He reigned as premier until the early nineties and then a former mayor of Calgary got elected as leader, who immediately privatized the liquor stores, resulting in the employees' wages being cut in half, and people from outside the province taking over the liquor trade and laying off all of the government highway workers and selling off all of the government's assets, with the roadwork in Alberta being taken over by large foreign companies to the detriment of small businesses in particular and all Albertans in general.

This hit small businesses who were involved in road construction in Alberta very hard with the big foreign companies being very hard to compete against, resulting in Alberta going downhill and proving to one and all how important it is to have a fair government in power. Now Alberta was a poor place to do business, very detrimental to the small contractor and supplier, proving once again how important it is for small business and professionals who contract or consult to the governments, and how important it is to have a government that is pro-small business and the working individual. In Calgary, the mayor and council who were elected in the early '80s were very detrimental to the city, with few roads being built, waste and mismanagement being rampant. This way of governing carried on through the '80s, '90s, and after the turn of the century to the great detriment of all Calgarians. Nevertheless, Alberta remained a good place to live due to its close proximity to the mountains for winter sports and summer activities.

The provincial government in the '90s became a disaster resulting in no new highways, no new streets in the cities, no freeways or overpasses being built, thereby causing congestion for Albertans, tourists, and truckers in the province.

Fifty percent of the hospitals were blown up, sold to foreigners, etc., resulting in hospital beds in the province being cut by 30 percent while at the same time the population of the two major cities grew from one million to two million people. This caused a disaster in health care. Few doctors and nurses were trained, resulting in wait times of up to a year for health care with hundreds of thousands of people suffering and thousands dying for the lack of proper health care. It was an unfortunate time for the province, almost equal to the Depression. Fortunately, Mattie's businesses were across Canada, and he was not totally reliant on any one province, but it was sad to see Alberta, his adopted home and headquarters, become like the Maritimes he had left behind. It was a disaster for the working man and small-business person.

Mattie was one of a dozen founders of the Reform Party whose motto was "The West Wants In." The party soon became the official opposition, and then in a coup won over the Conservative Party, becoming the government of Canada.

Mattie was instrumental in getting Stan Waters elected, the first elected senator in Canada, with the help of the prime minister and Premier Getty.

The Maritimes remained as always a disaster to do business in politically if you were an outsider, or as they said, "from away." But it's a wonderful place to live particularly in the beautiful summers with the friendly people, with Prince Edward Island with its lovely beaches, red soil, blue skies, and the nicest people. Quebec was a place where few outside small business would dare enter, for if you did, you could lose your shirt. Only big businesses that operated nationally would dare enter the province.

Ontario, depending on the government in power, was reasonably fair, and moving westward Manitoba always remained one of the best areas in the world to do business regardless of which party was in power. Saskatchewan would vary as it had a tendency to go from a left-wing socialistic government to a severe right-wing government, so small business never knew at any given time where they stood. Since Mattie had three branches in the province engaged in manufacturing, equipment distribution, and transportation. He had a large investment which left the success of his companies depending on the whim of which government was in power.

With Alberta now in a state of chaos for transportation with new rules continually being invented and the province being turned into a police state and large corporations from all over the world taking over the province, it was very difficult to secure construction jobs or to sell equipment as these worldwide companies could buy direct from the manufacturers and controlled the government to the detriment of small businesses.

Alberta had now become one of the worst places to do business if you were a medium-sized business. Even though Alberta, Saskatchewan, and British Columbia were situated on top of some of the greatest deposits of primary resources in the world, such as the greatest supply of uranium in the world, the greatest supply of potash worldwide, diamonds, the largest tar sands in the world, the largest oil shale deposits in the world, some of the biggest oil fields and natural gas fields in the world, extremely large coal deposits, hundreds of thousands of acres of lumber, hundreds of thousands of acres of some of the best farmland in the world, the resources of coal deposits and numerous rivers providing extremely cheap hydroelectric power. But even with all these substantial resources unlike anywhere else in the world, Alberta would take in thirty-two billion dollars in taxes and revenue from the various resources. It would still go billions in debt. Alberta would give away ten billion dollars per year, money that belong to all Albertans, to Eastern Canada. While in contrast, Arizona who took in only 8.6 billion dollars, less than Alberta gave away, would have superhighways, freeways, schools, and excellent hospitals. An example of how mismanagement and waste can destroy one of the richest areas in the world.

The Alberta government took on the judges trying to reduce their salary while the cost of living was escalating. The judges in turn ruled that they would double their salaries, showing the stupidity of the government.

When hiring lawyers, it is most important to get a referral from a prominent successful and intelligent individual as the outcome in court to a large extent depends on the lawyer and firm that represent your company and your associates. You may have to get different firms to represent your associates and your company whenever they need assistance for problems such as divorce, criminal law, financial matters, assaults, impaired driving, or corporate litigation. An individual with a number of companies and a large number of associates may need a minimum of a half a dozen firms, as you are always better to stick with the smaller law firms as the large firms are not interested in small business.

That is why it is extremely important to make connections with lawyers through charitable political community or church endeavors as it is important to establish friendships and a bond so that in time of need a small business and an individual can secure immediate and capable assistance to assist in important matters as they arise, for his or her small business and their associates.

History has proven that individuals and small businesses can succeed or fail in a large part due to their legal representation in their time of need. As it is extremely important to get a quote in writing before you start any proceeding in a court of law as Mattie found out in the case of *Bedfellow v. Ace Industries International Inc.*, and if in doubt always have your secretary send a letter to every lawyer in a particular city and then you'll be able to judge by the replies who are capable and dependable for your problems that will arise at any particular time in the future.

Mattie's group of over a dozen companies had at the peak over two dozen lawyers across Canada, all acquired by various referrals resulting in his companies winning cases against very long odds and recovering very large amounts of money from various firms and individuals who did business on the edge of society.

Mattie particularly used one legal firm of Williams, Moore, and Phillips for over a third of a century. There was one lawyer in the firm however—Brian Phillips, whose family had been friends of Mattie's for nearly half a century and whose son represented Mattie through all those years as a solicitor, barrister, and a friend, which was a rare and exceptional relationship.

Whether it was in politics or legal matters, Mattie came to rely on the friendships, relationships, and business dealings with the hundreds of lawyers that he had met across Canada throughout the years. This is extremely important to an individual and small business owner.

Mattie and a number of his friends, including a former premier, formed a public company on the stock exchange. This can be an extremely frustrating and costly experience. Mattie encountered several lawyers in the securities field, who made Al Capone look like a Sunday school teacher. Even though he had been in business for many decades, he was still unprepared for the greed in the securities industry. He was given a quote only to find out that the lawyer's word was like a flag blowing in the wind; you could never depend on what was going to happen in the next day, month, or year. This was proven in 2008 when the United States went into recession with Wall Street making billions while at the same time destroying the economy.

Fortunately for all concerned when the slowdown came after the turn of the century, Mattie's companies' shares had doubled in price in spite of the Depression, which the various governments called a recession with millions of people out of work and hundreds of thousands of businesses going broke. Pepsi, Coca-Cola, Interstate Batteries, McDonald's, and a few companies' shares held their value, with 99 percent losing considerable value. Mattie decided during the slowdown since his public company was profitable and his shares had increased substantially in value that he would get out of the security business, having sold all of his shares before the sharp decline in the stock market. He was now able to completely get out of the securities business with his pride intact. Since having been semiretired for many years, mainly dealing in property investments, he was able to continue with his charitable community, church, and political work, which, coupled with his traveling, left him busy with an extremely enjoyable life.

CHAPTER 11

Hard Work, Hardship, Health, Happiness, and Humor

Mattie grew up on a farm in the east on Queen Charlotte Island. Most of the farms were mixed farms, and the farming consisted of raising cattle, pigs, fowl, horses, etc. They also grew cash crops of potatoes, turnips, and grain. Straw and hay were put up for both feed and bedding for the farm animals.

In the spring, the land had to be cultivated with most farmers using four horses to a team as well as a small twenty- to thirty-horsepower tractor. Most farmers worked on the farms by themselves with some being assisted by their wives, where in other cases the women did not work outside the house unless they were teachers or nurses or worked in the retail stores.

Work consisted of getting up at approximately 5:00 a.m. in order to bring in the horses and feed them before harnessing them for their daily work. There would be anywhere from ten to twenty cows to be milked by hand as in the 1930s in the Depression and in the 1940s during the war years, and shortly after, there was no electricity for milking machines. Upon finishing milking the cows in the summertime, they would be herded back to the fields; while in the wintertime in the Maritimes due to the cold damp weather, they would be kept inside a barn, which also housed the hens, pigs, and horses.

Sometime during the month of May, the farmer would start to plant his potatoes and oats. Since Queen Charlotte was an island, a lot of farmers grew seed potatoes. These had to be planted by hand in order to get the top grade of seed potatoes. If the weather was good in the spring, the farmer hoped to have his crop in by late May or the first week of June.

In early July, the farmer would put up hay, usually with a hay loader towed behind a wagon and loading the hay into the hay rack. The wagon would be then taken to the barn where the farmer would stick the hay fork into it and then call for the person who was driving the horse on the end of a long cable to drive out into the yard, lifting a giant fork of hay into the barn loft. This process would be repeated for weeks until the barn was filled with hay, and any excess was put into stacks where it could be stored for feed for the winter months.

Usually in mid-August, the farmer would then cut the grain with a binder, and he would be followed by a hired assistant and put all the sheaves from the binder in stocks, which were then hauled to the barn and put in the lofts where they would be thrashed in the winter months with any excess being thrashed in the field and the oats stored in a granary. In later years, hay balers would bale the hay, and combines would cut the grain, which cut the work of harvesting by 75 percent.

In the fall, the famer would use either a digger with a round beater on it, which leveled the rows of potatoes or an elevator digger, which lifted the potatoes, tops and all. And while shaking out the topsoil, it would place the potatoes in a row, where ten to twenty potato pickers would follow the digger with each one having a section to pick. The pickers would pick the potatoes into twenty five-pound baskets, filling hundred-pound potato sacks, which would be hauled to the farmer's yard where they would be stored in a cellar under the farmer's house. With probably half the crop to three quarters being stored in outside sheds temporarily where they would then be graded and hauled to the wharf at the water's edge, and then loaded onto boats to be shipped to countries all over the world for use as seed potatoes.

During the winter, the farmer and whoever was available; for example, a hired man, his wife, and his family would help him grade the potatoes and ship these as table stock—in other words eatable potatoes —to markets in Montreal, Quebec, or to Toronto, Ontario, which were very large cities.

This was extremely hard work if you lived on a mixed farm, with a full day's work every day except Sunday, and chores such as milking, feeding the livestock, to be done early morning and late at night throughout the year even on Sundays.

During the winter months, there would be wood to be cut for the kitchen stove as well as the furnace. The wood would be cut in the wood lot and hauled to the farmyard where it would have to be piled in a large pile, and then one or two days a year, a sawyer would come with his machine and saw the wood into two- to three-foot lengths. This wood would then have to be manually split and piled into a woodhouse where it would dry for the winter's use. Again, a very cold, hard job. During the winter months, the roads would become nearly impassable, usually only with a horse and sleigh. In the spring, the roads would have very deep mud which made them almost impassable in the fall and spring except with a horse and wagon. It was only during the summer months that a car could be used. Health was the most important part of living on a farm, as even today without your health it is impossible to work and enjoy life to its fullest. It was very difficult for doctors to get to the rural areas as in those days the doctors traveled fall and spring in a horse and wagon during the winter months via a horse and sleigh and during the summer months with a car.

It was customary in each community to have a woman who was either a nurse, by training or inclination, or a midwife who would deliver babies, sew up cuts, and set broken limbs as these issues needed immediate attention as it would take hours to get a doctor from the nearby town and small villages did not have any facilities to speak of. The winter months were passed away playing cards, holding dances in the village hall, putting on fowl suppers, and going to various school events such as Christmas concerts, etc. There would also be plays put on by the women's institute as well as the various societies would put on events to entertain the community.

If there was a house or barn struck by lightning, the community would all get together and within a matter of a few days would build a new one for the unfortunate couple. And since it was common in those days to have large families of up to twelve or fifteen children, a couple needed a very large house. Some of the houses were very old having been built back in the mid-1800s, and as one chap said, he was very happy to have a wife who was very romantic because if she had not been so inclined, he would have frozen to death during the winter as the wind picked up speed when it blew through his house.

The schoolhouses were, as a rule, one large room with a potbellied stove in the middle. There would only be one teacher, and this teacher would have ten grades to look after. And on average forty to fifty pupils, it is a very difficult procedure to teach all of these children in all ten grades for ten subjects all during the same day while trying to keep order in the school. It was common for the children to entertain themselves by playing hockey in the wintertime and softball during the summertime. Children usually came to school on a bicycle or riding on a horse or in most cases, walking. There was no exercise facilities needed in those days as between the chores on the farm, the hard work all summer and winter, farm children were in better shape than any athlete in the top sports league in North America today.

If a farmer or his wife got sick or injured for any reason, the farmers would all gather. They would cut the winter's wood for the family. Neighbor women would visit daily to make sure that the person in the family who needed help was well cared for, as well as any assistance that needed to be provided to the children.

Since most farmers had their own beef, pork, chickens, ducks, geese, all their own frozen fish, bottles of strawberry, blueberry, and raspberry jams, they were almost totally self-sufficient. The only things needed to be bought from the store were items such as vinegar, molasses, salt and pepper, sugar, and, in most cases, flour.

The farm women were quite adept at putting up supplies for the winter, canning chicken, applesauce, etc., as well as baking delicious pies and cakes, which would melt in your mouth.

Since the famers lived in semi-isolation, the children in the neighborhood would get along, as a rule, quite well; and in the evenings, they would occupy themselves by playing crokinole, various card games, checkers, marbles, dominoes, and various other games to keep themselves occupied and happy.

Since the one-room school only went to grade 10, it was common on Queen Charlotte Island for the children to have to go to a larger town to go to high school. There they would board with some lady who took in various students, usually for the sum of forty dollars per month. Since the children were only fifteen to sixteen years old and were away from home for the first time, the various governments in the different provinces would allow the teenagers to write what was called the Maritime board; this would allow the young people to take eleven and twelve together in one year, which meant many a teenager could be attending colleges in the capital city at the age of sixteen years old.

From the turn of the century for fifty to sixty years, teachers only needed one year of training called normal school, yet these individuals who taught in the one-room schools, all ten grades turned out to be doctors, accountants, lawyers, and very successful businesspeople, some of the best in North America where today it is suggested that you get a university degree while many successful farmers, small businessmen, etc., have become millionaires without ever going to college.

There is an old saying that "hard work never hurt anyone." In fact, it did young people a world of good in preparing them for the workplace that they were about to enter, and as long as you had your health, no matter how much hardship you had to endure, you became all the better person for it. And this is true even after the turn of the century.

The most important part of enjoying life is to have a sense of humor, with a joke on your lips, and a smile on your face. This will carry you through life, as been proven for decades past.

CHAPTER 12

Travel

Mattie had always wanted to travel, so he decided as a late teenager he would leave Queen Charlotte Island by train for the capital of the neighboring province, which was Halifax in Nova Scotia. It's already outlined earlier in the book how Mattie walked mostly, with the odd ride, nearly a thousand miles in slightly over a month while at the same time seeing all of Maritime Canada and a good part of Eastern Canada when traveling into the main province in Canada, which is Ontario.

Mattie then stopped to pick fruit, work on farms at the harvest, and finally to pick tobacco which paid double the wages of anything else and gained an experience into how other farmers made their living, while at the same time meeting other young people who were also working in the orchards, neighbors on the grain and dairy farm. And while they were on school break, they assisted in the picking of the tobacco crop.

Mattie had now saved enough money to buy a nice car and drive all across Ontario and the western states to Alberta.

He then joined the oil industry which, over the next ten years, provided him with a vehicle, excellent wages, and the ability to see North America and parts of the world with all expenses paid.

In 1965, Mattie and his friend of ten years drove across the northern United States to the eastern seaboard to see the world's fair, and then down to the eastern states to Maritime Canada, where Mattie joined the oil crew and went to sea on the Grand Banks in the North Atlantic, which was his first cruise. It was completely paid for by the oil companies while at the same time, he was meeting a lot of different people.

He then started his own company which took him across North America with his drill rigs and finally in the summer of 1967 drove across Western Canada by car to Winnipeg, Manitoba, and then flew to Ontario and Quebec to see the world's expo with a lady friend at that time who later became his wife.

Mattie was now occupied full-time running his drilling business, but this still allowed him time for other activities such as cross-country and downhill skiing in the winter, water skiing in the summer, photography, golf, hiking in the mountains, boating across the prairies, in the mountains in British Columbia as well as on the Pacific on the West Coast and in the northern United States. Also riding his Arabian horses, flying the airplane to various job sites, and reading while traveling which was an excellent way to pass the time. He also became involved in politics, church, and charities.

The various charities were the Easter Seals Camp Horizon which was one of the nicest rural camps built in the mid-1960s and one of the nicest of its kind in Canada. Later on he assisted Camp Bonaventure which was another excellent camp within the city of Calgary in another terrific location, which was operated by a group called Between Friends. This camp specialized in taking children who were severely physically challenged and assisted each camper on a one-on-one basis, individuals which were not suited for Camp Horizon's camp.

Another excellent charity was the Society for the Prevention of Cruelty to Animals and the Salvation Army, which do excellent work for the homeless and many other people in need. The senior resource center which provides transportation to people who need various treatments for cancer, heart problems, stroke, etc., as these individuals would have no other way to get to and from their treatment centers and their medical procedures were it not for the kind individuals who work for the Seniors' Resource Center.

Purchasing vehicles for the Calgary HandiBus, which is another excellent organization that has over one hundred busses that also served the same purpose as the Calgary resource center and transport any person in need to and from any part in the city that they so desire. Dreams Take Flight is another excellent organization whose members are present-day employees of Air Canada airline, and their purpose is to provide trips to Disneyland or Disneyworld for physically challenged people, a very worthy cause. The Imperial Order of the Daughters of the Empire (IODE) is another great organization that provides thrift stores across Canada to help people in need.

The Children's Wish is another great organization, and Mattie helped organize the Queen Charlotte Islanders golf tournament which is held in June each year consisting of one hundred and forty-four golfers who raise one hundred thousand plus dollars for this excellent cause. The second golf tournament is held in July, usually the day after the Calgary Stampede ends with its proceeds going to Camp Bonaventure. The third and last golf tournament is held in October, and its proceeds are donated to Easter Seals Camp Horizon. Every December for forty-five years, Mattie has sold Christmas trees with the profits from the tree lots going to Easter Seals to be used for purchasing scooters and wheelchairs for the disabled. Also, he jointly works with the Calgary Boy Scouts who operate numerous tree lots, using the proceeds to go camping, skiing, snowshoeing, boating, and to attend Scout jamborees.

Other excellent causes that Mattie and his group have supported for years are the Battered Women's Shelter, Juvenile Diabetes Research, Crohns and Colitis Foundation, Heart and Stroke Foundation, and Cancer Fund.

From 1968 to 1970, Mattie was involved in traveling with the drilling rigs across North America as well as to various conventions in regard to his Murfinsky Equipment Distribution business. In 1970, Mattie and his wife crossed Canada for a month; and it's very important to remember when traveling that a good way is either to fly to Eastern Canada where at that time you could get excellent buys on cars much cheaper than in the west or, in later years when the Canadian dollar rose to par or better with the US dollar than it became much cheaper, you could save tens of thousands of dollars by buying a vehicle in the United States rather than in Canada while at the same time getting a free trip and enjoying traveling by motor car either to the east or to the south. If you went south, you could go to Mexico and get a complete dental work done for a few thousand dollars just across the border from Arizona, saving another five to eight thousand dollars.

In 1972, Mattie and his wife decided to go to Europe and ski the glaciers. Unfortunately, when they got to London, they met people who had been to Austria, Switzerland, Italy, France, and there was little or no snow. They then had to change their plans and went to Ireland where they toured Ireland, and while walking along the streets, they saw a sign by American Express advertising a charter flight to Spain to an area that was located by the Mediterranean Sea for next to nothing. They immediately took this trip and discovered an intense liking for Europe. Mattie's wife had been in to Europe 1966 for three months traveling with four other lady schoolteachers, so she was well versed in traveling throughout continental Europe.

The next four years were spent in skiing across northwestern United States and Canada in the winter as well as boating and golfing plus the many other sporting activities that they participated in.

From 1976 to 1985, Mattie traveled each winter on the ski trips as well as to the sun in places such as Hawaii, Southern California, the Valley of the Sun in Phoenix, Arizona, and Florida. While during the summer, they would participate in all activities that the warm weather allowed.

In 1985, Mattie, who had been an outside sales rep for American Express, in order that he might gain all the benefits—such as the 25 percent off cruises as well as cruise at 35 percent off the posted fare and get the half-priced reductions on cars, hotels, and tours as well as 75 percent off airplane flights—he and his wife then started to travel approximately 50 percent of the time.

If you do not wish to own your own vehicle when driving across North America, it is possible to get a car from places like Auto Driveaway or other similar companies who specialize in moving cars to various points, for large corporations who fly their employees along with their complete families from one part of America to another. Therefore you can get a car in Phoenix, Arizona, and drive it all the way to the Atlantic Coast for nothing. Probably receiving a free tank of gas and sometimes getting several hundred dollars for driving the vehicle to the employee's new location, where the large corporation will then take you to the airport and fly you back to where you picked up the Driveaway car.

An excellent time to do this is during the fall when the leaves are turning color across Canada in the months of September or early October. In the southern United States, late October or early November is an excellent time to drive across the southern United States as you see a lot of different terrain and encounter many different people.

Another way to travel free is to approach RV associations and RV dealers, as a lot of individuals who own motor homes will drive them across the country in order to see the various provinces or states, but rather than driving them back to their original destination, they will allow others to drive the vehicle back to where their trip originally started. Therefore giving a couple or a family the free use of a vehicle, and you can cook all your meals as you travel, and your only cost is your food and fuel.

Something to bear in mind is if you are on a budget, it's cheaper to stay in ordinary motels rather than chains because the majority of travelers prefer to stay in a chain because they have set standards that they are forced to meet which nearly always guarantees you an excellent room and food; whereas if you stay in a mom-and-pop motel, you will get a much better rate, but you will not have the guarantee that you would have in a chain of motels or hotels.

When it comes to eating, always eat at restaurant chains even if they're just fast-food outlets, as usually the food will be standardized and reasonably priced as well as clean.

Always when booking a hotel, get references from somebody you know, and it is always wise to book your room yourself by phoning the hotel directly because if you go through a third party, you will probably pay a third more for your room. And always remember it's easier to save money than make money.

If you're planning on being a traveler, always bear in mind if you go anywhere in the world when there's a major event, you will pay double to triple for your rooms. Traffic will be almost impossible, lineups at restaurants and at all events, and seating will be hard to get in restaurants with lengthy waits. In some cases, rooms will not be available, causing you to have to stay outside the city where the events are being held. One way to get around the excess crowds is to attend an event somewhat similar in small cities that have identical participants and shows.

If you're planning to watch major sports events, bear in mind that the American Hockey League has the same players as the National Hockey League. College football players will soon be playing in the National Football League, and you can see these second-tier sports events for half to a third the price.

For example, one of the best places in the world to see all sporting events is Phoenix, Arizona. There the desert gets cooler in November, and NASCAR will be hosting one of their nationwide car races. Also at the same time there will be NFL football, the very best available weekly. There will also be the NHL and NBA games being played as well as the Fiesta Bowl around New Year's which is equivalent of the Super Bowl, except it's college football which is just as good. They too will be playing in the senior football league in a year or two.

On the first of November, the golf courses will all be reseeded, and in the Valley of the Sun, there are over two hundred golf courses where you can play a round of golf at twenty dollars to up to two hundred dollars per person depending on the golf courses. There are also motels from fifty dollars per night to hotels at five hundred dollars per night to suit any particular taste.

Always remember when traveling to Australia, New Zealand, etc., that the seasons are reversed to North America. Should you wish to travel there in November, December, January, February, it can be up to one hundred to one hundred and twenty degrees Fahrenheit, resulting in a lot of people who are fair skinned not being able to utilize the beaches.

It's also wise when traveling to places like Europe, the Canadian and American dollar, if they are at par, are not worth nearly as much as the British pound or the Euro with a variation of up to a dollar forty. Add in a value added tax and a 15 percent tip, which is not normal in America. When you factor in everything, you could be paying double to see a country that is somewhat similar to America.

It is wise to remember that when you're traveling, you have the choice of going by train, which will take you from downtown to downtown, but you are at the mercy of the railroad. Having traveled by train throughout Canada, United States, Europe, UK, the Far East, etc., I find it a rather confined experience although places such as Europe and Japan have some of the best railroads in the world. Bus tours are another form of travel, but bear in mind that when you're traveling on a bus, you'll probably have to get up at six o'clock in the morning in the dark and have breakfast at seven, then travel all day which requires a lot of stamina, eating strange food as you stop where the tour operator wants you to stop, and then get back to your hotel in the evening and wait for the fifty-plus people on the bus to get served. You will look forward to getting to bed. The good part is you do not have to worry about hotels, food, rent-a-cars, etc., as the bus driver and tour guide will take full charge of you just as if you were in kindergarten. They will do everything except lead you by the hand, and if you need a wheelchair, they will probably provide that.

The other form, which a lot of people prefer, is to rent a car. Then you have the freedom to stay in an economical or luxury hotel or a bed-and-breakfast where you can talk with the owners who usually speak some English. And you will learn about the various food, animals, and crops grown in the area as well as the different attractions to see. Bed-and-breakfast people in Eastern Canada, the United Kingdom, and in continental Europe are usually very kind and generous, providing good food as well as information on their area.

If you are planning to ski, golf, etc., it is always wise to participate in these sports on weekdays as the locals will be all at work, and you will get more economical rates as well as not have to contend with the large crowds on weekends.

It is always wise to travel in the spring or fall as the children are in school, and certain groups of people such as teachers and couples with families always travel during the summer, causing congestion on the roads, in the airports, in the hotels and restaurants, etc., as well the prices will be considerably higher just as if you're attending a special event.

The only time not to travel in spring or fall is on a cruise ship as it can be very cold on a cruise ship in the spring and probably very wet. In the fall, the water can be very rough, and you may be confined to your cabin and quite possibly severely seasick; so even though the rates are at least half price in the spring and fall on cruise lines, you may not even get the value for your money.

Some of the better trips to take on cruise ships will now be outlined below in order to give you a few hints on some of the better ships, better prices, where to stay aboard ships, and what to do when you get into port.

Mattie and Bonnie have cruised on nearly every ship on all seven seas in nearly every area in the world. Caribbean cruises are very popular and can be purchased at excellent rates, particularly in the fall when the seas can get rough; but if you're lucky, you're only going to be on the ship for a week or perhaps two then you might get lucky and get reasonably calm weather. One of the better cruises in the world is the Alaskan cruise where you leave Seattle, Washington, or Vancouver, Canada, and cruise north in the inland waters to Alaska. It is wise to go ashore on places such as Ketchikan, Alaska, and look for a sign for a local sport-fishing outfitter to take you out for salmon. The large cannery is closed there now, but the fishing is excellent. In Mattie's case, he and his cousin who was with him reeled in beautiful salmon continuously that they took back to the ship and asked the maître d' if he would have the cook prepare and serve them to their table, which he did, and the fish was absolutely delicious.

In Europe, one of the best cruises is from Greece through the Black Sea where you will get to visit the Greek islands, the Ukraine, Romania, Turkey, where you will sail through the straits of Istanbul, which is the dividing line between Europe and Asia and an excellent place to purchase carpets. Then it's on to Venice and Rome. Venice is especially different with the gondola rides, a high point, and then on to Rome where naturally the Vatican is spectacular to behold. Rome, Italy, and Athens, Greece, have excellent ruins that go back several thousand years in time, an interesting piece of history.

Another top cruise is the Baltic cruise, which will take you from Amsterdam to Sweden, Denmark, Norway, Russia, which is the highlight of the tour, particularly Catherine the Great's palace which takes a full day to tour one of the greatest art and antique collections in the world.

When touring spectacular places of interest, it's always wise to watch for a local by the entry, who will probably speak English and be an excellent guide. At Catherine the Great's palace, they had a chap who, for eight dollars, spent the day outlining all the points of interest within her residence, which is called the Hermitage, an unforgettable experience in their lives. He then took Mattie and Bonnie down to the dock where he flagged a boat, and since Mattie and Bonnie were short of rubles, American tourists exchanged their money for rubles. And since Mattie and Bonnie were a little short, the American tourists gave then the balance. Mattie and Bonnie had a lovely boat ride and then went on land to tour Saint Peter's palace. The surrounding area was well kept up and absolutely beautiful. They were also traveling with a chap who they had met at breakfast who owned a steel mill in the United States, and he had offered to take Mattie and Bonnie with him, as he had a bus rented and had an extra few seats. He was quite elderly and had several generations with him with 80 percent of them being American-Irish, so he and Mattie got along great.

While the American industrialist was looking at the grounds, Mattie trotted up to the band and asked them if they could play "O Canada," whereupon they replied of course and said they could play "The Battle Hymn of the Republic" as one band member had been to Canada and one had been to the United States. As Mattie and the US tycoon were walking up the pathway to Saint Peter's palace, Mattie tipped his hat, and the band broke into a rendition of "O Canada." The American was very impressed that they would play the national anthem for Mattie. Mattie immediately pointed at his friend from the United

States, and the band started to play "The Battle Hymn of the Republic." The industrialist was very impressed, and they proceeded to tour the beautiful castle.

Mattie was impressed by the elderly ladies who were manning outdoor toilets, collecting twenty-five cents for the use of their facilities. Their guide then took them to a store where they could buy wine for a dollar a bottle, and the wine steward when tipped properly would serve it for Mattie and his table. They were also able to purchase triple distilled true Russian vodka called Stolichnaya. This is one of the best vodkas in the world. Since there was a rule that you could not take liquor aboard ships, everybody else had to throw theirs in a large crate as they went back aboard; but Mattie got a large tomato juice bottle, and he and his friends drank the tomato juice with ice cubes in it, which they filled up with vodka. So instead of paying five dollars a drink, they wound up paying more like fifty cents per drink. Also, rum was dirt cheap, so Mattie solved the problem by getting a two-liter bottle of Coke, which is available throughout the world, so they drank that throughout the day, saving part of it and then pouring forty ounces of rum into the Coke bottle. So when the others were sadly leaving their alcohol behind, Mattie and their crew marched aboard with forty ounces of rum and forty ounces of vodka, which shows that if you use your head, the system can be worked so that it's beneficial to the traveling individual.

In the Far East, Mattie flew on points. For twenty-five cents on the dollar as a businessman who buys everything for his companies on American Express or Visa will wind up with millions of points, which allows you to fly anywhere in the world first-class or business class for one hundred thousand points each, which, depending when you're traveling and how far, could cost you from ten to twenty thousand dollars. On several occasions, Mattie and his wife would fly around the world; for example, to London with Air Canada, then with British Airways into Europe and the Middle East and Africa, then to the Middle East to India, then Singapore, the cleanest city on earth. They would then take a cruise to Malaysia, to Thailand, with a brief flight to the Philippines, which was cut short due to either a hurricane or a typhoon, then back to Singapore and on to Hong Kong. They took a tour to China to attend a trade show in Guangzhou where they found China to be a very different culture but with very hospitable people; then back to Hong Kong to Vancouver, British Columbia, and then home to Calgary.

In the better hotels in the world, they will always have a room, usually on the ninth floor for business travelers and for people who want to eat various food from all over the world, which they know will settle easily on their stomach. Also, they can sample various dishes from that particular country while knowing at the same time that they will not get an upset stomach.

In Cairo, Egypt, upon deplaning Mattie and his wife were approached by a clean-cut young man who said rather than take a taxi, my uncle has a bus and he will drive you every day wherever you want to go for a reasonable sum of money. Mattie accepted his offer, and they traveled for days on end with the young man speaking good English and the uncle, having been a retired chauffeur for the president. They stopped numerous times during the day, some for the uncle and his nephew to lay out their prayer mats facing the east and say their prayers, which was quite impressive to Mattie. The next important stops were at McDonald's as both the nephew and the uncle loved to dine out at McDonald's since food is universal throughout the world at fast-food units, and they are very clean and staffed with young people who can give you information and directions on most anywhere you wish. Both Mattie and his wife always found fast-food units to be a great asset when they travel anywhere in the world.

It is very important when you are booking a cruise ship to always ask for the middle of the ship, up and down, and front and back. If you're too low in the ship the portholes are small with little or no visibility. If you're too high on the ship, there is a lot of roll; and if you tend to get seasick, you may not enjoy your cruise. Should you be at the front, you will perhaps even hear the waves as they hit the bow of the ship. And while you're at the rear, you can quite often hear the noise of the giant engines and the driveline.

In the middle of the ship, you are very close to the elevators which is convenient when you want to travel the seven to ten stories up and down for shows, meals, gym, outdoor pool, and restaurants. In later days, now they have extra restaurants where you can go and pay probably fifty dollars a person for a good meal, which is rather ridiculous since you have already paid for your food in advance. So why would you ignore what you've paid for, which is very good and all you can eat, and eat in the exclusive restaurant and waste your money. It is also very important that when you board a ship, as you meet each individual who is going to provide you with service, you tip immediately; and by all means be generous since 99.9 percent of the people getting aboard the ship will not tip till the end, when you are provided by the cruise line a list of how much to tip and an envelope to put it in for each person like the steward, the maître d', your table captain, your room steward, etc. Throughout your cruise you will receive excellent service, bearing in mind that nobody else has tipped, and of course when you finish your cruise, if you get exceptional service, you can tip more; but that is entirely up to you since you've already received double the service of anybody else aboard ship. On one occasion, Vinnie, our table captain on a cruise to Alaska, would take dollar bills and would fold them into frogs, and then we could bet on how far the frogs would jump. When we pressed their tails into the table, sometimes they would jump into drinks, coffee cups, off the table, or even into food. The table captain explained to us that in Hong Kong, this is how they gambled and taught the children how to play games. By showing them how to make toy frogs, they could all play with their little paper toys and gamble at the same time.

In Japan, we were amazed by the size of the city of Tokyo as we always were by the immense crowds of people—the big buildings and the major cities of the world such as London, Athens, Frankfurt, Madrid, Saint Petersburg, Moscow, Tokyo, and the other large cities too numerous to mention.

I will not go into detail on museums and historical buildings as I've seen so many, and really I expect if you only saw a few you would find them entertaining. But I in particular found them to be just another old building, although the art in some of them was worthwhile, but it's far easier if you live in Alberta, for example, to go to the Remington museum in Cardston, which is one of the biggest of its kind in the world of old-fashioned equipment and artifacts and the Heritage Park in Calgary, showing how work was done in days long ago with old hotels, steam trains, paddlewheel boats, etc. For twenty or so dollars per person, you can tour a site such as this and come away very happy, and it's very close to home for Canadians. Also included in the list is the Drumheller Badlands, which I happened to enjoy just as much as the Grand Canyon in the United States, having been to the south rim, the north rim, and having taken helicopter tours and Bonnie having gone down into the canyons and camped out, but she is the more avid hiker between us and therefore enjoys these sort of facilities to a greater extent.

It is the same in the United States; there are so many theme parks in the Anaheim area alone in California such as the Universal Studios, where Mattie was once informed that the hardest animal in the world to train was a house cat, so Mattie went back to Alberta and bought himself a cat, who he immediately trained to play football, hockey, etc., to his great satisfaction. There's also Disneyland and the Knott's Berry Farm, which makes this a particularly interesting area in the States.

Another interesting area is Las Vegas. Las Vegas is one of the few areas in the world with many different themed hotels such as the Stratosphere which is six or seven hundred feet high with a needle at the top that you can ride up and down provided you have the nerves of steel. There are hotels like the Venetian that you can travel around in boats; Treasure Island, which has pirate ships fighting at night out in front; the Bellagio, which has a tremendous fountain; and Circus Circus, which has free shows. You can also camp out in the parking lot with your RV, and you can go in and watch the shows, and you're pretty well in the center of the activities on the strip. Caesars Palace is another extravagant place and have shows such as Cirque Du Soleil and entertainers such as Celine Dion who performs with shows costing over one hundred dollars, but Mattie had always preferred to watch them on the TV, as it does not take any traveling and does not cost any money.

It's also nice to visit the Excalibur where they have jugglers, musicians, all different people performing at no cost to individuals staying in the hotel.

For people who have went decades ago to Las Vegas and return now since it's become an international and cosmopolitan area with visitors from all over the world, it has become exceedingly expensive.

If you like the water, cruise ships are probably the best value of all as well as the fastest-growing tourism industry in the world. In one trip to the Far East, Mattie and Bonnie disembarked in Tokyo after getting a trip overseas on points at a savings of 75 percent. They enjoyed the different culture of Japan where people are extremely friendly, and after touring the city, they caught the bullet train that traveled at two hundred miles per hour from Tokyo to Osaka. There they visited the surrounding areas like Kyoto and Osaka. There they were treated to a free guide, a lady who was the daughter of a very wealthy manufacturer, and it is the Japanese policy to not take any money for tour guides who do an excellent job of helping visitors. The only way Mattie and Bonnie could repay their wonderful guide was to send her an Anne of Green Gables doll, and since Mattie came from Queen Charlotte Island, it was very easy to buy the nicest dolls and send them to her in Japan where she, upon receiving the doll, sent back an excellent letter in English. When at the railroad station, Bonnie asked how they were going to find their guide again, so Mattie put currency in the pay phone, and immediately the lady's cell phone began to ring. And after looking around, they were able to find their guide. They then proceeded to a hotel where they slept on the floor, and then they proceeded to the lounge and restaurant to have a drink and have supper. The proprietor asked Mattie what they did with raw fish in Canada, as there they called it sushi, and it was very delicious. Mattie told him that in Canada they use the raw fish for bait; whereupon everybody in the room, tourists, and locals, all laughed hilariously. After a few drinks of sake followed by excellent Japanese beer, they told the proprietor they would go for a walk rather than have a raw fish supper, and fortunately down the road there was a McDonald's. They had lucked out again. They dined in style on a Coke, Big Mac, and french fries, a true American meal.

In cruising, it's always wise to try and depart first off the ship; therefore you will get your choice of a taxi driver who speaks English and will probably give you the best price in order to get quick business. And always remember that you ask for a table of eight or ten, so you now have many newfound friends, and it's always wise to ask them if they wish to share the vehicle with you depending on where you are in the world. This will cut your cost down considerably; for example, in China, in Shanghai a group of eastern Americans, some of them former Canadians, had met Mattie and Bonnie in the lounge and dance hall; and after a few drinks, they asked what Mattie was going to do the next day. He explained how he would go down to the dock, and he would try and get a ride uptown and from there, he would visit the various shops as he was interested in going to a communist store, which is very big in size and very cheap in price. Upon disembarking from the ship, there was a minibus waiting, and Mattie asked them what it would cost to be taken uptown. The driver stated that it would be free, as he had just dropped off some new crewmen for the ship; so if they wanted a ride, it would be no charge. The eight of them got a cheap ride uptown, where they toured the large state-owned store; and from there, they went to a market somewhat like a flea market in Canada or the United States, only it's very large with products priced very cheaply. Unfortunately, some of the people couldn't speak very good English, and with Mattie's group having no Chinese, it was very hard to converse and make a purchase. Mattie looked around for a chap who might speak English. After inquiring, he met a man who spoke perfect English, and Mattie asked him if he would interpret for them. The man said he would be glad to help out, so they spent all day together, traveling to various places of interest and shopping. Their newfound friend would flag down two taxis, as they were not very large cars and away they would go. The gentleman from Shanghai informed them that he was a professor at the university, and if they were interested, he would get his friend who had a van who would take their whole party, and they could go anywhere they wished day after day as the ship was only in port for two days. For a set price, he and his friend would meet them at the dock. Mattie's friends were amazed at the good luck, and they became friends for years, which was the usual occurrence for Mattie and Bonnie as this is generally what happened as they traveled. After tipping generously, they always got a large table with a nice group situated by the window.

It is very important when cruising to get a balcony if possible. You may even get it thrown in for free and also ask for an upgrade as this is common. On one cruise around the Hawaiian islands—and this is a terrific way to visit the islands—by touring the islands aboard ship, you could just get off, go where you want to go and charter a vehicle to tour the island. Absolutely it's a wonderful experience as the weather in Hawaii is always fantastic year-round with very little variation throughout the year. But you have to be careful in later years when you go through security, and if you set your purchases down, somebody else who has bought nothing may come along behind and pick up your purchase. And while you are getting frisked, they will be long gone aboard the ship, and everything you bought will have disappeared to your dismay. On that particular cruise, Mattie had booked late; therefore they had a berth lower down and towards the front of the ship, which was not what he wanted. And since he had tipped the purser a nice sum of money, he decided to approach the lady and ask for a cabin higher up in the center. She said she would see what she could do, and Mattie added a little more loot to what he had already tipped her when they boarded; whereupon she stated she said she would give it to the various staff, and they would appreciate it. Mattie always wondered since she was the one to receive the tip, she would be wise to keep it, which she no doubt did. Within minutes, there was a knock on the door, and they were moved up four levels on the ship; but lo and behold, there was a life boat in front of their beautiful big window, and they were going to be touring the islands where they wanted to see all the pleasant scenery. Mattie decided he would wait a few hours and try his luck again. Down he went to the center of the ship, and there's the same nice lady at the desk. "How are you enjoying your new quarters?" she asked. Mattie told her that it was situated far from the dining area, and as his wife had a bad leg, he would surely appreciate a little higher up, a little bigger, a little better location, and a balcony. She told him that those were a lot of requests, but Mattie just kept smiling and looking her in the eye and remarking on how pretty she was and how lucky she was to have such a pleasant personality, and how any young man would strike the pot of gold should he ever marry her, all the while pulling out more bills for her coworkers.

As her smile widened from ear to ear, and her eyes bulged she said, "Aren't you ever in luck." Then she immediately rang for two stewards, who quickly moved Mattie and Bonnie to a room that had everything he asked for, including a balcony as big as the room itself. Mattie tipped both stewards, as after all when you're paying thousands for a cruise, what's a few hundred in tips; and they rushed for snacks, appetizers, sandwiches, more Coke to mix with his rum, tomato juice to mix with vodka, in order for Mattie and Bonnie to celebrate their good fortune. The cruise turned into one of the better ones they had ever taken.

It is always wise when going on a cruise to book your meal at the same hour as you would be eating back in your home province or state; therefore if you were going eastward to the Caribbean, there would be a two-hour time difference, so naturally if you ate at six o'clock or seven in Western Canada, you would want to eat at an early sitting at six. If you were going westward, then six o'clock would be later to dine, so you want to dine at eight. When on a cruise if you are going to be stopping often, it is essential that you get a balcony so you can go out and sit on it and have refreshment and watch the ship tie up at dock, or even if you are on the ship in the afternoon, you can watch the activities on the dock. It's only if you are very cost conscious that you would get an inside room or if you're sailing on the ocean because there's nothing to see when you're traveling for several days out of the sight of land. Also, if you do not like confined spaces, an inside cabin is mostly just hallways and of course no outside view, so you would be better to save for a little longer and take the outside cabin, particularly if you're a veteran of cruises.

It is also important if you sail on the same ship or cruise line over and over. You will be part of the captain's club; therefore since you belong to this club, you will get better deals and quarterly newsletters on what is available at low prices.

It's very rare to get good last-minute deals as in prime time, which is when the weather is cold in northern United States or Canada, the ships will usually fill up early, and the discounts will no longer be available later on, nor will there be the kind of cabins available that you would want. You will either be put low down on the ship at the front or the back; therefore you will not enjoy as nice a cruise experience.

If you're young and do not spend much time in your cabin, as there is breakfast in the morning, a snack in between, there's lunch for the third meal, there's afternoon tea and pizza for the fourth meal, and dinner is the fifth, and then the sixth meal is a midnight snack, so you are forever eating. There is if you're close to land constant tours, or you may be up at the pool all day or at the gym exercising, maybe just walking around the promenade, in the library reading, and there are get-togethers for different people to play bridge or meet singles. There are various games you can play aboard the ship, so if you are going to be very active, you can take an inside cabin and save probably 25 percent, and it's worth it. Or if you are newly married or your lady friend is very romantic, then you may want to stay in your cabin for considerable periods of time. If so, it doesn't really matter as you will probably not be looking at the water or the shore anyway, so an interior cabin would be quite sufficient.

It's also important if you're travelling on a ship that is being repositioned from one part of the world to another. The fare can be as low as only 25 percent to 35 percent of what they would normally charge you, so for a money-conscious person, this is an excellent saving and a very economical way to see the world. For example, if you get a cheap flight to Hawaii, and then you were to take the ship for three weeks to Sydney, Australia, you could have a week in Hawaii, stop in Fiji, Bora Bora, and all the South Pacific islands on your way to Sydney. And you would have twenty-one days with nothing to do except enjoy the cruise.

Another form of cruising are the riverboat cruises out of New Orleans, up the Mississippi, and out of Portland, Oregon, then on the Colorado River on the paddleboat, with stops along the riverside to the Snake and the Willamette rivers; and riverboat cruises are totally different as there are only a few hundred people, and everybody becomes very friendly and spends a lot of time together.

There are also cruises that go up the Norwegian coast as well as cruises around the UK and Ireland, which are very interesting as there are lots of shore stops, and that is an excellent cruise as well. Going to South America is also very interesting to visit Brazil, as Rio de Janeiro is quite a city and then on down to Iguazu Falls, and the country of Paraguay lies adjacent to Brazil, and it has great duty-free shopping. And then from there while in Iguazu Falls, the dances don't start till eleven o'clock, so on the way over, Mattie got numerous bottles of Crown Royal whiskey, which is very cheap. So before the dances, they would always have a few shots, but unfortunately, the bottle had a picture of a penguin on it, and it was yellow in color. And to this day, Mattie still thinks it was penguin pee; nevertheless, in the morning Mattie got extremely sick. Varig Airlines flew him to Buenos Aires in Argentina, where the taxi fares were a ridiculous price and the airport was situated a long distance from the Sheraton downtown. So Mattie had one of the porters wheel him on a luggage cart down to the bus rather than take a taxi and tipped the bus driver well in order for him to get a fast trip downtown. The bus driver immediately took off like a racecar driver with the roads being full of potholes and speed bumps. Mattie was at the Sheraton in short order. Upon being helped to the desk, he asked for the manager who got in a doctor who worked for the major oil companies, Volkswagen, and Mercedes Benz. The doctor brought a nurse into the hotel where she stayed for four days, and the first payment was fifty-two dollars, but after that, he was happier to settle for a bottle of the Crown Royal, and he treated Mattie for four days where Mattie lost forty pounds. The doctor treated him with white yogurt with no fruit, in it and 7Up, which would be left to sit out for ten hours till the fizz had gone out of it, and charcoal. The doctor informed Mattie that he had acute intestinal colitis and that he would have him cured in four days. Mattie did not know whether it was the colitis or the trips to the bathroom to get clear of what was in his stomach from one end or the other that caused him to lose all the weight. In the meantime, Bonnie went on numerous tours; and within a few days, Mattie was back on his feet and was able to travel to Uruguay, having taken a day to look into selling used equipment in Argentina as it was in the mideighties, and times were extremely tough, with rich people paying ordinary folks to line up for a full day to get as much money out of the bank as they could because the Argentinean government was rationing the money. This was quite a change from back when Mattie was going to school when Argentina was the sixth richest country in the world, and now it was broke.

Another trip that was very interesting was Cuba because it is very much like Prince Edward Island back after the war, old tractors, old cars, red soil, green grass, mostly agriculture with the nice beaches, blue skies, and blue water. As was customary, Mattie rented a car and got the head concierge to travel with him. The roadside was full of hitchhikers, so they had the opportunity to meet many people, including police officers who would hitchhike out to where they were going to work, and there they would sit at a cheap table on the side of the road. When at the end of their shift, they would hitchhike back to the next larger town. Mattie had suggested this on numerous occasions to many police chiefs, mayors, and councilors that it's a way that the police travel in Canada thereby saving the taxpayers' hundreds of millions of dollars but as of yet with no success.

On one occasion, when Mattie finished work at five o'clock in Edmonton, Alberta, his wife asked what he was planning on doing. He told her that they should catch a flight to Yellowknife in the Northwest Territories and play golf in the midnight sun. Whereupon they promptly booked the flight, landing at ten o'clock in Yellowknife in the North West Territories and went golfing at midnight as there was only a couple hours of daylight. At that time of the year on June twenty-first, early in the morning they went fishing on Great Bear Lake, a gigantic lake with houseboats anchored in the bay all around Yellowknife. Evidently, the hippies had gone to Yellowknife in the sixties and built rafts; upon which they built little houses and painted them all the colors of the rainbow, a sight to behold. After fishing that same day, they caught a flight to Norman Wells and then on to Inuvik. Mattie had been up to Inuvik working for the oil companies decades before, but it was a first for Bonnie, and she enjoyed it immensely. The next day, they then took a charter airline Kenn Borek Air, who was a friend of Mattie's from back many decades, up to Tuktoyaktuk, and there they were on the Bering Strait. Bonnie dipped her toe in the Arctic Ocean, high above the arctic circle and got her picture taken with the taxi driver and his wife who drove them around town to meet the various villagers, as it's a community of only a few hundred people but was very interesting.

Research has shown that certain hotel rooms contain over 80 percent of fecal bacteria on most surfaces. The cross-contamination of bacteria by cleaning tools used by employees within different hotel rooms could be a cause of this. Exposure to bacteria causes the immune system to be compromised. Be careful when staying at hotels; try to wipe down surfaces with antibacterial wipes as best as you can, and wash your hands thoroughly to avoid being exposed to large amounts of bacteria.

One could go on for hundreds of pages on all the different places in the world, the different scenery, the different cultures, the different languages, the different foods, the different methods of transportation, the different nationalities, the various dances and activities, the different buildings and hotels, as in Shanghai where there were probably more cranes working than everywhere else in the world put together. And all the different architecture, the different dress and clothing worn by the individuals in each area as Mattie usually collected dolls from the various parts of the world clothed in the different attire of that country. So much to see, so much to do and life is so short. Nevertheless, hopefully the readers of this book will have the opportunity to see, travel, and enjoy enough experiences to satisfy most of their desires. Good luck.

CHAPTER 13

Conclusion

Mattie realized that one of the most important parts of his life was the environment in which he was raised; he had the good fortune to have a father who was a businessman and a mother who was a nurse, with both having dealt with people throughout the east and were only too willing to pass on everything they had learned to Mattie.

They always coached him in the value of money, how important it was, and how it was easier to save money than to make money and that throughout your life you had to be constantly reading and learning on a day-by-day basis. Mattie became an avid reader as a preschooler, progressing to reading five thousand pages per month as a late teenager, bearing in mind the words of a learned gentleman. "Tell me what a man reads, and I'll tell you what the man knows."

Mattie realized how important it was to not only have friendships within the community but within the family and always to be ever vigilant for a better deal just as when his friend broke his arm in Halifax, and they had to drive a hard bargain for a cash settlement to fund part of their trip westward to Ontario.

He also learned when he met with the driver examiner how important it was to be polite and plead his case for a driver's license in order that they might continue their way westward.

When applying for a job in Calgary, Alberta, he immediately stated his beliefs, thereby making an impression on the senior American who was in charge of the oil crew, thus getting a good job, a good pay, coupled together with a bright future in the oil industry.

He learned by associating with his older cousin in Toronto, Ontario, how to drive a hard deal when buying his second vehicle, a pickup truck. He then learned from his friend in Queen Charlotte Island how to buy calves on the mainland and resell them for triple what he paid, purchase bags of number 2 potatoes for next to nothing, and sell them for eight times what he had paid for them, thereby having a loaded truck both going to the mainland with potatoes and returning with the calves.

He also learned at the same time that buying and selling equipment was a very profitable business, and even though he was in his early twenties, he continued on buying, selling, manufacturing, and renting equipment for over fifty years.

He also learned that all the money he made in buying and selling when invested into a business where there was not a guaranteed return, such as farming and growing cash crops, he could lose everything that he had made in the retail business.

He also realized by making friends in the oil industry that this enabled him in his midtwenties to get into the oil field industry with his drill rigs. This was his original investment, and it paid off very quickly, making large amounts of money. In several years, he got into the maintenance and construction industry utilizing his equipment in the spring and summer, which gave him a year-round operation where his competitors worked either in the oil field industry in the winter and very little during the summer, or in the construction or maintenance during the summer and did nothing during the winter. By working year-round, Mattie was able to make far more money than his associates and rapidly build his business.

He then added his asphalt manufacturing operation which doubled his profits in the summer months, and since he had to hire trucks across Canada, it was only natural that he got into the transportation business as it went hand in hand with his asphalt manufacturing.

It was in his mid to late twenties that Mattie realized how important it was to be involved in politics, and at this time, he became very involved in the political field which was to give him an insight into how government and business were so closely entwined; and in order to be successful, you had to have an excellent knowledge of both.

Since Mattie spent a lot of time traveling and staying in hotels and camps, he had a large amount of time to read. It was then that he was able to read about various other people who were highly successful, and he would memorize their quotes and observations for future use, remembering his friend who said, "Tell me what he reads, and I'll tell you what he knows." It was only then that Mattie realized how important that simple statement was in life.

As Mattie met individuals from the people who worked in the lower paid jobs to the people who ran the jobs, he quickly learned that if you were going to make friends with them and be capable of doing good business, you had to have a sense of humor, as people would always remember you if you had a smile on your face and the capability to tell jokes with a sense of humor and be able to make other people laugh.

It was then as Mattie expanded all across Canada in his thirties that he realized that a businessman had to have access to hardworking, intelligent lawyers because he who did not have access to these people was certainly doomed to fail in business. Since a large number of lawyers are involved in politics, Mattie soon realized that through politics he would meet many lawyers who would be of great assistance to his companies across Canada. As the years went on, he immediately developed friendships with numerous lawyers from coast to coast, resulting in when the need arose to hire someone to represent or defend his companies, he was able, with a simple phone call, to hire excellent representation and ensure that his companies would not be penalized by having poor representation.

It was also in his early thirties that Mattie became deeply involved in church, community, and charities, realizing that if he took money out of the system, it was only right that he should put a large percentage of his earnings back into the community in general and support any and all good causes. This was to remain his goal for the rest of his life to dedicate both time and money to whatever causes that he felt were appropriate.

This book will inform the reader how you can start with a few hundred dollars in a strange and distant part of the country with no friends or relatives and by making acquaintances that would last for a lifetime and would assist you on the road to success, which various people come up with ideas such as the one in Queen Charlotte Island who gave Mattie the idea of buying and selling cattle and farm produce as well as selling equipment. And then Mattie realized a lot of things after three years. One, get into a business where it was supposedly a gamble and could turn out to be a losing proposition where you lost your shirt.

Two, getting into the oil business where oil is pumped from the ground twenty-four hours a day, three hundred and sixty-five days a year, he realized that it was almost impossible not to make money, and that your income was assured. Since the oil companies were making large amounts of money, it was only natural that it would flow down the pipeline to you.

Three, through his friendship with Reverend Olson, he was given the idea of the parking lot maintenance and construction, and this turned into a gold mine, all because of a simple friendship and the willingness to immediately take the gentleman's advice and act upon the advice, which he would later come to realize was one of the highlights of his life.

Four, upon attending a convention and meeting, he met Mr. Johnson who was the American vice president of a very large company from France who had a highly successful business in the United States and was willing to give Mattie the franchise for Canada and assist him on a twenty-four-hour basis for the rest of Mr. Johnson's life. This allowed Mattie to build manufacturing plants from the Atlantic to the Pacific in Canada and from the Yukon into the United States.

Five, Mattie then realized that he was hiring large numbers of trucks across the country that it would be wise to start up his own business in the transportation industry, and this proved to be another very successful venture.

Six, it was in the back room of a large hotel where Mattie was playing poker that he met Mr. Lorenzo who had sold his company for millions of dollars and offered Mattie the formula for making a new type of crack filler that revolutionized the maintenance of highways, parking lots, etc., throughout Canada.

Seven, through Mattie's friendship with Mr. Purdy, he learned the real estate business; and along with various individuals who owned large amounts of property, he was schooled in how to build economically and to own real estate with little or no money down. Resulting for example in buying lots at a lake outside Calgary for a thousand dollars that were later sold for a million dollars, buying rural property, and paying for it by doing roadwork into the subdivision, resulting in getting the lots for next to nothing and later reselling them for hundreds of thousands. Also, buying land in new industrial subdivisions for forty thousand an acre, which later became worth nearly a million dollars per acre and residential lots for a hundred thousand plus that would later become worth nearly a million dollars. Always remember the old saying, "Buy land because they're not making any more."

In closing, any one of the last seven paragraphs would be enough if an individual decided to take that route to success. He could go on to become a multimillionaire without borrowing large sums of money but simply relying on friendships.

CHAPTER 14

Investing

Upon graduation from high school, each individual needs to decide what path they're going to pursue in life. Small business is not for everyone because of the risks inherent to running one. The upside is that you get to be your own boss to a certain extent, as well as being able to take time off to travel, play sports, etc. Whereas when you work for the government, big business, or other small businesses, you have a commitment that does not allow you as much free time.

If you decide not to go into small business, then one option is to work for one of the various government bodies—municipal, provincial, or the federal government. Should you go to work for the federal government, for example trade and commerce, this position will allow you to interact with various businesses throughout the world. Should you choose to go international, with the pay when you become established in the range of one hundred to one hundred and fifty thousand a year, allowing you to pension out upon retirement with a pension of seventy thousand or more a year on average, you should work your way up the ladder over the years.

Should you decide to join the police force, fire department, or other service area upon graduation from high school? At the average age of eighteen, you will be able to pension out at approximately forty years old while working in these positions you will only work three or four days per week, allowing you to moonlight, running another business on the side. Upon retirement, you can then operate your business full-time as it will have grown over the past decades into a worthwhile occupation, and you will have no exposure to debt as your salary will act as backup to finance your own small business. Should you marry an individual who also works for one of the various government departments perhaps as a nurse or teacher or in the same line of work that you're in, the two salaries will give you an average minimum wage of one hundred and twenty thousand per year, allowing you to only pay thirty plus percent income tax in Canada or the United States, leaving you with a third to spend on your day-to-day living expenses with the other third of approximately forty thousand a year to be put aside to buy a house or invest in a business.

Should you decide to save for a period of five years, you will have two hundred thousand dollars in the bank, which is half the price of the average house in Canada, less in Atlantic Canada, higher on the west coast in British Columbia. Should you decide to live in a nice apartment and wait ten years, then you will have enough to pay cash for your house when you decide to build or buy one. This was what Mattie and his wife decided to do; therefore Mattie never had a mortgage in his life on any of the houses he built or on any of the industrial buildings or manufacturing plants that he constructed as everything was totally paid for out of savings or cash flow.

An example was a schoolteacher in High River, Alberta, who not only taught school but ran a travel agency as a side business while his wife was a nurse who also owned a ladies' clothing store, resulting in both individuals becoming very well-off. And when the husband retired, he then entered politics, a job which paid approximately one hundred and fifty thousand dollars a year plus expenses, which enabled both husband and wife to live all their life including retirement with a very high standard of living.

It is wise to start saving at a very early age as money put into a savings account adds up very quickly plus interest. When compounded year after year, it can add up to millions of dollars. When it comes the time to retire, if you're fortunate to choose the right occupation in life, working in big business is also an excellent path to choose for your future, as at one time for every dollar that the employee put in the pension plan, the company matched it with two more dollars. Unfortunately, pension plans nowadays with big business are not as lucrative. Not only as the years went on large companies went to hiring individuals who worked as consultants who now had to supply their own pension plan as well as provide their own benefits; benefits can be a large part of your salary. Normally, workman's compensation is provided automatically on all jobs if you work for someone other than your own company. Also, unemployment insurance is always included when you work for either government or big or small business. Usually, the employer pays a higher portion of Canada Pension Plan as well as unemployment insurance. Even in small business, it is wise to have a pension plan as the employee pays usually half with the employer paying the other half, which he normally pays a lesser wage to the employee to allow for the money that he pays to the pension plan on behalf of the employee. So in reality, the employer is not really paying anything into any plan because if he did not have to pay funds into the various plans, he would usually pay that percentage in addition to the employee's wages.

It is wise as the years go by to start investing for both husband and wife's future. Investing is very straightforward; if you want to put your money into stocks, it is wise to go with blue-chip stocks, such as utilities. For example, pipelines, electric and telephone companies, also railroads are a good investment; and as it is much cheaper to transport goods by rail as it is by truck. For example, the length of trains have doubled, giving the railroads double the profit. Also, railroads usually hauled one railcar hooked in tandem after another where now they load two containers onto the same railway car, resulting in again doubling their profit. And in Canada in particular, there are so many primary resources such as coal, grain, fertilizer, etc., that has to be hauled to Tidewater. The railways are very lucrative. With increased use of electricity and since once hydroelectric dams are built on the rivers and the power lines are constructed, electric utilities is pure profit. Telephone stocks are another growing industry with their shares going up in price and paying good dividends because with the advent of wireless communications, cell phones and Internet are other avenues that pay off handsomely over the years. There are many other stocks that do very well over the years such as Pepsi and Coca-Cola, McDonalds, Interstate Batteries, and any other manufacturer or retailer of consumer goods that have a very high markup. For example, Coke and coffee's basic ingredients cost approximately fifteen cents per serving and retail for around a dollar and a half, a thousand percent markup.

Another excellent investment is guaranteed investment certificates which do not pay a lot of return on your money, but if you want to invest for the short term, they are a safe and reliable source of income. When buying investment certificates, it's wise to buy on a twice yearly basis spread out over a five-year period which allows you to gain the best rate of return and allows you to average out your exposure.

Another form of investing is gold. For example, gold bought back several decades ago for two hundred per ounce has recently rose to a high of two thousand per ounce. Or if you bought gold three or four years ago at eight hundred or so an ounce, it is now worth an average of sixteen hundred per ounce, doubling your money over a period of four years, giving you a rate of return of over 200 percent or averaging a yearly return of 25 percent per year from 2008 to 2012.

When it comes to investing, nothing beats real estate. For example, Mattie has already outlined buying shore property for a thousand dollars per parcel and that same lot when subdivided into two was sold thirty years later for a million dollars, a return of 1000 percent on the original price, or land in an industrial subdivision that was worth forty thousand per acre that now sells at a rate of from four hundred to eight hundred thousand per acre, again an incredible rate of return over a period of several decades.

If an individual or individuals build warehouses and acted as a general contractor on their own buildings, they will save approximately 20 percent. This would normally be the down payment; therefore when the building is completed, your low initial investment return increases over the years not only will the building go up five hundred to a thousand percent, but the rents will also increase in value. For example, a building that is built on two acres of land purchased at forty thousand an acre will, over a quarter of a century, increase in land value to four hundred thousand dollars per acre; and the building and land which originally cost three to four hundred thousand dollars after a thirty-year period will be worth three to four million dollars if built in a growing part of the country, more in some areas and less in other areas.

Apartment blocks are also an excellent investment. Starting out with an up-and-down duplex which is very economical to build as the basement acts as the lower half of the duplex then progressing to fourplexes which also provide a good rate of return particularly if you can find an area that is located on a hillside or the lot can be built up allowing for a walkout residence, always making sure that the particular area is zoned for multifamily use. Then the owner or owners can progress to forty-two suite buildings with three stories being the norm with steps going into the lower area, which would normally be the basement. But when built four feet below ground level and four feet above ground level, utilize the basement as fourteen suites at a considerable savings. Then when you install an elevator four feet above ground level, you build another fourteen suites topped off by another fourteen suites on the third level, which is where the attic would be in a normal building. By building in this manner, you save approximately 20 percent. And when you act as your own contractor, you save another 20 percent resulting in the three-story, forty-two suite apartment building costing you little more than half what it would cost normally to build a building of this nature.

Another extremely lucrative real estate venture is to build mini storage facilities; the mini storage business was established in the mid-1960s mainly outside military bases in the United States, where personnel when transferred to the various bases needed extra storage for their possessions. Mini storage rents for an extremely high rate per square foot, resulting in very high profits on various buildings. For example, when the housing market crashed in 2008 in the United States, people were forced out of their houses by bank foreclosures and had to move into apartments, resulting in a high demand for storage space with the owners getting returns of 20 to 40 percent on their invested dollar, and investors in either private or public companies gaining extremely high rates of return on their investments.

For those who follow investments, the most highly successful investor in the world is probably Warren Buffett who, as a rule, strictly buys shares in companies that manufacture or retail consumer goods, utilities, railroads, etc. Mr. Buffett, even after giving billions to charity, still has a portfolio that varies from thirty to fifty billion dollars, and anyone who invests can follow and practice Mr. Buffett's investment strategies, which are written weekly in the various magazines outlining his investment strategies. Shares in his company average around one hundred thousand dollars per share mainly because it's very closely held. You can also attend his annual meeting, which is held in Wichita, Kansas, where he outlines his past investments and his plans for the future when you hold a share.

It is wise to bear in mind when buying stocks to always buy on a falling market, knowing that it's never possible to buy at a low point; but should stocks drop anywhere from 10 to 40 percent as they did for example in 2008, then if you start buying as the market goes down over a yearly basis, you will wind up with stocks at an excellent average price. And when the market starts to go up, you wait until you're able to receive a 10 to 40 percent return on your investment and gradually sell your stocks, making a decent profit while maintaining the blue-chip stocks that pay dividends of 4 to 7 percent, which is higher than inflation and gives you enough return to have an excellent standard of living.

You can invest in stocks by buying directly through a discount brokerage operated by a bank. You can also buy guaranteed investment certificates direct from the bank as well as gold, with the banks holding your stocks, investment certificates, and gold bricks for you at very little cost.

When buying real estate, it is wise to use a real estate salesman as it does not cost you anything for the services of a realtor and you gain his or her knowledge and experience. In later years, it is possible to sell your property yourself with considerable savings, but this is a personal choice whether you want to go the route of listing with a real estate agent or to the various companies that assist you in selling your own; there are advantages in using both services.

When starting a family, a lot of parents put money in a fund with various companies to pay for their children's education. Mattie never believed in investing money with somebody else while paying them to reinvest your own money mainly because in today's marketplace, a college student can work four months in the summer—May, June, July, and August—and during those months can earn anywhere from two to four thousand per month, allowing them if they live at home to save enough money to pay for their complete college tuition. Plus, even if they live in a rural area or a small town where there is no college, then they move to the larger city. There are always lots of part-time jobs for example either a waiter or a waitress and can usually receive ten dollars per hour and a minimum of another ten dollars per hour in tips working in the hospitality industry. This, coupled with working for three or four months during the summer, provides them with sufficient funds to carry them through college. It is always important to bear in mind when going to college that upon graduation with just one degree, it does not give the individual a much greater opportunity in the marketplace than if he or she just had a high school diploma. A decided advantage is if you get a master's degree as this will put the individual in a much smaller class of people looking for work, thereby he or she is able to get a job much more quickly as well as receive considerably higher earnings than the person who just has one degree rather than two.

It is also wise to consider that if you were to go to trade school for several months a year for four years, upon graduating it would have cost you very little to gain your diploma. Upon which, if you worked as a journeyman/tradesman with a firm for a few years and then opened your own firm, for example as an electrician or plumber and hired another five to fifty employees, you would wind up making up to approximately five hundred thousand per year. You would have to have a pretty good job in government or with another business to equal that sort of income.

It is also important to consider that when you open your own small business, and when you go on a holiday, there is no loss of revenue. For example, when a doctor, lawyer, or accountant takes time off from work, their income stops the minute they walk out the door; whereas, the small business person whose employees are still on the job under the supervision of a foreman or superintendant are still creating cash flow. And when the small business person is enjoying time off for sports, traveling, visiting relatives, etc., their business and employees are still making the money.

When starting a business, it is important to consider franchises. Franchises are usually available for anywhere from twenty thousand to two hundred thousand. This money can be saved by a couple usually in less than five years. By investing in a franchise, you have a well-known name and a greater chance of success. For example, some of the most successful franchises are Tim Horton's, McDonald's, and Dominoes Pizza. There are hundreds of different franchises available in America, and after doing due diligence and inquiring over a period of a year, you can decide whether it is better to invest in a franchise or start up your own small business. Always bear in mind that when you have a franchise, you might have a better chance of success, but you will also be working for somebody else as franchisers have very rigid rules on what you can and cannot do in their businesses. Should you decide to go into the food industry, this particular way of life entails long hours and constantly hiring staff as anything to do with retail is usually working from sunup to sundown, seven days a week.

Mattie found out during life that by making a lot of friends, reading every newspaper and magazine that was available, watching TV, and traveling a lot more than the average individual, he was able to spot excellent opportunities to make money; yet for every opportunity that he saw to make money, there probably were another hundred in every given year that he had missed and could have taken advantage of. Therefore, there are many opportunities in every walk of life to make money and give an individual the opportunity to be his or her own boss and have free time when he or she desire to do something. For example, Mattie's wife was a teacher, and they decided to take a trip in the early seventies to Europe, the UK, and Ireland in order to visit different parts of the world and enjoy a ski holiday, only to find out upon return that the school took a dim view of a teacher taking an extended holiday even though she had the principal's blessing. The school board replaced her for that extended period by another teacher at half the cost. It was then that Mattie suggested that since she was excellent at math, she might like to work for his companies in the accounting department, where she would be her own boss and work her own hours, along with taking time off to join him on a holiday whenever they so desired. This resulted in a much better lifestyle than working for a school board. Even though teachers are very well paid, starting out in Alberta at a salary of approximately fifty thousand per year with the opportunity to earn up to one hundred thousand with excellent lifetime benefits due to one of the strongest unions in the world because teachers have the advantage of having extremely strong support from the parents of their students. Mattie's wife also became a multimillionaire.

Another job that has an extremely strong union is working for the various police departments across the country, even John F. Kennedy said, "We have nothing to fear except fear itself." A quote from Shakespeare, the general public lives in fear, resulting in police personnel earning extremely high salaries with tens of thousands of dollars worth of overtime and a short work week, leaving them time to enjoy various activities or operate a small business with the backing of a government salary to ensure that there is little or no chance of failure, resulting in only having to work a few decades and then go to work in their small business full-time or for another government department or sit on many boards that is very common with retired policemen and other government civil servants.

Should you work as a government employee, it is quite common after retiring from one department to go and work in another department as senior retired government employees have a habit of hiring those that retire following their own retirement, resulting in government employees retiring with two-thirds of their salary and then usually earning a higher salary which when combined gives them about triple the earnings that they received on their original job. Nevertheless, you have to give a person credit that is successful and wisely chose the right path in life, which gave him or her excellent way of life with great benefits and the opportunity to get a second job upon retirement.

Although I'm sure most people would agree that the life of a police officer, with its long hours, weekend work, and possible injury on the job is not something that many individuals would desire.

In prior chapters, Mattie has experienced success due to the opportunities he had and the decisions he made in life, but it has not been mentioned the missed opportunities for success. One of which was the opportunity to invest in apartments that were being foreclosed in Fort McMurray, Alberta, where the main activity was mining the oil sands. A partner in one of Mattie's companies Mr. Mackie suggested when they were having a few social drinks of single malt scotch that Mattie give Mr. Mackie two hundred thousand dollars with Mattie's partner assuring him that he could turn the two hundred thousand into one to two million within the next few years, as he was meeting with a gentleman from Ottawa and that the federal government who owned hundreds of apartments were selling them off at fire sale prices. For example, an apartment that was worth fifty thousand dollars at that time could be bought for twelve thousand. Mattie decided after discussion with his wife that they would not invest in the apartments. Mr. Mackie the next day met with the federal government employee and purchased a large number of apartments, and upon his return to Edmonton, Alberta, he lent two hundred thousand dollars to his sixth wife, who in turn parleyed that small sum of money into approximately five million dollars in a decade as the apartments went from the initial twelve thousand to three hundred thousand. And when divided into condo apartments, it became worth four to five hundred thousand each, and the ones she held and rented out at a rate of from two to three thousand per month brought in extremely large sums of money beyond her wildest dreams.

Another opportunity that Mattie missed was when his friend Mr. O'Casey stopped by his office, inviting Mattie to join him for supper. During the course of the meal, he informed Mattie that there was an opportunity to buy a hotel in Banff, Alberta, for a million dollars, not really a large sum of money. Mr. O'Casey had been in the hotel-and-motel business for several decades and knew the business inside and out, buying, operating, and selling various buildings and businesses across Alberta, particularly in national parks. Mr. O'Casey informed Mattie that this particular hotel was owned by a gentleman who was very rich and was a very close friend of Mattie's and who happened to have his head office in a building situated on the same road as Mattie's office a few hundred feet away. After supper, Mattie and his friend Mr. O'Casey went to see the gentleman who owned the hotel, and as they drove, Mattie's friend outlined to him how the hotel in Banff was located in one of the few tourist locations that had year-round business. For example in Queen Charlotte Island, you could only run a hotel business for around three months out of the year in summer, whereas in Banff, you had a ski season of November through April, six months, and then you had a tourist season in the mountains of another six months.

Upon meeting with Mattie's friend Mr. Lars Williams, they were asked if they would like an after-dinner drink. Mr. Williams poured drinks all around, taking a half glass of liqueur for himself but giving Mattie an almost full glass. Mattie, upon observing the almost full glass of alcohol, inquired to Mr. Williams, "Why do you give me double the drink that you take for yourself?" Mr. Williams told him that since he was twice his age, he should only have to drink half as much. They all enjoyed a good laugh over the joke, and then got down to business about buying the hotel. Mr. Williams informed Mattie and Mr. O'Casey that since Mattie was a good friend of his, the price would not be a million, but would be eight hundred thousand, and the two hundred thousand difference between the price would be their down payment. This would allow them to buy the hotel with nothing down, an extremely lucrative opportunity, but he also informed that his partner was a rather shady guy and the manager of the hotel was helping himself to the profits, advising them that if it was up to him he would not participate as a partner in his hotel. After serious discussions with Mr. O'Casey and Mattie's wife, who did not think it was a good idea to get into the hotel business, and she was also the one who vetoed the apartment business in the north, Mattie decided not to become involved.

Unfortunately within three to four years, the hotel was resold to people in Red Deer, Alberta, for three million dollars; and in a few more years, it was sold to a group of investors in Banff for five million dollars. Should Mattie and his friend have bought the hotel, they could have made four million dollars in a decade, resulting in a gross profit of two million dollars each, showing how important it is when you are given the opportunity to make money so easily that you should immediately take advantage of the opportunity.

Mattie, in the late 1970's maintenance business was making nearly half a million dollars a year gross profit, which he built by putting together the snow removal, sanding, line marking, crack filling, sweeping, pothole filling, paving—the first in north America to do this. He should have franchised this business all across Canada and into the United States; he could have easily gotten fifty to one hundred thousand depending on the size of the franchisee's area and sold hundreds of franchises, resulting in earning tens of millions in franchise fees as it was very lucrative. Unfortunately, this was another opportunity that he passed on which could have earned him many millions of dollars.

A fourth opportunity would have been to sell his fourteen plants across Canada and the United States that were manufacturing asphalt products, as he had offers from oil companies and one of the richest families in North America in the range of ten million dollars for that segment of his businesses, but the offers came with a requirement for Mattie to stay on for five years and operate the companies as well as a no competition clause. Since Mattie was making large amounts of money, he felt it would be foolish to sell the businesses when he was only in his forties, as all he had to do was keep operating that particular manufacturing division, making the products and equipment to work within the industry as well as he had several dozen distributorships for construction equipment which they wished to purchase as well as he was the biggest manufacturer of asphalt products in Canada as well as the broadest distributor of construction equipment.

In a matter of five to ten years, he could make as much money as these companies were offering him for one of his businesses; and at the end of a short period of time, he would have made nearly as much money as they were willing to pay, retain his freedom to do what he wanted, and still have the businesses. Little did he realize that three of the largest companies in Canada, with one based in Eastern Canada and the other two operating businesses all over the world, would get in the asphalt manufacturing products. And when Mattie failed in his bid to purchase the Moose Jaw refinery, he had no source of asphalt that he owned while the other three companies all owned the largest refineries in Canada. The moral of the story is, when you have a chance to sell, sometimes a bird in the hand is worth more than any number of birds in the bush. Nevertheless, the land and buildings in some cases would be worth millions of dollars, and some could be turned into other uses to a good advantage; therefore in the long run Mattie did not win or lose by not selling the plants.

In the late eighties, Mattie had the opportunity to purchase a lot direct from the developer in one of the fastest growing areas in North America, which was southwest Calgary. Mattie bought the lot at cost, which later appreciated in a little over fifteen years by a thousand percent. His wife approached the developer for a building permit which allowed the house to protrude out twenty feet farther than the other established houses on the ridge overlooking the valley. The lady in charge turned her down. Mattie then asked his wife if there was anything in particular about the lady that his wife had dealt with. She mentioned that she was pregnant and in a month's time would be taking maternity leave. Mattie immediately went to see the new lady, outlining that he was going to build a garage that was sixty feet long instead of thirty feet long and use the back part as a rumpus room and exercise facility; and in order to compensate for the extra depth of the house, he would narrow the house in by a couple of feet on either side, allowing the people who were building across the road to have a much better view of the river valley, the city, foothills, and mountains. This would allow the developer to sell the lots across the street for a lot more money because they had a much better view. The lady thought this was a great idea, so she approved Mattie's plans immediately. Mattie next went to the city of Calgary as he also realized that this was a first for Calgary, but there would be advantages for the developer and the new owners across the street from Mattie's house. So he immediately stamped the plans, and Mattie was in business and ready to build. This gave Mattie a hundred and eighty degree view of the golf course, of the river valley, the largest urban park in Canada, the city lights, the foothills, and the snowcapped mountains in the distance. Over the long run, it caused the house to increase by a thousand percent.

Mattie decided that in order to preserve the view in front of his house, it would be wise to turn the river valley into a golf course as the land used to be a gravel pit, but since they had extracted all the material, the land was no longer in use for that purpose and had been turned into a provincial park. Mattie, having helped build Spruce Creek Golf Course and Cemetery in Calgary and purchasing all the peat moss from a friend who had hundreds of acres of a peat bog west of Calgary, and as the owner of Spruce Creek, he was an extremely rich gentleman and a friend who Mattie had worked for his oil exploration company and on one of the largest ranches in North America, it was quite easy to do a deal. Unfortunately, Mattie was able to get permission from his friend Ryan Law who was minister of environment in the government at that time, but when it came time to get permission to lease the land for the golf course, Mattie's friend Ron getty was no longer premier. A new premier was elected to head the government of Alberta. A man named Ron Klinker was elected the premier of Alberta, and Mr. Klinker had had problems, and he had to rely on three very important people in Alberta to save his hide. So in order to return the favor, he gave these three gentleman a ninety-nine-year lease for the Riverview Golf Course in front of Mattie's house. Golf courses can cost up to ten million to build since the water was adjacent to the property, and there were already ponds from the gravel excavating and the topsoil that had been stripped was piled at the ends and sides of the golf course. Mattie would have only had to mix the topsoil with peat, hire one of the best golf course designers around who lived seventy miles away in Kenmore and who Mattie was familiar with to design the course. And as he was just starting out on his own as he had worked for another worldwide golf course designer, he would have done a tremendous job at 10 percent of the cost. Once seeded out, and after a year's wait for the grass to grow, Mattie would have spent a million plus on the golf course, which would now be worth millions of dollars. Unfortunately, with Ron Klinker taking over the government, Mattie could no longer get a lease on the land in the park, which was also a wildlife sanctuary, so he thereby had to forfeit his claim to build the golf course. Later on, Ron Klinker was turfed out by his own party to Mattie's greatest pleasure, and shortly after he lost his health, including a large majority of the people who had competed against

Mattie and were both shifty and shady, Mattie was living happily with one of the best views in the world and one of the best businesses could take some comfort that at least when he was treated unfairly, eventually the people that were responsible either had passed away or suffered ill health or lost their businesses, proving that it pays to be honest and up front in life.

Mattie would never let anything stand in his way when doing business. When he was looking for work in the neighboring province of Saskatchewan, he would go to the capital and walk into the premier's office, informing the secretary that he had an appointment; and while she was searching through his records, Mattie would already be inside and shaking the premier's hand. And since both belonged to the conservative party and knew each other from the past, Mattie would be able to have a conversation and usually have his wishes granted.

On another occasion in Manitoba, he was unable to get major contracts, and the operations engineer in charge was a fellow called Mr. Goodbranden. When Mattie went to his office shortly after lunch, he was informed that the engineer was too busy to see him, so Mattie waited, sitting on a hard chair all afternoon until the secretary had gone home and everything became quiet in the office, and then the engineer decided to make a dash for the door. Unfortunately for him, Mattie raced to the door and grabbed the man's collar and told him they would have a talk about why Mattie was not receiving the contracts that he was low bid on. The engineer hemmed and hawed and would give Mattie no direct answer. Mattie simply memorized the excuses that he received from the fellow in charge and went a few blocks away to the parliament buildings, knowing that the premier and the cabinet would soon be taking time off for supper. The security guard directed him to the premier's chambers, a very well decorated large room with a long table with chairs all around. Mattie noticed at the head of the table was a very nice large chair, so he immediately took the chair at the end and proceeded to read the daily paper. Shortly the premier and a group entered the room. The premier, who was named Mr. Hawley, came to the end of the table. And when Mattie stood up shook his hand, the premier said, "I'm Premier Hawley, do I know you?"

Mattie informed him that he did not, but that he was there on important business. The premier told him that there was an empty chair a few chairs from the end of the table and told him to take it so they could discuss the problems. Mattie was building a new plant in the capital so the premier directed his questions to the MLA, who represented that riding. When Mattie started questioning him, this fellow seemed to be not all that interested, so Mattie invited him to supper where they could discuss the matter in detail. The gentleman said he had an appointment, upon which the premier interrupted and said, "Well, Larry Hay is the minister of highways, and he is a rancher an hour north of the capital, so you and he have something in common, and he has also worked in construction so why don't you and he go for supper, as he's responsible for the government division that you are dealing with." They did this immediately. Larry went to his own office, brought them out a bottle of whiskey, poured them each half a glass and said, "There's no reason for you to not be getting the contracts in Manitoba if you're low bid, and you're going to all the expense of building a plant here in the capital." Since up to this time Mattie was supplying product to the east half of Manitoba from his plan on the Saskatchewan-Manitoba border, the minister of highways after numerous drinks informed Mattie that in the morning he would be awarded all the work that he was low bid on. Mattie then had to inform him that the government was renting storage tanks from one of his competitors, and that he expected them to pull out their tanks immediately as soon as their competitor had gotten the work as they were a very low form of businesspeople. The minister of highways said that there was a few days left in the month, and he would hold them to their contract because if they were paying them a month's rent, they would get a full month's rental from their storage tanks, and that would give Mattie time to get tanks of his own..

Mattie immediately phoned his friend Jock Provost in Montreal, Quebec, in the east who phoned his branch in Toronto, Ontario, and instructed them to get four tanks ready to be shipped on the train that very night to Western Canada. Mattie then within the hour phoned his friends the Weinstrom brothers on the outskirts of Calgary who were the International truck dealers and asked them if they had any trucks coming west. They informed him that they had four ready to come west if they could find drivers to drive them as they were sold and their customers needed them immediately. Mattie said he would look after bringing the trucks west, and then phoned his Calgary office after hours and had them line up four drivers and get them on the midnight red-eye flight which would have them in Toronto at 7:00 a.m. His drivers arrived in Toronto the next day, picked up the trucks, hooked onto the tanks, and left for Manitoba, which was a twelve-hundred-mile drive westward; and by driving long hours, they made that in two days. Mattie then in a few days' time phoned his competitors and told them where they could shove their tanks because his own tanks were already on all jobs and the trucks by this time were back in Calgary.

On another occasion, Mattie was low bid on a large contract in Alberta, and his competitor, a major oil company that had a higher bid than his company was awarded the contract. Mattie drove in late afternoon to the job site, took a sample of his competitor's product, and had it tested that very evening. He then took the results that indicated that his competitor's product had failed the standards test in Edmonton to the lab where the chief engineer had also failed Mattie's product. Mattie informed him that he would have to award the product to the low bidder as both product samples had failed the test. The engineer in charge of the lab was not interested in what Mattie had to say, so Mattie went over his head to the deputy minister. Upon arriving at the deputy minister's office, he was ushered in and Hal Alton, the deputy minister, when hearing Mattie's story, said that since both products had failed and Mattie was low bidder, he would get the contract. Mattie thanked him profusely, and when Ron Klinker privatized all the government work in Alberta, awarding it to foreign companies, costing the taxpayers billions of dollars, Mr. Alton immediately resigned, knowing that the taxpayers' money was going to be wasted. And at his farewell dinner, Mattie presented him with a large check from the small business coalition of Canada, which Mattie was head of, and a wooden replica of a cowboy with a bull's-eye target drawn on the body, informing the very large crowd in attendance that Mr. Alton could spend his time shooting at the wooden cowboy, relieving his frustrations because he had ran one of the most successful highway departments only to have fifty years of hard work that he and his predecessors had accomplished destroyed in one hour by government mismanagement. That program is still in place to this day.

On another occasion, in the province of Ontario, the three senior positions in highways were all held by three engineers of Irish descent. Unfortunately, a major oil company had offered them all jobs in their asphalt manufacturing division, resulting in Mattie having great problems for a short period of time until he got a meeting arranged with an individual high up in the government who promptly overruled all three, and Mattie was able to get all the work he wanted for his plant in that province. The oil companies manufacturing division only hired one of the three at a much higher salary, resulting in the other two being offended. They immediately banned some of the oil company's products, so the oil company lost the work to Mattie and also lost other work that they were initially guaranteed, much to Mattie's delight.

When Mattie thought about small business, he remembered a quote that an elderly businessman had told him. It said,

You cannot bring about prosperity by discouraging thrift.

You cannot help the weak by weakening the strong.

You cannot establish sound security on borrowed money.

You cannot help the wage earner by pulling down the wage payer.

You cannot keep out of trouble by spending more than you earn.

You cannot help men permanently by doing for them what they should do themselves.

In many cases, small business can do work much more economically and much quicker than the government, and in rare cases, the government can do work more cheaply than small private companies. It takes very knowledgeable and intelligent politicians and civil servants to distinguish one from the other.

To illustrate one example is the street sweeping in the city of Calgary. Mattie owned one of the biggest fleet of sweepers in Canada as part of his maintenance division, enabling him to sweep the streets double shift around the clock, seven days a week if necessary, at approximately 125– 139 dollars an hour. The city of Calgary had a fleet of two dozen sweepers which they operated themselves with up to 50 percent breakdown where Mattie would only have 5 percent breakdown, and the city charging the taxpayers two hundred dollars an hour for their sweepers, which they stated was their cost, as well as charging two hundred dollars an hour for Mattie's sweepers, making a 30 percent markup. Yet on occasion the city would use their own sweepers only partially sweeping the city of Calgary, and while their employees were tied up for two months sweeping the city, their asphalt plant and three paving crews would sit idle while they waited for the sweeping to be completed in order to secure the services of the employees engaged in that activity, and in some years the asphalt plant did not even start at all while the potholes in the streets of Calgary grew bigger and bigger. And when thousands of complaints were forwarded to the city of Calgary superintendants, they would inform the taxpayers and residents of the city that the potholes actually acted as speed control; therefore they served a useful purpose.

When the city of Calgary hired an auditor who had saved the city of Ottawa, Ontario, five hundred million dollars on a city budget of two billion dollars on a population of a million people, she was then hired by the city of Calgary. After a lengthy period inspecting all the records, she presented to a council that the mayor and councilors and city managers and employees were wasting seven hundred and fifty million dollars on a budget of two and a half billion caused by waste, mismanagement, and some corruption. In a vote by fourteen councilors and the mayor, the motion to take the advice of the auditor was defeated by fourteen to one with the city deciding to waste the money and quickly firing the auditor, an example of why taxes are so high in Canada compared to in the United States. For example, Mattie's house in Mesa, Arizona, with a main floor square footage of two thousand feet or less, the city taxes are eleven hundred dollars. On a house in Calgary, Alberta, with the same square footage, the taxes could be up to seven thousand dollars, an example of how some cities manage their money well while others waste hundreds of millions.

In Alberta, one of the richest areas of the world, with some of the primary resources such as coal, water for hydroelectric power, light oil, heavy oil, the biggest oil sands in the world, an abundance of natural gas, cattle, grain, lumber, etc., the province takes in over thirty-two billion dollars in revenue yet goes in debt 9.6 billion dollars a year, spending a total of forty billion dollars. In contrast, the state of Arizona in 2012 had a budget of 9.6 billion dollars to operate the complete state while at the same time having five times the freeways, far more schools, and a health system where you are able to procure operations the next day rather than waiting for months or a year in Alberta. Alberta voters would be wise to send the politicians and senior bureaucrats from the provincial government to Arizona to learn how to run an efficient and effective government while getting full value for the taxpayer and voter's dollar.

Two items of great importance Mattie learned through doing business across Canada and in the United States.

1. When dealing with the government, you are better to go ahead with a project because it's far easier to ask forgiveness than permission.
2. When expanding your business from province to province and across the country, you can always multiply your problems by the miles as the farther away you are from the home base, the more problems you will have because you're not as familiar with how the governments and various businesses operate, as well you will not have the connections in order to get assistance from the government in order to do proper business.

For example, companies in the United States such as the Carson Group's three founders together earned more than four hundred million according to a document filed with the Securities and Exchange Commission in the United States. Another group, the Whitstock Group, when prepared its public offering in 2007, it reported that in 2006 its executive shared in seven hundred and seventy one and a half million in cash distributions, the full compensation at the time. The CEO was paid three hundred and ninety eight million, and the chairman was paid two hundred and twelve million, an extreme example of how large companies can make fortunes yearly, not just in a lifetime. They're ably assisted by high government officials such as in the case of Hank DePalo, a former defense secretary who was hired from the government to act as chairman for ten years for one of the companies. Another individual by the name of Jack Bigger who was secretary of state to the president of the United States and was hired by a company as head of their defense division in order to assist in making good deals with the government.

Now that you have grown older and have made your millions in one of a thousand different businesses, it will be time to make a will to pass on your money to your family and favorite charities. One way is to make a revocable living trust. This particular trust allows you to control your money and property while at the same time letting you decide who you will leave it to in your will. It is important to do this as sometimes trusts can be more efficient than wills. It is important to bear in mind that trusts can be expensive to put in place, maintain, and update. In order to be worthwhile, you should have a large amount of money and property before deciding to draw up a living will or a trust.

It is also important to pick one or two executors. These individuals should be in the same state or province that you live in and that most of your assets are located as it will cost a lot for an executor to travel across the country if necessary and some provinces do not allow outside executors.

It is also important when you are semi-retired, older, and traveling to have health insurance, particularly important in the United States as health care costs in the United States are much higher than in Canada. When applying for insurance, it's always wise to get all information in writing from the insurance company, and then it is extremely important to take it to your doctor. If you have any problems such as a heart condition, stomach pains, or diabetes, it is important to have all of this filled out in detail. As the insurance company, after you have received a bill for twenty to two hundred thousand in the United States, they can refuse to pay the claim, leaving you stuck with the bill. If you are an older senior and do not have a lot of cash on hand, you can be forced to sell your primary residence in order to pay the bill.

It is important to bear in mind if the insurance declines your claim, you fight it in the public eye. As now in later years, you can establish a social media blog and post to let other people know the problems that have happened to you; and when hundreds or thousands of people reply to your blog, they can join you in a class action or even just a joint action against the insurance company. By letting people know and getting the word out, you can have thousands of people join you to put pressure on the insurance company.

It is also good to know that in the United States, the hospitals usually settle at 40 to 50 percent of medical bills when you are paying cash, as they only get paid that amount from the insurance companies and are paid usually 40 percent or less by US Medicare and sometimes only half of that from Medicaid when they are paid by the federal government.

Mattie semi-retired when he was in his late forties, leaving him time to do the things that he and his wife wanted to do. Even though from he was in his thirties, he was able to take time off when he wished to travel throughout the world to various sporting events and see the various parts of the world that they were interested in. Another good thing about owning your own business is that you can attend conventions for business purposes, and this is a tax write off. Therefore, if you are in the high thirties or forty plus percent tax bracket, you save almost half the cost of your travel. Factor in that if you are connected to the travel industry you are traveling business class for twenty-five cents on the dollar; sailing on the cruise lines all over the world for thirty-five cents on the dollar; and getting cars, hotels, and tours for fifty cents on the dollar. You are traveling for next to nothing while staying in the best of hotels, driving luxury cars, and flying business or first class. It is wise to remember that if you are spending large amounts of money for a small business, if you use the right credit card, you don't have to pay for a month, and you receive at least a point for every dollar. Simple math dictates that a million dollars gives you a million points, and considering that two people can fly around the world for a few hundred thousand points, business class, it's an enjoyable way to travel. Plus when you're associated with a travel agency, or own one, you receive information daily from all the suppliers engaged in the travel business, making it very easy to be well informed on where, when, and how to travel so that you have a much more enjoyable holiday.

It is extremely wise to invest in real estate, owning your own house, your own place of business, which should be large enough whether it's a warehouse or a strip mall, that you have up to a dozen other tenants, as these tenants provide a buffer if you have difficulty in business. Plus they also provide revenue because as you grow older, you raise your rents which assists you in fighting inflation over the years since the price of groceries, gas, travel, etc., always goes up over the years so does your rents and the value of your buildings. That is why when you look around you in a city or on a farm, you see all the land and the expensive buildings. It is only then that you realize that some clever individual has invested over the years and now owns all these assets, making his and her family millionaires many times over.

It is always wise to advise your family, friends, and employees that it's much wiser to marry into money and inherit it than it is to try and make it, and again one can never repeat often enough. Whether male or female, it is wise to marry someone with a profession that enables them to make good money, with a guaranteed income with very little chance of being out of work. Also, the second income will enable you both to have excellent credit at the bank and may even allow you to run a business on the side on your days off, nights, and weekends. Usually, good jobs have pensions, including health benefits so that as you grow older, you can rely on one or two pensions and the health benefits that go with your pension.

If you do not have a business or a government pension in your future, then it is wise to remember to put away the 5 or 10 percent of your salary monthly, or if you get a chance to work overseas as a young person, it is wise to take the opportunity as a lot of overseas jobs allow you to not pay any tax and of course all your expenses are paid for, just like working up north in Canada. This way you will have 100 percent of your money with the exception of the income taxes that you will have to pay to put in the bank for your future house, business, real estate investments, blue-chip stocks, or cash in the bank or something such as gold that can be easily cashed in so that when you see a good deal to purchase, you're able to act immediately where other people will not have the money or have it in ready cash that they can make the purchase.

When Mattie originally started in the oil business, it was a difficult time for others even though Mattie—because of his maintenance business which was recession proof, and a new type of drill rig was in demand by the oil industry—was able to get cheap shop space, good help at reasonable prices, and, in a number of cases, was able to take over the payments on trucks and equipment with some people even paying him to take over their debts so that they could preserve their credit. Not only did Mattie get equipment for nothing, but he got cash on the barrelhead to boot, a deal that was very hard to beat; and it's always wise to remember that whether its stock, real estate, equipment, etc., you buy when the market is going down. You may never know what the low point will be, but you will rest assured that if you buy on the way down, sooner or later history has proven that it will always go up, leaving you with a very high rate of return on your investment. For example, on Queen Charlotte Island back in the late 1950s, Mattie bought land at a bankruptcy sale for twenty dollars an acre. Several decades later, this land was worth two thousand dollars an acre. This made it a very lucrative investment indeed.

Another excellent idea is to put your money in the registered retirement saving plans or RRSPs. These allow you to invest your money and pay tax only when you take your money out of the plan. This can be advantageous, but one always has to bear in mind that should you grow older and be lucky and successful, you will be in a much higher tax bracket than when you put it in. Therefore, it is important that you weigh the pros and cons of this investment because later on in life, when you turn seventy, you will have to put it into another plan and start withdrawing a minimum of ten thousand per year. Now if you have bought a house after you and your wife saved enough money to do so and hopefully paying cash for it and owning both your vehicles now, as the years have passed by you'll have a debt-free house, vehicles, either one of you has an excellent pension for your retirement, plus health benefits, and you have the equity in your business or your profession. Also, if one does not have a pension from your job, then if you were in your own business all your life you have your RRSP, which is going to pay you a minimum of ten thousand a year. Now, if we add up that each person at sixty-five is going to receive close to ten thousand in Canada Pension Plan or Social Security plus an old age pension of five thousand, you are going to have fifteen thousand per year each for a total of thirty thousand dollars gross. Now add in the ten thousand of the small businessperson's RRSP and you are at forty thousand. Then add in the teacher, nurse, policeman, firefighter, pension of forty to sixty thousand dollars. You have a total of eighty thousand dollars, and as a rule, the small business person will have from property, etc. that will bring in one hundred to two hundred thousand per year minimum from their real estate investments. Now you're at one hundred and eighty thousand dollars of income per year; that's ninety thousand for husband and ninety thousand for the wife in Canada. Anything over sixty-eight thousand and they will claw back your old age pension. So if you're taking in a lot of money, not only will you both move into a higher tax bracket but you will lose ten thousand in your old age pensions, and you will pay more taxes because you are in a higher tax bracket. It is easy to see if your plan for your future when you're a late teenager or in your early twenties that you can wind up with far more money than you will ever need for your retirement. As Mattie has stated prior, in today's society children can work at high-paying jobs as well as working during the summer, evenings, or part-time when they go to college. So it's very easy to put themselves through college or save enough money to start a small business if they so desire while graduating without debt. The wise student, if he does not plan to go on and get a master's degree for any reason, will work towards a trade certificate which will in most cases if he starts his own business make far more money; and even if he just works for someone else providing he picks the right company, he will still make as much money if he had an ordinary degree. And if he owns his own trades business, he will make even more than if he had a master's degree or a doctorate.

It is always wise when investing to never buy in small startup companies because one in five companies over a period of five years will be successful and only one in one hundred will be wildly successful. And one has to be very careful that you don't get involved with a company either as an employee or an investor such as Enron in the United States or Nortel in Canada, resulting in you losing your job. This happens to hundreds of thousands of people in North America on a yearly basis, and it is wise to be aware of these pitfalls.

We've already gone through the advantages of living in an apartment and not having to pay property tax while saving as much money as you can to buy your house for cash, and once you buy your house for cash, never invest in somebody else's venture, invest in yourself. Nobody knows the capabilities, honesty, and intelligence of other people. You may be told about it and read about it, but there is no guarantee like investing in yourself for you and your partner's future.

It is always wise when buying a vehicle to buy one a year or two old as you can save at least a third, as vehicles depreciate usually 30 percent in the first year that the original owner has in possession. Therefore, there is no quicker way to make money than buying a used car with warranty or a used boat or RV because as a rule, boats and RVs are never used very much, and the vast majority is still good as new when you go to buy them. For example, when

Mattie would buy an RV if it was worth twenty-five thousand dollars and the original owner had it for one or two years and had hardly ever used it because it was not what he and his wife wanted, Mattie would buy it then for twelve or thirteen thousand dollars and fifteen years later it would be still in like-new condition because it was properly looked after, and it would retain its value. Mattie still has one RV that is eighteen years old and is proof that with proper care, it is still like new, and one of his five boats has been owned for thirty-six years, and it was bought in the midseventies and there were only a dozen made, so it's now a collector's item. And since Mattie bought it for 50 percent off since the factory had burned down, the boat is now worth more as an antique, and it still works like brand-new.

Mattie also bought a 1986 Mercedes Roadster convertible. This car cost one hundred and thirty-seven thousand dollars new because the Canadian dollar was only 62 percent of the value of the US dollar. Mattie has driven this car for decades and having bought it used from his eye specialist for thirty thousand dollars, the car is now a classic and can be fully insured for one hundred and eighty-four dollars per year; and since it was never driven during the winter, it's worth more used than what Mattie paid for it, and he's had the free use of a luxury car for all those years.

Mattie in 1995 used a sixty-thousand-dollar Cadillac to pull his thirty-foot RV. He still owns this car which has only about eighty thousand miles on it and has only spent a few thousand dollars on it in seventeen years and only paid twenty-nine thousand dollars for it because the country was in a recession in the midnineties, and he was able to purchase the car for half its value, even though it was only a year old as the owner was going to file for bankruptcy. He also bought a two-thousand-square-foot house in Arizona, the Valley of the Sun, for under one hundred thousand dollars. This house today in Calgary would be worth half a million seventeen years later, and all those years Mattie had the house, which he allowed his friends to use it for free in a lovely community surrounded by mountains with an excellent PGA golf course located within its perimeters.

Probably the best place in the world to retire would be in Arizona where food is priced at half the cost in Alberta. During the winter months, you hardly ever require heat or air-conditioning; therefore, your utilities are very low. You're able to get an extension of your TV in Canada for five dollars a month, so you can get Canadian TV together with the US TV on Canadian and US channels for next to nothing. It is easy to hook up another wide screen TV, and you can use that to get the local US channels as well as play all your DVDs so that you have TVs in separate rooms. The house had two bedrooms, two bathrooms, a dining area in the kitchen, a formal dining room, a family/living room; there's another room which is used as an office and computer room, complete with a wet bar, exercise room with a pull-out couch bed which makes it into a third bedroom and is separated by glass sliding doors with curtains so that you have complete privacy. The lot is landscaped with 50 percent desert landscaping which requires no water or care, and the other half is landscaped with blooming shrubs and trees to add color. Large trees protect the house from the sun during the summer as well as adding character to the landscaping.

It's always wise when buying a used house to look for someone who is selling due to a death, divorce, or are quite elderly. You can purchase these houses for half price and usually get the furniture thrown into the deal for little to no extra charge. It is always wise to buy within a mile of a freeway as you can travel at much higher speeds rather than the slower main streets of the cities, but even the speed limits in cities such as Scottsdale and Mesa, Arizona, have speed limits on the city streets of forty-five miles per hour; whereas in Calgary the city streets are only thirty miles per hour, usually taking into consideration the congested traffic and poor road infrastructure twice to three times as long to drive wherever you want to go.

The Phoenix valley gets approximately 345 days of sun per year and very seldom goes below freezing. It is surrounded by dozens of lakes in close proximity where you can fish and boat, plus enjoy the benefits of golf, baseball, football, basketball, hockey, NASCAR, PGA golf tournaments, surrounded by mountains for excellent hiking. And if you live in a fifty-five or older community, there will be no children with quiet cul-de-sacs plus a golf clubhouse which will include a large restaurant and bar with dance hall without having to drive outside your community. A good community will also have a community center which will include a pool hall, woodworking shop, library, ceramics shop, and a smaller hall for various activities. When you factor in the ideal weather, it's one of the best places to live, as it hardly rains in the winter and the sun is always shining, resulting in your living for five to six months in the winter in the closest to heaven you'll find on earth. Although Mattie, having lived in Calgary for well over half a century as his main base when he traveled for work, business and pleasure throughout the world, Calgary has more sun than anywhere else except two other cities in Canada and also has all the amenities for hiking, fishing, skiing, and has all of the sporting events you could wish for as well. Therefore, in Mattie's opinion, the perfect two places to live are Calgary in the summer and the Phoenix valley in the winter. History has proven in the past that people such as Franklin D. Roosevelt, the president of the United States and Henry Luce, the founder of *Time* magazine used to write in the fifties, sixties, and seventies that the Valley of the Sun was the best place to live in the winter months; and Roosevelt always stated that it was nice to live near the water or the mountains during the summer due to the fresh breezes blowing over the mountains or off the water. That is why Mattie enjoys the ocean in the summer on Queen Charlotte Island, and from when he was in his early twenties, the mountains in Alberta, then from his thirties in Hawaii and Florida and then traveling to Arizona in his forties and taking up winter residence there in his fifties. So it is wise to pick your future homes with care should you be lucky enough to live to and grow up on a beautiful island such as Prince Edward Island, one of the prettiest in the world, and then to live in a city such as Calgary during your working years while being able to visit Hawaii and Florida during your working life and semi-retire or fully retire life if you so desire in Arizona, Florida, California, or Hawaii during the winter months.

We have talked about RRSPs and then transferring them over to RIFs in Canada, but if you are a US resident and the United States is ten times the size of Canada, then you would put your money into an IRA as contributions to an IRA are tax deductible, and they are very good if you do not participate in other retirement plans such as profit sharing in your company or a Keogh plan; then you or your wife may make a tax-deductible IRA contribution no matter how much you're making. Your spouse can make a fully deductible donation as long as your gross income is not more than one hundred and fifty thousand dollars. People who are covered by retirement plans can only deduct IRA contributions if your gross income is fifty thousand or less. Single people can deduct contributions if your gross income is thirty thousand or less. Once your income exceeds those levels, naturally your IRA contributions drop on a percentage basis gradually. IRA stands for Individual Retirement Account and are funds set up by people who have earned through wages, salary, self-employment income, professional feeds, etc. A lot of people today work as consultants rather than full-time employees; therefore, they have to look after their own retirement plans.

It is good to get the advice of a financial planner or tax consultant when you are starting up your plan. The main reason for starting savings and retirement plans is that you get in the habit of saving 5 to 10 percent per year. It's usually good to try for 10 percent. While saving, you can always put aside a small amount extra to buy a used car, several years old, which are usually good as new and still have warranty for at least another year and the balance of the five-year warranty which if your car is two years old will be three years. This way you have the benefit of the cost savings as well as still having warranty, and if you pay cash that you have saved, you will not have any payments to make. If you continue saving at the rate of 8 to 10 percent per year, it will not be long before you have enough money to purchase a house, condo, or other residence. This will give you something that you can own without having to pay too much in the way of an initial price. It is always wise to look towards the future, and then if there's a possibility that you personally or the company you work for may transfer you in the not too distant future, then its better just to rent rather than own because the cost of real estate fees, lawyer's fees, etc. when you're buying or selling will add up, and you will not make very much money on the deal.

If you wish to buy a house or start a business, it is always wise to borrow against your savings, as this will not disrupt your plan and way of life and will also establish credit with a bank; and in the future you can always borrow against what money you have saved from your sweat equity, and you can pay this money back over as short a term as possible. And it's always wise if you are buying a house, equipment for your business, etc. to make sure that if you borrow; then you must buy insurance to cover the loan so that if anything went wrong, the loan would be totally paid for in full.

When buying shares, it's always wise to buy in companies that shares are easily sold. If you buy shares in a small company, it's sometimes very hard to sell them should the need arise that you may want to cash out and use the money for something else. Again, it can never be impressed upon individuals enough that it is wise to buy in blue-chip companies as we have mentioned before such as railroads, banks, utilities, and others that have a decided advantage in the marketplace and also pay dividends as well as being easily traded in the marketplace.

You may wish when your business gets started that you give your employees the option of buying shares in the company as this will give you a ready market should you decide to sell the company in the future. A number of large companies such as PCL in Alberta, Canada, use this plan, selling shares to employees who have been with the company for a period of time with the agreement that if they move on to another job or retire, they will in turn sell the shares back to the company. This is an excellent idea as the company will continue to grow and prosper in the future as there will always be employees with a vested interest and therefore will work harder and smarter, causing the company to thrive compared to the other companies where employees do not have such and interest and therefore the employee turnover is much greater.

Should you own your own company or be in a profession such as the legal or accounting fields, it is easy to continue working when you are semiretired while having younger people run your operation on a day-to-day basis, and at present with wireless communications, one can live anywhere in North America and operate their business or profession from many miles away. This is a distinct advantage for the self-employed; whereas, if you work for the government, an employee does not have this option. Should you work for big business, you can also work when you retire as a consultant. This provides an opportunity to earn two-thirds of your salary plus another third to a half of your salary in consulting fees resulting in no reduction in your income or standard of living and allowing you the freedom to travel or to live during the winter months in a warmer climate.

Over the years, women have entered the workforce in large numbers. Also, North American couples are having fewer children than they did in the past resulting in higher disposable incomes, allowing married couples to travel when they are at a younger age as well as having a much higher standard of living.

In 1980, Mattie built a new house, and the interest rate was at 11 percent. The following spring, interest had gone to 24 percent for a mortgage, more than doubling. Fortunately for Mattie, he was in the business of buying and selling equipment, and he had acres of used equipment; therefore it was easy to pay off the cost of building his house by selling a few pieces of equipment, which gave him a debt-free house. Upon selling a piece of equipment to a very rich individual, Mattie was surprised when the sale was completed by one of the girls in the accounting department, stating that the purchaser rather than signing his name had only placed an X on the dotted line. Mattie informed the employee that the man was older and had got very little schooling. Even though he was one of the richest men in Alberta, he could not read or write. This totally amazed Mattie's young employees who found it hard to believe that an individual who had hardly gone to school for any length of time was able to make millions of dollars in business.

If you are buying a used house, it is always wise to bear in mind that you buy one of the lower priced houses on a nice street and fix it up as the other expensive houses will raise the value of your house when you have put in new carpets, painted the interior, installed a fireplace, and other minor repairs as nowadays you can buy an electric fireplace for a few hundred dollars and install it in a matter of a few hours, which will give your house the same atmosphere as if it had a wood burning or gas fireplace, which are much more expensive. It is also wise when building or renovating a house to landscape the property to the best of your ability as first impressions when potential buyers drive up to your house are very important and often will help sell the house much faster than houses that do not have beautiful landscaping. It is also wise to give consideration when buying or building a house if you want a pool as an outdoor pool can only be used for a short period of time, particularly in the majority of America—as the weather will be too cold or rainy to swim and the cost of maintaining an outdoor pool is extremely expensive with the weekly if not daily cleaning of the pool plus the high cost of heating it. In Mattie's case, the house he built in 1980, the estimates for an outdoor pool were over one hundred thousand dollars. Mattie built the pool himself for less than fifty thousand, including the building that enclosed the pool. When Mattie sold the house in 1995, he gave the pool away even though the new buyer had young children and planned to use it. He was unable to get any return on his investment, but he did get more than his cost back on the enclosure, as he informed the buyer that even when the children grew up and should he not want to use the pool, then he simply had to drain it and put a floor over the pool area and then the building could be used for a racquetball court, squash, dances, a party area, or an exercise room. Upon hearing this, the buyer had no problem with buying a swimming pool.

Mattie listed his house for over a year as he already had a lot in Calgary with a tremendous view where the lot outside the city limits at that time was approximately twenty miles. With traffic very hard in the wintertime to commute back and forth to the city, even though at that time the town where Mattie lived two miles west was only seven thousand people, but thirty years later it was nearly fifty thousand people, and during the winter months the congestion was unbelievable. But during the fifteen years that Mattie lived in the rural area, he was very close to the international airport, approximately ten minutes away; and since he flew weekly on business, this provided a decided advantage. Also at this time, he owned a lot in Washington state in the United States with a view of the mountains, the marina, the water, etc. It was possible to catch a flight from Calgary to Seattle, Washington, with a stop in Blaine, Washington; and with Mattie's boat in a marina only five minutes from the airport and the flight only lasting one hour, Mattie could go from his house north of Calgary to his boat in less than two hours, which was faster than driving the few hundred miles to the lakes in neighboring British Columbia. This US property increased in price over 500 percent in less than ten years, a 50 percent return on his money per year.

In the United States, interest on your mortgage payments is tax deductible, offering an advantage over mortgages in Canada. It is also wise should you wish to do so to allow prepayments on the principle without penalties, and always bear in mind that depending on the length of the mortgage, you will wind up paying double for your house. And if it's a long-term mortgage, you may wind up paying triple depending upon the interest rate. It is also wise to get a fixed-rate mortgage due to the fact that interest has a habit of fluctuating up and down; and if you do get a mortgage on your house and the interest rate rises rapidly, you may lose your house due to the increased rate.

One of Mattie's friends had a son, and he was able to purchase a condo with nothing down. The real estate agent simply added a small portion on to the cost of the condo to allow for a down payment. The young fellow then went on to the furniture store to get enough furniture to fill the condo with nothing down and no payments for six months. He then went to the auto dealership where he bought a new truck with nothing down while at the same time selling his own good used truck for a substantial sum so at the end of the day he was a proud owner of a fully furnished condo, a new truck, and had a substantial check in his pocket for his used truck. Now he had to worry about the large payments that he was faced in the future.

It is wise when making a purchase to always look for a foreclosure or a distressed property if it is in real estate, as there are many disasters caused by death, divorce, etc., that will allow you to purchase at a fraction of what the real estate is really worth. It is always important to get an inspector to check your property or your vehicle before you buy it to make sure you are not buying something that you or no one else will want. It is also important if you get repairs done such as a roof shingled to get a roofing inspector to check that the job is done properly. However, Mattie became familiar with many of his friends and business acquaintances having new roofs installed only to find out that they leaked, resulting in the water going through the ceiling, the floor, and right into the basement, leaving a damage of several hundred thousand dollars.

One can never emphasize enough that saving approximately 8 to 12 percent of your income and investing it for long-term growth where it would build a retirement fund and using this investment to borrow against to buy real estate or start a business can never be beaten as a way of enriching yourself for your future; and if you do your due diligence and homework to make sure that you have done the right thing, then you have no worries whatsoever about the future. It is always wise to remember the quotation of a wealthy individual who stated that he did not plan on giving his children all the money they wanted, but he would give them all the money that they needed, emphasizing the point that there is a big difference in what you may want and what you need. It is always wise to get a credit card early on in life as credit cards are an excellent vehicle for establishing credit; plus if you charge your purchases on the right credit card, you will have thirty days to pay your bills. In addition, a large number of credit cards that also give points which if you put all your purchases on that particular credit card, you will wind up with thousands of points per year. If you run a small business and charge parts, fuel, etc. on your card, you may get up to a million points per year, which will allow you to travel at no cost, always bearing in mind that the farther you travel at any given time, you will gain much greater benefits from your points than if you only use them for short flights. Mattie was always amazed by people who used a charge card where the money was immediately taken out of their account at the time of purchase while the buyer never received any benefits whatsoever; whereas on a good credit card, you get insurance on your rental car when you're traveling as well as on theft, etc., and on some cards when you purchase specific products you receive double the points, allowing your account to grow at a much faster rate.

It is very important to learn early on how the art of bartering when you go to purchase. Always for example if you are buying a vehicle and the owner wants fifteen thousand you would naturally offer ten thousand dollars, and then if the owner comes down to fourteen thousand dollars, you would up your offer to eleven thousand. And if the owner said thirteen thousand, you can offer to split the difference at twelve thousand, and usually this will allow you to purchase a vehicle with a considerable savings, bearing in mind that if you save twenty-five hundred dollars this is equivalent of earning over four thousand dollars before taxes, again outlining that it is much easier to save a dollar than to earn a dollar.

When Mattie started up his first business, he borrowed to put in his crop as well as purchase a new car, equipment, and other necessities on time, plus investing all of the money he had saved over a three-year period as well as all that he'd earned buying and selling produce, livestock, and equipment, resulting in being in the business that a number of people called a gamble, which in turn really was not a gamble at all. As Mattie lost all his investment and wound up owing money, which took another three years of hard work to pay everybody back in full. Mattie would have been better off going to Las Vegas and spending all his money there, as there was probably a higher chance of winning; whereas in farming you never know what is going to happen to your investment because you have many battles to fight in farming or in construction, particularly with farming because you have to battle the weather, you have to keep your equipment running and functional, there is always diseases along with weeds and bugs to kill your crop. You can have a good crop of grain turning amber in the fall and along will come a hailstorm and beat it into the ground. If the hail does not hit you, the wind may cause your grain to shell (kernels falling out of the heads) so bad you lose half your crop before you cut it; it may be too wet to take your crop off. You may have an early frost which between the wet weather and the cold your crop will freeze, and the quality will drop, causing you to aerate your bins and dry the grain. And after you have fought all those elements, you have to contend with perhaps a low price, so the odds are that to win all your battles is a long shot because usually the end result is on a large number of occasions you lose the war. This is something to bear in mind when you're starting out or when you retire as a lot of people upon retirement like to get into farming or ranching as a hobby, which can turn out to be a very expensive retirement. Mattie always said that if he had millions, he did not need or want, then and only then would he be interested in going back into farming or ranching. Even though it might be an excellent way of life and an interesting hobby, he could not see any future in it. There are families who are farming or ranching and have watched their half section of three hundred and twenty acres grow to ten thousand acres yet find themselves asset rich and very cash poor resulting in a lot of farmers and ranchers living poorly and dying rich, but nevertheless, they continue on through sheer stubbornness in order to protect and grow their investment.

One can never emphasize enough that when you're purchasing investments, make sure they're insured by the Federal Deposit Insurance Corporation no matter what good rate you are earning. For example, when certain institutions are only paying 1 to 3 percent in 2011–2012, other institutions are available for your 401K, IRA, CD, or savings funds at up to 7 percent, which are excellent for guaranteed income, savings, and allow you to withdraw monthly interest. Always make sure they're guaranteed and insured fixed annuities through the various insurance companies, and always bear in mind that not only are they insured and your savings and income protected but you are able to withdraw should you really need to take out some of your money. Although they are excellent investments, you will be able to borrow from a bank against those savings.

On occasion, by borrowing you will force yourself to save and in the meantime you will enjoy your purchase, but you must always be able to live with the stress of borrowing and exposure to debt, bearing in mind that alcoholism, divorce, family breakup, deteriorating health can all be caused by too much debt. You'll find it easier to sleep when you're earning interest than when you're paying it. Borrowing always has the advantage of forcing you to save, and it also has all the disadvantages that Mattie learned to his dismay in the late fifties. Mattie never bought any gas, repairs, or motor vehicles that he could not write a goodly portion off on his taxes as these items were all tax deductible. When he traveled, he had to pay for his gas, but upon arriving in Calgary and getting hired by the oil company, he received mileage and all expenses for his vehicle. For the next fifty-five years, he was able to write off his vehicle with the exception of personal use, which when added up over a long period of time, it amounts to a substantial savings.

It's also important to remember that a bottle of alcohol may sell for twenty dollars but can be manufactured for only two dollars; therefore, should you buy the same bottle of alcohol in a bar, the same two dollar bottle will cost you one hundred dollars, so Mattie always wondered why anybody would drink in a bar when they could enjoy a sociable drink with their friends for a very small cost. Another item was tobacco. On one of Mattie's trips, he was in Georgia, and he saw a large sign saying, "Cigarettes, $1 per package." At that time these cigarettes were selling in Canada for five dollars a package and a short time later, selling for ten dollars a package. Mattie smoked for only a few years, but upon seeing the sign, he realized that he was throwing good money after bad, and he quit smoking on the spot. For example, in the United States, you can buy fifty-two ounces or the equivalent of two bottles of Canadian liquor for ten dollars where those two bottles of liquor would cost you forty dollars if purchased in Canada; simple indications of how easy it is to save money.

When Mattie was a young man, he took a pledge in church not to drink alcohol until he was twenty-one, which was an excellent idea as this allowed a young individual to save money as well as not encountering the problems that often occur through the use of alcohol. When Mattie was a boy, soda pop was seven cents a bottle. If you drank it in the store, you could return the bottle for two cents, resulting in the drink only costing a nickel. Mattie's mother strongly emphasized that you could buy a package of freshie for a few pennies which when mixed with water and sugar in any flavor that you wished, it would make a gallon rather than twelve to fifteen ounces. Therefore, for the same amount of money you could have over fifty ounces for the price of fifteen. Mattie never forgot that lesson in economics, and very rarely in his life did he ever drink pop, always enjoying milk and water which have been proven to be very beneficial to your health. When working for Mr. Levine buying cattle, Mr. Levine strongly emphasized that the time you took having coffee breaks when added up twice a day over a lifetime, the results are like saving money, with the interest compounding was almost unbelievable. He also advised Mattie never to drink tea or coffee or take coffee breaks as not only would it be better for his health, he would save money as coffee costs less than ten cents and was selling for more than a dollar. Mattie was very impressed with the many ideas Mr. Levine had for making and saving money, and as each one was outlined to him, he made mental notes never to forget what the elderly man had told him, as he was a fine example of an extremely wealthy businessman. Mattie knew he would be wise to follow in his footsteps.

Mattie learned early on to buy no-name brands as they usually sold for half the price of brand name products, and on the vast majority of purchases, they were just as good as the brand names. Mattie also learned the advantage of taking on partners early on in business. The majority would only last for a few years and then decide that they want to leave the company and go on to something else, which is normal, leaving Mattie now owning a bigger share than ever. Although he did have one partner, Mr. Mackey, who was involved in business and real estate with Mattie until his death. This was the gentleman who offered Mattie the share in his endeavors in Fort McMurray, Alberta, for two hundred thousand which would have turned into millions. Mr. Mackey throughout his life had the Midas touch when it came to investing money and making real estate purchases; therefore it is wise in life to keep an eye open for people such as this who have the canny ability to see opportunities which others miss and have the ability to make money as easily as falling off a log.

Mattie always believed in incentives for the people who worked with him, including company vehicles, bonuses; and his companies were one of the few in the world who gave away free Rolex watches at year-end. The watches would bear the inscription: "To John, thanks for a job well done, Mattie." When the employee's friends saw these very expensive watches, they always inquired where they got the watch. The employee would then answer that the company they worked for gave away these watches after the employee had five successful years with the outfit. The acquaintance would remark that they must be a pretty good employee or it must be a very good company in order to participate in a program like that, which not only made the employee feel good; it spoke well for the company and was one of the major ways that Mattie's companies became successful, and Mattie acquired new employees.

Mattie always enjoyed a few drinks of alcohol. Even though he thoroughly disliked the taste of wine, beer, or hard liquor, he enjoyed the sociability and the relief from stress that alcohol provided although as he looked back in time, he realized that to a lot of people alcohol caused more harm than good. Having taken many people to enroll in AA, where Mattie always was amazed at the serenity prayer: "God, give me the serenity to accept the things I cannot change, the courage to change the things I can, and the wisdom to know the difference." Mattie at one point came to town and spent a week drinking with a group of his friends and co-workers. At the end of the week, two of Mattie's friends were having problems with the drink and went to AA, so Mattie went along to see what it was all about. After a couple of meetings, one of the senior individuals in the group took Mattie to a bar where he drank tomato juice, and Mattie and a few of his friends ordered up drinks. Mattie would order a drink of rum with a beer chaser shortly, but someone called for another round of drinks. Mattie would have another double drink of rum with a beer chaser while they would just have a single drink or a beer. Mattie's new acquaintance quickly remarked how he was not an alcoholic, simply a hard drinker, and told him that he should learn to drink the same as the vast majority of people. Slowly while enjoying the sociability of meeting with his friends, Mattie realized that this was an excellent idea as this man had quit drinking alcohol and went on to form one of the biggest companies in Canada, impressing Mattie with his business acumen as well as his intelligence and work ethic, so Mattie tried in the future to follow the advice of his newfound friend even though he was not always successful.

Mattie's partner Mr. Mackey explained that God invented whiskey to keep the Gaelic people from taking over the world. Mark Twain once wrote, "There are two times in a man's life when he should not speculate, when he can't afford it, and when he can."

One can never emphasize enough how even if you're a fireman, policeman, teacher, nurse, or other service job you can start a small business on the side which will result in you doubling your income and having the ability to gain tax deductions, which can amount to large savings over a lengthy period of time. And if you're associated with the travel agency, you get many benefits that have been outlined before. It is also wise to bear in mind that in all companies and government jobs, you will have workman's compensation if you get hurt on the job, but it is wise to consider disability insurance. You do not need to have a large amount of insurance, but you should have enough that you do not have to worry what would happen to you or your family should you become disabled. And always remember as a student that you pay no taxes, and should you stay at home and work at a good-paying summers job hopefully in the field of endeavor that you're majoring in at college while working part-time during the winter months, you will be able to put yourself through college without having your parents put money in a fund for your education or graduating deep in debt.

Mattie started out raising fowl on the farm at the same time that he started school, which allowed him to get an early knowledge of business. It is wise as a young child in the city to have a paper route as nowadays a paper route can bring in from ten to twenty dollars an hour for a few hours in the morning, which is a very good wage. Working for your neighbors, friends, or relatives at cutting grass, snow removal, babysitting, and other odd jobs are other sources of income that will help you earn money as well as develop a work ethic for the future. It will also give you an insight into a way of life where time is a very valuable commodity even though you're only a very young person or through life until you become a senior and then time becomes even more valuable. And as a working individual, you must always provide for your retirement years so that you have proper health care which in Canada is usually free, but in the States during your working life, it can cost a family up to one thousand per month for adequate health care. Always remember KISS—Keep It Simple, Stupid. In life, no matter what you do or what others tell you, it is always important to stick to the basics as this will be of great importance throughout your life. Also remember the cliché "Tell me what a person reads, and I'll tell you what the person knows." There are so many magazines that are available on the market today, such as *MoneySense*, *Bloomberg Businessweek*, the *Economist*, which will keep you up to date worldwide. Another two excellent publications, the *Canadian Geographic* and the *National Geographic* are excellent publications going back several hundred years.

Two phrases Mattie remembers that a chap told him who had taken a Dale Carnegie course as well as other courses and they were

1. Do not get stressed, give stress.
2. Put the monkey on somebody else's back. In other words, if you need to get things done, try to get somebody else to do it.
3. Remember to think everything through.
4. Never ask a question that you do not know the answer to.

Since this book is about making money, we will touch on one product that can help you with your problems and save you a lot of money over your lifetime, and that product is vinegar. Not only is vinegar a condiment that you would put on fish and french fries or chips as they are called in the old country. It can be used in cleaning, laundry, and home medicine. In the last century, vinegar was used in World War I to treat wounds; and today it can be used for rashes, bites, and other minor ailments. Over the years, vinegar can improve the taste of many foods as well as for personal hygiene and takes the place of many specialized cleaners. Over the years, vinegar has been used as a condiment, a preservative, a medicine, an antibiotic, and as a detergent. Vinegar is excellent when used as a cleaning solution, but one can also use Coca-Cola along with a scouring pad to take rust off your vehicles, which amounts to considerable savings rather than buying a rust remover. Vinegar has an acidic nature and is self-preserving and does not need refrigeration. White vinegar will remain virtually unchanged over an extended period of time. Even if the color changes, this does not harm the product and can still be used successfully. White distilled vinegar is very economical when used for cleaning glass, pots, and as a detergent or disinfectant. It is also excellent for pickling old Gaelic recipes, such as making chow-chow from green tomatoes and mustard pickles and relish, which are delicious and utilize white distilled vinegar as a main ingredient. Vinegar also contains elements such as lactic acid, calcium, iron, and zinc which are needed in the human body and is excellent when cooking and making salads, stir fries, sweet and sour dishes, as well as pickling. Vinegar is usually made from grapes, and the longer the grapes are left in the field, the better the vinegar is with balsamic. Being one of the better vinegars, there is also fruit vinegar and vinegar high in sugar, which is the one that can also be used in making pickles, mustard relishes, etc. Vinegar is excellent for removing labels. Just soak the label or sticker with vinegar and leave it till it is soaked, and it will usually peel off. It can also be used for cleaning collars and cuffs by mixing vinegar and baking soda together and then remove the stain. It can also be used as a fabric softener and for a static cling reducer. Just use it as you would with a fabric softener. It will also cut down the lint on the clothing, putting in five ounces into your rinse cycle to reduce the lint on your clothes. White vinegar can also be used to prevent your colors from running when filling the washer with cold water and then adding soap and clothes. Mattie was involved in the tar business and utilized vinegar quite often on the stains before he put them in the washing machines. A lot of people do not like the odor of bleach, so it is wise to add a cup of vinegar to the final rinse in the washing machine. Another problem is cola stains from soft drinks that can be sponged away by putting white vinegar onto the stain and rubbing the spot. It's also useful for removing the smell of smoke from clothes by using a cup of vinegar and zinc in hot water. It's also good for getting clear of bugs in your garden as well as keeping ants from entering your house if you pour vinegar across the sill in the door opening.

Vinegar can also be used when mixed three parts of water to one of vinegar as a weed suppressant and will also repel mosquitoes if you mix apple vinegar to a quart of water. It is also useful for keeping flies from your swimming pool if you pour it around the edge of your pool as well, as vinegar and baking soda cause a chemical reaction when combined and will break down the fatty acids and can be used as a drain cleaner, etc. It can also be used for removing paint from glass, as it can be very frustrating when you get paint on the glass when you are painting, so heat up some vinegar and use a cloth to wipe up the paint. It can be very helpful in cleaning windshields. When Mattie had a twin-engine plane in the mid-1960s, he and the pilot would mix three parts vinegar to one part water and wipe this with a damp cloth on the windows. This combination would keep the windshields clear of ice and frost. Vinegar can also be used to take off marks and stains by applying vinegar directly to the area you wish to clean. The best vinegar for cleaning is usually distilled white vinegar. Vinegar can also be used to clean refrigerators and microwaves, and the usual mix is 50:50 with the other half being water. Another cheap cleaning solution is one-third white vinegar, one-third rubbing alcohol, and another third water combined with a quarter teaspoon of dishwashing liquid. Mix this into a used clean spray bottle, and you have the equivalent of a floor cleaner. Just spray and then wipe up; it will also deodorize the room at the same time. Needless to say, this solution will make an excellent toilet cleaner when brushed on the bowl. You can also leave several cups of white vinegar in the bowl for an hour and then flush, which will make it easier to clean. As a deodorizer, it removes the smell of onions and garlic from your hands and it is also a general hand cleaner if you rinse your hands with vinegar and then wash them.

When cooking, a lot of times eggs will crack when boiling, so it is helpful to add several tablespoonfuls of vinegar to the boiling water. It will also reduce bacteria when preparing food for cooking such as chicken and other meats.

Vinegar has health benefits, and numerous people speak highly in that the use of apple cider vinegar contributes to healthy veins, blood vessels, and arteries when taken in small amounts as it also helps with digestion. It also contains potassium along with bananas and potatoes, which is good for your eyes, sinuses, etc. Mattie had a problem with a tooth where the gum was decaying. He went to the dentist, whereupon the dentist sent him to the periodontics where he was informed that it would cost several thousand dollars and did not have even a 50 percent chance of preserving the tooth or the gum. Mattie had read prior to this happening that if you mixed sodium peroxide, baking soda, salt, and water and rinse your mouth morning and night, it was ten times as good as any mouthwash for killing germs that cause bad breath, plaque, and the gum disease gingivitis. Mattie has used this product for over twenty-five years, and he still has the tooth, proof that simple cures are more efficient than anything else on the market and tens of thousands in savings. When speaking of teeth, Mattie's wife spent tens of thousands in dental bills. Mattie, because he drank several gallons of milk a week, which is full of calcium, his bones were as strong as if they were made of iron and never had to see a dentist. Upon years of playing hockey, he got three teeth broken, and upon arriving in Calgary, he went to a dentist called Dr. Henry Hopkins, who made him a plate with three teeth on it that lasted for over fifty years. This plate eventually got broken while at the same time it damaged a tooth that the plate was fastened to. Mattie was on holiday for a few months, and he was informed by a friend that if he went to Mexico, he would only pay one-fifth the cost as this friends was quoted twenty-two thousand in Alberta for a large amount of dental work but got in completed for two thousand dollars in Algodones Mexico, just across the border from Yuma. And when he smiled, Mattie was amazed that the chap who had been a superintendant building houses for Mattie had all new perfectly white and shiny teeth for such a good price. Mattie then went down from Phoenix to Yuma and went across and met the recommended dentist who did a root canal, placed a cap on Mattie's tooth, made a new state-of-the-art plate out of plastic, which is extremely comfortable as well as capping all of Mattie's front teeth for several thousand dollars, which would have cost him ten thousand dollars in Canada. While the dentist was doing the work, he got into a violent argument with Jose who was making up the caps for the teeth. Since they were speaking in Spanish, Mattie knew the dentist was chewing Jose's butt out, but he could not tell what they were saying. Nevertheless, two of the caps cracked within months and he had to go to a local dentist in Canada and get the caps replaced at eleven hundred dollars each; nevertheless, he still saved six thousand dollars on a ten-thousand-dollar bill.

If you encounter sunburn, it is wise to cover the burn with a towel soaked in water and vinegar overnight. It will smell, but it is wise to repeat it several times for good results. Mattie also drinks a glass of water with several teaspoons of cider vinegar and two teaspoons of honey several times a day, which is good for his arthritis; and since Mattie worked in the oil fields for many years, his hands are badly crippled, twisted, and sore from arthritis. But he finds vinegar as well as spraying WD-40 on the joints to keep them lubricated which is a great help. Also, if you enjoy sitting in the sun around the pool reading like Mattie does, it is wise to soak your feet in vinegar and water for three evenings in a row as it is excellent for athlete's foot, which is common in pool areas. Vinegar is also good for cold sores as anyone who works outside or does a lot of cross-country or downhill skiing, if you apply vinegar to cold sores, it will dry it up and sometimes prevent further outbreaks.

Mattie has suffered for decades with sinus trouble and nasal congestion and has found relief by adding apple cider vinegar to his diet as well as inhaling a mixture of baking soda and salt in water also using the mixture of hydrogen peroxide, salt, baking soda, and water that he uses as a mouthwash as a nasal rinse at night, clearing his sinus passages so that there is no trouble breathing. The reason Mattie uses vinegar for swelling and pain on his joints is that his father and grandfather used to wrap the legs of the farm workhorses as well as the racehorses in a vinegar and cloth bandage, leaving on for four to five hours, which helped to reduce the swelling. Vinegar will also remove stains where wet glasses have been placed on wood furniture when mixed with olive oil and rubbed and polished for good results. It's also useful for softening paintbrushes, cleaning eyeglasses, and for removing salt from shoes when using a tablespoon of vinegar to a cup of water, which is very helpful in Eastern Canada and eastern United States where they use a lot of salt to prevent the streets from becoming too slippery. It is also wise to add two tablespoons of vinegar and one of sugar to a quart of water and use this for cut flowers to make them last longer. It will also work on Christmas trees to keep the tree from dropping its needles. The drink 7Up is also good for this purpose.

This outlines how just one product can save an individual or family thousands of dollars per year and is very convenient because it is available in every household. Now since we have discussed how to make money, how to enjoy money, and how to save money, let us outline briefly how the government is wasting money, particularly in Canada.

1. In Abbotsford, British Columbia, the hockey team received 1.3 million dollars as part of an agreement to guarantee that the team would not lose any money. The problem is that nobody buys tickets. They might as well buy tickets because one way or another, the people of Abbotsford are going to pay.

2. The federal government gave a blizzard of funds to Quebec snowmobile clubs, a total of nine groups who received a windfall of 1.5 million and over the past three years have received a total of six million. The Ontario government, just to show how generous it is, gave five hundred thousand for loop trails of its own.

3. In London, Ontario, since 2007 two of the city's taxpayer-owned golf courses lost more than six hundred thousand dollars amid a glut of public and private courses in the region. Reminds me of one of the sweetheart deals that Ralph Klinker gave to the owners of the Riverview golf course in Calgary.

4. In Viscount, Saskatchewan, a community of 250 the federal government gave nine thousand to convert an unused curling rink into an energy efficient archery center. Probably only a couple of people in town owned a bow and a few arrows.

5. The city of Windsor spent a million to rebuild sand traps at the golf and curling club, which the city owns.

6. Vancouver taxpayers paid two million for the Vancouver Canucks Stanley Cup riot. While the Canucks were a profitable private company (playoff tickets earned the team forty-four million), it makes you wonder why taxpayers need to subsidize a party for its fans.

Meanwhile, Ottawa, Ontario, put five million towards marketing and celebrating the GreyCup in Toronto. While British Columbia paid five hundred and fifty thousand for a GreyCup party in Toronto and Ottawa, Ontario paid twenty-eight thousand for hockey tickets while raising rates to cover increased business costs. Auditors in Winnipeg found six semiprivate golf clubs pay just a dollar a year to lease public land, even though city-owned courses racked up eight million in debt. The city of Ottawa spent twenty-one thousand on a five-minute video on how to use bike lanes.

12. In New Brunswick, taxpayers had to cough up four million to fix a bridge thirty-six hundred kilometers away.

13. Prince Edward Island spent $330,000 building a parking lot for trucks for times when the Confederation Bridge is closed due to stormy weather, but it never gets used because it's in the middle of nowhere. During a windstorm in October, when the bridge was closed for thirty-six hours, only three trucks used the lot while the rest parked on the road.

14. Infrastructure in Quebec is so shabby that the government paid $170,000 to keep heavy trucks off of Montreal's Mercier Bridge twenty-four hours a day.

15. Ottawa is spending $1.16 million to design a pedestrian bridge over a busy highway, even though no decision has been made on whether the bridge is actually needed. (It depends on future plans for a nearby stadium.) The province is widening the highway and wants to know the proposed bridge's dimensions, in case it ever gets built.

16. Quebec paid $1.2 million to send transport officials overseas to study the latest in engineering technology, including trips to Burkina Faso and Algeria.

17. In its rush to qualify for federal stimulus dollars, the city of Ottawa spent $1.8 million to buy land it would have eventually gotten for free under a right-of-way arrangement with the landowner.

18. The feds forked out $268,000 for a footbridge in Forestville, Quebec.

19. There's lots of talk in Ottawa about cutting fat, but since when? Did that mean the government is getting into the weight loss business? In October, the Federal Economic Development Agency for Southern Ontario (FedDev Ontario) invested $249,000 in Newtopia, a company based in Vaughan that offers genetic testing for obesity and online weight loss counseling. Founder Jeff Ruby was ecstatic, "Banks can give us money, but the government of Canada provides great credibility."

20. In July, Ottawa poured $190,000 into New Brunswick doughnut maker Mrs. Dunster's—famous for making its doughnuts out of pure lard. Meanwhile, the provincial government is putting together a program to fight obesity.

21. The region of Durham, Ontario, threw a $75,000 party to celebrate a new garbage incinerator, complete with air-conditioned tents and sushi.

22. You can never have too much cheese, or too many cheese companies, apparently. Last year the federal government invested nearly $700,000 in a pair of start-up fromageries. One of the new businesses, in the town of Asbestos, will produce "cow's and goat's milk specialty cheeses."

23. A 2011 audit of the Toronto Community Housing Corporation uncovered millions in questionable contract spending, such as the $90,000 the agency spent for Christmas parties in 2008 and 2009, complete with a chocolate fountain, crème brûlée, grilled calamari and mussels.

24: Prince Edward Island served up $65,000 to produce a series of YouTube videos starring celebrity chef Michael Smith to promote local food.

However, most of the eight-minute clips have attracted fewer than 1,500 viewers.

25. Toronto spent $87,000 to determine whether city-owned facilities could dedicate half their purchasing budgets to food produced in Ontario—the answer was "No."

26. Despite the millions of dollars provinces spend to prop up their wine industries, the feds handed $1.05 million to Calona wines of British Columbia to double the output of its boxed wines, even though 80 percent of the wine it sells is imported.

27. New Brunswick taxpayers learned they would have to pay $11 million over a failed job-creation plan involving a Norwegian solar company. The province owes Umoe Solar the money for land and equipment after plans for a $600-million solar panel plant fell through in May 2010. Three months earlier, the federal government had said it would grant the company $3 million to support R & D work.

28. Ontario's green energy plan was supposed to boost employment, but according to the province's auditor general, each new "green job" that's created costs the province between $100,000 and $300,000, and also results in the loss of two to four other jobs as a result of higher electricity prices.

29: Quebec gave IQT, a US firm, $670,000 to set up two call centers in the province in 2000, but in July, ITQ shut its doors, laying off 1,200 employees. The reason—Nashville offered it $1.5 million to move south.

30. Ottawa awarded $87,000 to PurGenesis Technologies of Montreal to commercialize its "line of anti-aging products based on certified organically grown baby spinach leaves." The money followed an earlier government "contribution" of $282,000 in 2009.

31. Several towns in Nova Scotia learned last year they'd have to cough up $790,000 after a controversial regional development agency went bust in 2010—mere months after Ottawa pumped in $80,000, claiming the South West Shore Development Authority contributed to "the cultural vitality and quality of life of [the] community.

32: Even as Rio Tinto Alcan and Alcoa said they would invest $15 billion to modernize operations in Quebec, the province and Ottawa still gave the industry $125,000 for a trade show.

33. The feds granted a company called SolarPro $54,000 to commercialize tanning beds.

34. An audit found that a $284-million program to get Ontario tobacco farmers out of the industry in 2008 actually funneled half the money to people who didn't farm tobacco in the first place.

35. Vancouver council voted to grant the Environmental Youth Alliance Society $5,000 for a project called Lawns to Loaves, through which thirty homeowners in the city could replace their grass lawns with wheat.

36. About 115 new Canadians were taken on a camping trip partly funded by taxpayers. The Learn to Camp project aims to teach the recent immigrants how to "put up a tent, how to start a camp fire, [and] how to make some S'mores," according to a Parks Canada spokesperson. There's still no word on exactly how much it will cost, or how many cases of Molson will be consumed.

37. Environment Canada spent $1 million to buy 14,000 "weatheradios" for schools, girl guides, and scout troops. The devices, which look like a radio alarm clock, provide twenty-four-hour weather-related broadcasts and sound a special tone to alert listeners to impending weather emergencies. Or they could just leave a regular alarm clock radio tuned to a twenty-four-hour news station with weather updates every ten minutes.

38. It's no secret that Canadians love the outdoors. We have to. There's just so damn much of it. Yet Environment Canada still spent $456,000 on a national survey on the importance of nature to Canadians—the fifth time it has done so since 1981. Have our attitudes about trees, lakes, and birds really changed that much over the years?

39. In 2008, the British Columbia government created the Pacific Carbon Trust, a Crown corporation, to make the world a greener place, apparently by picking the pockets of the province's school boards and

other government agencies. It was revealed in August that school districts were forced last year to buy $4.4 million in carbon credits to seek penance for such sins as heating their schools. The trust then spent its windfall so companies such as Encana and Intrawest could reduce their emissions, recycling money that might be better used by students rather than profitable corporations.

40. Montrealers came to the rescue of Bixi, the troubled bike-sharing program the city owns, with a $108-million bailout package made up of loans and loan guarantees. The nonprofit, money-losing company has faced problems as it expanded to Toronto and Ottawa, but Mayor Gérald Tremblay insisted taxpayer money would all be paid back once Bixi becomes an international bike-sharing powerhouse. Not so fast, warned the city's auditor general. Montreal taxpayers could suffer significant losses, he said, because "basic rules of management were neglected or circumvented."

41. Ontario taxpayers were handed an $18.6 million bill by an industry group over the province's failed eco-fee program.

42. Campaigns to ban bottled water exposed just how much provinces and cities pay to buy packaged water, such as $750,000 in Manitoba from 2004 to 2010 and as much as $7 million by Ottawa since 2006.

43. Environment Canada paid consultants $41,300 to find out the value of Canada's polar bear population. Turns out each one are worth $400,000 or $6.3 billion for the lot. Just think of the dent that could be made in Canada's deficit if we sold them off.

44. The Yukon government spent $1 million to build two "wildlife culverts" for an expensive new subdivision in Whitehorse so moose would stay off the newly constructed road. That's commendable, except the culverts helped push the price of lots in the government-owned development to as much as $218,000, and one-third of the thirty lots failed to sell.

45. The feds gave $717,000 to establish the International Centre for Sturgeon Studies at Vancouver Island University, the latest in a string of government funding announcements, going back a decade, all meant to jump-start the industry. To date there is only one producer of farmed sturgeon in Canada.

46. The city of Toronto tore up a dog park it had built just two years earlier at a cost of $40,000 after several nearby homeowners complained of the noise.

47. Going up? Users of Montreal's spiffy new bus station, which opened in December, are privy to a striking oddity—escalators to nowhere. The station, located on the lower floor of the Université de Québec à Montréal's Îlot Voyageur, was meant to be the school's commerce and residence hub, but today largely remains a $300 million taxpayer-funded concrete skeleton. Nine escalators were installed to take users to the mezzanine, at a cost of up to $200,000 because it has been abandoned—and won't be used anytime soon—a wall was built straight across the stairs.

48. The Canada Revenue Agency spent $750,000 on an ad campaign warning against "under the table" home renovations, then gave another $113,000 to a polling firm to find out the ads "did not have a statistically significant impact."

49. Environment Canada spent $140,000 to store office furniture for a year, only to eventually sell it off at auction and replace it with new workspaces.

50. British Columbia school boards paid an estimated $350,000 to mail out blank report cards after teachers refused to fill them out as part of a job action.

51. Fredericton, New Brunswick, bought the city's only strip club, North Star Sports Bar Pub and Eatery, to shut it down. The property was assessed at $364,900, but the city paid a premium price of $500,000 to buy it, then turned around and sold it for $400,000, incurring an immediate $100,000 loss.

52. Manitoba's publicly owned insurance company handed out $41,000 to eight convicted car thieves injured in stolen vehicles between 2006 and 2011.

53. The city of Edmonton spent $500,000 on licenses for software that an auditor said hardly any employees ever use.

54. Canada donated $36 million to China, a country that's accumulated US$3 trillion in foreign reserves.

55. The Royal Canadian Mint spent $7.3 million to make 486 million new pennies at a cost of roughly 1.5 cents each.

56. Calgary must spend $1.6 million on "public art" to go on the walls of a new traffic tunnel being built under the airport runway simply because of a rule that says all projects must include an art component.

57. A dog-eat-dog world—it was revealed that the federal government, through the Atlantic Canada Opportunities Agency, gave more than $180,000 in loans and grants to a Sydney, Nova Scotia, concert promoter to bring Snoop Dogg to the city to perform in 2010.

58. U2 isn't just a rock band; it's a billion-dollar, multinational corporation. But when Bono and crew swung through Montreal for a two-night show in July for their 360° tour (which incidentally earned them $740 million worldwide), the city subsidized the event by spending $450,000 to build a temporary stadium just for the show.

59. Montreal budgets about $150,000 annually to pay for murals painted by graffiti artists around the city. Another $1 million is spent helping boroughs get rid of murals that were, um, painted for free.

60: Ottawa handed over more than $83,000 to promote a bluegrass festival in New Richmond, Quebec.

61. Even though the conservative Members of Parliament want to cut off taxpayer funding to the CBC, the Harper government gave $82,000 to support a radio service in Bonne Bay, Newfoundland.

62. CBC documents showed it spent at least $6.6 million celebrating its seventy-fifth birthday.

63. Ottawa's National Capital Commission installed seven new ice shacks along the Rideau Canal for skaters to lace up in. Each shack cost $750,000. By comparison, the average house price in Ottawa is $360,000.

64. Ottawa doled out $354,000 to build nineteen yurts and teepees at a new glamping (glamour camping) park in Debiens, Quebec.

65. Ottawa gave $1.5 million to Parc Safari zoo in Hemmingford, Quebec, in part to build a "wolf observation tunnel."

66. The city of Hamilton spent $500,000 to recreate a tiered landscape design in Battlefield Park that dates back to the 1920s. To turn back the clock, city workers chopped down several trees in some places and planted new trees in others.

67. Calgary spent $800,000 to rebuild two Second World War aircraft that have sat disassembled in storage for decades.

68. Ottawa spent $455,000 to build an RV park in Grand Marais, Manitoba.

69. Toronto spent $50,000 on yet another plan to overhaul the city's port lands, this one including a doomed proposal to build the world's biggest Ferris wheel.

70. A glut of conference centers in North America didn't stop the feds from giving Thunder Bay $250,000 to plan for yet another in the northern Ontario city.

71. A federal agency coughed up $120,500 to improve a marina in Clarenville, Newfoundland, with just forty slips.

72. Another federal agency spent $1 million to modernize a municipal campground in Péribonka, Quebec, creating eight jobs—at $130,000 a pop.

73. Ottawa paid $160,000 to build four eco-tourism cabins in Gaspé, Quebec, at Chalets du bout du monde Inc., loosely translated as "the ends of the earth chalets."

74. A Richmond Hill, Ontario, councilor claimed $1,200 in expenses for new golf clubs, shoes, and a bag. Carmine Perrelli said he gets invited to a lot of charity tournaments and that by getting taxpayers to buy him new equipment, he actually saved them money on rentals. He also

said the gear remains the property of the city. Who wouldn't want a pair of old golf shoes?

75. David Hahn spent eight years at the helm of BC Ferries, a taxpayer-funded corporation. During his tenure, the British Columbia government doubled his annual salary from $500,000 to $1 million. In September, at sixty-one, Hahn retired, bowing to pressure to step down before he turned sixty-two, when his pension would have grown to a dizzying $314,000. He'll still retire after less than a decade of work with an annual pension of $77,000.

76. A Toronto city councilor charged taxpayers $300 to have his office blessed by a Baptist pastor.

77. BC Hydro hit its financial targets last year, prompting the public utility to give an eyebrow-raising 99 percent of its employees a performance bonus. But an internal memo revealed BC Hydro hit its yearly numbers by raising electricity rates and using some nimble accounting to defer debt payments. It also raises the question: how bad did the 1 percent have to be at their jobs to *not* qualify for a bonus?

78. Provincial governments are gaga for Apple products. In 2010, Alberta paid $276,000 to buy 1,400 iPod Touch devices to give away during the Winter Games while British Columbia taxpayers have spent roughly $250,000 to outfit senior government officials with 268 iPads.

79. It emerged in December that Defense Minister Peter MacKay spent $2,904 last year for a two-night stay at Munich's Bayerischer Hof, a lavish hotel where Bavaria's King Ludwig I used to take royal baths. MacKay's lowly staffers slummed it eight minutes away at the Hilton for $239 a night.

80. Speaking of MacKay, his controversial airlift from a personal fishing trip to the airport in Gander, Newfoundland, cost $16,000.

81. In the three months before he was found guilty of fraud and breach of trust in March, then-senator Raymond Lavigne was allowed to expense more than $32,000.

82. The feds created a job for Cecil Clarke, a Tory candidate defeated in last year's election, and gave him a salary of $133,000.

83. Thirteen members of former British Columbia premier Gordon Campbell's inner circle walked away with $2.4 million in severance payments.

84. Bruce Carson, the disgraced former adviser to Prime Minister Stephen Harper, claimed $28,000 in personal expenses to a federally funded think tank in Calgary in one month alone.

85. Paranoia will cost you. The city of Montreal has spent nearly $537,000 since 2008 spying on its own employees. It's not clear which employees were being watched, but early last year, Montreal auditor general Jacques Bergeron, who has regularly criticized city officials, filed a lawsuit against municipal employees who hacked into his email.

86. Following the earthquake in Haiti in January 2010, the Department of Foreign Affairs spent $26,500 on banners using Conservative party colours for a ministerial conference on the crisis. As reports noted, that sum is roughly thirty-nine times Haiti's per capita gross national product.

87. Two years ago, the government of Alberta spent close to $4 million to come up with a new slogan: "Alberta: Freedom to Create. Spirit to Achieve." When Alison Redford became premier last year, she scrapped the expensive, meaningless mouthful.

88. In the months leading up to the 2011 federal election, the conservative government spent $26 million of public money advertising the Economic Action Plan stimulus program.

89. Ottawa spent $424 for special gold-embossed business cards for Foreign Affairs Minister John Baird last year.

90. It was revealed the Harper government paid $2 million to spruce up Deerhurst Resort for the G8 meeting in June 2010, including $1,600 to move a bed and $3,500 to adjust light fixtures.

91. Ottawa also spent $1.9 million to monitor what media said about it in 2010.

92. The federal finance department and Privy Council Office separately paid Ipsos Reid a total of $200,000 for two focus-group surveys that both concluded, "Generally speaking, participants were not looking for a quick fix to Canada's budgetary deficit."

93. The Public Health Agency of Canada plans to spend $55,000 to study how to combat Montezuma's revenge—otherwise known as traveler's diarrhea—in the Caribbean.

94. Barrie, Ontario, spent $118,000 in preparation for a ban on commuter train whistles at railway crossings after five hundred residents complained of the noise. Among the steps taken was $10,000 for a "whistle cessation study." The city also assumed full liability for any future crossing accidents involving the silent trains.

95. The federal government paid consultants $19.8 million, or $90,000 a day, to suggest ways to trim budgets. Here's betting "overpriced outside advice" doesn't end up on their list of recommended cuts.

96. Last January, the city of Summerside, Prince Edward Island, filed a lawsuit against an American concert promoter over a worldwide Michael Jackson tribute concert that officials thought was going to kick off in their little town. The city wired $1.3 million in two separate payments to the promoter between 2009 and 2010 after they were allegedly promised that Beyoncé, Justin Timberlake, and Usher were lined up to perform in Summerside.

97. The city of Calgary spent more than $65,000 fighting a controversial street preacher in court over a $100 bylaw fine.

98. A November report called the British Columbia government's decision in late 2010 to cover $6 million in legal fees for Dave Basi and Bob Virk—two former political aides who pleaded guilty to charges of corruption—"highly unusual."

99. Ontario judges and justices of the peace spent close to $600,000 for three conferences at the Deerhurst Resort in Muskoka.

100. The city of Calgary built a bridge for twenty-five million dollars which they contracted out to a firm from Italy when Calgary shops were badly

in need of work. Not only did the bridge cost five times what it was worth or 500 percent of what it should have cost, it was not needed in the first place. A total waste. As well, the bridge took five times as long to draft, contract out, and build. No doubt someone connected with the city will build a high-rise at either end of the bridge, and this will benefit them immensely as there is always a reason for every project whether it's for the good of the taxpayer or whether it's a waste of money. An example in the United States would be Senator Ted Stevens, who was charged by the Federal US Justice Department. And even though the case was later dismissed, the justice department spent several million dollars on their own legal fees, which was a total waste of money as Senator Stevens never should have been charged in the first place.

101. In the state government of Arizona, Jan Brewer unveiled a budget on January 14, 2012, of 8.9 billion. This budget will restore funding for schools, give state workers their first pay raise in five years, and will assist Arizona's technological infrastructure. In Alberta, they will unveil a budget of approximately forty billion, over four times the amount of the state of Arizona's, and with the result that the infrastructure, schools, and health care system is about one quarter as good in Alberta as it is in Arizona. One would wonder where the other thirty billion dollars goes in the first place and secondly why a province which is one of the richest areas in the world does not have education, health care, and infrastructure like the state of Arizona, which has little or no primary resources other than tourism.

Canada is one of the richest countries in the world with world's most nickel, uranium, and pot ash, etc., including large quantities of diamonds, agricultural products, oil, gas, oil shale, oil sands, timber, coal, etc., and many other primary resources too numerous to mention. Yet it has a budget deficit each year as well as a very large overall deficit of tens of billions.

An excellent book on your tax dollars not at work called *Money Well Spent* an ironic title by Micheal Grabell, three hundred and eighty-nine pages. An ironic title as it illustrates exactly the opposite. Mr. Grabell does a good job of cataloging misdirected funds and misplaced priorities, which makes one wonder how he settled on the inquisitive title, page after page seems to answer with a resounding "no." There were many items such as the large grant to the failed solar panel maker Solandra, which is now under federal investigation. Other worthy competitors are the $783,000 grant given to study why young people drink malt liquor and use marijuana, and the $218,000 grant to study the hookups of college students (perhaps these research efforts could have been combined). Then there is the $92,000 spent by the army corps of engineers (on costumes for mascots for Bobber, the water safety dog). If the aim was to underwrite vital structure products, why did an Alaskan village called Ouzinkie, population of 167 receive a fifteen-million-dollar airport? By contrast, the author notes that major hubs such as New York and Las Vegas didn't get any stimulus money; and Atlanta, the busiest airport in the world, didn't receive any amount of grants. Only about 10 percent of the spending or eighty billion was devoted to infrastructure, and very little of that went to critical work. Even though bridges too numerous to mention are in need of repair as well as repaving roads that are a necessity, less than 12 percent of the infrastructure spending went to bridges or roads. Money was allotted in an effort to weatherize American homes, but at the end of 2009, only ninety-one hundred homes had been weatherized nationwide out of a total of nearly six hundred thousand in three years. In California, a total of twelve houses have been weatherized.

Trillions were given to Wall Street and the banks who promptly took the money out in salaries and bonuses, paying off their own bills while at the same time refusing to give loans to the small businesses and people who were in dire straits. A further example is the American International Group (AIG), who, through mismanagement, went in debt to the total of one hundred and eighty-five billion dollars, resulting in the federal government promptly bailing the company out. AIG is one of the largest insurance companies in the world; it employs over forty thousand people whose main job is to go over insurance claims and deny a large portion. After AIG failed, they changed their name to Chartis, and Mattie had the unfortunate experience to place insurance through a broker who in turn placed it through another broker in Central Canada who then in turn placed it with the new name Chartis. They are also now called Travel Guard Insurance in the States. The companies had a plan where instead of spending five days getting your medical insurance, the broker would simply phone you, ask you a few questions, and then get your credit card number; and in five minutes, you would be completely insured you thought. Unfortunately, when the time came to pay a small claim of thirty thousand dollars, the group of two brokers and Chartis refused to pay the claim for dubious reasons with the end result that Mattie will have to take action and hire a lawyer to have his claim paid to the companies and individuals in the American medical system who he dealt with in the spring of 2011. This is another example of how big business works against the individual and small businesses including all taxpayers and consumers. On the positive side, the infrastructure spending helped put a floor under the construction industry, and the government did fund a large number of useful projects. Of course it was poorly designed—politicians designed it—but given the resulting joblessness, the American people have reasons to give thanks, and taxpayers and consumers can only hope for the future.

The government does create opportunities for small business and the consumer to receive compensation through small debts court, and example is where a woman in southern California won in a big way. Los Angeles superior court commissioner Douglas Carnahan ruled in January of 2012 that Honda Motor Company mislead Heather Peters about the potential fuel economy of her hybrid car and awarded her over nine thousand dollars, much more than the couple of hundred dollars cash that a proposed class action settlement was offered to the various Honda owners. Honda disagrees with the judgment and plans to appeal according to a company spokesman. The lady who sued stated, "Wow, fantastic. I'm absolutely thrilled." when she was informed of the decision. Sometimes justice comes in small packages. The judge included with his twenty-six-page decision a long list of misleading representations by Honda that Peters had correctly identified. Among them were that the car would use amazingly little fuel providing plenty of horsepower while sipping fuel, and that it would save plenty of money on fuel with up to fifty miles per gallon during city driving. However, the actual performance of the plaintiff's vehicle did not live up to these standards, the judge said. Peters opted out of the class action lawsuit so she could try and claim a larger amount of damages for her 2006's failure to deliver the 50 MPG that was promised. In small-claims court, there are no attorney's fees in cases that are decided quickly. Peters had hoped to inspire a flood of small-claims lawsuits by the other two hundred thousand people whose cars are not covered by the proposed settlement. If all two hundred thousand people sued and won, it could cost Honda Motor Company two hundred billion dollars. Peters launched a website Dontsettlewithhonda.org. Instead, she was contacted by hundreds of other car owners seeking guidance if they opted out of the class action case. Legal experts say it's unlikely many owners will take this route because of the time and energy involved in such lawsuits. This is a prime example of how big business tries to get out of their responsibilities.

An example of representative democracy is shown when Edmond Burke warned his Bristol electors in England in 1774 that he would not take instructions from them and would not deliberate in parliament in the national interest, not theirs. However, in the following election in 1780, Burke lost his seat when seeking another. He said, "The people are the masters" and wrote that "no man carries further than I do the policy of making government pleasing to the people. I would not only consult the people, but I would cheerily gratify their humors." Somewhat older and perhaps wise, he noted that he never conformed himself to the humors of the people. He could not say that the opinion was indifferent to him, but he would take it if he could as his companion but never as his guide. This would be good advice for politicians today.

A prime example in the United States is the republican nominees already with just a few months in 2012 in the debates Madam Brockman, Mr. Perry, and Mr. Cain have already flamed out; and strangely Mr. Romney who is the present leader for president has stated that he is not interested in the poor, but that they have their own support system. This is probably a safe statement to make as the poor rarely vote; they realize that their cause is a losing one, and there's not much sense in voting as there is little chance that they will better themselves. Nevertheless, it is an example of a very rich individual wanting to be president of a very large nation, indicating publicly that he is not interested in one segment of the population.

Another example of government supporting big business is that not only did the government give several trillion dollars to Wall Street brokerages and banks in New York; they also keep lowering the interest rate, which makes it very easy for the ultra rich billionaires to buy up the homes and businesses of the ordinary individual and middle class.

President Bush cut back on the regulations on big banks and big Wall Street brokerages, allowing them to do as they wish resulting in the recession/depression of 2008. These tough times have been going on now for four years and will continue on for at least another four while the gap between the extremely rich and the ordinary people continues to widen. An example is almost eight thousand beneficiaries of life insurance policies have received over two million as a result of a push to get companies to comb through their records and look for overdue payments. The early results from this effort come as other probes sweep across the country in what regulators and other state officials describe as a widespread problem that hits lower-income families the hardest. Under this approach, tens of thousands of customers appear to be losing out on proceeds from insurance, and there are believed to be families with smaller policies that don't have lawyers keeping track of their money matters. Regardless, insurers say they are behaving lawfully, but regulators and state attorney generals, including in New York, have probed the matter and saying enforcement action and possible penalties are being pursued in the future.

Another problem in the United States is that corporate America's top lobbyists are trying to curb powerful antibribery law known as the Foreign Corrupt Policies Act (FCPA), which has risen to the top of the agenda, sparking a widespread debate on how the legislation is enforced. In the past five years, enforcement of the US law has led to about four billion in penalties. The law prevents companies from paying bribes to foreign officials to win business, and violations can result in criminal prosecutions. Congress passed the law in 1977 after the Watergate scandal revealed the use of corporate slush funds to bribe foreign government officials, but it was sporadically enforced until the recent years. Justice department officials have attributed the recent enforcement push, in part, to the 2002 Sarbanes-Oxley Act, which requires corporate officers to certify the accuracy of their financial statements. That has led to more companies discovering potentially illicit payments on their books and disclosing them to the Securities and Exchange Commission and the justice department, they say. High-profile settlements involving both American and foreign companies, including Siemens AG, Halliburton Co. and Johnson & Johnson, have burnished the law's reputation as a major force internationally. In the Siemens case, the department accused the company of funneling more than $50 million in bribes through consultants and agents to officials in Argentina, Bangladesh, Venezuela, and elsewhere in return for contracts. Siemens, in 2008, admitted wrongdoing and agreed to pay record penalties of $1.6 billion to the United States and German authorities to end the probes. But as the FCPA's stature has grown, so has resistance from companies, which have thus far responded by paying for multimillion-dollar compliance programs that help them identify bribery risk in their dealings abroad. Now, amending the law is a priority for the US Chamber of Commerce, the largest lobbying organization in Washington. In the first three quarters of this year, the chamber paid outside lobbyist's large sums of money to represent their interests.

In a majority of countries around the world up until the last few years, bribery was legal and is still practiced in a large number of countries throughout the world. Without paying bribes, companies would unable to do business with the various governments throughout the world.

On the positive side, corporate employees help and scope out opportunities in development countries; for example, Ms. Benetti, a twenty-seven-year-old customs and trade coordinator for Dow Corning is working in India helping women examine stitchery and figuring out prices for garments to be sold in local markets. She and nine other colleagues work nine hours a day and sleep in a lodge frequented by locals that has plenty of access to hot water and electricity, and even though it's very hard work, the Dow Corning employees consider it a plum assignment due to the satisfaction they receive for working for the poor. Dow is just one of a growing number of large corporations including PepsiCo Inc., FedEx Corporation, Intel Corporation, and Pfizer Inc. that are sending small teams of employees to developing countries such as India, Ghana, Brazil, and Nigeria to provide free consulting services to nonprofits and other organizations. A major goal is to scope out business opportunities in hot emerging markets. At least twenty-seven Fortune 500 companies currently operate such programs, up from twenty-one in April and six in 2006, according to a survey by CDC Development Solutions, a Washington, DC, nonprofit that designs and manages these programs. At a cost of $5,000 to over $20,000 per employee, the programs require a significant investment. It costs International Business Machines Corporation (IBM), which has the largest such corporate volunteer operation, roughly $5 million a year. IBM has sent 1,400 employees abroad with its Corporate Service Corps since 2008. Its projects have produced plans to reform Kenya's postal system and develop an eco-tourism industry in Tanzania. IBM credits its program with generating about $5 million in new business so far, including a contract, awarded in April 2010, to manage two public service programs for Nigeria's Cross River State, says Stan Litow, vice president for corporate citizenship. The overseas assignments can act as a training ground for future leaders. A vice president of corporate responsibility and president of the Pfizer Foundation, says some of the 270 people the pharmaceutical giant has sent abroad describe the experience as "a mini MBA." "They build skills, in part because they are sometimes thrust into situations outside of their comfort zone, which tends to make people more creative," she says. A professor at Harvard Business School says his research that alumni of the program remain on the job longer than peers with similar performance and tenure. By offering something like this, they can retain these people for longer, and it is a very smart investment.

An article on Tuesday, January 23, 2012, in the *Washington Examiner* by Walter Williams states "I Love Greed" and so should you. In his article, he states capitalism made it possible to become wealthy by serving one's fellow man. Capitalists seek to discover what people want and then produce it as efficiently as possible. What human motivation gets the most wonderful things done? It's really a silly question because the answer is so simple. It turns out that it's human greed that gets the most wonderful things done. He states, "When I say greed, I am not talking about fraud, theft, dishonesty, lobbying for special privileges from government, or other forms of despicable behavior." Evidently he had never worked for big business. He states, "I'm talking about people trying to get as much as they can for themselves. Let's look at it." Texas ranchers work very hard to look after the cattle. In order to ensure that Americans can enjoy beef. Idaho potato farmers toil in blazing sun, dust, and dirt to ensure that Americans have potatoes to go with their beef. The reason they do this is because ranchers and farmers want more for themselves. In a free market system, in order for one to get more for himself, he must serve his fellow man, which is a very true statement. This is precisely what Adam Smith, the father of economics, meant when he said in his classic "An Inquiry into the Nature and Causes of the Wealth of Nations" (1776). "It is not from the benevolence of the butcher, the brewer, or the baker, that we expect our dinner, but from their regard to their own interest." This is very true. He asks how much beef and potatoes Americans would enjoy if it all depended on the politically correct notions of human kindness. He personally feels that without capitalistic greed, the world could not succeed, and he does have a point. He further goes on to say that free market capitalism is relatively new in human history. Prior to the rise of capitalism, the way people amassed great wealth was by looting, plundering, and enslaving their fellow man. Capitalism made it possible to become wealthy by serving one's fellow man, and the nature of the successful capitalist and entrepreneur is to discover what people want and then produce it as efficiently as possible—the author's own words. The hostility towards free market capitalism when he said, "People of the same trade seldom meet together, even for merriment and diversion, but the conversation ends in a conspiracy against the public, or in some contrivance to raise prices." Mattie learned in his business experience the above the hard way.

In Japan, Tokyo Electric Power Company said Tuesday it would raise the electricity rate for corporate customers in April. As the utility faces higher fuel costs after the loss of its nuclear power general capacity following last year's accident at its nuclear plants. The rate increase of about 17 percent will be used by the electric company to buy fossil fuels as many of its nuclear facilities remain off after the tsunami-related disaster in March. One would wonder what kind of tsunami hit Alberta, Canada, in the past few months, as electricity has increased from 6.3 cents per kilowatt to 14.8 cents by the giant provider ATCO Utilities to the province. One would wonder does it have anything to do with ATCO's billion-dollar investment in Australia as the rivers are still running as usual, the coal is still in abundance, and the power lines are all constructed. Unless they're planning to build new ones to sell power to foreign interests and charge the cost to the Alberta consumer. Another reason might be that from time to time the various utility owners such as Direct and ATCO would like people to sign contracts, and as long as the consumer is receiving a reasonable rate, they would have no interest in signing the contract. Therefore the simple way would be to increase the prices dramatically and then advertise and door-knock with a slightly lower rate, and many people will sign contracts, figuring that they are saving money. In the past, people have signed contracts at higher prices only to find that the utility rates have gone down. As old P. T. Barnun said, "There is a sucker born every day."

Mattie has outlined in prior paragraphs in this book how by investing in real estate you can become very wealthy. Unfortunately, when one considers how big business and big government controls the economic future of a nation, this is not always true; therefore we should outline just a few examples of how even large outfits lose substantial sums of money. The California Public Employees' Retirement System, CalPERS, after the bubble burst suffered losses on a number of deals, losing more than nine hundred million in one deal alone. While its real estate portfolio lost half its value or about ten billion from March 2008 to June 2009, CalPERS says it has now rebounded more recently. When the bust hit in 2008–2010, the giant California pension fund wrote off a five-hundred-million-dollar equity stake in Manhattan Sprawling Stuyvesant Town and Peter Cooper apartment complex, another one of the biggest pension fund losses in the real estate collapse. CalPERS wrote down nearly a billion investment to LandSource, a venture that owned thousands of acres of land in Southern California as well as Lennar Corporation, the pension funds partner on the deal, which later bought a stake in LandSource for a fraction of what CalPERS initially invested. This goes to prove that in real estate and the stock market, anytime there is a loser, there is also a winner, and vice versa. It is up to the individual investor to make sure that they have done due diligence and inquired from their wealthy friends where and when they should be investing.

Mattie has also mentioned the phrase "Tell me what an individual reads, and I'll tell you what they know." This does not always work either as you will rarely be informed by a financial planner how to stop doing dumb things with your money and stocks. Selling stock when it's going down and buying when it's going up is irrational, writes Carl Richards in a book *The Behavior Gap: Simple Ways to Stop Doing Dumb Things with Your Money.* The book is full of sarcastic advice like, "Don't just do something, stand there." When the market soars or hits a rough patch, there is a natural tendency to do something fast. A natural reaction is to sell after the bad news (when the market is already down), and buy when the news is good (after the market is already up), thus indulging our fear and our greed. It's an impossible strategy. He states, "Find out who you are and what you want. Then you can stop wasting your life energy on stuff that doesn't matter to you." Mattie learned this lesson very early on in life when he bought back in the late fifties the big car, the new farm equipment, all the items in life that were totally unnecessary while foolishly financing these items while investing in farming which turned out not to be a gamble but a license to lose money. Mattie has found out that the wise thing to do is find a spouse, friend, or anyone you trust and walk them through your answers to the question: what impact will it have if I'm wrong, and have I been wrong before? Mr. Richards states when speaking of advice, to ignore it. He said. "Let's face it, most of the advice we get is useless. People tend to give their opinions based on their own fears, their own experiences, and their own motivations. Following a tip you read about is just dumb." He further said, "If you read about it in the economist, a magazine that sells more than a million copies a week, so did a whole bunch of people who think they are being clever in exactly the same way, at exactly the same time. This happens with the numerous money magazines and financial newsletters that are sent out across the nation to millions of people. If these people all read that a certain railroad stock is a great buy, feel quite sure that they'll be buying that stock on the same day with the end result that you have to get in very quickly on the ground floor 'cause without a doubt the positive side is they will drive the price of the stock up in the very near future." So Mr. Richards's advice is not totally correct because anytime people read that a certain stock is an excellent investment, then if hundreds of thousands of people invest in it, then the stock will go up in price and you too will be the beneficiary of a rising financial investment. This is outlined quite clearly when you read about the insider trading, which is quite common in the stock market. In fact, when a lot of lucrative companies go public, they limit the shares to buyers who are blue-chip investors in particular stock broking firms, and you will only be able to buy the shares after the individuals in the inner circle acquire all they want. And only then when the market has gone up will the ordinary Joe be allowed to purchase stock. This is very unfair, but it is a practice that is extremely common throughout the stock market. Mr. Richards goes on to say, "When planning for retirement, don't get hung up on how much money you'll need to have your dream house. Make sure there's enough in the budget to visit the kids, travel wherever you wish, pay for your golf club dues, and have additional funds in the bank for when things get bumpy." "If you're buying or selling at the wrong time," Richard says, "one alternative is to swear off the stock market forever." He states that whatever the experts may claim, steering clear of the stock market isn't stupid. Richards, the founder of Prasada C. M., confessed he doesn't know when is a good or bad time to buy, and this frustrates friends and family. "It's bad enough that I don't know where the market is going. People are more confused when they find out I don't even care. Believe it or not, the ability to build and protect wealth is often inversely related to knowing what is going on in the market. I tell people it is a terrible idea to try and predict the market's movements, whereas it may make them anxious, and anxious people screw up." "Focus on personal goals," he writes. "If your financial goal is to send your kids to college, tracking the performance is not going to help you reach that goal." He tells a story of an older woman who was worried about how trouble in Lebanon may affect her portfolio; he told her two things. First, Lebanon is not going to play a major role in what happens to you, and second, there is not a thing you can do to influence events in Lebanon. Then he asked her, given those two facts, why are we talking about Lebanon? In short, this just goes to prove in one man's opinion that you pick stocks for a particular reason. If you find out that railroads are going to lengthen the length of their trains, that there's going to be a big demand for coal, grain, goods coming from offshore to the ports of New York and Los Angeles, and then you also find out that they're going to ship from offshore in containers and the railcars are going to be carrying two containers instead of one as they update their tracks, then you will realize, as Warren Buffet did, that railroads are one heck of a buy. And since there are always commodities moving, you can't go wrong. Second, if gold has dropped to a low price like it did when Mattie's brother bought a lot of gold or when Mattie had lost faith in the stock market and decided to buy gold and silver because he thought they were reasonably priced and had a chance of going up, perhaps even doubling, which proved to be a very lucky move and a sound investment. Third, when Mattie realized that banks in Canada were paying a very good dividend and were a very sound investment plus eventually they would rise in price, he realized that he had three ways of making money on bank stocks, and he immediately invested. Fourth, if Mattie found out through his friends or acquaintances that an individual or group of small individuals had left an oil company, he felt secure in the knowledge that they would take with them the experience and expertise that they had gained at the successful oil company that they were leaving and were fully aware of potential plays where they perhaps had already acquired a land position, and there was no way that by investing in their company that you could not succeed as not only were you investing in real estate and oil rights, but you were able to realize excellent profits. If and when they struck oil and most people do not realize that when you strike oil you strike natural gas, butanes, propane, etc., so not only in 2012 are a lot of oil companies producing oil at twenty dollars a barrel and selling it for almost one hundred, a 500 percent profit, and that when oil goes up at the pump a dollar a gallon, few people realize that the oil wells that were found in Leduc, Alberta, Canada, in 1947 continue to pump oil for fifty years. So the idea that the price is going up at the pumps because the cost of oil is increasing in cost to the oil company is a bit of a fallacy as the oil keeps pumping day and night, thirty days a month, 365 days a year. That is why there are so many very wealthy oilmen, and of course when the oil company goes public at a dollar a share and then the shares increase from a dollar to ten dollars to fifty dollars such as Hurricane Hydrocarbons, a company with vast interest in Kazakhstan in Asia, the country adjacent to Russia and located on the Caspian Sea, where Mattie was fortunate to buy shares at forty cents per share as he read in an article that one of his friends was buying a very large number of shares, so Mattie bought as well. Unfortunately, Mattie started selling the shares at lower amounts, but his last check when the company was sold to Petro China was for fifty-five dollars per share, an excellent rate of return and all made possible just by reading various oil publications. Mattie's friend by the way it was reported made fourteen million on the deal, a substantial amount of money in anyone's books.

Mattie has always had a built-in hate for cell phones and finds it perfectly ridiculous to compare Henry Ford and Steve Jobs because Henry Ford invented the motor vehicle which provided a form of transportation that changed society. With Steve Jobs, who revolutionized cell phones, which are a nuisance as Mattie finds—even though he has a large number of them—that they are not safe to use on the road as they distract you from driving and cause numerous accident and are banned in every province in Canada and numerous states in the United States. When Mattie meets with someone and they keep glancing at their cell phone, he often wonders during the meeting or dinner if they are first, brain surgeons that abruptly left during the surgery and are checking in to see if they ought to go back and finish the surgery; second, are they current politicians high up in the government and are searching for important messages or just scores of athletic events; three, are they applying for a job and checking to see if any offers have come their way and do not want to be tardy in replying. He wonders if you do not fit into any of these categories, perhaps you can hold off on using your phone until you can pretend to need to use the bathroom, but later he finds out that you went there to tweet the result of your friend's tennis game.

To continue on with investments, one would think that Las Vegas that used to be one of the most rapidly growing cities in the world where houses were doubling in price yearly, now you can buy a house that was worth two hundred and fifty thousand and is now for fifty thousand dollars, an excellent investment which has numerous flights to the Vegas airport, and it is possible to attend shows and various events such as a national rodeo and a large number of conventions. Although it is wise to book ahead as room rates double on weekends as well as when conventions are being held for example, the big electronics show CES that's held in Las Vegas or the giant equipment show that's called ConExpo that draws over one hundred thousand people to these events, making it very difficult and costly to get hotel rooms, food, and attend the various events, etc. There are numerous large projects in Vegas which have been put on hold and are only half built with most of these properties being in litigation. One example is a group of debt holders have gone to court to block a deal for JW Marriott Las Vegas resort and spa. There are giant firms who specialize in taking over real estate that has fallen on hard times or companies that are underperforming and investors who put money in these companies such as Genworth Financial Inc., Pacific Investment Management Company, Blackstone, Carlyle Group, and Bane Financial outfits make a practice of getting money from extremely wealthy investors and taking a 15 percent management fee for investing it. Since they have built up considerable credibility, they have no trouble finding investors who place their money with these corporations, and the controllers and shareholders make fortunes by receiving 15 percent of the profits on the successful investments while at the same time only paying 15 percent taxes where the average American or Canadian would be lucky to get away with a 35 percent tax bill. This is an example of how the very rich make fortunes with little risk or responsibility.

While talking about investing search for a safer bet in 2012 in these recessionary times, and dividends have gone from being an afterthought to one of the top items on many investors' minds. These periodic payments from companies to their investors are taking an oversized role in the markets. Given the stock market's disappointing performance last year and lackluster targets for 2012, investors are happy taking what they see as a safer bet. That craving for dependable, albeit not guaranteed, dividend income could continue, given that interest rates remain low, analysts say.

"People are throwing in the towel on the horse race," says an individual of Harris Private Bank. "They want a dividend program that can deliver." Therefore it's wise to consider that dividends were the sole source of return for many investors in 2011. The return by Standard & Poor's 500 last year was entirely due to the dividend yield, says S&P Capital IQ. That's the highest contribution of dividends on investors' total return since 2008 when the stock markets 38.5 percent decline was partly upset by a 1.5 percent dividend. Dividends were the biggest returns since at least 1988 if the years the stock market fell are excluded. Not only did investors enjoy cash from stocks that paid dividends; they avoided more disappointing losses too. Stocks that paid a dividend gained 1.4 percent on average in 2011 versus a 7.6 percent average loss for S&P 500 stocks that didn't pay a dividend, says S&P Capital IQ. Dividend-paying stocks have been beating the market. The S&P dividend ETF rose nearly 4 percent last year, edging out the 0 percent gain of the S&P 500. Looking into 2012, investors have high hopes for dividend-paying stocks. Nearly three quarters of S&P 500 companies are expected to boost their dividends in 2012. Investors are likely to see at least an 11 percent increase in dividends and possibly more, meaning dividends could top the previous record set in June 2008, according to S&P Capital IQ. Some investors believe it's more likely that companies will raise dividends than that economic growth will boost stock prices, says Rick Helm, portfolio manager of the Cohen and Steers Dividend Value Fund. An increase in yields from treasuries and other safe investments could make dividend-paying stocks relatively less attractive, says an individual at the Alpine Dynamic Dividend Fund, but unless that happens in a big way, investors looking for income see dividend-paying stocks as the best alternative. Another interesting individual is James Altucher, the managing partner of Formula Capital and the author of several finance and motivational books based on his career—he has made millions, lost it all, and recovered it again, suffering emotional breakdown along the way. His website Altucher Confidential has been viewed more than ten million times since its launch. His latest self-published book *I Was Blind But Now I See* is now among one of the top-rated motivational books on Amazon's Kindle Store. Altucher was a columnist for the London *Financial Times*. His self-help books focus on his losses and failures, and when asked what has struck a nerve with people, he says that he thinks everybody is ashamed that in 2009 the tide came in, they either lost their job, their marriage, or they had trouble paying their mortgage than at any time in the past fifteen years—they didn't make as much money as their friends did. He feels that his book gives him permission that that is okay. As we've all been through it. When asked if most of his readers were Wall Street–types, he stated, "No, it started that way. A little over a year ago, it was all Wall Street people, but now it is people from all over." When asked when he lost it all, and he would pace the floor at 3:00 a.m. contemplating suicide, was there a point where his life needed to change? He stated, "Several times I reached that point. When you're in the middle of losing everything but you don't want to, you have to make a change. Life is a roller coaster." When asked about his successes and failures and how many businesses have he failed at, he stated, "I've had hundreds of ideas. I've probably failed at a good seventeen different business attempts, and I've had three successes." This is something that Mattie can relate to. When asked, "Does everybody have the talent to be creative?" He answered, "Yes, it's not a talent, it's a learned ability. You start every day with ten ideas, what people you should talk to, what business should you start, and what books should you read. It has to be a solid, doable next step. You'll have a lot of bad ideas, and it's only then that you'll start coming up with good ideas. It's not that your ideas are so good; it's the sheer quantity that you come up with." When asked why he is a big critic of the belief that people should own a home and go to college, because he has made a lot of money having done that, he stated that he doesn't want to connect the two. If two thousand equally ambitious and aggressive people and gave half of them a four- of five-year head start with no debt at the end, they're probably going to do very well. Just like they've done very well throughout history. It's only in the last thirty or forty years that a college degree has become mandatory in American society." This is something Mattie totally agrees with. When asked would he have gotten a job in the investment field without a college degree, he answered, "No, you would probably need a degree." But the best job he'd had was because his boss was a good chess player but ranked lower than him, and that helped him get the job. And in Mattie's case, the reason he got the excellent job with the oil company when he arrived in Alberta when he was eighteen years old was simply because he had came a thousand miles farther to Calgary, Alberta, then the boss had came from Dallas, Texas, which really impressed his new boss-to-be. When asked that after "working for others he started his own company, which he eventually sold. He answered, "Yes, in September 1998 I did very well. I sold at the right moment. I cashed out at the right moment, and then suddenly I went stupid. I did everything you could possibly do wrong for the next year and a half, and this proves when you get a good offer for a going business, it's usually wise to sell in Mattie's opinion." When asked why he made mistakes for eighteen months, he stated that he thought he was the smartest guy in the world because he had made all the money, which is the first mistake people that make money think. "I said I made all this money on the business which was a great thing, and that the future is in the Internet, so I decided in March 2000 I was going to buy every Internet stock I could and keep doubling down. That didn't work. I lost a million a week in the summer of 2000, and then it went to zero." The only place this works in Mattie's opinion is when you're playing blackjack. You start out with the bet, and if you lose, you go to a two-dollar bet. And if you lose, you go to a four-dollar bet, and if you lose, you go to an eight-dollar bet. If you lose again, you go to a sixteen-dollar bet, and if you lose again, you go to a thirty-two dollar bet. This is a winning combination as the law of averages, and if you're able to remember and if you've got a good memory in order to remember the cards and in blackjack, there's about a ninety-plus percent chance of winning, you cannot lose until the managers in the casino find out that you are extremely successful, resulting in you being booted in the butt out the door. When asked, "You write about watching your bank account goes from fifteen million to zero in two years, which sounds terrifying, he said, "It was and also very sad. A few years later, my dad got sick, and I could have maybe helped him more if I'd had that money. But I was like a foolish, drunken rock star." He was then asked, "How did you come out of that funk?" To which he replied, "I had to figure out how to support my family. So I got healthy again instead of just lying on the floor. Emotionally, I got rid of anybody who was negative. And I started writing down ideas. After writing hundreds, some of them started to work. I built an entirely new career, from scratch. Ironically enough, it was in investing." He was asked, "You talk about your 'daily practice' to becoming healthier." He replied, "Yeah, when I sold my apartment after going broke and I was kind of in exile, I needed ways to cheer myself up. I was really depressed, so things like flying a kite and sitting on a swing where you step out of your normal rhythm does cheer you up." He was asked about one of his ideas to become a psychic on Craigslist. He replied, "Right around the time I had separated from my first wife, I don't know. I was feeling lonely, and I was feeling totally down and out, and I just wanted to connect with people, so I put an ad on Craigslist that said, 'I'm psychic. Ask me any question you want, and I'll answer.' And in all my answers I was fair. I gave just my opinion. I viewed it more like Craigslist therapy than Craigslist psychic powers. It was fun, and I have Facebook friends now that I met that way." When asked if he would describe himself as happy now, he said, "Yes, I do. It doesn't mean I have $100 million or a yacht on the Mediterranean. I ascribe happiness more as a feeling of contentment." Which is very correct in Mattie's opinion. When asked where money fits into the equation, he replied, "Money's extremely important to support yourself and to support your family and to be as comfortable as possible, so somewhere in between, you know, being a billionaire and being somebody who sits in a cave all day by yourself, there's the right amount of money that produces contentment." An excellent statement. When asked if there is an interesting headline in the book. he said, "You need to quit your job right now," which is a message that probably a lot of people would find appealing, but I'd venture not many people will follow. His reply, "Well, you know, let's look at that question broadly. So why does somebody want a corporate job? Because they think it means safety. A corporate job is not safe. It's much safer to develop ideas and to have multiple streams of income, just like I was able to do where I was not only investing other people's money, but I was writing about it, and I was also doing deals and transactions." This is what Mattie has outlined in the previous hundreds of pages. It's not totally safe working for big business as so many people have found out, and working for government does not always bring happiness. And more often than not, it can bring unhappiness, plus there's also the problem of being transferred hither and yon which has proven to cause considerable unhappiness in so many families across the world. Whereas in Mattie's opinion doing deals and transactions are the ultimate in challenges and can be extremely rewarding. That is why he outlines this individual's opinions, which he believes are very interesting. When asked if he was a big proponent of the American economy, and what was his forecast for the next few years, he replied, "There's going to be an enormous boom, and the reason is there's a lot of cash lying around looking for something to do. The banks have almost $3 trillion, the nonbanks have another $2 trillion, and pension funds have another trillion or so in savings. There's $5 trillion in this economy that's all potential customers and investors, so I think this money's eventually going to filter through and benefit all of us." This gentleman is an extremely interesting individual, and when one is considering his or her future, they'd be wise to check James Altucher's website headed under Altucher Confidential as evidently if it has ten million hits, other people are extremely interested in his thoughts and activities. He has also self-published a book, which, as we have already mentioned, is among the top-ranked motivational books on Amazon's Kindle Store. The above should all prove interesting to anybody interested in a way of life and another person's success, failure, and thoughts on investing and business.

Chapter 15

Politics

An excellent candidate for US president Mr. Romney, who has been extremely successful and is an outstanding gentleman, made an unfortunate statement in the Florida, primary stating that he is "not concerned about the very poor, because they have an ample safety net." He later apologized saying he misspoke, but this indicates how a simple statement can cause a candidate serious problems in an election. On the other hand, back a few elections ago in the United States, Bill Clinton, when he was running for president and was behind another candidate, used the statement suggested by James Carville, one of his senior campaign individuals. "It's the economy stupid," and that statement alone went a long way to winning him the presidential election.

One of the better candidates running in the United States primary in 2012 is a gentleman who is a doctor by profession, Ron Paul, and he goes out of his way to show the extent of his frugality—and goes into great detail when it comes to filling out his expense reports, down to one hundred and sixty-four separate entries for expenditures of a dollar each in his reports. When he eats out, he buys value meals at McDonald's and eats at truck stops and other fast-food restaurants. Even though Ron Paul is one of the most honest, intelligent, and up-front individuals, he will not get elected simply because people don't trust a person who comes out as a completely honest individual. If people have a chance to vote against something, that's the route they will take rather than vote for something that would be better for the country. In the United States, there is an Ohio candidate called Joe the Plumber, and he pays himself a salary before he even gets elected out of his campaign account. And evidently, it's perfectly legal for a candidate to pay themselves with campaign funds according to the Federal Election Committee rules although the newspapers comments are that this practice is relatively unusual.

In some countries such as Canada, the federal government is building more prisons; and rather than rehabilitate people who do wrong and have them pay taxes, they are locking them up in prisons at a cost of fifty to one hundred thousand a year, which is a burden the taxpayers can no longer afford. For example, in California hundreds of prison employees got layoff notices in the last month, as the inmate population declines to comply with a federal court order resulting in fourteen thousand fewer inmates than four months ago. Five hundred and forty-eight employees were laid off in an order backed by the US Supreme Court that gave the state two years to reduce its prison population by thirty-three thousand inmates. In California in the last twenty years, they have built over twenty prisons and one university while now with the recession/depression, they have to close these prisons down and lay off employees.

Another way that municipal governments could save hundreds of millions would be through installing public transport systems that would reduce pollution and frequent accidents. Cities should be building large parking lots and rapid transit systems with dedicated lanes for busses and cars with two or more people in each vehicle in order to reduce pollution and cut the time of commuting to downtown areas by half. A farther way would be to put in roundabouts like they have in Maritime Canada or in England where instead of stop signs and traffic lights, where all traffic comes to a stop for minutes, there are two-lane roundabouts where the traffic never stops. The vehicles enter and go around to the street where they decide to exit, and this causes the traffic to go at three times the rate that it does with stop signs or traffic lights.

Japan entered the Second World War in 1942 because the United States put tariffs against the goods that they wanted to export to the United States. Now seventy years later, the US government has put a tariff against China, which has ignited a tit-for-tat low-grade trade war over US exports such as broiler chickens, disrupting business elsewhere and deflecting energy from trade issues. Spokespeople at the ITC, the commerce department, and the Office of the US Trade Representative say that they have no comprehensive analysis yet on the broad effect that the tariff has had. The Steel Workers Union believes the tariff has been a success, adding jobs to the United States. It cites anecdotal and other evidence of production expansion across the industry. The bad news is that any decision by the administration will have on the tariff in 2012, an election year. The good news? The statute under which the tariff was issued expires at the end of 2013 and so would any extension. In the meantime, the price of tires across North America has been raised by 20 to 50 percent due to the tariff, which, along with the cost of food, gasoline, etc., creates inflation and increases the cost of living.

A major problem with the various governments, municipal, provincial, or state and federal is when it comes to procurement, the people charged with doling out and monitoring contracts are unparalleled experts. Tickets to expensive sporting events, invitations to luxury suites, free golf, and free lunch plus fishing trips have been doled out in abundance, another reason for costs to escalate.

In Canada last month, the C.D. Howe institute warned that the lucrative defined-benefit pensions of federal employees now all but extinct in the private economy represent 146 billion unfunded liabilities, even according to the numbers in the Public Accounts of Canada. Using fair value accounting with realistic asset yields, the institute said the figure is more like 227 billion. Factor in the total for the defined-benefit pensions of provincial public-sector employees—teachers, nurses, civil servants—and you have a twelve-digit financial promise that must either be broken by the governments or covered by the taxpayers. For example in Flint, Michigan, General Motors workforce has shriveled to eight thousand from eighty thousand in the last decade, and the city population has dropped to about half of the 1960 figure. This is a problem in a lot of cities in the United States where property values have dropped, and hence revenues continue to drop to municipal coffers. Flint, Michigan, has seven hundred employees but pays pension and health care for three thousand retirees. Retirees benefit obligations are estimated at more than eight hundred million. In the United States, the Democratic Party is divided in two with the Liberal Democrats on one side and the Unions on the other side fighting with each other while the ordinary conservative republicans are in a fight with the right-wing Republicans who have formed their own group called the Tea Party movement. The Tea Party group is all for bailing out big out-of-state corporations, raising property taxes on homeowners, and attempting to raise income taxes for almost 90 percent of Americans even though many homeowners are barely able to keep their heads above water. Politicians should be working together to grow the economy, create jobs, and help out the middle class—not working against the people who have been hit the hardest by the recession. For example in the past few months Canada has lost fifty thousand jobs while the United States has created two hundred and fifty thousand jobs. In North America, a large number of high-up ex-government employees either go back to work for the government, drawing full pensions and benefits while collecting an additional salary making more money than they did when they were on the job, which is called double dipping. In the United States, a lot of ex-politicians and government senior bureaucrats work as lobbyists, resulting in big corporations having laws passed that favor their interests to the detriment of the taxpayers.

In Canada and the United States, revenues increase as well as deficits services are being cut back. For example in the United States, chiropractors are barely able to survive with the price for chiropractic services. In Canada, they are averaging fifty dollars per visit while in the United States it is now being cut to fifteen dollars per visit. In Canada, visits to physiotherapists were paid for up to a limit of ten to twelve visits, whereas now, no longer are the treatments paid for individuals who have paid taxes for decades. Instead, you have to pay seventy-five dollars per visit with a lot of working families and seniors unable to afford the costs of physiotherapy.

When the head of Barrett-Jackson's car auctions, one of the largest firms of its kind in the world, was asked how would he improve the way government operates, he replied, "I tend to believe government is more inefficient than not. I like steps such as establishing a state or provincial commerce authority, which enlists the skills and spirit of the private sector to help government operate best. For example, if you run for elected office in Canada, there are no qualifications for a political job in any other field of endeavor. There are certain criteria you should be required to meet to be a member of the municipal, provincial, or federal governments. There should be boards established of probably three individuals comprised of one successful big businessperson, one successful small businessperson, and a successful professional such as an accountant. These three individuals would accept your resume, and if you did not have the necessary credentials to be capable of managing budgets in the billions of dollars, then you would be denied the opportunity to run for political office.

It is now possible for an individual to run for political office with less financing than at any time in the past one hundred years as there are numerous ways that you can connect to your constituents via social media, allowing you to get your views to the public that were unavailable to candidates in the days before the Internet. And by moving the conversation online, it means more people can take part. Yet despite the low barriers, entry blogs do impose some intellectual standards. Errors of fact or logic are spotted, ridiculed, and corrected. Areas of disagreement are highlighted and sometimes even narrowed. Some of the best contributors do not even have blogs of their own, serving instead as referees, leaving thoughtful comments on other people's sites and often crossing party lines. This debate is not always polite, but was it ever? The arguments between John Maynard Keynes and Friedrich Hayek in the 1930s, some of them published in academic journals, were not notable for their tact. Observers often likened their exchanges to the brawling of cats. Both men, one suspects, would have relished taking their battle online. When we read in the media or on the Internet articles that we do not agree with and we may not like what people say, but still we must defend their right to say and publish their own opinions."

In the United States, billionaires fight with other billionaires. An example is the Koch family versus the Pickins family over subsidies and tax credits. It involves Pickins, a longtime oil and gas man who has been lobbying for natural gas subsidies for decades. His cause has become particularly urgent this month. Pickins owns options to buy fifteen million shares of Clean Energy Fuels at $10 per share. According to SEC filings, if congress could pass the NATGAS bill this month, the price of his shares would skyrocket. If the act might drive up Clean Energy shares owned by Pickins, he could exercise his fifteen-million options at ten dollars per share and make more than one hundred million dollars risk free. If the bill does not pass and share prices fell—which have steadily dropped since their mid-November rally—the options might become worthless or at least risky. The Clean Energy Fuel bill is meeting resistance. Because unlike many subsidies which tax everyone a few pennies to give millions to a few special interests, the Pickins bill would severely hurt some powerful players. Pickins's gain would be at the expense of everyone who uses natural gas, which will spike in price. Thanks to increased demand. Primary among natural gas users is the fertilizer industry. One of the world's largest fertilizer sellers is Koch Fertilizer. Koch (owned by pro-free-market businessmen Charles and David Koch, who are in the top 1 percent of the Forbes 400) has led the resistance to Pickens's bill. So in this age of multiplying bailouts and subsidies, what does it take to thwart a billionaire seeking federal handouts? It might just be two multibillionaires not willing to pick up some other guy's tab.

Throughout the world, various countries and their different levels of government are coming up with formulas for reform in austerity. Recession hit countries such as Greece, Portugal, Ireland, Spain; all are finding ways to save money and pay down their debt. Unfortunately, in cities across Canada, little or no effort has been made to find ways to better manage the taxpayer's dollar and deliver more and better services for the revenue received from the taxpayer. Another example is the searches at the various airports, which are conducted at great inconvenience to travelers in general. Ron Paul, one of the candidates for president of the United States, states, "The police state in this country has grown out of control. The government searches at the airport grope and grab our children, our seniors, and our loved ones, and neighbors with disabilities. They do all this while doing nothing to keep us safe." This is an example of what happens when countries go to war in far and distant countries where they kill women and children and the elderly by mistake, while at the same time the young people who are fighting in these wars are being killed and crippled and their way of life destroyed for no good reason. Imagine in North America if the trillions that is spent on war was instead spent on health care, saving the lives of tens of thousands of people and the millions who are suffering from lack of health care, with the funds that is spent on the war effort instead being spent to provide a better quality of life for all that need it. A good example of the police state growing out of control is cameras at red lights and police sitting alongside the road with radar giving out tickets. In Calgary, Alberta, a red light ticket costs approximately three hundred dollars; whereas in Seattle, Washington, the same ticket would cost one hundred and thirty-five dollars. In Los Angeles, red light cameras have been totally eliminated. In Sioux City, Iowa, the mayor says he wants to lower the fine for people caught on camera speeding or running a red light, as the city has become too dependent on revenue from the fines, making it more about money than safety. At the city council's meeting in February, the mayor will introduce an ordinance that will reduce fines from one hundred and eighty-five dollars to one hundred dollars, which would be more in line with common sense and good judgment because it's the people who have to drive daily in order to make a living that have to face the consequences of these overly high fines. For example, Calgary, Alberta, in Canada takes in over thirty million in traffic fines while Edmonton, Alberta, the capital, takes in over fifty million. Washington, DC, the capital of the United States, takes in over ninety million, which shows that fines are being used as a revenue producer rather than a deterrent.

In these inflationary times, if you are retiring in 2012 or in the near future, you would be wise to do the following:

1. Start keeping close track on your spending. Start by going back over the past few months of bills and expenses to get a detailed picture of your spending and expenses. Plan on keeping close tabs on a continuing basis, remembering that some spending may be seasonal such as holidays and presents. Budgeting tools such as Mint.com will enable you to highlight certain spending that won't continue after retirement, such as commuting costs.

2. Fine-tune your income expectations. Recent years haven't been kind to savers. A lousy decade for stocks has been compounded by interest rates that are at historically low levels and seem likely to remain low for years in order to assist the large corporations and billionaires, enabling them to borrow low and buy up assets at fire sale prices. Unfortunately, 401(k) calculators typically don't rely on current yields when projecting your income during retirement. Instead, they usually rely on historical patterns, says a number of financial advisors in the United States.

3. Start thinking about Social Security. Central to your income planning will be Social Security benefits. You won't know the exact size of the check until the first one arrives, but the Social Security Administration can provide an estimate that should be relatively close. You can get an estimate at SocialSecurity.gov, on the phone or in person at your

local office. Be sure to check if you're due additional benefits if you are widowed or divorced. All this leads to one of the most important decisions regarding retirement planning: when to start taking Social Security benefits. In the United States or Canada pension delaying benefits means larger checks in the future, but it may require eating into your savings up front.

4. Build a cash reserve. One thing you want to avoid in retirement: being forced to sell during a steep selloff in the stock or bond markets in order to raise cash to pay bills. The solution is to keep enough cash on hand that you can sell investments when you are comfortable. Many advisers recommend at least a year's worth of money.

5. Get emotionally ready. Amid the focus on financial planning, don't lose sight of the fact that for most people, retirement is a completely new and different experience that can be challenging on an emotional level. While many people can't wait to get out of the 9-to-5 grind, there are those for whom a career was more than a job. It was an identity. You would be wise to consider a part time job, even if it's just something relatively small that you are energetic about and this is something you get to do right now. You will enjoy having something to do and the additional cash flow.

In closing on the part of government inefficiencies, once can never emphasize enough the value of circular infrastructure. Having driven on roundabouts throughout the world, Mattie has found them much more efficient than stop signs or lights. For example, when asked whether visitors struggled to navigate the town's many roundabouts in Carmel, just north of Indianapolis, they responded more than any other city in America. But while locals love them for their speed and efficiencies, visitors are apprehensive; one reason that an out-of-towner was so afraid of the strange formations that he preferred to travel by taxi. The mayor of Carmel built the first roundabout in 1997 after seeing them in Britain. Instead of a four-way intersection with traffic lights, a circular bit of road appeared. It was so successful that today Carmel is the roundabout capital of America, and the mayor plans to rip out all but one of his remaining thirty traffic lights. The modern, safe roundabout first entered service in Britain back in 1966, after it adopted a rule that at all circular intersections traffic entering had to give way or "yield" to circulating traffic. This innovation, along with the sloping curves of the entry and exit of a roundabout, which slow traffic down, created a design that is now found worldwide. Though tens of thousands of roundabouts exist across Europe, America still has only three thousand of them.

One of their main attractions, says Mayor Brainard, is safety. The Insurance Institute for Highway Safety, an independent research group, estimates that converting intersections with traffic lights to roundabouts reduces all crashes by 37 percent and crashes that involve an injury by 75 percent. At traffic lights, the most common accidents are faster, right-angled collisions. These crashes are eliminated with roundabouts because vehicles travel more slowly and in the same direction. The most common accident is a sideswipe, generally no more than a cosmetic annoyance. What locals like, though, is that it is on average far quicker to traverse a series of roundabouts than a similar number of stoplights. Indeed, one national study of ten intersections that could have been turned into roundabouts found that vehicle delays would have been reduced by 62-74 percent (nationally saving 325,000 hours of motorists' time annually). Moreover, because fewer vehicles had to wait for traffic lights, 235,000 gallons of fuel could have been saved. It is amazing how the various municipal and provincial governments have not moved to build roundabouts when evidence has clearly shown that they are the ideal way to move traffic in a town or city.

When business magazines rank the best and worst airport terminals in the world, the best are as follows:

1. Jeddah in Saudi Arabia
2. Eriksson Terminal in Iceland
3. Seoul in South Korea
4. Wellington Terminal in New Zealand
5. New York JFK Airport Terminal 5
6. Singapore Changi International Airport Terminal 3, and it is worth noting that bureaucrats should be sent to Singapore to see for themselves how a city is kept perfectly clean, with traffic moving along at a desired rate, as well as one of the safest cities in the world.
7. Marrakech–Menara Airport Terminal 1 in Morocco
8. Madrid–Barajas Terminal 4 in Spain
9. Carrasco International Airport, Montevideo, Uruguay
10. Bilbao Airport Main Terminal in Spain

The worst airports in the world are as follows:

1. New York JFK Airport Terminal 3
2. Manila Airport Terminal 1 in the Philippines
3. Sheremetyevo Airport Terminal B/C in Moscow
4. Paris-Charles de Gaulle Airport Terminal 3
5. Queen Alia Airport in Amman, Jordan
6. LaGuardia Airport Terminal 5 in New York

7. Newark Liberty International Airport Terminal B
8. Paris Beauvais Airport
9. Chicago Midway International Airport

In 2010, the disaster of the sinking of the *Costa Concordia* has raised questions about the safety regarding the ever-increasing size of cruise ships. Even though experts say that these new megaships have the latest safety and navigation technology and pose little risk to passengers. The *Concordia*—a ship more than 250 yards long—was carrying more than 4,200 passengers and crew when it hit a reef on the seventeenth of January 2012 off the Italian coast resulting in the ship being flooded with water and listing to one side. At least a dozen have died and another twenty are unaccounted for. Industry watchers also placed the blame on human error. Mattie has traveled on nearly all cruise lines and on all major oceans in the world during his lifetime, and he and his wife prefer not to sail on a ship larger than fifteen hundred people due to the extensive and lengthy searches now performed since 9-11. He feels that he has been inconvenienced by the lengthy delays, which really serve no useful purpose.

Mattie noticed during a recent visit with a friend who was celebrating his ninety-first birthday that the elderly gentleman kept eyeing the various ladies at the swimming pools at the clubhouses and in restaurants when they were dining out, so Mattie has decided to comment and provide some statistics on singles in America as even though many people maintain that they pay no attention to others, they certainly enjoy ogling others throughout the day whether at work, driving on the streets, or traveling on holidays. The majority of people wonder do individuals have sex on their first date, a questionnaire in *USA Today* states that 55 percent say they have. Particularly says sex therapist Laura Burnam, noting that many people meet online and feel that they know each other by [the first date]. She quotes, "It's almost as if by the time they've had the first physical date, it might have been the equivalent of three dates." And she thinks this online sharing has definitely escalated some of the familiarity and quickness which people get into sexual scenarios, she says. The online dating services have taken the place of the old mail-order brides back in the early days of the Wild West when communities were mostly all male, and these men would have to send away by letter to acquire a bride to share their home and future in the West.

Among other romance-related findings are the following:

- 58 percent of singles have had a one-night stand (65 percent of men and 51 percent of women)
- 44 percent had *not* experienced infidelity; of those who had, 36 percent

said a partner had been unfaithful, 8 percent had personally been unfaithful, and 13 percent said both were

- 60 percent said a partner having a series of one-night stands was "more unacceptable" than a three-month affair with one person; 40 percent said a three-month affair was worse

In a survey of men:

1. Over 20 percent said if they met a partner who makes more money, it would make them more acceptable.
2. If the individual was career driven 30 percent, said it would make them more acceptable.
3. About 25 percent would be impressed if they were not driven to have children.
4. And 5 percent did not care about the ladies' career.

If you agree with these statistics, then it will satisfy your curiosity, if not, feel free to conduct your own survey. Good luck and enjoy.

CHAPTER 16

In regard to the future in 2012, the outlook is very poor for the next four to five years as companies such as HSBC Holdings, Europe's biggest lender, announced that it is laying off thirty thousand people by the end of 2013. Bank of America, the second largest US lender, said it too would be cutting thirty thousand jobs. Both banks are trimming about 10 percent of their workforces. In November, BNP Paribas, France's largest bank, said it will cut thousands of jobs in its corporate and investment banking unit; and UniCredit, Italy's biggest bank, said it plans to eliminate over six thousand positions by 2015. Faced with higher capital requirements, the failure of exotic financial products and diminished proprietary trading, the industry may experience more than a slight dip investment bankers have now been convinced that we are living in a limited period where things are much more difficult and could be a substantial period before the world comes back to normal, says the chairman of Zurich-based UBS.

In general, banks, insurers, money management companies in North America have announced fifty thousand job cuts this year. That's more than twice last year's total. That coupled with the several hundred thousand jobs that were laid off in 2008. It is predicted that Wall Street will not regain its lost jobs until about 2023, states an economist at Moody's Analytics. Several hundred thousand are being laid off in Western Europe. As well as three hundred thousand in the city of London while in interviews, dozens of people who have lost jobs at the Royal Bank of Scotland, and Jefferies described a growing pessimism about their future prospects, still companies such as Goldman Sachs set aside ten billion which is equal to two hundred and ninety-two thousand, eight hundred and thirty-six dollars for each of its thirty-four thousand two hundred workers as of September thirtieth. That's almost six times the median household income in the United States, where 49.1 million people live in poverty according to the Census Bureau data, which indicates that there is an ever-growing gap between the rich and the poor.

The big central banks get infusions of cash from the federal government but still loathe lending. Banks are hoarding rather than lending, a record four hundred and eighty-nine billion Euros, equal to six hundred and twenty-five billion US dollars that has been injected into the banking system, thwarting attempts by policymakers to avert a credit crunch. Almost all the money loaned to the five hundred and twenty-three Euro area lenders wound up back on deposit at the banks.

Lenders across Europe have vowed to trim at least a trillion in loans from their balance sheet over the next two years, either by selling assets or not renewing credit lines according to data combined by *Bloomberg Businessweek*. This will continue to keep Europe and the United States economy weak as banks shore up their own finances and refuse to lend, thereby stifling the economy in general.

The Carlyle Group is a Washington buyout firm that is preparing to go public this year, wants to bar future shareholders from filing individual class actions. The firm revised its offering documents to say that investors that buy company shares must settle any subsequent claims with Carlyle through arbitration in Washington that could limit the ability of stockholders to win big awards for securities-law violations such as fraud, state several attorneys. This would result in banning the shareholders' rights to file lawsuits.

We have discussed statements made by various individuals in the financial sector who state, "Sometimes it's better to do nothing. Other times if you do receive a tip that has been made public that tens of thousands of others will also know about a particular company, and since they will invest, there will be little opportunity for you to make money." Mattie has always found that the vast majority of individuals will wait to make up their mind, so if you should get word in any way that a company has the potential such as a utility with a new pipeline, a railroad that has a tremendous future, or an oil company that has just made a very large strike, then it's wise to move immediately and buy the shares. Even though they may have possibly started to rise, you may still wind up making large amounts of money in a very short time.

Mattie will list a number of companies that he feels are good investments for 2012. There a lot of people traveling on Canada's major airline, Air Canada; and since it trades at only a dollar and forty cents as of the end of October 2011, it could be a good buy. ATCO, an Alberta company, has also has extremely large holdings in utilities in one of the fastest growing and most profitable areas in the world and as of the end of October trades at sixty-two dollars, this could show an increase in the future and is a very stable stock. Any bank in Canada, as there are only a half a dozen major banks, whereas the in the

United States, there are a thousand and the banking system is in much better financial shape than other banks in the world. Banks such as the Bank of Montreal, Bank of Nova Scotia, Canadian Imperial Bank of Commerce, the Toronto Dominion Bank, and the Western Bank which are located in one of the most prosperous parts of the world are all good potential investments. In communications such as BCE Bell, Bell Aliant, Tellus, etc., are other good investments. Canadian oil sands in the oil and gas business as well as a fast-growing company called Canadian Natural Resources, Canadian Tire in retail which is almost as successful as Wal-Mart, Canadian Utilities, and Gas Transmission Lines. Both Canadian National Railway and Canadian Pacific Railway (CPR) in transportation although Canadian National Railway is now trading in the seventy-five-dollar range and has had a rapid increase in recent times. Enbridge and TransCanada in pipelines are both good companies including the world's largest Caterpillar dealer, which trades at twenty-one dollars at the end of October 2011, is also a good investment including Flint Energy Services, which is a major oil and gas service company and only trades at eleven dollars. Fortis Inc., which trades at thirty-three dollars, is another good investment. The Mullen Group, which is big in transportation and oil and gas services and trades at the twenty-dollar mark always does well when oil is at a high of around one hundred a barrel. But always bear in mind with oil and gas stocks that when the oil boom picks up and oil goes from thirty dollars to the hundred-dollar range, the oil stocks will double or triple; and when oil drops back to fifty dollars a barrel, they will drop back down, and this will let you know that it's time to buy their stocks when oil drops in price per barrel. Gold and silver is high at present, but should it drop back in price, then it is wise to buy companies that are in mining such as Barrick, Pan American Silver, etc. PetroBakken Energy only trades at eight dollars per share and is located in one of the largest oil fields in North America and therefore could have some potential. Potash Corp of Saskatchewan only trades in the fifty-dollar range and has traded at a high of over two hundred dollars, and since the price of agricultural crops is at an all-time high, this company has a good future. Research in Motion, a company involved in technology which has been highly successful with the Blackberry but now has had difficulty competing with Apple's iPhone, has dropped to the sixteen-dollar range, and this could be a good stock for the future. Royal Bank of Canada is one of the largest banks in Canada trading around the forty-eight-dollar mark, which should be a good investment, including Suncor Energy, which is in the oil sands in northern Alberta and trades around the thirty-dollar mark with increasing demand for oil and the potential for major pipelines to the United States to the south and to the west coast to supply China could have a good future. TransAlta is another Canadian company held by Mattie, who is engaged in electric utilities and trades in the twenty-two dollar range. This company could also see a rise in its share value. WestJet Airlines has grown from a few airplanes based on the Southwest Airlines model, and Southwest has been one of the few airlines in the world that has continuously made money; and as WestJet is planning to buy another seventy to one hundred planes in the near future and is only trading in the thirteen dollar range could pose as a good buy.

Mattie was a large holder of stock in Yellow Media, which prints the yellow pages for the phonebook market, with the rise of the Internet, he felt they had no future, so he sold out when they were very high in 2007—when they were trading at forty to fifty dollars per share. They are now trading at twenty-two cents. This is an example if you're going to be in the stock market, you either have to be lucky or able to anticipate the future.

One can never repeat often enough how wise it is to buy land in the best location possible, depending on how much money you have to invest, and bearing in mind that it's always wise to take in partners as over time for one reason or another they will eventually sell out, and you will wind up holding a valuable piece of property, plus land that is suitable for subdivision grows in price. It is always wise to buy land that has the possibility to be zoned for residential or industrial use as once you get land zoned for development, it grows in price astronomically. Always bear in mind that it should have the following:

1. Proximity to urban infrastructure
2. Good road access and allowances
3. Bear in mind the timeline because it's getting tougher to find land that has not already increased in value, and you may have to buy farther away from major municipalities; therefore you should be prepared to hold the land for a longer period of time and be financially capable of doing so.
4. Always bear in mind the potential of various environmental issues. Many individuals and companies have bought land only to find out that it had environmental problems which resulted in them losing money rather than making money.

It's getting very hard to buy land with mineral rights, but if you can, you will be able to make a killing, but you have to be careful and investigate that property and mineral rights can be contained in two separate deeds in almost every province. But this information is a matter of public record, so you only have to go to the government office to get that information, or a lawyer that is well versed in the type of purchase of these sorts of resources.

If you're just starting out in the residential market, it's wise to buy an older house in a good area and remodel it. Particularly if it has a basement suite and is zoned for two-family living, you can either live in the top level and rent out the basement, or you can rent out both top and bottom levels and double your source of revenue. And if you have renovated the property and rented both levels, you can probably double or triple your money.

If you don't have enough disability coverage and you cannot afford more, there is other help available if you paid into Canada Pension Plan for a set period of time, usually for four of the last six years before your disability occurred; then you may be entitled to collect from the federal government CPP disability benefits program. The injury may have been long ago, but the CPP does cover disabilities that prevent you from working.

When traveling, it's very important to buy travel insurance as some areas such as the United States hospitalization costs and medical bills can cost anywhere from fifteen thousand dollars a day to twenty thousand dollars per day. For example, a two-day stay in the hospital for infection can cost you thirty thousand dollars, and if you have a plugged artery, a stent will be one hundred thousand plus, and bypass surgery or a stroke can cost you two hundred thousand plus. And you have to make sure that you have a form made-up and take it to your general practitioner and specialist and have him fill it out if you had any pre-existing conditions; otherwise the insurance company will deny your claim. But it's important to bear in mind that if the insurance companies have a habit of denying claims, you can launch a class action against them as well as settle with the various parties involved for fifty cents or less on the dollar as this is quite common, particularly in the United States, and is something well worth knowing. The same also applies that if you're needing services that have a lengthy waiting period in Canada or England for example, you can get these done almost immediately in the United States and wind up when paying cash getting the services for fifty cents on the dollar.

Another way, when purchasing home furnishings or other items such as a new coffee table that sells for approximately fourteen hundred dollars, but should you wish to buy an imitation of one of the name brands, you can purchase an identical table for four hundred and fifty dollars, a third the price. This is only one example of a thousand knockoffs that you can buy for 10 percent to a third the cost that you would pay for the real thing, and nobody will ever know the difference. Theo Fleury states that making millions and losing it is a tough way to learn, but it is one thing that can teach you that money doesn't make the man; it's what you do with your success. If you don't teach other people how to be successful, then you have wasted your time. If you don't pass on what you have learned, what you know, and inspire others to become better people, then success in itself means nothing. This is why Mattie felt there was a real need to write this book.

CHAPTER 17

Health

The most important thing in your life is health because without health, the quality of your life is diminished, and it's extremely important to eat the proper diet as well as keep your weight down as low as possible and exercise as much as you have free time for. With regard to diet, it's recommended by nutritionists and dieticians that you stay on a diet that's low in fried and fatty foods, a limited amount of alcohol, not eat too much sweets—such as candy, cookies, and cakes— and processed foods. In addition, eat 60 percent or whole wheat bread rather than white bread, keep dairy products to a minimum, and eat very little at fast-food outlets and junk food.

Should you be traveling and encounter bouts of diarrhea, avoid raw fruits and vegetables, high-fiber foods, and foods that will cause gas in your stomach such as onions, beans, cabbage, spicy foods, and soda pop. Also, stay away from rich fatty foods, caffeine, alcohol, and chocolate until your system returns to normal. Remember the brat diet (bread or banana, rice, apple sauce and tea). Alcohol in moderate consumption may cut heart attack risk by raising your HDL cholesterol and thinning your blood. It may also protect the brain against age-related dementia and may provide happier moods. On the minus side, it can provide mood swings, aggression, and can be addictive. It can also interact with your medications and can, over time, cause cancer. It has been stated that green leafy vegetables, orange juice, corns, asparagus, peas, lean meat, fish, poultry, eggs, whole grains, etc. are good to ward off Alzheimer's.

It is also recommended that you drink eight glasses of water per day in order to ward of dehydration as lack of water can cause fatigue, headaches, etc.

It is wise to cut saturated fats by eating leaner cuts of meat and cut back on the size of your meat portions, as well as eating low-fat cheese. It is also recommend cooking with olive or vegetable oil instead of butter or margarine and eating baked potatoes instead of fries and using low-fat yogurt. Bananas are an excellent source of potassium and vitamin B as well as fiber, and they make an excellent snack. Beets are also another good source of fiber and potassium. In order to control your blood pressure, fresh vegetables and fruits are good for your diet, and it is wise to limit canned and processed foods because they contain added salt. Again, it is wise to limit fatty foods if you have high blood pressure. Blueberries are an excellent source of vitamin C, and for those with celiac disease, it is wise to limit your intake of bread. Butter and margarine are good sources of vitamins A and D but are high in calories which come from fats and may increase the risk of heart disease. Also, both butter and margarine may be high in salt.

Mattie never drank tea or coffee and only on rare occasions drank soda pop, and even though he had a sweet tooth, he always tried to limit his sugar intake.

Low-carb diets are followed by a number of people, but sugars are a major source of energy and fiber. Another, carbohydrate is also good for your health, so although some carbohydrates are bad for your health, not all are problematic. It is also a good idea to watch the newspapers for advertisements listing ultrasound tests of the heart and arteries as these are good prevention packages for heart disease, stroke, and aneurysm. Usually you can get approximately six tests for under two hundred dollars, which is very reasonable and give you notice of various problems that may be arising of which you are not aware. If there is a history of heart trouble or stroke problems in your family, or any type of cardiovascular disease in your family, it is wise to follow a heart healthy diet, which is available from dieticians and nutritionists, and will extend your good health for many years as well as add years to your life. Carrots are not only a good source beta-carotene and vitamin A as well as fiber and potassium. Carrots also prevent night blindness and helps lower your cholesterol levels. Not only are they a very delicious vegetable. Cheeses are high in protein and calcium as well as vitamin B, and a number of cheeses prevent tooth decay. The negative side of cheeses is that they are high in saturated fat and sodium.

Type 1 diabetes is another disease of the young people; whereas type 2 diabetes attacks older individuals. It is important if you have diabetes to keep your weight down, drink plenty of fluids and shower in warm—not hot—water, keep your skin moist with daily application of a lotion after bathing or showering, and wear cotton underclothes and use a humidifier to prevent your house from becoming too dry in the winter due to forced air heating. Diabetes can affect up to one in five people, so it's a very common disease, and individuals should check their blood sugar to make sure that they're not suffering from high sugar levels. It is also good to be careful to not believe everything you read as a sullen chef on TV had diabetes while continuing to dish up deep-fried, high-calorie, high-fat recipes on television. People who followed her cooking shows would certainly be misled with regard to diabetes and dieting.

When traveling, it is wise to consume plenty of bottled water should you be hit by a case of diarrhea, and it is wise to eat a diet rich in bananas, rice, applesauce, and tea. Baked potatoes are good, providing you do not eat the skins. Boiled or poached eggs or any other bland food will help your stomach. The bread/bananas, rice, applesauce, and tea is called the BRAT diet. It is also wise to avoid juices, salads, fruits and whole grains, alcohol, and caffeine for a minimum of seventy-two hours. If you want to keep your weight off, some tips are as follows:

1. Eat breakfast and don't skip meals.
2. Choose your carbohydrates carefully.
3. It is wise to avoid cornflakes, white rice, and mashed potatoes while at the same time choosing bulky foods that contain lots of fiber also downsize your portions to approximately half and eat slowly while drinking plenty of fluids, particularly water, and this will help you with your diet. Also, it is wise to have small portions of your favorite foods in order to treat yourself to the foods that you like.

Eggs are an excellent source of protein, B vitamins, vitamin A, zinc, and iron as well as a good source of antioxidants; but it is always wise to cook your eggs well as they can be a source of salmonella. When storing food, it is always wise to bear in mind to keep bacon in the refrigerator for seven days or in the freezer for no more than a month, butter up to three months, and in the freezer for nine months. Chicken or fowl up to two days or in the freezer for up to one year, eggs up to five weeks in the fridge, and eggs cannot go in the freezer. Lunch meat in an open package should be kept for two weeks in the fridge, two months in the freezer. Milk, seven days in the refrigerator and three months in the freezer.

If you are planning to lose weight, fruits, vegetables, and berries are the most appetizing and some of the best foods to eat such as apples, pineapples, grapes, bananas, peaches and pears, oranges, etc. Not only are they tasty, but they are extremely healthy and will help you keep your weight down. Tomatoes are an excellent food rich in compounds that have reduced risk to various diseases. Articles have been written that tomatoes are excellent in preventing cancer, diabetes, heart disease, arthritis, etc. Mattie always ate tomatoes at least twice a day for over half a century and continuously ate either a tomato sandwich or a bacon, lettuce, and tomato sandwich. As we have mentioned before, garlic lowers high blood pressure and cholesterol, and some articles state that it may help fight certain cancers as well as infections and nasal congestion. On the negative side, it can cause bad breath and indigestion if eaten raw, but at present, there are capsules, particularly the Kyolic brand, and Mattie gives credit to these capsules for extending his life from heart disease for twenty years.

Mattie also had a problem with a hiatal hernia, but he was able to keep it in control by eating small, frequent meals, high-fiber foods that included lots of vegetables, while at the same time not drinking coffee, very limited alcohol, controlling his weight, avoiding soda pop, fatty foods, smoking, etc. Legumes contain more protein than any other plant-derived food; they're also a good source of starch, B-complex vitamins, potassium, iron, zinc, and other minerals. Most are high in fiber. All legumes need to be cooked, and in some people, it may cause intestinal gas. Lettuce and any other greens salad are low in calories and high in beta-carotene, vitamin C, calcium, and potassium but should be well washed before eating because they can cause stomach infection and never eaten in third world countries. People who suffer from muscle cramps should consume low-fat dairy products for calcium; potassium-rich foods such as bananas, citrus fruits, potatoes, milk; carbohydrates such as rice, legumes, and pasta; whole grain breads and cereals; and lots of water to maintain the circulation and flush waste products from your circulation. Avoid caffeine, soda pop, salted foods, and smoking. Oats are an excellent source of soluble fiber as well as calcium, iron, vitamin E, and other vitamins. Mattie always ate oatmeal every morning with low-fat yogurt rather than sugar in milk, which made for an excellent breakfast. While on the weekend, he'll be having ham and eggs with toast and on occasion potatoes. Oranges and parsnips are both excellent foods with parsnips particularly high in calories and fiber and coupled with potatoes and carrots, which are an excellent source of vitamin C and potassium. Peaches are also excellent as a source of beta-carotene, and they can be eaten fresh or preserved or in pies, jams, etc. Rhubarb is another plant that contains vitamin C, potassium, and fiber and is excellent as a jam or in pies particularly if coupled with strawberries. Salsas are made by mixing fine-chopped vegetables or fruits with garlic, citrus juice, and other ingredients. Homemade salsa from fresh fruits or vegetables is virtually fat free, high in fiber, and low in calories as well as rich in vitamin C and beta-carotene. Mattie would buy frozen pizzas for a dollar a pizza on sale; and upon putting them in the oven to cook, he would top them up with extra onions, tomatoes, bacon, ham, salsa, mushrooms, etc., resulting in a pizza that was three times as thick with a very thin crust and three times the flavor and would serve it to guests. They would all comment that they had never eaten a pizza as delicious and would ask where they could get a similar pizza. Mattie would then inform them that these were bought pizzas for a dollar instead of ten dollars and enriched with all the various ingredients, which were homemade. It is very important to develop a strategy for coping with stress because if you have symptoms of rapid heartbeat and chest pain, this can be caused by stress and will ultimately lead to heart disease. Also rapid breathing, dizziness or lightheadedness, tingling sensations in the hands and feet, backache, frequent headaches, diarrhea or constipation, heartburn or other types of digestion problems. Stress will cause difficulty in concentrating and sleeping, and chronic fatigue, resulting in not getting proper rest, anxiety, no appetite, and difficulty coping with life in general and decreased enjoyment in various activities and events. Yoga is an excellent way of getting clear of stress. Also, simply just sitting relaxed and deeply breathing in and out while quoting any simple phrase over and over again will help relieve your stress. It is wise to set aside a few minutes each day to sit quietly with your eyes closed and relax. Also, exercise regularly which will help lift your moods; listen to your favorite music as you are practicing your relaxation techniques with yoga, meditation, and deep breathing exercises. Do not rush or worry about things that need to be done. If you have problems, it is good to talk them over with a friend. And for people who like animals, a pet can be a very relaxing companion.

For people who have had strokes, it is important to eat lots of fresh fruits and vegetables for vitamin C, potassium, fish, oat, bran, vegetables, fruits, and garlic, which helps to prevent blood clots while at the same time limiting dairy products, high-fat animal products, and salt which will raise your blood pressure. Limit alcohol and avoid smoking as well as it is very important to keep your weight down.

It is recommended in numerous articles to drink green tea as it may help cholesterol problems. Researchers have stated that people who drink a half a dozen cups of green tea per day have better cholesterol levels, and people of oriental heritage who drink large quantities of green tea usually live long and healthy lives. Turnips are another vegetable which are rarely served in restaurants or at any meal. Although they are a useful source of vitamin C, calcium, and potassium, a low-calorie source of fiber, and it has been suggested that they may help protect against cancer. Turnips come in various colors such as white, yellow, or pink. Since we have been through the various foods alphabetically starting with A and now with W, water is the most vital ingredient in life. Water has no calories or nutrients, but a human can only go a few days without it. As suggested previously, a minimum of eight glasses of water a day is needed to keep the bodies system functioning properly. If an individual's urine is pale then this indicates that they are drinking enough water. Should it be dark or bright yellow, then you should increase your water intake. It is not necessary to buy bottled water as there are excellent filters on the market now that can filter your water in your residence or place of business at a quarter the cost of buying filtered water. These filter systems can be as cheap as an inexpensive countertop pitcher, an under-the-sink unit that can cost you up to one thousand dollars, or a lot of modern fridges have built-in filtration systems in the units when you buy them. One of the best foods you can eat is yogurt, an excellent source of calcium and phosphorus and contains vitamin A and B. Low-fat yogurt is much more digestible than milk for people with a lactose intolerance, colitis, etc. There are excellent brands of yogurt that have been manufactured in Greece originally and now all over the world, which are excellent for individuals who have various health problems.

It is wise to be careful when eating meat products as many livestock farms use antibiotics to kill drug-resistant germs. According to various studies, eating large quantities of meat can lower your resistance to antibiotics, should you encounter a stomach infection of which there are a large number. In Mattie's case, he had the unfortunate experience of contracting a stomach infection in Arizona, and while in the hospital, he caught *Clostridium. difficile*, more commonly known as C. diffile. This hospital infection, as a rule, kills 99 percent of the people who contract this infection; and because it is usually caused by poor hygiene in restaurants or hospitals, health care officials usually put the cause of death not as *C. difficil* but as old age, heart failure, or pneumonia as they are always concerned about lawsuits. This infection hospitalized Mattie for three months and caused him to lose over fifty pounds. By the time he got an excellent specialist after months of hospitalization in Calgary, Alberta, an intestinal specialist called Dr. Kareemi who gave him a newer type of a very strong drug called Vancomycin. Upon taking this particular drug, Mattie was able to check out of the hospital within a day and had to learn to walk again as he was so extremely weak caused by going to the bathroom up to forty times per day. At least as one of his friends said people could no longer say he was full of crap as he had lost fifty pounds. In the United States, a noted singer was unhappy with her surgeon, and she posted on a website her problems, only to find out to her dismay that a jury in Phoenix, Arizona, awarded the surgeon an outrageous settlement of twelve million dollars, which was rather immaterial as the singer was spending money in a lifestyle that she had become accustomed to and didn't have a million dollars to her name; nevertheless, he wouldn't repeal the judgment, so not only can you have severe problems in hospitals, but you have to be careful what you say as it can come back to bite you in the butt. It is also wise to have a blood pressure monitor and take your blood pressure morning and night as Mattie has known of hundreds of people who have taken strokes who had high blood pressure and did not get immediate treatment resulting in becoming physically crippled or resulting in death. If you feel the signs of a stroke such as the ones outlined before, including confusion, unresponsive, not understanding what others say, shakes with no known cause, vision problems, facial problems, slurred speech, weakness on one side of the body, numbness, tingling and possibly pain, difficulty walking due to lack of balance or coordination as well as dizziness or nausea, it is important to get to the hospital immediately. Mattie has had a stroke and fortunately was within ten minutes of a hospital and with an ambulance within minutes resulting that the cardiologist was able to give TPA (tissue plasminogen activator), a drug that can break up blood clots, resulting in Mattie being out of the hospital in several days and fortunately returning back to normal.

Other problems that can be very serious are when you get problems with your joints such as what Mattie had on one occasion from golfing, and he went to a walk-in clinic where they gave him prednisone, which caused a reaction with his heart medication resulting in giving Mattie a heart attack in which he was very lucky to survive, but there is little chance of success in suing a small clinic and trying to prove damages. And should you go for surgery on knees or other joints, it is very important, studies have shown, to have a surgeon do it, who has done hundreds of operations. Should your surgeon only have done a dozen operations, the chances of success are much less than if you hire a surgeon who is fully experienced with your particular type of operation.

February is heart health awareness month, and if you're willing to take the trip to Arizona where you can golf, watch NASCAR, play hockey, join spring training for baseball, plus dozens of other activities. You can also visit over one hundred and fifty clinics such as wellness clinics which includes diabetes, CPR, blood pressure, etc. Alzheimer's, general support groups, cancer support/networking groups, various groups for arthritis, and other clinics for seniors, where you can become aware of nearly every health problem that you may encounter in the future.

It is important to get various checks for cancer such as colonoscopies at least every five years when you reach the age of fifty as well as ultrasounds, x-rays, and MRIs so that you can stay on top of your health before something drastic occurs.

We can never repeat often enough in regard to preserving your health. Again some of the suggestions that you can do is everything that is good for the heart is good for the brain as well. So it is important to not smoke, stimulate your mind, avoid high blood pressure; and if you have either disease, manage them properly. Watch your weight; do exercise as it is important for people to be physically active throughout life and beginning with adulthood, if possible even if it is only walking. Avoid head injuries; eat right, stay away from diets high in bad fats and consume plenty of fresh fruits and vegetables, whole grains, etc. Avoid excessive alcohol or drugs as alcohol abuse can put you at risk for stroke. Report all your problems to the proper medical authorities. If you suspect a problem, get evaluated by a doctor who is knowledgeable and experienced on the subject, a specialist if possible. Don't ignore stroke signs, as a stroke can change your brain function almost instantaneously.

It is important to live a lifestyle and make a New Year's resolution to have the courage to live an enjoyable life. Do not overwork; if you're unhappy; express your feelings as it is foolish to stay angry. It is very important to stay in touch with your friends and family, and in general let yourself be happier and healthier while enjoying your family, your time on a daily basis.

People recovering from a heart attack or severe chest pain are unlikely to suffer another heart-related problem if they take a new blood-thinning drug along with the standard anti-clotting medicine. One large study has pointed out the drug xarelto, but this benefit has a cost, a greater risk of serious bleeding usually in the digestive tract. Nevertheless, a low dose of the drug substantially cut the risk of dying during a large study.

Xarelto is approved now in higher doses for preventing strokes in people with irregular heart rhythm and preventing blood clots after joint surgeries. It is stated that it works in a better way than aspirin and older blood thinners do. The drug is expensive, and the higher doses now cost approximately seven dollars a day.

Drugs are made all over the world at present, and fake drugs have become big business; counterfeiting no longer solely occurs in poor nations. An example is the discovery of a fake version of the well-used cancer medicine Avastin, which is circulating in the United States and raising fears that the multibillion-dollar drug counterfeiting trade is increasingly making inroads in the United States. The practice has largely been relegated to poor countries with lax regulations. But with more medicines and drug ingredients for sale in the United States being manufactured overseas, American authorities are afraid more counterfeits will find their way into this country, putting patients' lives at risk. The Avastin discovery follows other recent instances in the United States of counterfeiting, involving such drugs as Viagra, the cholesterol medicine Lipitor, and the weight-loss pill Alli. Therefore, it is wise to read up on all drugs to make sure that you are purchasing the best possible pharmaceuticals.

Another three ways to protect your heart is getting your teeth cleaned regularly; or as Mattie has done for the past twenty-five years, mix up a solution of hydrogen peroxide, salt, and baking soda. This solution will protect your gums, keep your breath fresh, and will result in hardly any cavities or gum disease over the years. Secondly, it is wise to not drink anything with sugar in it as people who drink beverages that contain sugar-sweetened drinks are four times as likely to have high levels of unhealthy blood fats when compared with people who do not drink sodas. Thirdly, it is wise to check your vitamin D level as well as well as blood pressure in order that you do not suffer from heart disease.

When receiving medical treatment, always be aware that a large number of people, including those who are in the hospitals, doctors, etc., have a high rate, which is caused by slow payment by the insurance companies. As a rule, insurance companies and in the US Medicare and Medicaid only pay 40 to 50 percent of the medical bills actual cost; therefore, if you're insurance does not wish to cover your costs, you may wish to negotiate a lower price with whoever you are dealing with, particularly in the United States. Mattie was hospitalized for two days with a stomach infection in Arizona, resulting in a bill for almost thirty thousand dollars. His insurance broker in Alberta had used a new plan from a company in Toronto, Ontario, called World Travel Protection where rather than mail you forms, they asked you a few questions over the phone. Mattie answered the questions that he was asked by the insurance agent on the phone, which only took a few minutes and then was asked for his credit card, and that was the end of the discussion for travel insurance. Normally they would send out a form, and Mattie or his doctor would fill it out to make sure there was proper coverage; but in this case, the broker in Alberta was using this new type of application. The insurance was put through with AIG, a company which stands for American International Group, a company out of New York. AIG changed its name to Chartis in Canada and in the States to Travel Guard Insurance as there was a claim of looting of $4.3 billion in stock. AIG was basically broke and received one hundred and eighty-five billion dollars in bailout money from the government of the United States; therefore when the time came to pay Mattie's claim, they refused, stating that he had not answered all questions regarding his health. Simply, this was not Mattie's fault as the agent did not ask him very many questions and filled out the questionnaire herself, so the fault totally lies with the one insurance broker, with the placement agency in Toronto who had come up with the new program, and with the bankrupt American insurer who states in their Internet information that they have forty thousand people who work on reviewing and denying claims. So if you have any health problems, it's very important to have your doctor fill out your application in order to make sure that you have insurance, although in most cases insurance companies will not insure for preexisting conditions. Therefore, if you've had a minor heart attack, they will not insure you should you have another heart attack in the future; but should you break your finger, they will come to your rescue and pay your claim. This is another example of insurance being good for the insurance company and those involved with them and in many cases being of no use to the insured. In Mattie's case, he is going to launch a class action lawsuit as well as participating in a media program on the problems concerning travel insurance.

When traveling for brief vacations, the main areas are Mexico, Cuba, Dominican Republic, and Jamaica. These make up the vast bulk of the traffic to the Caribbean and for good reasons. The larger islands are going to be cheaper, and they have well-developed tourist industries and infrastructure. There is competition between resorts and numerous flights in and out. The smaller islands are much more expensive and cater to a more upscale clientele. Cuba is a low-priced area for a holiday, and Mattie had found it much better than the Dominican Republic or Jamaica as he had been to both; he did not enjoy his holiday as he paid almost a thousand dollars a day and found out to his dismay that he got a holiday that was worth approximately one hundred dollars a day. After complaining to Air Canada Vacations, the large Spanish hotel chain, etc., he was unable to get any satisfaction therefore would not recommend either place, including Air Canada Vacations or Sol Melia Hotels due to the fact that even though they are expensive, you can have a detrimental holiday. They provide all-inclusive meals, but in a lot of cases, the staff does not understand English. The meals are mostly buffet, which you can get in America for ten dollars a meal, or otherwise eat for approximately fifteen dollars a day and get a hotel in the southern United States for sixty to one hundred dollars a day so why pay more for less. They also include all the free liquor you can drink, but in a lot of states in the United States, due to low taxes, you can buy fifty-two ounces of alcohol for ten dollars. This would cost you fifty dollars in Canada; therefore, alcohol is almost as cheap as soda. It is wise to do substantial research before you book your vacation, or you will be disappointed because there is a common misperception that all-inclusive are all the same everywhere—they're not. Some have shoddy hotel rooms, are situated away from the beach, and serve poor restaurant meals and cheap brands of liquor. Nor can you judge the quality of the resort solely by the number of stars it's been accorded because they can have a four- or five-star rating and be the equivalent of a two-star hotel in America. Some people like to check websites such as Tripadvisor.com to see what previous guests have had to say about their stay, although you have to bear in mind that people are more likely to write in to complain rather than to praise a particular resort; but if you see a bunch of negative comments, then you may want to stay away. Different resorts come with different price points. When cost is the sole concern, you are going to notice it in the food quality and service quality. As stated by a lot of travel writers, it is important when going on all-inclusive trips in the sun or cruises to you go through a regular travel agent who will be there to help you when problems arise. For young people who just want a beach and a lounge chair, then you can purchase this sort of accommodation, but they are not luxurious. Nowadays a lot of travelers bypass agents and book directly online; this is promoted as cheaper than dealing with a regular travel agency, but this is a misstatement of facts as well as last-minute sales. Mattie has been in the travel agency business and, at one time, owned the fastest-growing travel agency in America before he sold it and last-minute seat sales are usually sitting back by the toilet in cramped seats and perhaps with a stop en route to your destination; therefore it is highly recommended if you're going to buy, you can check online and see what's available. But always at the end, when doing all-inclusive or cruises, go directly to a specialist and then you will be almost positive that you will have a most happy holiday. Again, one can never emphasize enough that you book early because prices usually increase on a day-to-day basis. The closer one gets to the actual departure date, although if you are ready to leave on a few hours' notice, you can find heavy discounts, especially if you're not too picky about where you go. You will have few options, but the savings can be substantial on rare occurrences. Also, consider booking during the shoulder season. December through April is always the high season in the sun, and the summer months are the high season for a lot of cruises, but you can usually find substantial savings by booking the shoulder seasons on either side like late November or May. It's always a balancing act between getting the great weather and the low prices.

Now that you're reasonably healthy and have saved your money, invested well, and are looking for retirement in your fifties or sixties, make sure you buy in an area where you will be happy; and the only way to do this is to rent for a small part of time prior to buying a winter or summer home in a retirement area. If you like to golf, then areas such as Florida or Arizona have numerous golf courses at prices from forty dollars for eighteen holes to hundreds of dollars for the same golf privileges. Some areas will have RV sites, double-wide trailer homes, condos, duplexes, or houses. It is important to check out with an experienced real estate and friends and business acquaintances who have already bought to find out just what is right for you and yours in your retirement.

The Arizona desert can probably not to be beaten for the numerous activities such as golf, NASCAR racing, spring training baseball games, hockey, football, basketball, car shows, hiking, fishing, boating, etc. And if you wish to participate in a lot of different activities, it is important to move into a community that may have bus tours, ceramics, quilting, pool, woodworking shops, dancing, picnics, and dozens of other activities that will keep you on the go every day throughout your holidays.

Why do I have a variety of friends who are all so different in character?

How can I get along with them all? I think that each one helps to bring out a "different" part of me. With one of them I am polite. I joke with another friend. I sit down and talk about serious matters with one. With another I laugh a lot. I may have a drink with one. I listen to one friend's problems. Then I listen to another one's advice for me.

My friends are like pieces of a jigsaw puzzle. Together they form a treasure box. A treasure of friends! They are my friends who

*understand me better than I do myself, who support me through good
days and bad days. We all pray together and for each other.*

*Real Age doctors tell us that friends are good for our health. Dr. Oz calls
them Vitamin F (for Friendship) and counts the benefits of friends as
essential to our well being. Research shows that people in strong social circles
have less risk of depression and terminal strokes. If you enjoy Vitamins
F constantly you can feel up to 30 years younger than your real age. The
warmth of friendship stops stress and even in your most intense moments
it can decrease the chance of a cardiac arrest or stroke by up to 50%.*

I'm so happy that I have a stock of Vitamins F!

*In summary, we should value our friends and keep in touch with them. We
should try to see the funny side of things and laugh together, pray for each
other in tough moments, and thank God often for our many blessings.*

Chapter 18

Retirement

It's very important to live a retirement for you, the individual, not for someone else. This allows you to be free to do what you want and enjoy life. Way back seventy-five years ago, when Mattie was born, life was much different as there were no pensions that there are now, and it was left up to the generation after their parents to support their mother and father. There were no seniors' homes and similar facilities; therefore, the parents enjoyed a much better standard of living being with their family.

People who have gone on to engage in some sort of activity, work part-time, volunteering, helping others in any way they can, as a rule, are much happier than those who are not involved in their community.

In the coming years, it's going to be much more difficult for the next generation to support themselves as they will be faced no doubt with a higher cost of living and more competition in general in the retirement years. It will be much harder to sustain your standard of living as income and payroll taxes will increase, and as big business controls more and more government, no doubt interest rates will drop in order that the big businesses will have cheap funds to buy up most of America. It will also become more difficult to find a job due to the new technology, and with millions of jobs being shipped overseas in America and Europe, it will be much more difficult to find meaningful employment.

Prior to 2008, the savings rate in the United States was in the negative territory. People were actually spending more than they earned. One good thing about an economic crisis is that people all of the sudden start to save, which is going to help them substantially in the coming years.

In the future, retirement means freedom, but it is necessary to have money to be able to enjoy that free time as you please. It's also important to be able to vary your lifestyle as you grow older so that you're happy with your various types of retirement and have a purpose, whatever it may be, in order that you may enjoy whatever you decide to do with a desire to start over at something new or expand upon the activities you have been carrying on in the past. It is also important to learn to live within your means as large numbers of rich athletes, movie stars, and singers go broke due to a lifestyle which is totally unnecessary. Or they give the vast sums of money that they have made to some financial planner to invest for them, and all of the sudden they find out their savings has disappeared, and this can happen very quickly to individuals who have good government jobs or who have worked for big business or ran a very successful small independent business of their own. So it's a matter of "buyer beware," and as we have outlined prior in the book, it is very easy if you invested your money into revenue-producing property or you have your money in utilities or banks which pay good dividends and over time will increase in value regardless if there are slowdowns and the stock market drops when the very rich are playing games with other people's money.

If you start to work in your midtwenties and decide to fully or semi-retire in your mid fifties, you will have worked twenty-five or thirty years and, with luck, could live to eighty, giving you another twenty-five to thirty years to enjoy your savings and retirement.

Again, one can never emphasize enough that in retirement, you should have a purpose in life that you enjoy; practice sound money management, keep in touch with your family, friends, and the business or professional people that you've worked with over the years. And it's very important to exercise, eat the proper diet, and maintain your health; and if you do not feel you are kept busy enough, it is wise to add additional leisure and lifestyle interest. Heart attack and strokes cause the death of the majority of Americans; therefore one can never say enough to stay clear of stress. Keep your blood pressure down, maintain your cholesterol, exercise on a daily basis, watch your weight through diet, and alcohol moderation and do not use tobacco under any circumstances.

Money, it has been said, is the root of all evil when in essence it gives one the freedom to do what you wish throughout life. Another old saying is that money does not grow on trees, advising you to save and not waste your money, which is an excellent suggestion. When we talk about money, we state it as a fact not to blow about how much you make because Mattie always had the greatest respect for the people who saved their money and were able to retire and enjoy an excellent lifestyle. A half century ago, it was stated that we should save our money for a rainy day, and that is why the Alberta Heritage Fund was created but only wound up with ten to fifteen billion dollars in it; whereas in Norway, over the same period of time their heritage fund for a rainy day had over six hundred billion in it, which meant that Norway could always enjoy the standard of living to which they've become accustomed to due to the sound money management of their government.

It is always wise if you want to know how to manage your money that you talk to any individual who has saved his or her money as well as investing it wisely; and when it comes the time to retire, they have a large income yearly from their rental properties as well as having money in a pension or retirement savings fund as well as cash in the bank and investments in gold as security should the governments mismanage your country.

When you retire, it is a good idea in Mattie's opinion to write a book outlining your experiences whether they'd be good, bad, or indifferent throughout your life, as this allows the next generation to read about your experiences and allows them to do what is best for them and not make the mistakes that so many others have made. You can save all your life, and then with one bad investment, it is possible to lose your life savings. So that is where it pays to ask for advice from people who have been successful, and the majority of them will be only too happy to help you out as this does not cost them anything and gives them a great sense of satisfaction that they may be helping others along the pathway to success when they follow in the footsteps of the older generation.

When you retire, if you have very little to do, you will find that when you get up in the morning and do nothing all day, your work is never finished; and tomorrow you start in and again do nothing, every day you never get to feel a sense of accomplishment so that is why it is so important to keep your mind and body working to the best of your ability.

Some of the things you can do in retirement is get up when you feel like it; you can do what you want instead of doing what others want you to do. You no longer drive in rush hour traffic. Mattie never drives before 9:00 a.m. or after 3:00 p.m., always avoiding the rush hour and enjoying the pleasure of driving wherever he may wish to go. He also never drives on slippery streets or roads and drives as little as possible at night and is always back in his house at the latest by 8:00 p.m. and in bed no later than 10:00 p.m. And if he sticks to a regular schedule of going to bed and getting up at the same time every day, he finds that he can sleep through the night quite soundly when others complain of having trouble sleeping. You also don't have to deal in the office or in business with people you find to be a pain in the butt. You're able to take holidays to travel by RV in the mountains or sit by the beach or go to the sunny south in the winter. You can also decide to do each and every day what you want on that particular occasion, which means a lot when you are semi or fully retired. You are also able to take vacations whenever you want and travel with your friends or just meet for lunch, etc. You can cut down your travel by plane, which has become more a nuisance than good due to the scare tactics of the various governments throughout the world. Mattie rarely flies as it is more enjoyable to take the bus than to fly on an airplane; and since Mattie got paid as a teenager to travel on a bus as well as his hotel room and wages, he doesn't want to pay a tour company to travel on buses throughout the world. Mattie always finds time now to have a nap as when you grow older and go from rocking horse to rocking chair, you usually go back in time as a senior to when you were a little guy; and it's nice to lie down and have an afternoon nap, allowing you to wake up fresh for supper and enjoy the rest of your day. You're also able to travel during the week, and at times when other people are on holidays you wait until everybody is back to work and then you can travel when it is less crowded and much more enjoyable.

Soon-to-be seniors and retired individuals always talk about how they're going to enjoy their golden years. Mattie has seen too many people whose health has failed them and the only thing golden about their golden years is their urine.

Numerous well-known people have never retired such as George Burns, Frank Sinatra, Bob Hope, or Warren Buffett, these people keep on working and doing what they enjoy into their eighties which is what Mattie plans to do should his health permit him to do so; and it's an excellent thought for anyone who thinks about total retirement. It is wise to look at the other side of the coin and see how you could keep yourself fully occupied at anything that you might enjoy.

Mattie has seen too many people golf five or six days a week while some on a year-round basis. In fact, they have turned their retirement into golf as work if only golfing occasionally, as Mattie always felt if you golf too often. Golf has a habit of spoiling a good walk, especially if you get uptight when you're playing and losing, or if you find it too hard on your body to golf continuously.

It is always wise to bear in mind that people who are in their fifties only about half enjoy excellent health, and in your sixties approximately 40 percent, and in your seventies approximately a third of your fellow senior Americans have good health; therefore it is always wise to bear in mind that the sooner you enjoy the lifestyle endeavors and traveling to the various parts of the world that you would like see, it is important to do these things at the youngest age possible.

It is wise to consider your newfound freedom to be an opportunity to do the many things in life that are possible for seniors in today's society because if you do not do so, then you have wasted an opportunity to help yourself as well as to help others. It is important that you feel useful in life and are committed to various activities and lead a productive life in society. It is important to go to the auto driveway services should you wish to travel across North America as they will provide you with a new or late-model car which they will give you and provide a full tank of gas and on occasion hundreds of dollars, allowing you to drive nationwide and see the country at the appropriate time of year. For example in Canada in the springtime when the leaves are coming out on the trees, and the trees are in blossom and the flowers are all starting to bloom and the fields are full of farm animals, which makes for a beautiful scenery. In the fall of the year, the leaves are turning color in Eastern Canada, and in eastern United States in September or early October while in November it is an excellent time to drive across the southern states as in the hill and mountain country, the trees are all turning color later in the season, and you get excellent rates on motels and hotels and gas is usually priced at a lower rate per gallon. A lot of people find in retirement that no matter how much they dislike their job, they still find being occupied and doing some sort of work is more enjoyable than spending your time trying to have fun.

A lot of Mattie's friends work for the senior resource center on a volunteer basis where they get supplied with the gas for the vehicle, and they drive people to doctor's appointments, hospitals for various treatments, etc. This allows them to meet new people and gives them a great sense of satisfaction. Another occupation that people enjoy is working on a golf course as this is summer job, and you are able to get paid a wage and get free golf as well. So this has several advantages. Working in the tourism and travel, as a travel agent is another occupation where you can meet people and learn about the various places that you can travel, and in some cases, you can get excellent discounts. Some people, if they enjoy meeting others, open a bed-and-breakfast in their house, which does not cost them anything but allows them to meet and make new friends. In tourist areas across America, one can always become a tour guide; or if you enjoy driving, drive a tour van or bus, chauffeuring various individuals around your area. Another good idea if you wish to travel cheaply is to trade your house for one in the UK, Europe, the United States, or in Australia or New Zealand. The house will probably come with a car and neighbors, and this will allow you to only have to pay for gas, food, and airfares which do not amount to a lot and allow you to see other countries at a discount. There are many firms listed on the Internet which provide a service in trading houses.

When Mattie finishes writing this book in the spring of 2012, he intends to write several more books on various countries, including one solely on travel. Therefore his future is already booked up with things to do.

Too many people spend their time watching a lot of TV and movies, going to the bar and socializing, eating more than necessary, going to casinos, watching spectator sports, window-shopping in various malls, etc. These activities will not keep your mind mentally active; you will find that you are not old, but you will just feel old. In retirement, one can never emphasize enough that you should be extremely active because in order to be happy and feel a sense of satisfaction, you must be very active and involved in a great many different activities as it has been often stated that the real fun is having to do a lot of things and being able to make the choice not to do it.

The more one maintains their mental health by reading books and watching informative television shows coupled with a good diet and a half an hour to an hour of exercise per day will preserve your health for years to come. In Mattie's case, by changing his lifestyle and following what he has already suggested in this book, he was able to extend his life by twenty years to the spring of 2012, and with good luck and the help of the Lord, he should be able to live a number of years yet in enjoyable retirement.

It is estimated that in America, half a million Americans die prematurely due to physical inactivity and poor diets. Another activity such as smoking is estimated that it kills another five hundred thousand people in America, and now in the last few years, it has been impossible to smoke in public buildings, in a lot of restaurants, most people's houses, in cars, busses and other transportation. So it is when one considers the health hazards with smoking and lack of exercise while not practicing a good diet that one can see all the people who have passed away.

Buddha, it is reported, has stated that health is a gift and to treat your body with care, and while Mattie traveled to the Far East and saw the statues of Buddha, he felt that he was considerably overweight. So this is why it is not always a good idea to practice what somebody else preaches as it may not always be correct, or it may not be the lifestyle that they are following.

When Mattie was playing sports as a young teenager, he weighed one hundred and sixty-four pounds, and now sixty years later, he weighs one hundred and seventy-five, so there is not a lot of change in his weight over six decades where he has been fortunate in being able to maintain this weight.

Mattie now only eats on a plate half the size of the normal dinner plate and donates the money he saves to the food kitchens that serve meals to the unemployed, which gives him a lot of satisfaction and certainly allows him to maintain a much better weight than if he ate the food himself. Mark Twain has said if you want to stay healthy, it is wise to eat what you don't want, drink what you don't like, and do what you would rather not.

A lot of people buy gym memberships and travel to various facilities where they work out with others. Mattie was always concerned about catching colds, the flu, or other illness in these places, so he bought a complete gym for each one of his houses, when this equipment was on sale at half price. Therefore, rather than paying five hundred or a thousand dollars per year, within a few years he would a have each gym paid off. Some of that exercise equipment is thirty years old, and yet after having used it for a half an hour to an hour per day, it is still in good working order. And Mattie can watch a TV tuned into his favorite programs as he exercises, which usually passes the time very quickly. When he listens to the commentators on the news talk about the political state of the nation and what the various governments are doing to make it worse, he gets concerned and exercises much faster, which causes him to sweat and lose weight even more quickly.

A friend of Mattie's back in the eastern part of Canada where he was born, Howard Day, always said, "Work when you see fit, eat when you are hungry, and sleep when you are tired." And Mattie believed this was an excellent statement for people to practice in their future. It is always wise to remember that money is only important if you do not have any and then only if you need it. For example, if you have twenty dollars and you are going to buy a meal for your friend and yourself, if you can eat for ten dollars each, then the twenty dollars will cover your food, and that is all the money you need at that time in life. Mattie was always told that a true friend would give you the last dollar in his pocket, perhaps even borrowing from his friend to help you out, and that is why Mattie soon realized that people in general did not have many true friends.

It is not necessary to be good-looking in life, but only to keep fit, healthy, and dress well in order that you may look good. Dale Carnegie always said get the monkey off your back and put it on somebody else's shoulder, this way you do not suffer from stress. That is why it is so important to go for a walk in the park, on a sandy beach, or take a trip to the mountains through the week, or if not possible on the weekend in order to relax and enjoy the outdoors as Mattie as a lover of nature felt that he never could get enough of the mountains, the water, and the wilderness. And essentially, nature is the cheapest form of entertainment that an individual can find and enjoy.

Mattie always stayed in touch with his friends and relatives, throwing parties for fifty to one hundred and fifty people. Even if he was not going to buy something, he would keep an eye open for a good deal, and he always kept watching for somewhere to travel in the near future. Always tried to inquire and read about new opportunities in the business world, and as he has always done his own investing, by and large he found it very interesting. For example, a stock broker friend suggested that Mattie invest in the shipping and ship-building industry. Mattie decided that if there was a slowdown in the economy, the shipping industry would be the first to feel the pinch, and fortunately, he was proven right as the recession of 2008 proved him correct with many ship-building firms and shipping lines going broke.

Mattie instead invested in railroads, utilities, and banks, which paid good dividends and easily retained their value. Mattie had many friends who would travel the world staying in hostels, and after considering many various hostels in the world, they would travel to these places to stay while saving thousands of dollars. He was informed that the Elderhostel had thousands of sites throughout the world and was a nonprofit organization which provided excellent lodging at a very reasonable price. In fact, Mattie was staying at an expensive hotel in southern Spain by the Sea of Cadiz, and while he was paying two hundred dollars a night for his lodgings, his cousin was staying at a hostel closer to the beach for only twenty dollars per night. The cousin was much younger and was traveling the world on a very low budget, and where Mattie seldom got to meet anybody during his travels, his young cousin made hundreds of friends during that summer that he traveled throughout Europe. Mark Twain stated that good friends, good books, and a good nap made for an excellent life. It is always good to start making as many friends as possible in your school days, and then when you go to college, you should try to make as many as possible and carry out this practice throughout life in your profession, business, work, etc. As if you have friends in a time of need, you will be able to call upon them, and you will find them invaluable.

Before Mattie left to travel across the country, he was warned that people in general are ashamed of you if you are poor, and at the same time many of them will be jealous of you would become rich, so always remember that it is only your true friends who stick with you through the good and the bad. Mattie learned this very quickly in the early years of his life.

Mark Twain stated that a true friend will support you when you are in the wrong because anybody will support you when you are in the right. People who agree with you all the time or want you to do what they want, or want you to financially back them or tell you what to do are usually not a friend. Look for a friend who does not care if you are rich or poor, does not matter what you do in life, and stick with you when you have problems, and who you can converse with when times are tough and will always stand up for you should anybody try to run you down. So these are a few clues to what you should look for in friendship.

Mattie found when moving to a retirement community several decades ago in the United States that a lot of people worked very hard at making new friends; they were always having happy hour, parties, traveling to various places, inviting you to their house for meals, inviting you to join them for supper in the various restaurants in the area, in their various outings, and making you part of their way of life which is why Mattie says it is so important to look at dozens of retirement communities and find the right one for you. For example, many of Mattie's friends pay two hundred in condo fees, six to eight thousand per year for the rental of the property that they have their double-wide home on. Mattie only pays fifty dollars per month in his retirement community in Mesa, Arizona, and golf is less than two thousand per person per year; so when you consider all the facilities that are available, it is an excellent place to live, in fact one of the better areas in North America today.

In the retirement community where Mattie lives at, there are dozens of activities going on in a continuous basis, such as ceramics, a pool hall, woodworking, hiking, bus trips, dances, working with charitable organizations, a community church, a dog park, computer club, and half a dozen major grocery stores and large restaurants in the immediate area, making it an excellent place to live and enjoy your retirement. One of the rare areas in the world where over fifty people have joined together over the last-quarter century to plant all different types of desert plants, trees, flowering shrubs, etc. and where this group meets Saturday mornings at eight o'clock during the winter months and keep the place looking like a park. In fact, they have won awards for being the best kept area in the Valley of the Sun. They also meet after work at ten o'clock to have breakfast together, which is an ideal chance to get together and make friends; and should one of their group pass away, they will hold a memorial service of several hundred people in the community church, which shows their dedication to their fellow residents of the community.

Two forms of entertainment that are very reasonable, costing little or nothing are hiking and photography. Mattie has over the past forty years taken nearly fifty albums of pictures, many filled with his travels all over the world so that when he finds a free hour, he is able to sit and reminisce by himself or with others about where one can travel in the world and what there is to see. At the same time, his wife is an avid hiker going out with groups at least three days a week and making many friends who travel back and forth between Canada and the United States to enjoy their favorite pastime. It is wise to always remember that the Internet is not always the cheapest place to book your travel and if you encounter problems you will not be able to go back and get help that is why travel agents are still by far the best place to discuss your travel adventures and purchase your tickets.

A lot of people who like to travel to the sun are nervous about traveling to Mexico. Mattie and his wife have been to all the sunspots in Mexico and have not had any problems but are very careful to eat only cooked meals such as pizzas, soups, etc., and to only drink pop or bottled water and not travel at night as Mattie never felt it was safe. Mexico can be very economical; otherwise, if you stay where the high-end resorts are, it can be very expensive. When you are looking to exchange your home with somebody in a foreign land, you can always try the website www.seniorshomexchange.com. This allows you to trade houses in other countries. Mattie belongs both to Canadians Association of Retired Persons (CARP) in Canada and American Association of Retired Persons (AARP) in the United States, allowing him to get discounts at motels and hotels. There are also other clubs such as Vacation Exchange Club at 1-800-638-3841.

One must start planning for their retirement when they are very young. Mattie started when he was fifteen, deciding what he was going to do for the future. He was in college, and he was talking to the girl next to him when the professor in the math class said, "Mr. McFinsky, I'm speaking to you, would you put up your hand." So Mattie put up his hand, and the professor said, "I said would the person who made nothing in math please put up his hand. Why did you not put your hand up?" Mattie replied, "I'm surrounded by people who are better qualified to make nothing in math than I, sir." To which the professor replied, "Stay after class." Mattie stayed after class, and the professor, a Lieutenant Colonel McKinley, said, "What are your plans for the future?" to which Mattie replied, "Well, sir, you are a very clever man, and therefore you are a class 1." To which the professor said, "And what about the rest of the class?" Mattie answered, "They are all class 2s." He was then asked what he considered himself to be. Mattie answered, "A class 3." And the professor asked, "And what does a class 3 person do?" Mattie said, "Well, these other people are going to be accountants, engineers, lawyers, and I intend to hire them and at the end of the year, make money off each one. With the end result being I will be better off than any one of them." To which the professor replied, "I'd like you to come and see me in ten years' time and let me know how you make out." Mattie replied that he would, and on his way to visit the professor, who had now become the lieutenant governor of the island, he had a few drinks at a blind pig (bootlegger), and he did not turn quick enough resulting in hitting the power pole that supplied the energy to the lieutenant governor's house with the result that the lieutenant governor was out of power. Nevertheless, Mr. McKinley was glad to see him, and they discussed Mattie's past and future as he was already well on his way to achieving his goals.

Early on in Mattie's life, he had difficulty speaking to groups, and on one occasion, when he was asked to give the toast to the bride at his cousin Kim's wedding, he got up at the podium without a few drinks first and nothing written on paper, resulting in him having great difficulties in delivering the toast. This frustrated him to no end, and he drowned his sorrows that night resulting in the next day when he got to the office he was still feeling it. He was to attend a meeting of one of his competitors at the large convention center in Calgary. This competitor was a major oil company and had just sold part of its empire to a large corporation in the United States. When Mattie got to work, his secretary suggested that she drive him down to the meeting; and upon arriving at the hall, Mattie walked up to the front of the group and sat down beside the microphone. When the president of the oil company got up to speak and then after a short talk asked for questions from the audience, Mattie stood up and posed the question—how long would it be before this Canadian oil company would soon be sold to foreigners, which would be to the detriment of all the Canadians. Upon making this remark, the crowd all stood up and clapped. Mattie then left the hall. As he and the secretary were driving back to the office, she said, "Mattie, who was the crowd clapping? Was it for you or the president of the oil company?" Mattie replied, "I do not know." And to this day, he has often wondered if it was his question and little speech that got the enthusiastic response, or was it for the oil company president and his short speech. After that, Mattie never had any problems speaking without notes for any length of time.

In 1985, oil prices had dropped from forty-two dollars a barrel to nine dollars a barrel for West Texas Crude, and times were really slow in Western Canada, resulting in Mattie losing a million dollars in one company in one year. He decided to shake it up resulting in the next year that company made a million dollars. When his chartered accountant Leo Kelly, a top chartered accounatnat and a mountain climber, had finished the year-end, he and Mattie along with their wives were having dinner together at a hotel and talking over the past year, Leo asked if Mattie minded if he took the year-ends for 1985 and 1986 and showed them to people as he was head of the chartered accountant's society for the province. He was quite an achiever in mountain climbing as he and his son had climbed to the top of Mount McKinley in Alaska, and also his son had made a successful climb of Mount Everest in Nepal while Leo was unable to make it quite to the top due to the health of his guide. And in answer to Leo's question, Mattie asked why he would want the statements. Leo told him that it was quite a feat to lose a million and then make a million the following year, to which Mattie replied that he did not see it as being a success story, as he worked two years for nothing. It was in the mideighties when Mattie was in his early fifties that he decided to start to sell his businesses and take semiretirement as he was beginning to reflect on where he had been and think more about what he wanted to do with the balance of years in his life. This was accelerated in the early nineties when he suffered a severe heart attack while fishing in a national park, which resulted in his heart stopping and luckily he was fortunate that the paramedics were only a few minutes away. And as soon as they arrived, they used a defibrillator to get his heart started, and again on the way to the hospital which was about ten miles away, they had to stop again with the attendant in the back yelling to the other paramedic to stop the ambulance and get the paddles. As they opened the door and the cold air hit Mattie, he thought, "Here I am dying, and these two guys are going to go canoeing," not realizing that the paddles were part of the defibrillator. While at the hospital, he had a few more heart attacks, and his cardiologist was on speakerphone to the hospital in Banff where Mattie was being worked on, this time by two doctors and a number of nurses, but because of the delay in getting from the lake to the hospital, the doctors could not get the magic drug into his veins as the blood had almost stopped flowing; then all of the sudden the helicopter arrived to take Mattie to Calgary, which was about eighty miles to the east, and the paramedic came in from the outside and said that the helicopter was waiting, just like the little chap on the Fantasy Island TV show. The doctors informed the paramedic that the cardiologist stated that Mattie could not be moved until they had gotten an intravenous hooked up and the drug to disperse the blood clot injected into Mattie. With that, the paramedic said that he would do it, as he was looking forward to the helicopter ride, and with that, he took Mattie's socks off. And when the nurses saw Mattie's feet, which were black as could be, they could not believe it, but because Mattie had been in the lake when he pushed his boat into the water, the dye in the cheap socks had dyed Mattie's feet. The paramedic never missed a beat but just stuck the intravenous needle into Mattie's feet, and it worked immediately; and within a matter of minutes, Mattie was on his way to a major hospital which only took a little over a half an hour in the helicopter. Before he left, the doctors informed him that he might only live for a couple of hours; nevertheless, Mattie informed them that he would be back skiing in the mountains the following year, and he would stop and see them and bring them chocolates and flowers and cigars for the paramedics. The following spring, Mattie was back in Banff skiing and stopped at the Mineral Springs Hospital to see the people who had saved his life, and they collected a large crowd of the staff who were on hand and were overjoyed to see that they had been successful after all. This resulted in Mattie deciding in the early nineties to speed up his semiretirement and to cut his business interests by two-thirds and to increase his work with the various charities by double as he was also fed up dealing with big business and various governments.

He immediately put his asphalt manufacturing plants across Canada up for sale and sold his interests in Ontario to a group of his competitors on the condition that he would move the plant to Brantford, Ontario, to a site where one of the investors had a large operation, but it was conditional that he would receive the million dollars for his investment in the province if he would have the plant delivered no later than June the thirtieth of 1993. He hired a chap called Frank Gropo, who had moved a bunch of equipment from Florida back to Toronto, Ontario, to move the plant which consisted of one dozen plus loads from Toronto, but he had to wait to get everything assembled and was going to move it on a Saturday morning. A gentleman he knew who worked with the Ontario provincial police informed him that the weigh scale on a major east-west highway would be closed on Saturday morning, so Mattie left before daylight on Saturday morning. And sure enough, when Mattie went ahead of the trucks with the rental car, the station was closed so they had clear sailing. As the plant was mounted on highway trailers which were quite elderly and would not pass inspection, but were quite fine for a stationary plant. Within a short time, Mattie arrived on the outskirts of Brantford and was breathing a sigh of relief when the truckers pulled over to the side of the road at a Tim Horton's coffee shop for coffee and donuts and just at that moment an Ontario Provincial Police car arrived on the scene and saw all the trucks parked along the road with the officer inquiring who owned the plant. They directed him to the rear of the convoy where Mattie and his cousin Ed were getting ready to go up and see what was the cause of the holdup, but as they were ready to pull out, the policeman pulled up beside Mattie's rented car. And as he was getting out, cousin Ed said that they would lock his equipment up for the next ten years, and that Mattie was done unless he could talk his way out of it. The night before, Mattie could not sleep, so he was reading that Wayne Gretzky, one of the greatest hockey players in North America, was starting to invest in businesses. So when the policeman came over to the car, he said to Mattie that those were the nicest trucks he had ever seen, but that the trailers sure look pretty rough, but Mattie said that they were pretty good, and that they had made it all the way from Toronto. The officer asked who owned the operation, and Mattie informed him that Wayne Gretzky had bought the plant. With that, the officer just shook his head, as Wayne Gretzky had been born and raised in Brantford, Ontario, while remarking, "What will that guy buy next?" He then offered an escort to the buyer's location. Mattie thanked him profusely but said that it would not be necessary, although Mattie asked the officer if he could help him get the convoy moving and get the truckers out because Mattie was still in a state of shock. Within a matter of minutes, they had the entire plant safely deposited in the buyer's yard, and Mattie was a million dollars richer; but he had also been within minutes of losing the deal, only for a large amount of good luck and God's help.. He and his cousin then inquired where the local legion was, and Mattie and his cousin toasted to their luck and the good business deal. Over the years, cousin Ed told that story over one hundred times, about how on the verge of having all the equipment seized that with good luck and the help of the lord, they were able to consummate the deal.

Mattie had three very close friends who all came from the same island that he was born on, and were of the same nationality, religion, age, and political persuasion; and they looked forward to the day when they would all get together and make a golf foursome as well as travel as a group. Unfortunately, Hermon Connor, the first chap who was a schoolteacher and was a very close friend of Mattie's as well as a relative, passed away from cancer in his forties. The second friend, Al Ross, who was high up with a major oil company, dropped dead of a heart attack while Mattie and a dozen of his friends were out celebrating Saint Patrick's Day. Unfortunately, when he was only in his midfifties, the third friend took cancer, and while Mattie was skiing at Sun Valley in Idaho, he got a call from a friend and another one from his buddy's wife asking Mattie to be a pallbearer as his dear friend, Bert Dunn, had just passed away. So he drove all night back to Calgary, Alberta; and as he returned from the cemetery, he thought about how three of his closest friends were now gone and he was the only one remaining, that it was time to slow down and smell the roses and enjoy life more.

When Mattie was talking to a number of his friends, he found that probably the most exciting thing in their lives was when they got an ice cream cone on a warm day, and they really had to work at licking around where the ice cream met the cone in order for it not to run down on their hand, so Mattie made up his mind that he would not totally retire and would try to keep his life as interesting as possible. By this time, Mattie had hopefully at least twenty years of retirement to look forward to, and he did not want to be like some of his older friends who had gone from the rocking horse to a rocking chair as seniors and in a lot of cases had become like little kids. Although he was told as he was growing up that idle minds breed mischief, but in the case of seniors, he could see in a lot of cases that they did not breed much of anything.

When it comes to retirement in a lot of cases, husband and wife spend a lot more time together; and since there is usually not a lot of conversation unless it involves children and grandchildren, one has to be prepared to compromise, communicate clearly, be a good listener, know how to settle difficult issues, and learn how to solve problems.

In Mattie's case, Mattie's wife liked to hike, bicycle, dance, ski, and travel while Mattie liked to read thousands of pages a month as he had always had a great interest in reading and found it an excellent way to pass the time, and he always pities some of his acquaintances who only read a few hundred pages a month.

Money was not a concern as Mattie had saved all his life and had invested in property across the country, and by the time he was in his late fifties, he already had a guaranteed income, which was more than he needed to live on. Certain things such as playing bridge did not interest Mattie as it was a slow game that took a considerable amount of patience. He found the same thing with bowling and curling and was unable to develop an interest in either. He did like fish, but he had been fishing for over half a century, so he was beginning to get a bit tired of this sport. But on occasion, he would go fishing with his father-in-law and his two brothers-in-law. These trips ended when all four went on a fishing trip in northern Saskatchewan, and their accommodations were a camper on the back on the of the farm pickup of Mattie's father-in-law. After supper, they looked at the inside of the camper, and it was Mattie and his brother-in-law who was a professor who shared accommodations in extremely small quarters above the cab of the pickup in the camper. In the middle of the night, Mattie was always in the habit of putting his arm over his wife, so he naturally put his arm around his brother-in-law, who, thinking that Mattie was giving him a hug, somehow managed to jump over the top of Mattie and down out of that small camper and out the back door in a matter of seconds. That ended that particular type of sleeping arrangement on future fishing trips.

In 1995, Mattie put up a Gaelic cross for a tombstone in the cemetery of the church where he attended service when he was a young boy. When he phoned the manufacturer of the headstones on the mainland, the owner wanted to know why he was putting up a monument before he died. Mattie informed him that when he got the tombstone up to send him the bill; he would then send him the check and phone him with an answer to his question. Within a month, Nelson Monuments in New Brunswick had the tombstone erected, an excellent bit of workmanship, and Mr. Nelson phoned him telling Mattie he had sent him an invoice and asked why he had put his tombstone up while he was still alive. Mattie said that he had been quoted twenty thousand for the tombstone, and he had bought it from him for sixty-six hundred. "Could you see me negotiating with you after I had died and getting so much off the price?" Whereupon Mr. Nelson replied that fortunately not everybody thought like Mattie, and that he could see how he had driven a good deal. And that's when Mattie informed him that if it isn't a good deal or on sale, then he goes to buy it, or does not need it. Mattie used to go to auction sales, and since they were always cash on the barrelhead, he would buy and then over the next few days or months, he would resell at a much higher price resulting in a good profit. But nowadays, when you go to a sale, you can be bidding against the auctioneer, against the owner of the equipment, other interested parties, plus bidders who are supposedly bidding on the Internet so you never really know whether you are getting a fair deal or not.

When Mattie had semi-retired, he found that he always had extra time on his hands, so on one occasion, he took his wife to Vegas for four days and then they were going on for three days to Palm Springs, California. Unfortunately, Mattie liked to play poker all night long while at the same time he would be treated by the casino to complimentary drinks. On this occasion in the morning, there was an oil company plane going back to Calgary, and they offered Mattie a free ride back. Mattie forgot that his wife was with him and flew back with his newfound friends. His wife called his Calgary office, spoke to the secretary, and wondered why Mattie was not at the hotel room at his normal time. And as Mattie always phoned the office in the morning, Bonnie wondered if they had heard from him. They said that they didn't have to get a call, as Mattie was already there when they got to work. Mattie's wife then flew back to Calgary, and upon getting to their residence out in the country, he found Mattie playing cribbage for ten cents a point with his taxi driver. His wife informed the taxi driver where to go, and he set a speed record getting out of the house. Mattie realized that the time had come to change his ways, so he immediately gave up gambling, smoking, and drinking. And in the following years, he never smoked nor did he ever play cards, but a few years later, he would take the occasional drink and found that life was easier if you passed on some of the pleasures that were rather unnecessary.

Some couples like to discuss their goals for the future. What kind of lifestyle do they want? How much will they need to retire? What kind of financial resources do they want to leave after they pass on. Do they need an emergency fund? In some cases, they may not feel comfortable making these decisions on their own; therefore, they may wish to discuss them with a financial planner, and they may want to draw up a will and name an executor or have a bank act as executor for them. If you have made the decision to work for the government, then you will no doubt have a sizeable pension as well as health benefits that will cover you in the future. If on the other hand you went to the other extreme and started your own business in order that you could enjoy more free time and take time off as you wished, then hopefully you have invested in property and in blue-chip stocks, gold, and cash in the bank as well as a retirement fund that you can draw on to supplement what you receive in the form of social security in the United States or old-age security and Canadian Pension in Canada which will allow you to enjoy your retirement without having to worry about money. If you have worked with big business, you cannot be guaranteed a job like when you work for the government or in your own business, as big businesses have a habit of hiring and firing. But you will have probably earned good money, and you and your wife in anyone of the three vocations will be in a position to retire in comfort.

When some people retire, they can be susceptible to depression; therefore it is wise if you are aware of the signs and symptoms such as irritability, fatigue, lack of interest in various activities, changes in appetite and sleep patterns, needing sleeping pills, alcohol, and concerned with death. You will be fortunate if you believe in a life hereafter, which is better than the one you have lived in the past and have no fear of death whatsoever.

Mattie and his wife used to love to horseback riding and had a stable of beautiful Arabians. Over the years, one of the horses that he owned, her half sister became the North American champion, and it was a great experience to ride in the evening on the prairie as the sun went down. Therefore a few years ago, Mattie and his wife were staying up in a provincial park an hour's drive west of Calgary, and as they were driving through the mountain, they saw a sign that said Horseback Rides, so they decided to go for a ride. Upon paying for their two horses, Mattie was the first one to mount up, and one of the ladies suggested that they bring along a stool for Mattie to stand on as he mounted. Mattie could not believe how the years make a difference as a cowgirl had to give him a hand up in the saddle, and his wife had even more problems. After riding for a few hours, they returned to the stables, and it was time to dismount. The same cowgirl who had helped Mattie mount up now came along and helped him get his foot up over the rump of the horse and then slide down onto the ground where he almost fell down. When it came time for Mattie's wife to get off the horse, she could not swing her leg up over the horse's rump, so an old cowboy about Mattie's age came over and suggested that Mattie and he would each take one hand on the bridle and one hand on one of the ears of the horse and pull its head towards the ground, letting his wife slide down the neck of the horse. As they walked away, the horse kept staring after them and shaking its head, and Mattie could only think what was going through that horse's mind because after all it's years of giving people horseback rides, he never had anybody dismount over the front in that manner.

Statistics have shown that 75 percent of seniors in America want to remain in their own homes as they grow older. In Mattie's case, his father took a heart attack at sixty-five, and he was having severe chest pains at home as he suffered from heart problems, and Mattie's mother who was a nurse said she didn't think he was going to live to the morning. Whereupon, Mattie's father said, "Keep the land, take your mother with you wherever you go, have a son and call him Daniel after me. Do not burn your bridges behind you as you may have to cross them later, and always let your word be your bond." His last words were, "I have enjoyed working with you." They then shook hands, and Mattie's father then drifted off to sleep and died within minutes. Mattie's mother lived an additional eight years, and of those she spent three with Mattie on the island, two in Calgary with Mattie and his brother while Mattie worked in the oil field and his brother taught school, and the last three years in Edmonton, Alberta, where Mattie's brother took a dentistry degree. In her sixty-ninth year, she had a stroke and was in a coma for a day. Mattie was not there, but it did not matter as she was not able to communicate, and he had gone back to the island to ready the house so that she could come back for a trip. But unfortunately, she came back by train to be buried in the family cemetery beside her husband. Mattie had no children, but his brother had a son, who he named Daniel after their father who now resides on the farm. When Mattie was a boy going to the school two miles away, there were thirteen families on two and a half miles off the road consisting of over sixty people. Now in the year 2012, twenty years later, there was only the one farm left on that stretch of road, and it is the one Mattie was raised on. A sign of the ever-changing times which is not really for the better.

When you do decide to retire, it is wise to consider availability of a hospital, affordability, climate, the age of the people in the community, taxes, cost of living, crime rate, shopping, and amenities which you may wish to participate in such as golf, tennis, swimming pool, fitness center, hiking, walking, and biking. Also, you have to consider how far it is to the water or the mountains should you enjoy either one. Finding a retirement community that will suit you takes time, and again you will only learn by asking friends and doing your homework and due diligence; otherwise, you can wind up in a place where you are not happy. You also need to find out what are the yearly costs, what services are provided, or are there additional condo or homeowner fees. If you are the people who enjoy pets, ask what are the rules, what happens if you need the assistance of a caregiver as you get older, and ask if this service is available, etc.

Becoming involved in charity work is one of the most enjoyable and one of the better ways to give back to your community. It is wise to look at all the various charities in your community, including working with the seniors, the handicapped, the homeless, the poor, etc. as this can be one of the most enjoyable and satisfying ways to spend your retirement if you've already been involved in the past. Then it will be very easy to increase your work and interest in whatever field of endeavors you wish to participate. When people retire, either partner may wish to participate in totally different endeavors from what the other partner wishes to enjoy. At this point, it is important that you are able to each find your own path in retirement and follow it to your utmost enjoyment. When Mattie was leaving the island, his friend Ed Reid who he had known all his childhood years—and since their families had been friends since the early eighteen hundreds—met with Mattie and told him to always remember that people say they have hundreds of friends, but in reality you are a lucky if you have a few dozen. And if you can count your real good friends on the fingers of your hand, then consider yourself very lucky because you can have business partners, a wife or a husband, family, etc. But if these people are not your very good friends, then you will have a gap in your life. Because a lot of marriages do not work out, various family members wind up not speaking to each other, relatives become distant, and you hardly ever see them. Business partners that were once very close in business and in friendship dissolve their partnership and split, so always remember that friendship is the most important thing in life after your health.

Now that you have decided on a place to retire, you may want to sell your existing house and may wish to move somewhere else in Canada or the United States. If so, you need to hire an experienced real estate agent to give you the information you need to successfully complete your sale. For example, ask them about a past failure they had in their real estate career and how they handled it. They should tell you how they turned failure into a learning experience. If they stumble in response, that's not a good sign.

Request statistics, ask all the candidates for data on the homes they've sold in the past six months. In each case, what percentage of the list price did the homeowners obtain? And how many days did the property sit on the market before it sold? Be cautious against hiring an agent who promises to get you much more than others say your home is worth.

Screen for frankness and tact. You should consider only those agents who are candid in assessing the changes needed to make your property sell for its full market value. But you don't want someone who is overly blunt. You may need to know, for example, that a themed bathroom must be painted over. But a good agent should be able to tell you tactfully. You should tell all the agents how much money you have for presale upgrades and then ask them to give you a list of priorities. Ask for their gut reactions and whether, for example, you would be better off spending the money, you have to plant flowers beside your front entrance or to paint your bathroom. The right agent should have good suggestions that fit in your budget.

Look for experience. Make sure you hire an agent with sufficient experience to do the job. A bad agent can ruin a sale. For example, if during the six months they had your listing, and they failed to advertise your house, the result will be zero traffic and the loss of a lot of prime selling time. " If something like this happens, after the first agent's listing agreement expired, interview several replacement candidates. You can hopefully find a seasoned agent who is successful in selling the property for a good price in just a few weeks.

Select a second agent who has been in the business forever, is a great negotiator who knows how to market the house and also prices the house correctly, which is very critical,. Sellers should carefully screen potential listing agents through interview questions that help draw out their track records. Ask them to walk you through the methodology they use to market homes and how they've met challenges. Past performance is always an indicator of future performance.

In retirement or when you are going through life, you may wish to drive an ordinary vehicle as in Europe now the police check individuals who are driving luxury cars and perform roadside checks on the drivers, assuming that the people who drive luxury vehicles may be cheating on their income tax or charging these luxury vehicles as tax deductible.

An example is Apple's Tim Cook who received 378 million in his first year on the job according to an article in *Bloomberg Businessweek*, and they asked the question, "Is any chief executive officer worth one hundred and eighty-nine thousand dollars per hour?" This is one of the main reasons why the United States is sixteen trillion in debt, and in Canada health care is a disaster. Individuals who are high up in big business receive absolute fortunes for which no individual is worth that sort of money. It's the same in Alberta, Canada, where the head of a health region was receiving million dollars a year plus a fifth of a million in an expense account and received millions more when he retired from the civil service even though the health care system was a total disaster with hundreds of thousands suffering and thousands dying unnecessarily. In the United States, an individual by the name of Steve Judge, a lobbyist was named president and CEO of private equity growth capital council in Washington which is a fancy title for saying he is head cheerleader for some of the richest companies. He receives million dollars a year, and his main job will be protecting the 15 percent tax rate for private equity managers at companies such as the Blackstone Group, Kohlberg Kravis Roberts (KKR), Carlyle group, and Bain Capital plus numerous others. *Bloomberg Businessweek* had an article on a chap called Michael Wodford who worked for Olympus Corporation out of Japan. He stated that Olympus sold endoscopes that cost a couple of thousand dollars to make for forty thousand dollars each to hospitals. This is just one example of hundreds of thousands that clearly indicate why health care in the United States and Canada are totally out of control. Mattie was informed by a salesman for General Electric who sold ultrasound, MRI, and cat-scan equipment to hospitals that the province of Alberta was divided into two regions, with one foreign company having the northern half and another foreign company having the southern half as their territory, selling equipment to the Alberta health regions at whatever price they saw fit. It is a small wonder that health care costs so much and is in such disarray across North America.

In letters to the editor in a March issue of *Maclean's* a lady from Maple Ridge, British Columbia, wrote a letter regarding old-age security, stating that Canadian members of parliament can take their pensions at fifty-five and that for every dollar the member of parliament puts into the pension fund, the Canadian taxpayers contribute $23.30 and immigrants to Canada can collect a pension after only ten years of contributing to it, but Canadians must work for over forty years to have the same benefit. At present, the Canadian government would like to extend the age limit on when you can draw old-age pensions. The big question is would somebody still be healthy enough to work till they are seventy, and secondly how many companies or governments would hire anyone in their sixties? So I think the few sentences in which I have just outlined the problems with big business, the various governments, etc, clearly show that the 99 percent of ordinary Americans and Canadians must look out for themselves. And hopefully this book will have provided some help to those who are starting out in life as well as individuals partway through life or ready for retirement. Good luck in the future, and hopefully this book will be of interest and help to those who read it.

Now that you have been fortunate enough to have good health and have been successful in your profession, working for big business, or operating your own independent small business as an entrepreneur and have picked a retirement community where you can live during the winter months. So now besides all the activities that are available in the area where you live in North America and in the retirement community where you have moved to for several months during the summer, you may wish to do something else with your time. The most satisfying is working for charity with helping the physically challenged, or seniors, two of the most satisfying. Another way you may wish to help others is by helping people start up small businesses who wish to gain from your experience and expertise that you have gained over your working lifetime.

I am now going to give you some information on the small business administration in the United States. This will provide an insight into a government program that is very helpful to entrepreneurs starting up in business. We hear a lot about the vital role of small business in the United States, especially in election years. But that raises the question, how vital is the role of the federal government in promoting the role of small business in America? And specifically, how vital is the Small Business Administration in that promotion? The following is quoted from The Wall Street Journal

The SBA's supporters argue that it plays a crucial role, guaranteeing billions of dollars in loans for small businesses each year and providing an army of counselors and information resources for those who need help. It particularly focuses on those who, some say, have been failed by conventional lenders.

But the SBA's critics say that the agency's loans do more harm than good. The loans go to only a tiny fraction of the small businesses in the country, for example, and help the recipients compete with small businesses that aren't similarly subsidized. Thus, instead of playing a crucial role in the U.S. economy, the critics say, the agency really is directing resources where the market has determined they aren't needed.

Small businesses created two of out three net new jobs in the U.S. from 1993 to 2009. About half of the people who work in this country are employed by a small business. With unemployment still over 8%, now is not the time to eliminate one of the most important resources available to America's job creators.

The power of the SBA isn't just measured by the number of loans it makes. The Small Business Administration helps keep capital, contracts and know-how flowing to small businesses. In fiscal 2011, the agency guaranteed $30.5 billion in loans to about 61,000 companies, helped small businesses win nearly $100 billion in government contracts and mentored one million entrepreneurs through its network of business counselors, such as the 13,000 volunteers of Score, a nonprofit association of business counselors.

Through its Small Business Development Centers, Women Business Development Centers, and similar facilities that help minorities, women, veterans and other business owners, companies of fewer than 500 employees can learn about marketing and forecasting, and how to navigate the federal contract system. Some 14,000 counselors and trainers, including Score volunteers, help entrepreneurs get started and help established owners take their companies to the next level. The training resources are mostly free and are delivered in person or through a variety of media.

Such training gives these businesses the greatest possible opportunity to succeed. The SBA further collaborates with many private nongovernmental organizations to offer additional training, resources and technical assistance. Even if the number of loans made by the SBA is relatively small, the aid goes to some of the most important, and most in need, sectors of our economy. In a 2009 study, the Urban Institute found women and minorities were three to five times as likely to get a loan through the SBA as they were through conventional lending.

I spoke recently with a woman who, after failing to get bank loans to launch a small manufacturing company, obtained an SBA loan within 45 days. Now, a year and a half later, she is preparing to meet with SBA counselors to expand her business and begin exporting her goods. She has two employees and several contractors, and is looking to hire. Women and minority business owners play a substantial role in our economy already, but could contribute so much more. Get rid of the SBA, and they will contribute so much less.

The argument that SBA loans are given to applicants with poor plans and prospects, as judged by the market, misses a key point: The market too often is misjudging the viability of many of these businesses. Research shows women start their businesses with less capital than men, and there's a widespread perception that it is harder for women- and minority-owned businesses to get loans from financial institutions than it is for similarly qualified white men to get loans.

This isn't because women-owned businesses are less likely to succeed; it's because the market mistakenly perceives they are less likely to succeed. The SBA is an advocate for small businesses with lenders at all times, but its role is especially important during economic downturns, when the squeeze on commercial credit can disproportionately affect small businesses. The SBA played a key role in arguing for policies to force the nation's biggest banks to resume lending to small businesses after the financial crisis hit in 2008.

The agency also worked closely with community banks to encourage more lending during the recession, and recently worked with 13 of the largest banks in the U.S. to increase their commitments by $20 billion over the next three years. President Barack Obama recently elevated the SBA to a cabinet-level agency. Making SBA Administrator Karen Mills a cabinet member gives small business a seat at the government decision-making table like never before.

Those who wish to abolish the SBA cite research that makes the puzzling assertion that it is young businesses, not small, that drive job creation today. I doubt that any small business will understand this argument. Small and young businesses are one and the same. Small businesses employ about one-half of U.S. workers. Of 120.6 million nonfarm private-sector workers in 2007, small firms employed 59.9 million and large companies 60.7 million. About half of small-business employment is in second-stage companies (10 to 99 employees), and half is in firms 15 years old or older.

For our economy to grow and to become competitive again, we must increase our investment in our people and our resources. On the surface, crowd funding sounds like a good idea—letting companies tap into a new source of funds and giving average people new opportunities to invest. But it creates problems for people on both sides of the transaction, and there are better ways to get capital into the hands of entrepreneurs.

Let's start with the problems it brings to investors. When average citizens buy traditional stocks, they have access to audited financial statements and disclosures, and they can sell their shares to a market of buyers at any time. Investing in a small business as a member of the crowd gives the investor none of these things.

The proposed law would not require audited financials on capital raising under $1 million, meaning people in the crowd could buy something that's valued based on potentially flawed numbers. And there could be hidden liabilities—such as workers' compensation claims, lawsuits and back taxes—in the company that the crowd now owns.

And the crowd would be stuck with those problematic holdings, since there's basically no way to sell the investments. They're about as illiquid as you can get. From the entrepreneur's perspective, meanwhile, equity-based crowd funding raises just as many problems. Let's start with a basic issue: Yes, small businesses need capital. But they need a lot more than that. And by focusing simply on capital, equity-based crowd funding would rob small companies of access to everything that traditionally comes with capital.

Investors, for instance, often bring industry experience, market intelligence and a valuable contact list. Everyone's money is green, but it's what comes with the money that is often more important. By selling equity through crowd funding, an entrepreneur could be stuck with a crowd of investors who may not know anything about the market or industry—or investing, for that matter— and may bring no other value.

Instead, that crowd of investors could bring a whole host of new problems that were never contemplated. For example, managing investor relations and communications with a larger number of potentially unsophisticated investors will take time away from running the business, making sales and executing on strategy. Not to mention the potential legal and tax ramifications that will need to be addressed.

An entrepreneur is better off raising larger amounts of money from a single angel investor with experience and connections than trying to hunt down smaller amounts from many investors with nothing to offer besides the money. Angel investors understand how to value companies, have the liquidity to make investments, and often have the experience and connections to help the new venture make the most of the investment.

Of course, as proponents of crowd funding say, companies with low growth potential are generally not good candidates for equity capital. Experienced investors look for innovation, scalability and a team that can execute, and many small businesses simply aren't in that category. Even if equity-based crowd funding is legalized, angel investors will continue to get access to the best small-business investment opportunities while the crowd picks over the rest.

But that's precisely the point: Many of these companies are not good candidates for equity capital—either from experienced investors or crowds. If experienced investors have passed them by, there's probably a good reason. But those reasons may not be apparent to unsuspecting crowds.

For small businesses that don't attract interest from experienced investors, there are other options available that are better than crowd equity. For example, they already have access to crowd-sourced capital, but they don't have to trade equity for it. There are several popular crowd-funding sites that help entrepreneurs raise money through donations. This connects a funder's desire to make a difference to the entrepreneur's need for capital without diluting ownership or creating future problems.

As another alternative, we could craft policy that would make it possible for the crowd to step up and provide debt capital where banks will not. For the business owner, debt is ultimately less expensive than equity, and it solves the problem of raising capital without all the hassles of taking on shareholders. People in the crowd benefit by earning interest at a higher rate than they would get on a bank deposit, while participating in a company for which they have a passion.

An entrepreneur with a truly innovative, scalable business opportunity will still have to work hard to access capital, but there is no doubt that it is out there. Crowd equity does not fill a gap in the capital market, but rather it creates more problems for small-business owners, as well as for the crowd.

Entrepreneurship can't be taught in a regular classroom any more than surfboarding can. To learn it, you have to get your feet wet in the real world. Why? Entrepreneurship is messy. For an entrepreneur, there are rarely clear-cut right or wrong decisions day to day. Real life gives entrepreneurs the ability to better make those kinds of judgment calls.

Entrepreneurship is also a team sport, not a solo skill. We all know the myth of the "lone wolf" entrepreneur, tucked away in a basement or garage tinkering with an invention. In reality, an entrepreneur has to deal with lots of different people daily, all of whom present social barriers to overcome, whether it's geography, culture, language or just plain distrust.

Entrepreneurs have to understand people well enough to get them to surmount their barriers and deliver their best efforts. Those kinds of skills can't be taught in a formal classroom, and they can't be fully developed in the span of a semester or even a few years. Entrepreneurship is learned through the aggregate experience of a life that is lived.

That's why comparisons with traditional business education don't hold up. M.B.A. training helps you learn to allocate resources and calculate risk, which are skills that can be quantified and taught. The life skills needed for entrepreneurship can't be.

I have seen successful executives who left corporations and joined start-ups and were unprepared for the experience. They knew how to manage, but they weren't ready for the uncertainty in almost every aspect of decision-making, informal handshakes in place of formal agreements, raw conflicts among company founders and investors and the need to do everything oneself—from emptying garbage cans to fixing jammed copiers.

Leading a start-up also demands a deep understanding of people that can only come from real-world experience. Imagine a potential employee who's trying to decide between joining a large company or a tiny start-up. Just looking at the numbers, it would be insane to go with the smaller firm. You would almost certainly make less money, you would take on huge personal risk and emotional burden, and you could even wreck your reputation if the venture failed.

An entrepreneur has to help that potential employee see beyond all of the negative incentives, to see why joining this little company is worthwhile. One person, for instance, might want a chance to change the world. Another, meanwhile, might be motivated by the joy of adventure, the thrill of a challenge or the love of novelty.

Which approach is going to work best with the prospective hire? You're not going to find that out sitting in a classroom, talking to the same people day after day. The same logic applies to every aspect of running a start-up. Imagine you've got a new product to sell that promises to change your industry. But having a better mousetrap isn't enough. You must be able to read your potential customers and answer crucial questions about them.

For instance, who's the right person to pitch someone who will really understand your idea and be in a position to act on it? What are the buyer's incentives to take such a huge risk with a start-up product?

Admittedly, there's a booming interest in entrepreneurship education these days, and its proponents claim that there's more science behind the subject these days. But I think that much of what traditional entrepreneurship classes teach—the best ways to avoid mistakes—is misguided.

Telling entrepreneurs to avoid failure risks causing them harm. They're tempted to fall into endless planning and product engineering, without real-world experimentation. Failures and mistakes are inevitable and are the equivalent of testing hypotheses and learning in the scientific world. Just as we would never tell scientists to avoid running experiments that might fail, we shouldn't tell entrepreneurs to avoid making mistakes and risking failure. Entrepreneurs hone their craft through experimentation and collaboration in the real world. They learn best by rolling up their sleeves and building companies, while surrounded by a supportive mentor and peer community.

We can't teach entrepreneurship in the traditional sense. But we should come up with ways to help entrepreneurs help themselves to learn more effectively. This means finding ways to provide them with a network of mentors and advisers and nurturing a business culture around them that says: dream big, open doors and listen to new people, trust and be trusted, experiment, make mistakes, treat others fairly and pay it forward.

Working this way means looking beyond the traditional focus on individual entrepreneurs and finding ways to cultivate the communities that surround them. But it's a move that can pay tremendous dividends.

Now that you have thought over whether or not you may wish to help independent business which is one of the most worthwhile endeavors that an individual can do in their retirement years because any help you give to small business, they will pass on the savings, which can be up to 50 percent, to you and the rest of the taxpayers and consumers in your community in Canada or the United States—as small business can operate at a lower cost than larger operations as they work in and manage their business on a day-to-day basis and usually you can have considerable savings over the years if you support the small entrepreneur.

Much has been publicized in the media about what and who makes gasoline prices raise. Quite simply, natural gas in the winter of 2012 is selling at a little over two dollars per thousand BTU (British thermal units). This is very cheap as it is almost the cost of finding and producing natural gas. This has been a boon to the consumer as the cost of heating their residences and businesses in North America have been very economical over the past several years, as there is at present approximately a one-hundred-year supply of natural gas in North America.

In one area of Canada, the utility company has invested a billion dollars of profits in a foreign country. While increasing the cost of electricity from 6.3 cents per kWh to 14.4 cents per kWh, instead of the government taking action in regard to this outrageous increase, they awarded the main shareholder a medal. This just goes to show how the government and big business work hand in hand.

With regard to gasoline, oil wells pump day and night every day of the year except for some downtime when they are servicing the machines, and the norm for a good oil well is to pump continuously for twenty years. Therefore, when gas goes up by a dollar or two dollars a gallon, there is no reason for it as the cost of oil remains basically the same from year to year. Over the past decade in North America, major oil companies have merged and closed 50 percent of their refineries resulting in the few major companies that are left buying product from each other in various parts of the country. It is quite legal for an oil company to raise its prices to whatever it sees fit when selling to one of its competitors, resulting in increases at the gas pump for really no valid reason.

The Organization of Petroleum Exporting Countries (OPEC), a consortium of major foreign oil companies have joined together to fix the prices and amount of oil they'll produce per year; therefore, this creates an artificial market and constantly increasing prices, even though 82 percent of the oil in the world is controlled by various countries.

A major reason for oil to go up is the various wars that have been ongoing for the past four thousand years. If there is a threat of a war or an invasion in a country that is a major producer of oil, then prices will escalate very rapidly. An example was when oil was selling for forty dollars a barrel and the oil company raised it to eighty dollars a barrel and at that time Wall Street and the speculators entered the market, raising the price to eventually one hundred and forty-seven dollars a barrel. They did this by filling all the tanks in the Middle East and North America as well as loading all the ships with oil so that they created a shortage; the end result was that the two major automakers in America had to get large bailouts from the federal government and the taxpayers to stay in business.

The vast majority of ordinary North Americans do not understand why wars are constantly being fought; it's an ongoing affair for the past four thousand years as outlined in the *Historical Atlas of the Bible* written by Dr. Ian Barnes. Another excellent book which is over three hundred pages which describes the various wars in the past is the *Historical Atlas of the Celtic World*. Both of these books by Dr. Barnes make excellent reading and show quite clearly why there will likely be wars for the foreseeable future. Without wars, the manufacturers of all of the military products would be out of business; and since these large corporations donate millions of dollars to the federal governments all over the world, they are able to keep the various leaders of nations throughout the world consistently engaged in war even though it is the women and children and the elderly who suffer greatest in wartime as well as young men who go to fight throughout the world in various wars. The author would suggest that instead of sending people who are eighteen to thirty-eight off to battle, that the politicians and people high up in the military, big business, and government who are from thirty-eight to sixty-eight should all have to go to serve at least two years on the battlefield along with another young family member or relative. This would probably cut the war efforts by at least three quarters.

CHAPTER 19

Tips on Taxes

Billions of dollars in credit card debt that was charged off during the Great Recession—some of it decades old—is coming back to haunt the borrowers in the form of unexpected tax bills.

Now as we get close to the end of the book, we have talked about starting a business or a profession, going to work with the government or big business. If you decide to run an ordinary business life may be most enjoyable by and large, it is only when you decide to move into the playing field of the large corporations that business gets extremely tough, dishonest, and can become a very unhappy place in which to participate.

Mattie in one state was dealing with two of the major oil companies in particular, and after causing one of the largest companies in the world to close out in his particular field of endeavor, they then sold out to one of the richest families in America. And Mattie was able to force them to sell out their operations; but unfortunately, they sold to a group that was part of a large oil company who had their own refineries in Central Canada and the West, which made it even more difficult. And unfortunately, as we cited before when he went to buy with two of his friends one of the major oil companies in Western Canada, the prime minister sold it to several of his friends as they all belonged to the same political party as the prime minister, where Mattie was only one against seven and his two friends who also had one of the largest businesses in Canada were very apolitical. As a result, the refinery was sold to the lowest bidder rather than the highest bidder. This refinery was sold three times in the next twenty years and each time at double the price, clearly indicating that the government is not interested in making money, but more interested in patronage and corruption.

In the same state, Mattie had to deal with a government where the majority of the elected politicians were charged with criminal offenses, a rarity in North America. Nevertheless, Mattie was able to continue on until three of the largest companies in Canada ganged up on his company that was in the manufacturing of asphalt products, and it was at this time Mattie decided to take a serious look at getting out of that particular industry while he was still ahead and had been so lucky and successful to become the biggest in Canada in that particular field along with two of his other companies which he took coast to coast—north to the Yukon and south to the United States.

In the United States where he had a plant, he was doing large volumes at good prices until there was an election and the government changed, and the commissioner, when Mattie phoned him, stated, "One of your competitors gave a much larger donation than you did, so even if you are low bid, you will not be getting any work." Mattie then resold the plant which he had bought from a US oil company and immediately stopped conducting operations in that state.

Back in the States, where he had political problems with the government, and politicians who were charged, he had to deal with another major international oil company who consistently offered the government bureaucrats jobs, hiring the occasional one from time to time at a much larger salary with considerably longer holidays. Mattie could not or did not want to compete in this unethical manner, so he took a further look and decided that the time had come to cut back his operations and deal only in medium-sized businesses, investments, and real estate and take semiretirement as it had become such a vicious and unethical war that neither he nor his employees could find happiness in this particular business. His senior employees who had built the companies and had seen the unscrupulous competitors, bureaucrats, and politicians did not wish to continue on in or buy the business, so Mattie sold to other small independent businesspeople who, in a lot of cases, had used the facilities for a different operations and business; however, Mattie kept some of the properties for rentals across Canada.

He also encountered a company with many partners who built one plant in a large province with their friends as shareholders, and as unbelievable as it may sound, they sold shares to their friends conditionally that if their friends wanted to sell their shares, they had to sell them back to the small group that controlled and built the manufacturing facilities, resulting in their friends getting little or nothing when they went to sell their shares. Nevertheless, the vast majority of the major shareholders in this company have been dead for years, and that goes for the other large corporations that Mattie dealt with in big business and in the government which clearly indicates that there must be a heaven and a hell—because Mattie dealt over a third of a century with tens of thousands of people and the vast majority of them being hardworking, honest, and very decent individuals where the other shifty, shafty, and sneaky individuals who would do anything to succeed even though in a lot of cases they were rich beyond their dreams. Therefore in Mattie's opinion, there has to be a place in the hereafter for the good guys as well as a rather inferior place for the people who wreaked havoc on their country and community in their life. It's a very simple explanation, and one that should convince any atheist that people who have lived a decent life and worked for the good of their country and their fellow human beings should be rewarded for the rest of their life in the hereafter, while the ones who did not should be dealt with in a different manner.

When traveling in the United States, an individual must be prepared to pay costs for health care incurred while traveling at ten times the rate of any other country in the world. You may have bought insurance before you left your country of residence, but the big business insurance companies will try to weasel out of paying your bill which could amount to hundreds of thousands of dollars per hospital visit. This has happened to Mattie as well as hundreds of thousands of other US visitors, businesspeople, and tourists. If you buy insurance, make sure you have a doctor in your city where you reside to fill out your forms so that it is difficult for the insurance company to refuse to pay your bill, which can be extremely high.

The following is an article by Benjamin Skinner published in the February edition of *Bloomberg Businessweek*:

On March 25, 2011, Yusril became a slave. That afternoon he went to the East Jakarta offices of Indah Megah Sari (IMS), an agency that hires crews to work on foreign fishing vessels. He was offered a job on the *Melilla 203*, a South Korea-flagged ship that trawls in the waters off New Zealand. "Hurry up," said the agent, holding a pen over a thick stack of contracts in a windowless conference room with water-stained walls. Waving at a pile of green Indonesian passports of other prospective fishermen, he added: "You really can't waste time reading this. There are a lot of others waiting, and the plane leaves tomorrow."

Yusril is 28, with brooding looks and a swagger that belies his slight frame. (Yusril asked that his real name not be used out of concern for his safety.) He was desperate for the promised monthly salary of $260, plus bonuses, for unloading fish. His wife was eight months pregnant, and he had put his name on a waiting list for the job nine months earlier. After taking a daylong bus ride to Jakarta, he had given the agent a $225 fee he borrowed from his brother-in-law. The agent rushed him through signing the contracts, at least one of which was in English, which Yusril does not read.

The terms of the first contract, the "real" one, would later haunt him. In it, IMS spelled out terms with no rights. In addition to the agent's commission, Yusril would surrender 30 percent of his salary, which IMS would hold unless the work was completed. He would be paid nothing for the first three months, and if the job were not finished to the fishing company's satisfaction, Yusril would be sent home and charged more than $1,000 for the airfare. The meaning of "satisfactory" was left vague. The contract said only that Yusril would have to work whatever hours the boat operators demanded.

The last line of the contract, in bold, warned that Yusril's family would owe nearly $3,500 if he were to run away from the ship. The amount was greater than his net worth, and he had earlier submitted title to his land as collateral for that bond. Additionally, he had provided IMS with the names and addresses of his family members. He was locked in.

What followed, according to Yusril and several shipmates who corroborated his story, was an eight-month ordeal aboard the *Melilla 203*, during which Indonesian fishermen were subjected to physical and sexual abuse by the ship's operators. Their overlords told them not to complain or fight back, or they would be sent home, where the agents would take their due. Yusril and 23 others walked off in protest when the trawler docked in Lyttelton, New Zealand. The men have seen little if any of what they say they are owed. Such coerced labor is modern-day slavery, as the United Nations defines the crime. (The South Korean owners of the *Melilla* ships did not respond to requests for comment.)

The experiences of the fishermen on the *Melilla 203* were not unique. In a six-month investigation, *Bloomberg Businessweek* found cases of debt bondage on the *Melilla 203* and at least nine other ships that have operated in New Zealand's waters. As recently as November 2011, fish from the *Melilla 203* and other suspect vessels were bought and processed by United Fisheries, New Zealand's eighth-largest seafood company, which has sold the same kinds of fish in the same period to distributors operating in the U.S. (The U.S. imports 86 percent of its seafood.) The distributors in turn have sold the fish to major U.S. companies. Those companies—which include some of the country's biggest retailers and restaurants—have sold the seafood to American consumers.

Yusril's story and that of nearly two dozen other survivors of abuse reveal how the $85 billion global fishing industry profits from the labor of people forced to work for little or no pay, often under the threat of violence. Although many seafood companies and retailers in the U.S. claim not to do business with suppliers who exploit their workers, the truth is far murkier.

Hours after Yusril arrived in Dunedin, New Zealand, the *Melilla 203* officers put him to work unloading squid on the 193-foot, 26-year-old trawler. The ship was in bad shape, and the quarters were musty, as the vessel had no functioning dryer for crew linens or work clothes. Yet the conditions seemed comparatively decent to Yusril. Two years earlier he had worked on the *Dong*

Won 519, operating under the auspices of Sanford (SAN), a 130-year-old, $383 million New Zealand company. On that boat, Yusril says the officers had hit him in the face with fish and the boatswain had repeatedly kicked him in the back for using gloves when he was sewing the trawl nets in cold weather. Most unnervingly, the second officer would crawl into the bunk of Yusril's friend at night and attempt to rape him. When asked for comment, Chief Executive Officer Eric Barratt said Sanford's observers, which the company placed on all their foreign-chartered vessels (FCVs), reported that the ships "don't have any issues with labor abuse."

When the *Melilla 203* set sail for the deep waters of the Southern Ocean, conditions worsened, according to the accounts of Yusril and a dozen other crew members. The ship trawled for up to two months at a time, between 12 and 200 miles offshore. The boatswain would grab crew members' genitals as they worked or slept. When the captain of the ship drank, he molested some of the crew, kicking those who resisted. As nets hauled in the catch—squid, ling, hoki, hake, grouper, southern blue whiting, jack mackerel, and barracuda—the officers shouted orders from the bridge. They often compelled the Indonesians to work without proper safety equipment for up to 30 hours, swearing at them if they so much as asked for coffee or a bathroom break. Even when fishermen were not hauling catches, 16-hour workdays were standard.

The resulting fatigue meant accidents, which could bring dismemberment in the cramped below-deck factory where the fish were headed and gutted by hand, then passed along conveyor belts to be frozen. Over the past decade at least two crew members of the *Melilla* ships have died, according to local newspaper accounts and reports by Maritime New Zealand, a government regulatory body. Dozens of *Melilla* crew members suffered injuries, some crippling.

When Ruslan, 36, a friend of Yusril's on the *203*, snapped two bones in his left hand in a winch, it took three weeks before he was allowed to go to a hospital. The morning after his discharge he was ordered back to work but could not carry out his duties. The company removed him before any follow-up medical appointments. "I was a slave, but then I became useless to the Koreans, so they sent me home with nothing," he says. Today, back in his home village in Central Java, Ruslan has a deformed hand. While IMS, the recruiting agency, finally paid him $335 for three months of work, it has blacklisted him, according to Ruslan, because he spoke to investigators, and it has refused to help with medical bills.

During the last decade, New Zealand authorities repeatedly fined or seized the *Melilla* ships for ecological infractions, such as a 2005 oil discharge in Lyttelton Harbor, which the country monitored by satellite and occasional inspections by Ministry of Fisheries observers. Crimes against humanity were secondary. Scott Gallacher, a spokesman for New Zealand's Ministry of Agriculture and Forestry (which merged with the Ministry of Fisheries in July), explained that "observers are not formally tasked" with assisting abused crew, though they may report abuses to the Department of Labour. Yet Yusril said that when he once whispered a plea for help, an observer expressed sympathy but said it was "not my job."

New Zealand authorities had plenty of prior evidence of deplorable working conditions on foreign vessels like the *Melilla*. On Aug. 18, 2010, in calm seas, a Korean-flagged trawler called the *Oyang 70* sank, killing six. Survivors told the crew of the rescuing vessel their stories of being trafficked. A report co-authored by Christina Stringer and Glenn Simmons, two researchers at the University of Auckland Business School, and Daren Coulston, a mariner, uncovered numerous cases of abuse and coercion among the 2,000 fishermen on New Zealand's 27 foreign charter vessels (FCVs). The report prompted the government to launch a joint inquiry. The researchers gathered testimony from New Zealand observers who saw abuses being committed even after they had boarded ships. "Korean officers are vicious bastards," one observer said, as quoted in the report. "Factory manager just rapped this 12kg [26-lb.] stainless steel pan over [the crew member's] head, split the top of his head, blood pissing out everywhere." The observer said he gave the Indonesian fisherman 26 stitches.

After eight months aboard the *Melilla 203*, Yusril and 23 other crew members finally protested their treatment and pay to the captain. Their move came after a Department of Labour investigator, acting independently, visited the ship in November 2011, when it was docked in Lyttelton. The official gave Yusril a government fact sheet stipulating that crew members were entitled to certain minimum standards of treatment under New Zealand law, including pay of at least $12 per hour. When deductions, agency fees, and a manipulated exchange rate differential were subtracted, the fishermen were averaging around $1 per hour.

The captain dismissed the document and threatened to send them home to face retribution from the recruiting agency. Believing that the New Zealand government would protect them from such a fate, Yusril and all but four of the Indonesian crew walked off the boat and sought refuge in Lyttelton Union Parish Church. Aided by two local pro bono lawyers, they decried months of flagrant human rights abuses and demanded their unpaid wages under New Zealand's Admiralty Act.

Ten miles from Lyttelton, in neighboring Christchurch, stands the headquarters of United Fisheries, the company that exclusively purchased the fish that Yusril and his mates caught. The building features gleaming Doric columns topped with friezes of chariot races. It was designed to resemble the temples to Aphrodite in Cyprus, the homeland of United founder Kypros Kotzikas.

The patriarch started in New Zealand with a small fish-and-chip restaurant. Some 40 years later, his son, Andre, 41, runs a company that had some $66 million in revenue last year. Although three *Melilla* crew members, citing abuse, had run away nine days before I spoke with Kotzikas, he told me he had heard of no complaints from crew on board the ships, and he had personally boarded the vessels to ensure that the conditions "are of very high standard."

"I don't think that claims of slavery or mistreatment can be attached to foreign charter vessels that are operating here in New Zealand," he said. "Not for responsible operators."

In an e-mail, Peter Elms, a fraud and compliance manager with Immigration New Zealand, cited a police assessment that found that complaints from crews amounted to nothing more than disputes over "work conditions, alleged (minor) assaults/intimidation/workplace bullying, and nonpayment of wages." Elms said his department had two auditors who visited each vessel every two or three years, and they had found nothing rising to the level of human trafficking, a crime punishable in New Zealand by up to 20 years in prison. Kotzikas said that while New Zealand's labor laws are "a thousand pages of, you know, beautiful stuff," he believed they did not necessarily apply beyond New Zealand's 12-mile territorial radius.

Half of United Fisheries' annual revenue is generated outside New Zealand, spread across five continents. In the U.S., which imports an estimated $14.7 billion worth of fish annually, regulators are beginning to pay attention to the conditions under which that food is caught. The California Transparency in Supply Chains Act, as of Jan. 1, requires all retailers with more than $100 million in global sales to publicly disclose their efforts to monitor and combat slavery in their supply chains. The law covers some 3,200 corporations that do business in the state, including several that trade in seafood.

In our interview, Kotzikas said his company sold ling, a species of fish caught by the *Melilla* crews, to Costco Wholesale (COST), America's largest wholesaler and the world's seventh-largest retailer. As is true with many seafood exports from New Zealand, the exact quantity of United's sales to Costco was untraceable through public shipping records. Costco representatives did not respond to requests for comment about the sales and the abuse allegations.

Dean Stavreff, managing director of Quality Ocean—the Christchurch-based company that exported the fish and whose largest shareholder is Kotzikas—said Costco purchases ling that is processed through the facility at United Fisheries headquarters. While he did not oversee that process, Stavreff insisted that all of the ling that Quality Ocean sold Costco had been caught on "longline" vessels operated by Talley's and Okains Bay, two fishing companies that "stay well away from the alleged slave labor that is associated with the *Melilla* ships." Costco advertises that it offers only chilled, longline-caught ling to U.S. consumers. The retailer, which annually audits United's processing facility but not its vessels, had issued the company a six-page Supplier Code of Conduct, which laid out minimum labor conditions and specifically prohibited "slave labor, human trafficking... and physical abuse of employees."

In New Zealand, there is no independent auditing of catch method once a fish has been landed and processed. Ling caught by longlines is considered to be of higher quality and more environmentally sustainable than ling hauled by trawlers. As a result, longline-caught fish can fetch double the price, providing incentive for fraud and mislabeling. As recently as 2008 the *Melilla* ships were fined more than $300,000 for "trucking," which means misreporting catches from one fishing area to another. New Zealand officials have not, however, accused them or any other vessel of trying to mislabel trawler-caught fish as longline-caught. Costco offers only chilled, longline-caught ling to U.S. consumers, and Stavreff said that thawing frozen ling would degrade it so as to make fraud implausible.

Other large U.S. retailers also do business with United Fisheries. (Thirteen employees at nine seafood companies contacted for this article agreed to speak only on background.) P.F. Chang's China Bistro (PFCB), a Scottsdale (Ariz.)-based chain with more than 200 restaurants worldwide and more than $1.2 billion in annual revenue, purchased squid exclusively through Turner, a California-based importer. According to Import Genius and Urner Barry shipping records, Turner bought at least 568,554 lb. of squid from United since November 2010. Squid was one of the most common seafood species caught by fishermen held on the *Melilla* boats, according to Yusril and other crew members. Turner did not respond to requests for comment. A representative for P.F. Chang's declined to comment on record.

Honolulu-based importer P&E Foods has also bought at least 48,940 lb. of squid from United since November 2010. According to P&E's president, Stephen Lee, his company sells squid to Sam's Club, the 47 million-member wholesaler. Lee said he was unaware of allegations of abuse on ships chartered by United, a company with which Lee has done business for "20, 30 years." He added that he did not know whether any of P&E's buyers required him or his suppliers to sign a code of conduct for labor practices. Carrie Foster, senior manager for corporate communications at Sam's Club, said her company does require such signed agreements from their suppliers.

Another New Zealand company with ties to U.S. retailers is Sanford, the country's second-largest seafood enterprise. On Nov. 3, I interviewed crew members of the *Dong Won* and *Pacinui* vessels, charters catching fish for Sanford, near the docks at Lyttelton. These men risked punishment by speaking out: Less than a week earlier three *Pacinui* crew members who had complained were sent back to Indonesia to face the recruiters.

A *Dong Won* deckhand said he felt like a slave as he simulated a Korean officer kicking him on the ground. Their contracts, issued by IMS and two other Indonesian agents, were nearly identical to those signed by the *Melilla* crew. They reported the same pay rates, false contracts, doctored time sheets and similar hours, daily abuse, intimidation, and threats to their families if they walked away. After several desertions over the past decade, New Zealand labor audits of the *Dong Won* ships turned up some of the same complaints. In 2010, Sanford assured the government that it would improve oversight of foreign-chartered vessels and address allegations of abuse or wage exploitation. Barratt, Sanford's CEO, said observers of his company's foreign vessels did not find instances of abuse and that three deported *Pacinui* crew had returned voluntarily.

According to Barratt, his company exports to the U.S. through at least 16 seafood distributors, the majority through Mazzetta, a $425 million corporation based in suburban Chicago that is the largest American importer of New Zealand fish. Mazzetta sells the same species caught on the *Dong Won* and *Pacinui* ships to outlets across the country. On Feb. 21, after the publication of an online version of this article, CEO Tom Mazzetta sent a letter to Sanford's Baratt demanding an investigation of labor practices on Sanford's foreign-chartered vessels.

Sanford also supplies to $10 billion supermarket chain Whole Foods Market (WFM), according to Barratt. A Whole Foods spokesperson, Ashley Hawkins, said that "for proprietary reasons we cannot reveal who we source from for our exclusive brand products," including the chain's Whole Catch New Zealand hoki products. Asked about allegations that FCVs in New Zealand employ slave labor, Hawkins said Whole Foods is "in compliance with the California Transparency in Supply Chains Act. According to the U.S. Department of Labor, New Zealand is not considered high-risk."

Other buyers of Sanford's fish include Nova Scotia-based High Liner Foods (HLF), which sells products containing the same seafood as that caught by the indentured fishermen on the *Dong Won* and *Pacinui* ships. High Liner's customers include U.S. retailers such as Safeway (SWY), America's second-largest grocery store chain, and Wal-Mart Stores (WMT), the world's largest retailer. When alerted by *Bloomberg Businessweek*, spokespeople for both retailers pledged swift investigations. "As with all of our suppliers, we have a process under way to obtain documentation that [High Liner] is complying with the laws regarding human trafficking and slavery, and that [they are] reviewing their supply chain to insure compliance," said Brian Dowling, Safeway's vice president of public affairs, on Feb. 17. "We have not yet received certification from High Liner. However, we are following up with them immediately and asking that they provide us with certification."

Henry Demone, High Liner's CEO, said he "abhorred" slavery and labor abuse and that his company "tries very hard to do the right thing." He said that in the case of the FCVs used by Sanford, "we bought from a company whose labor practices in the [processing] plant were fine. We audited that. We didn't audit the fishing vessels. But we relied upon a well-known New Zealand-based company and their assurance of 100 percent observer coverage."

It is unclear exactly how much seafood caught by indentured fishermen ends up on the plates of American consumers. Public shipping records—which do not report seafood imported on planes, and only detail some seafood imported to the U.S. by boat—are sparse, and seafood distributors rarely disclose their specific suppliers. Alastair Macfarlane, a representative of New Zealand's Seafood Industry Council, declined to comment on which American companies might be buying fish from troubled vessels such as the *Melilla 203*.

However, an analysis of several sources of data—including New Zealand fishery species quota and FCV catch totals made available by the Ministry of Agriculture and Forestry—suggests roughly 40 percent of squid exported from New Zealand is caught on one of the vessels using coerced labor. Perhaps 15 percent of all New Zealand Hoki exports may be slave-caught, and 8 percent of the country's southern blue whiting catch may be tainted.

Despite the prevalence of foreign-chartered vessels, which in 2010 earned $274.6 million in export revenue and hauled in 62.3 percent of New Zealand's deepwater catch, some New Zealand companies have determined they are not worth the risk.

"The reputational damage is immeasurable," says Andrew Talley, director of Talley's Group, New Zealand's third-largest fishing company, which submits to third-party social responsibility audits on its labor standards, a condition of its contract to supply McDonald's (MCD) with hoki for its Filet-O-Fish sandwiches. "New Zealand seafood enjoys a hard-earned and world-leading reputation as a responsible fisheries manager, with a product range and quality to match," says Talley. "There is nothing responsible at all about using apparently exploitative and abusive FCVs."

The main thoroughfare that bisects Yusril's Central Java village feeds into a chain of divided tollways that run all the way to Jakarta. Travelers along the road quickly leave the briny air of the fishing kampungs and pass through green rice paddies dotted with water buffalo and trees bearing swollen, spiky jackfruit. Sixty years ago, Yusril's grandfather worked that land. Today, thousands journey along the highway to seek new lives.

When I found him last December, Yusril was back in his in-laws' modest home, tucked well off a side road. He was out of work and brainstorming ways to scratch out a living by returning to his father's trade, farming. IMS, the recruiting agency in Jakarta, had blacklisted him and was refusing to return his birth certificate, his basic safety training credentials, and his family papers. It was also withholding pay, totaling around $1,100. In total, Yusril had been paid an average of 50¢ an hour on the *Melilla 203*. (An IMS attorney did not respond to repeated e-mails requesting comment. When I showed up at the agency's offices in Jakarta, a security guard escorted me out.)

Two of the 24 men who walked off the *Melilla 203* returned to work on the ship rather than face deportation. The ship's representatives flew the remaining 22 resisters back to Indonesia. When they returned to Central Java, they say, they were coerced by IMS into signing documents waiving their claims to redress for human rights violations, in exchange for their originally stipulated payments of $500 to $1,000. Yusril was one of two who held out. On Jan. 21, when I last spoke to him, I asked why he had refused to sign the document.

"Dignity," said Yusril, pointing to his heart.

As Shakespeare said, "You've got to be honest and truthful, because all your fellow individuals have to gauge you by on your way of life is not only what you have done for yourself, but what you have done for others." No matter what mistakes you make, in the end you have to hope that the people you are closely connected with family, and friends and in business will turn out okay over the years, nothing is forever.

CHAPTER 20

As Mattie nears the end of his career, he is very concerned about where America and the world are heading in the future. Headlines in the media indicate that Stockton, California, is on the verge of becoming the largest United States city ever to go bankrupt. Barring a last-minute reprieve, Stockton, which has a population of three hundred thousand people, will file for bankruptcy in late June of 2012. At one time, this was the transport hub for the gold rush 160 years ago. At the height of the economic boom, three thousand houses a year were being built. However, Stockton spent money on an $80 million glass concert arena, a five-thousand-seat ballpark for the local minor league baseball team, and $42 million super yacht that a casino dominates.

During its glory days, the city also paid $2 million to a chef from California in order for him to open up a restaurant which did not last long. Stockton spent $35 million on a building that was supposed to be a city hall, but the city never moved in and was repossessed by the bank along with its three multistory parking garages. Inside the crumbling city hall, the tap water is not drinkable, and the building is full of rats. Because of its massively inflated housing marking and soaring debts, Stockton was hit like a freight train when the recession came after 2007 subprime crisis. Its home foreclosure rate was the highest in the United States, property values dropped to 75 percent, and business went under. Unemployment is now at 19 percent, the city's revenues from property and sales taxes were decimated by the downturn. In addition, it had given away benefits to the city employees, including lifelong medical care for each employee and their spouse. This health care plan left them with an estimated liability of $417 million.

City officials are in talks with creditors over $350 million the city owes bondholders. These talks will not likely concede, and bankruptcy will follow. The city has already slashed public sectors staffing and pay. The 425 police forces have been cut by 25 percent. Less than a mile from a marina, the morning queue at the food bank starts an hour and a half before opening time. More than four hundred people line up each day for a box of donated food.

This is an example of what is happening across North America. The question is, why? The answer is simple. In Calgary, Alberta, a list of the city's top fifty earners indicate the Shaw family corporation pays out $50 million to their top employees, including three family members. One family member, who is retiring at age fifty-four, is getting a $5.4 million pension per year. It would be hard for anyone to imagine what an individual could do to earn such a large sum of money yearly for doing nothing, and how one could possibly spend this much money in a lifetime.

The book written by Bruce Livesey *Thieves of Bay Street: How banks, Brokerages, and the Wealthy Steal Billions from Canadians* is a sobering read. Canada's financial sector was increasingly being dubbed, prior to 2008, as the Wild West by journalists and foreign critics as they do in many countries in Europe. The yellow pages have dropped in stock value per share from $50 to less than $1.

Why is Canada so prone to fraud? CEOs live in the same neighborhoods as their boards of directors, and corporate lawyers send their children to the same school. Canadian regulators are criticized for being toothless and seemingly incapable of putting anyone in jail.

It was only when Wall Street's recklessness caused the US economy to spectacularly explode that everyone suddenly forgot about Bay Street's seedy underbelly, but nothing ever changed. Policy makers clearly need to be prodded to take this problem seriously.

When talking about wages, the Queen of England's yearly pay jumped by 20 percent, another reason for her to be cheerful in her Diamond Jubilee year. Her annual pay is about to jump to US$57 million. Another example in Canada is Encana Corporation, an oil and gas production company located in Calgary, Alberta. This was once Canada's premier oil and gas company; then they decided to concentrate on natural gas—the fuel of the futures. We all know how that bet turned out. Now the company is shutting down gas wells and exploring for oil and other liquid fuels. The CEO Randy Eresman got paid $9.2 million in one year. The directors each got at least $340,000 in stock and cash. David O'Brien, the chairman, was there when the company was formed a decade ago. In the old days, he used to run Canadian Pacific Railway. Encana has been in the news for environmental problems in America, paying fines of a few million dollars, which amounts to nothing but a tap on the wrist. This company was sold by the premier of Alberta in 1993 for $2 million. Two years later, it was worth $6 million; at its peak it was worth $60 to $100 billion. What a terrible loss for Albertans!

If you are investing in the stock market, beware of RONA Inc., a retailer and wholesaler of hardware supplies. The *Globe and Mail* Report on Business states that its share prices have gone down 56 percent over the past five years, even though Canada is supposedly in a housing boom. The CEO and directors blame it on bad weather. Another company is AGF Management; the family that controls this mutual fund company has been trading its shares for the last fifteen years in the $11 range.

The other side of the oil business is that while many are thriving off of the oil sands in Fort McMurray, others are struggling, and the need for social assistance persists. The north is a place of extremes. At 9:00 a.m., a lineup is already stretching from the doorway and down the street where a thrift store is about to open for the day. In it are bins of bread, free for the taking while upstairs are offices and a homeless shelter. Each of its thirty-two beds is typically in use at any night. Welcome to the Salvation Army, where staff and volunteers are off in the front line for those in need, even in the heart of Alberta's booming oil sand sector. One night last week, the Salvation Army soup kitchen served over one hundred people. Typically they would expect no more than seventy-five people. Vacancy rates are low and rent is high, and lucrative jobs are not guaranteed while big foreign business are making billions in profit out of the area.

In Canada, the banks are warning Ottawa over lending rules, particularly the TD and RBC banks, who caution that new maximums on government-backed mortgages could dampen economy. They state it is hard to argue that the government shouldn't be doing something to slow the economy down. It is not good to pull too tightly on the reigns. In other words, it is suggested that Canada should be like the United States and drive the country into a recession or depression in some particular areas, causing over 40 percent of the people to lower their standard of living and lose their jobs and homes.

We mentioned earlier on about Encana coming under scrutiny in the United States. There is a fine irony in the fact that two of the highest towers in North America near completion, the company is experiencing major cracks in its foundation. Not only has Encana's fortunes sagged along natural gas prices, the company is now dealing with reports that the US Department of Justice is investigating accusations between it and the second largest US natural gas producer. No matter how anyone slices this one, it doesn't look good for either company. It all began with a report by the Reuters news agency that claimed Encana had collaborated with another company so that neither company could bid up the price on a sale, hence the reason for the justice department's reported scrutiny.

The airline industry is another area of concern for Canadians. For example, if you were to book flights in Europe twenty-one days in advance, your bill would be $689 of which taxes and fees are 36 percent of the total. Now consider a US comparison; flights to the United States between New York to Washington just for a return amounts to $840, with taxes and fees of 61 percent. Compare the totals with return flights in Canada—Calgary to Victoria is $1,800 including taxes and fees of 28 percent. Even though you would fly a longer distance in Europe than you would in North America, Europe has better fare-friendly skies.

As the United Kingdom gets ready to celebrate the British Olympics, its financial sector is in turmoil. This tragedy has not yet received much attention in the New World, yet the scale is breathtaking. With bankers in disgrace throughout the world, and patience with them worn thin, how many more punches can the precarious economies in the world take? The public is outraged over the fact that banks have been rigging interest rates for their own benefit. These practices seem to be common in the industry.

Do fines really matter to energy firms? It is debatable if the penalties make companies change their ways or just deter others. A $125,000 against TransAlta for manipulating the electricity market in Alberta, or the $3.7 million fine proposed for Enbridge after its oil spill in a Michigan River would amount to no more than a small error on a corporate balance sheet. It has been stated that all these fines are buying the regulator one or two days of newspaper headlines.

An article in the *Globe and Mail* states that the origin of the crisis the world economy has faced in the recent years lies in the greed of "takers," the speculators responsible for the initial collapse. Perhaps if governments made a better effort to ensure that the large "takers" gave back proportionally as much as the little ones, there would be no need for argument and some of the very rich corporation CEOs deplore. Young people would graduate without an enormous amount of debt rather than have to protest on the streets for better tuition fees.

Banks and drug companies used to enjoy good reputations and were relatively highly trusted. Most people regarded them as useful industries that created products and services that benefited society. Sometimes the people who ran these companies lived down the street from the average person. Those times are long gone. Today, these people are movie villains. They will do anything to turn a dollar. Judging by current events, this characterization is all too true. Some of the most powerful people in this line of work will lie, cheat, and steal until they get caught, all the while assuring us that they are adding value to our society.

What happened? Both banking and pharmaceuticals went global, and the stakes and rewards shot up. Today they count their sales and profits in the billions. Today they make more money than most people could ever dream of. Their compensation is linked to stock prices, which means they have every incentive to boost short-term results. This is called aligning management's interests with the shareholders, and for years was thought to be a good thing. Unfortunately, it is not always a good thing for the public. Simple logic dictates that if the risk is small and the reward is great, the temptation to lie, cheat, and steal will occasionally prove overwhelming. Those billion-dollar fines are just the cost of doing business. Shame doesn't count for much in our culture. We do not expect those who participate in wrongdoings to fall on their swords. Bankers are not drummed out of political society, and pharmaceutical executives are not booted out of their country clubs; they will not suffer any serious financial penalty.

It is a very similar market in the oil industry throughout the world. Oil has slid over 30 percent from US$100 to US$80 per barrel, yet prices seem to keep rising. US consumption is in decline, and North American production is soaring. In the absence of a miraculous economic recovery, the benchmark price of a barrel of West Texas Crude should stabilize between $70–$90, with lower prices radiating across the economy. Early drillers dumped waste materials into streams and rivers and spread toxic drill mud on the land. Producers used most of the natural gas in the 1920s–1930s in order to get to oil. Flaring across America made the nighttime landscape look like a birthday cake covered in candles. These were common practices at the times and are no longer acceptable. During the past century, industry and government collaborated to solve these problems, and many more. Now as pipelines are becoming older, breaks into rivers and lakes should be added to the list.

There have been oil wells that have blown wild. The conservation boards are taking control of these runaway wells, the oil spills, and sometimes the entire oil field. The employees are working with the industries best technical experts to try and prevent the kind of spills that have occurred throughout the last few years. Government and industry leaders must take a stand on pipeline integrity. The mess each spill makes threatens our future. A social license to develop our petroleum birthright is special. If repeat offenders need to be penalized with huge fines, then the government should demand them. It is embarrassing and worse for our government leaders to have to defend pipeline leaks; it is time to bury them in the past. In ordinary business, a large bank in Canada is suing a US businessman and a group of alleged Canadian associates, stating that they ran a check-kiting scheme that targeted several banks and cost the large bank $20 million dollars, involving $750 million in fraudulent US checks.

One is only to look at Mongolia's boom, who are now having an election on a referendum on whether primary resources has enriched a few at the expense of many, with the middle-class saying that they don't want people coming in and escaping with whatever hot profits they make. Ordinary Mongolians state that right now, Mongolia is rushing to give away its land and resources to foreigners.

Endowed with some of the world's largest reserves of gold, iron, copper, and coal, Mongolia has become a magnet for foreign money. The nation's ten biggest deposits are worth more than$1.3 trillion according to estimates, yet close to one-third if the country's people still live in poverty. With the average Mongolian stating that the economic growths from the last few years has not trickled down to the people and is creating social tension, pressure for more policies is growing. Sound familiar?

In May, lawmakers approved a new foreign investment law that requires parliamentary approval for deals in which overseas investors owe more than 49 percent of the equity for more than $75 million in sections deemed strategic, including media, telecommunications, banking, and mining. The legislation was sparked in part by the Aluminum Corporation of China to purchase mining assets in Mongolia, causing the people to have concerns about losing control of their resources to foreigners. Throughout the world, 82 percent of the primary resources are controlled by the governments of each individual country in order to protect these very same resources the residents of the country. In Western Canada, the premiers and energy ministers are all heading to China in order to make deals to sell off their primary resources. A lot of residents of Western Canada feel that as those primary resources are sold and the profits flow out of the country, the residents across the nation will be left with the environmental problems and will have to pay much higher prices for their own resources, as natural gas in Western Canada is worth $3 per MCF while in China it is selling for $15 per MCF. If the governments and large corporations together can sell the resources outside the country, then the very residents of that country will end up paying five times for their own resources what they are normally paying at present.

The Canadian oil sands are an obvious example of new hydrocarbon reserves, where we must acknowledge the epic complexity and risks of most of these new finds. Alberta, Canada's oil sands are the obvious examples. Here, on average two tons of earth must be strip-mined and seven barrels of water heated to steam in order to produce a barrel of oil. It takes barrel-worth of energy to produce three barrels of oil. Thirty years ago, it would have been one hundred. In 1985, only 6 percent of the oil from the Gulf of Mexico came from wells drilled in water more than three meters deep. Shell, for instance, has spent $4 billion preparing to drill on the shores of Alaska, without yet producing a single barrel. Farther north, the federal government opened the bidding on a million of hectares of the Canadian Arctic sea floor.

These extremes go a long way to explain why oil is at $100 a barrel, which in turn helps explain why major oil companies are now keen to start pumping in Peru's Amazon. It has been stated, "Big money, big problems." It must be noted that major companies will not work where they do not have majority community support.

There has considerable debate on the Keystone Pipeline from Western Canada to the Gulf of Mexico. This pipeline was unsuccessful when it tried to go through Nebraska's US aquifer and was unable to get a permit. Now, a pipeline that was sending oil north to Oklahoma has been reversed, and oil has flows to be refined along the Texas coastline, results in less of a buildup at the Oklahoma terminals and more products for the Texas refineries. Since that time, it looks like a pipeline will be run eastward across Canada to the refineries in the eastern provinces of Ontario, Quebec, and New Brunswick, which will provide cheaper oil for Eastern Canada while at the same time not having to rely on a Venezuelan off shore crew and providing jobs for eastern Canadians and a sense of security for the consumers of Eastern Canada. Also relating to the oil industry, Enbridge Inc. is battling industry complaints in the United States that is favoring oil sand companies over producers from North Dakota's prolific Bakken field, as a shortage of capacity cost the companies over billions in revenues. This dispute underscores a growing scramble for pipelines and transportation space.

The Canadian Association of Petroleum Producers have cited an urgent need for addition transportation infrastructure as a key risk factor that oil sands production will double to three million barrels a day by the year 2020 from 1.6 million barrels today. Producers in Alberta and Saskatchewan aren't the only ones facing a problem; companies in North Dakota are resorting to transporting by road and railway. Enbridge states that they continue to believe that a High Prairie pipeline company claims are without merit and have filed a response with the Federal Energy Regulatory Commission (FERC) asking the commission to dismiss their complaint as it denied their earlier protest.

Risky investment drives improved productivity, which in turn drives higher wages and living standard for the poor and the rich. This is standard trickle-down and is not much in dispute. Today there are a lot of single people and couples without children. The economy is much more subject to global competition. Young people are willing to move and change jobs, and businesses are much more willing to move production to other countries. Governments can't simply raise taxes on parts of the population anymore, though they can get revenues to fund all the public services that the older population has been promised in terms of pensions and health care. Health care in both Canada and the United States has grown very costly and is no longer sustainable. In the United States, fifty million people do not have access to health care. In Canada, the wait for an operation can be a year or two. Therefore, if you have paid taxes for forty to fifty years and find yourself needing either system, there is no doubt that you will find both systems out of reach.

Countries use monetary fiscal stimulus to emerge from the 2009 recession. This has been the worst recovery of the last eleven US recessions, with poor employment response. Effectively, entitlements have become less affordable in certain countries throughout the world, with the main result being dangerous debt. A lot of debt occurs because people believe they have the right to the lifestyle of other people around them. A lot of people think that whatever their neighbor have, they should also have. All this has resulted in a battle of generations, with the entitlements being taken away from younger people. These are things that are harder to take from older people from a standpoint of politics, as baby boomers are getting into retirement, and they are a big voting block. It is harder to pull pensions and health care from people who are sixty to seventy-eight years of age because they can't begin working again at that age.

At present, governments throughout the world are filing lawsuits against tobacco in an attempt to recover smoking-related health costs. Among the allegations, none of which have been proven in court, is that the companies designed tobacco products to be highly addictive, deceiving Americans by minimizing the product's addictiveness and harm and falsely denying the health risks of exposure to tobacco products. Provinces and states have collected $1 billion annually in tobacco taxes while a $10 million lawsuit is the base for a lawsuit against tobacco-related topics. These cases drag on for years. In some cases, lawsuits have been filed in the '90s, and no Canadian case has gone to court. In 1999, the United States tobacco industry settled with forty-six US states by agreeing to pay almost $250 billion over twenty-five years. That deal featured restrictions on how tobacco products were marketed and sold.

The lawsuits lay out a long list of negative health effects from tobacco use, including lung cancer, cardiovascular disease, chronic obstructive pulmonary disease, and overall diminished health and increased risk of morbidity and mortality. The Coalition of Anti-Smoking Groups states that tobacco kills anywhere from three thousand to five thousand provincial or state inhabitants per year.

Mattie has been a Union supporter, but many people wonder as America has been in a recession-depression for the past four to five years with the Unions gaining raises and additional people being hired, how America can remain competitive in a global economy. This is something that is of great concern to the majority of Americans as we become less competitive, and costs go up, then our living standards have only one way to go—down, resulting in other countries with lower wages being able to take away the European and American market.

"Bribery Hushed Up by Wal-Mart," an article in the *Globe and Mail* states that there is reasonable suspicion to believe that Mexican and US laws have been violated by Wal-Mart by participating in corrupt dealings with politicians. One of the senior people, who resigned from Wal-Mart in Mexico in 2004, said he helped organized years of payoffs. He described personally dispatching two outside lawyers to deliver envelopes of cash to city officials. They targeted mayors and city managers, who issued permits in their favor; another example of big-business corrupting bureaucrats throughout the world.

In an investigation, new allegations arise in SNC-Lavalin probe. A businessman claims he lost an infrastructure contract for refusing to pay a bribe of $100,000. He claims he was shot out of a big construction project because he refused to pay a bribe to one of the Canadian's top company executives; another example of corruption throughout big business in the world. Protestors target General Electric's tax rate in a newspaper, an employer of a specific company writes nearly one hundred protestors in an attack against the US low tax rate. The General Electric chief financial officer stepped up to defend against the protestors, saying that they were complying with every law around the world on how they pay their taxes. A 2011, report claimed that GE had an effective negative tax rate which the companies deny. Hundreds of people affiliate with the Occupy Wall Street movement. In an interview, the company's CEO told reporters that GE supports the idea of reforming the US tax code and that it reflected write-offs.

In a western province in Canada, a salesman for GE stated that he used to work for a Far East manufacturer of hospital equipment, but he could not sell anything because GE from the United States had divided the province up between the two companies. He quit Toshiba to go and work for GE, resulting in getting double his salary, working out of his house beyond belief while he laughed at the stupidity of the provincial government. Upon further investigation, Mattie found out that the budget for that Canadian province was $16 billion of which Mattie, when working out the cost of supplying health care to a little over three million people, could be cut by $10 billion as the government, through waste and mismanagements, were throwing away over 50 percent of the health care budget resulting in lengthy wait times in the public health care system. It has been stated that many patients stay in the hospital longer than the four-day benchmark for surgeries, resulting in every hour that an acute care bed remains occupied by a recovering patient that doesn't need to be there is an hour in the same bed that cannot be occupied by another patient who need surgery.

Public health care suffers from many ailments, and it is going to take years to solve the problems that have developed over the past several decades, resulting in a terrible health care situation in Canada. It has been stated in Canada that older immigrants cost the health care system $3 billion a year just in hospitalization alone. It has been suggested that the government, which isn't shy about favoring the economic immigrants, wasn't just trying to be fair and doing nothing about the backlog, but it also has grave concerns about accepting low-earning immigrants.

The cost of education for large immigrant families is not often taken into consideration. The education system already a disaster, whereas the schools and universities should be run half the time for one group of students and the other half of the year for another group of students, cutting the cost of education in half. Unless the plan is put in place, the education system in Canada and the United States is going to go broke in the near future. There are more people drawing pensions than there are working.

Bureaucrats have taken control of the universities. No longer do academics set priorities for the university. Administrators take control and make the rules. When professors were at temporary administrative assignment, they never forgot the purpose of the university. Today there is a fundamental conflict between academics and administrators. Across the continent, administration has become a growth industry at a time when budget constraints are said to compel the reduction of full-time faculty positions. Recently some universities offered mostly senior faculty a onetime buyout with no guarantee that their positions would be replaced. Such a commitment would reduce administrative flexibility.

One reason administrators have won is because there are too many of them. At most universities, the executive team, besides the president, has six vice presidents and two lawyers. The first VP listed cannot do his job fund-raising without the aid of a senior director, four executive directors, thirteen directors, and more associates and lesser officers. Many of these people have their own assistants, and this is not the largest administrative unit. The question is, what do these administrators do? They meet, attend conferences, and organize retreats. Sometimes they have joint retreats with administrators from other conferences, which is the very opposite of academic discover and insight that they should be doing.

In today's university system, most professors use undergraduates to do their work while they draw huge salaries for doing research or travelling throughout the world attending conferences. If you wonder why universities are expensive to operate today, follow the money to the administrators and their support staff. When students come to universities, they are more likely to find whatever educational value exists in the underpaid work of part-time seasonal instructors. Money spent on administrational activities cannot be spent on academic programs. It's about time that there is a measure so that the ordinary taxpayer and student could tell how their money is being spent.

When discussing the inequality of the present system in the western world, many people have written books stating that we should be worried that in the U.S. the top 1% claimed 20% of the national income. Should we be more concerned that the middle is lagging or that the very top is soaring? Until recently, economists mostly ignored these questions. The financial sector broadens the income gap and destabilizes the economy. With President Obama proposing a millionaires tax and even republicans haranguing the republican Presidential Hopeful for the sin of getting rich. His time is certainly good. Inequality is shaping up to be a defining them of the 2012 election year in the U.S. Do democratic institutions promote equality? In general, I believe they do not.

By inference, inequality should be regretted. There are few solutions, aside from state involvement. Inequality varies from the level of development, thus all agrarian feudal societies and all advances technological economies will resemble each other more than they resemble other countries. There is a shriveling of the welfare state. Nonetheless, with the encouragement of central banks and other official bodies, the financial industry now captures a far higher share of total income than before.

Increased inequality is a warning sign that something is not going right. What might that something be? A very smart man once wrote, "The inequality of the past three decades—driven by the stock market and the rising role of finance, lead inexorably to instability and chaos."

Another waste in the western world is fluoride, which in various cities is now being put into the water in a large number of cities. This was a total waste of money as water that was used for flushing toilets, watering lawns, used on streets and roads, etc., contained fluoride—a total waste of the taxpayer's money.

In Canada, Teachers' Pension Plan joins Calls for Change at Canadian Pacific Railway. CPR, a railroad which was built over 150 years ago and completed across Canada in the mid-1980s, has now been taken over by a Wall Street firm totally backed by the Teachers' Pension of Canada. This is what I like to refer to as the Great Canadian Sellout.

Some states and provinces have been taken increases of 30–40 percent in a one-year period. This sets a very bad example for the people who provide the goods and services in any state or province. Recently there was a $4 million payout to the CEO of the Calgary Regional Health Authority in Alberta, Canada, and expenditures of over $200 million to purchase hardware and software, including $15 million in severance payouts for departing MLA's cushy and high-paid jobs that were not advertised for competition, but given to friends of the people in power, plus $21,000 per month for four years to pay members of the assembly. You'd wonder why more people would not be concerned when the government wastes so much money.

In Canada, the Canadian Association of Petroleum Producers' (CAPP) most recent handbook indicates that in 2010, this industry sold over $100 billion in gas but paying only $12 billion in resource royalties. Even people from the government who are for large foreign oil companies can only come up with $22 billion, which includes all general taxes applicable to all industries but still only amounts to one-fifth of over the $100 billion.

On the positive side, an American investor in the Canadian oil industries has donated a ranch worth $11 million to the Calgary Stampede, one of the biggest outdoor shows on Earth, and excellent show which lasts ten days and draws over one million people to Calgary, Alberta. His eight-thousand-acre ranch, which dates back to the late 1870s, has several subsequent owners and expanded over the years. At one time, it was going to be a military training ground and artillery range when an Alberta business, Daryl Seaman, bought it to ensure that it remains undeveloped. After this man died, someone stepped in and bought it and made a gift in 2012 on the one hundredth anniversary of the Calgary Stampede. This land has been protected from development and oil drilling and will stay in its natural state. The Calgary Stampede has celebrated Alberta's culture for the past one hundred years, and this gift will encourage that for the next one hundred years. Certainly, a fine example of a transplanted American in a foreign country who has built a very large oil business while donating millions to charity.

The Financial Services section of the *Globe and Mail,* a Canadian-wide newspaper, states that a global investigation in the manipulation of interbank landing rates widened with Britain's fraud squad taking up the case. Germany's markets regulator had launched a probe into the Deutsche Bank. Authorities in the United States, Europe, Canada, and Japan examined more than a dozen banks over suspected rigging of the laundering interbank rate. Britain's Barclays has so far been the only bank to admit wrongdoing, agreeing to pay a fine of nearly half a billion US dollars.

The Canadian government is proposing a new set of standardized rules to government how complaints against big banks are handled, but the government has formally given banks permission to pick who will hear customer's disputes. The new rules followed the departure of the Royal Bank in 2008 and Toronto-Dominion in 2011 from having complaints heard by the federal government's employee. Critics have been quick to pounce on the announcement with the Public Interest Advocacy Centre called the regulations week and said they would destroy "the Ombudsman for banking services and investments," stating that the bank is choosing the individuals who are going to settle the complaints, as well as paying for them, it doesn't sound like an independent process.

Mattie decided that these are the same two companies that want to keep interest rates low resulting in seniors getting no return on their money that they have worked all their life for while the big businesses get their hard-earned money at next to nothing, 1–2 percent, while lending it out at 15–18 percent on credit cards—a complete rip-off. These very same two banks are also raising the charges on the seniors' accounts, something that the seniors cannot afford.

Mattie solved his problem by quitting the Toronto Dominion and Royal Bank and moving to the Canadian Western Bank and Scotia Bank, which he finds are much better banks to deal with.

In the United States, the tally of people charged by the US Attorney's Office for the southern district in New York now reads that sixty-nine people charged since October 2009, with sixty-three convictions and five cases pending, with one remaining defendant on the run. Evidence has shown that one individual who had an excess of $100 million in personal assets and also had a position on the boards on some of America's largest companies and tied to numerous universities, while there seemed to be an endless demand for his services. Given all of this, the jurors still convicted him which is a good sign that individuals on Wall Street which have destroyed over 40 percent of the middle-class Americans' standard of living will finally be taken to task.

The side effects of low interest rates are causing problems throughout the free world. For example, in its latest annual report, the Bank for International Settlements (BIS) points to a number of other problems that negative real rates might provoke. First, the fall on financial cost may promote ignoring balance sheet problems resulting in these individuals getting deeper in debt. The result could be that the problems are left to fester, making it impossible for central banks to raise interest rates to a normal interest rate to a more normal level in future years for fear of the damage they might cause. The BIS also worries that low interest rates in the developing world may have had spillover effects in emerging markets, pushing up exchange rates, causing asset bubbles such as Chinese property and, until recently, inflating commodity prices. Finally, the BIS frets that easy monetary policy may be letting politicians off the hook, remarking that "it would be a mistake to think that central bankers can use their balance sheets to solve economic and financial problems."

There will be something wrong if in five years time, real interest rates are still negative. Capitalism depends on having given a positive return to suppliers of capital, which would be a mistake to argue that the central banks should attempt to raise interest rates soon. The European Central Bank's (ECB) decision to tighten monetary policy last year looks like an even bigger error in retrospect than it did at the time. Savers will have to keep suffering.

Another concern in North America is universities researchers stating that medically impaired drivers are taking the place of drunk drivers on the roads, silently sneaking up on motorists with their particular band of peril. While medical issues increases as people age, effecting vision and physical requirements needed to drive, age alone isn't a good age of whether or not someone is road-worthy. "The most pressing need is for the public and medical community is to shift from older drivers to medically-at-risk drivers," states a university professor. "It should be as socially unacceptable to drive when medically impaired as when you are drunk. But it isn't." These same professors state that people of any age can have medical issues impairing their ability to drive safely. The professors also state, "Driving is a very complex task," but after searching statistics, Mattie found that only 6 percent of seniors are involved in accidents, and these are mostly minor fender benders.

Mattie personally has driven over two million kilometers throughout the world on slippery roads, through snowstorms, driven cars, trucks, tractor trailers, etc., without ever having an accident that was the result of his driving. Now, at seventy-seven years old, he is a better driver than 99 percent of the people on the roads in North America. Mattie's solution to this problem, which does not exist, is to fire these professors immediately and use the money that is being wasted on their salaries to help fund health care for the hundreds of thousands of seniors and the tens to thousands who are dying because of a lack of proper health care.

What we are wasting on education and mismanagement in both health care and education is costing us in America billions of dollars. This does not include lost productivity and suffering by people who have to wait in Canada up to a year or two for health care assistance. Big business and the rich have called, as a group, for tax cuts for the last quarter century. We have now got them, and in Western Canada, we have lost half of our hospital beds whereas Americans who have health care insurance usually get excellent treatment.

US politics has become a race for money. The candidates are attending at least three fund-raising events per week since the beginning of the year, raising in one month alone from $60–$80 million. If you think those sums are large, you haven't seen anything yet. To be a politician in the United States is to be a full-time pursuer of cash. It wasn't supposed to be this way; in 1971, Congress passed the Federal Election Campaign Act that tried to put limits on spending and contributions. In exchange for these limits, public financing was introduced for presidential campaigns. What has become an endless game of Whack-A-Mole, the Supreme Court struck down any limits on spending. On the contribution side, money streams into political parties. These superpowers are created by party activists and make no bones about which parties they support. A large number of donors who have given at least $300, 000 in turn have already raised over $60 million for one party.

The party in power in Canada raised $25 million in 2011, more than twice the sum raised by the opposition parties. Unfortunately, money can have a deeply corrupting influence on politics. Not just because of the expectations in favor of the money received, but because it diverts so much attention away from governing to seeking cash. The US Supreme Court has been complicit in the corrupting influence of money on US politics and government.

CHAPTER 21

In ending this book, Mattie feels that there are a number of items in North America which are of great importance to every individual in America. At this time, he is going to address that what he feels are both sides of the various issues.

1. Abortion
   Abortion should be legal if a child is going to be born and grow up in a home where it will be mistreated and have a poor quality of life. On the other hand, with so many families now going overseas to adopt, would it not be wise to give birth to the children even though they are unwanted and adopt them out to these families who are so desperate to have children?

2. Banks
   Should banks and the stock market be regulated? Of course. Recessions and depressions over the past one hundred years have been caused by stockbrokers and big banks that draw very high wages and extremely large bonuses. Without regulation, these two corporate endeavors would destroy the free world. Capitalism is a great system, but if allowed to run rampant it will destroy civilization in itself over the long run. On the other side, too much regulation can destroy free enterprise.

3. Big Business versus Small Business
   If there were no regulations to help small businesses, then big businesses would simply run countries to the detriment of that country's citizens. As the bottom line for big business, or any business, are profits. For example, Husky and Esso Oil are very tough companies to deal with;

where Pacific Petroleum and Gulf Oil were probably some of the best businesspeople that Mattie ever dealt with. Unfortunately, both are out of business while Esso and Husky are thriving. This is a clear indicator that if you will do anything to make a dollar, you will survive, while other companies with a high degree of business ethics will go out of business. On the other hand, if the government regulates big business in favor of small business, that can be looked upon as detrimental to the economy.

4. Birth Control
    On the positive side, birth control in the third world countries keeps the population down. Even though the majority of religions are against it, it is still being practiced by a large percentage of North Americans. On the other side of the coin, there is very little to be said for not practicing birth control if couples do not want children or are not ready for them.

5. Class Actions
    Class actions in North America have been criticized and the lawyers who pursue them. This is the only way that many people have a chance to receive justice in a system that is stacked against them. On the other side of the coin, a number of wealthy lawyers receive large settlements from these class actions, but one must bear in mind that the lawyers take a chance that if they do not win, they do not receive any money.

6. Capital Punishment
    Mattie used to be for capital punishment, but after reading in the media how in Illinois over 50 percent of the people that were put to death were later declared innocent by a DNA, he is now against it. In states such as Texas, police and attorney generals withhold information that sends people to their death. On the other side, some may state that if you do a horrific crime, you deserve the ultimate punishment. This is something that is usually only practiced in states such as Texas and other areas of the deep Southern United States.

7. Chemicals
    Nearly all the food we eat is contaminated by various drugs and chemicals, such as antibiotics in farm animals. Mattie found this out to his dismay when he got a stomach virus followed by a hospital infection caused by unhygienic conditions in hospitals that resulted in ninety days of hospitalization and two months recovery to learn to

walk again because the antibiotics used by the hospitals in the United States and Canada were incapable for months of curing the stomach infection. A doctor from the Far East, a very intelligent and sincere individual, saved Mattie's life when he only had several days to live. On the other hand, if farmers, fruit growers, cash crop farmers did not use chemicals including herbicides and pesticides, it would be very difficult to carry out their agricultural endeavors. There are positive and negative sides to using chemicals.

8. Debt
Debt can destroy individuals, businesses, or governments. An example is the US government, which is $16 trillion in debt, most held by offshore countries. On the other side, without debt, businesses, individuals, and governments would find it very difficult to operate.

9. Divorce
When Mattie was a teenager, there was no divorce, and couples who engaged in divorces were highly frowned upon. On the positive side, it is better to divorce than live in an unhappy marriage. Adversely, divorce is not a very fair situation as one person is often successful, and when it comes time to divorce, the other party can take half the assets and can take children, if there are any, far away from the other party.

10. Drinking and Smoking
It has now become a negative to drink and drive and to smoke anywhere in a public place. Mattie has not smoked for over a third of a century, nor has he drank too excess and personally feels that with the police stopping vehicles in places such as Western Canada solely to check if an individual has been drinking is taking away your rights, and the new rules only allow for a very small blood alcohol level. This law, which has just been put in, will be no doubt be challenged in court. On the other side, a lot of people who are against smoking and drinking, such as Mothers Against Drunk Driving (MADD), will continue to lobby against alcohol abuse.

There is also a great concern by the seniors losing their rights, should a graduated license program be put in place that would restrict nighttime driving and high-speed driving for those over sixty-five. The majority of seniors feel this is age discrimination. Some doctors across Canada believe that seniors are in more fatal car crashes than any other age group. It is time for the seniors to stand up, or else they will lose their independence. If the provinces in Canada were more focused on making safety improvements that would benefit all drivers and build better roads, many problems would be eliminated. It is time to listen to the people who have done due diligence and know what they are talking about. New rules in Canada have taken away your privacy resulting in a loss of rights.

11. Drugs

Illegal drugs should be regulated and taxed just like pharmaceuticals. Throughout the world now, for example, British Columbia states that the problems with drugs are overblown, and those lethal dangers only arise when the chemicals are polluted by money-hungry gangs who sell it. One way to solve the problem would be to give lengthy sentences to drug dealers and for the immigration of any country to stop bringing drug dealers and criminals from third world countries. For example, Uruguay is planning a radical approach to the legalization of marijuana by proposing the sale of the drug being controlled by the state. Countries such as Holland have done this for years. On the other side of the coin, a large number of people still feels that drugs cannot be controlled to legalization.

12. Education

A fortune is being spent on education and health throughout the world, with many individuals in the United States having no health care. Whereas in Canada that has a public health care system, health care is much more economical but has wait times which are detrimental to the health of the sick. Public versus private health care has been debated thoroughly, with each side having their own positives.

13. Environment

At present, large companies engaged in primary resources such as mining throughout the world pollute the environment. On the other side, these large corporations state that if they are overregulated, they will not make money and will have to close down, driving up the costs for the consumers.

14. Euthanasia

If your mother or any other member of you family were suffering, should you allow them to suffer? While if your pet was suffering and you did not put it out of its misery, you could receive up to thirty days in jail. On the other side, a large number of people believe that euthanasia goes against their religion. Even though places such as Switzerland and

Holland all allow euthanasia. Mattie has become part of the Farewell Society which won a court case making euthanasia legal in British Columbia in Canada. No doubt the federal government will try to overturn the judge's decision, but this is a debatable point with people on both sides believing in their own convictions.

15. Flat Tax

It is now time to go in North America to a flat tax. A number of people have come up with a fair and balanced plan to eliminate corporate income tax. For example, raising rates on long-term capital gains is the first step towards tax reform. We need to get corporations out of politics, improve North America's competitiveness, bring home more than a trillion dollars in offshore earnings, increase wages, end the double taxation of company profits, and improve return for many shareholders.

This could be achieved if Congress in the United States and Canada would agree to a simple deal—lower marginal rates, long-term capital gains and dividends at the same rate as regular income, and eliminate the corporate income tax. The system now leads to Herculean tax-avoidance efforts, as the rich hire armies of accountants to manipulate their incomes to get their preferential rate. When there is a matter of inheritance, when the wealthy die, any gain in their investments passes on tax to their heirs. The current system often also amounts to double taxation since income earned by a business is subject to the 35 percent corporate rate, and then taxed again when it is paid out as a dividend.

As it now stands, the tax system prompts executives to take out over sized pay because their salaries are a deductible expense. It reduces wages, and its burdens fall heavily on labor; it makes an attractive investment in the world of mobile capital more difficult. And as mentioned above, the corporate income tax invites the double taxation problem which encourages companies to pass along their tax expense to consumers and employees and discourages payments.

Ending the tax break for specific industries would also help get the government out of the dreaded practice of picking winners and losers and providing corporate welfare. Much of the vast corporate lobbying that pervades the US capital would be neutralized, and companies could repatriate the more than $1 trillion in overseas earnings that they are holding to avoid taxation.

In the interest of compromise, we should all endorse such variations on our proposed deals. It is important to remember that none of these reforms will result in fiscal utopia, and there will surely be complications.

16. Gambling

On one side, many people believe that gambling is a sin and should be outlawed. On the other side, people who gamble for things such as charity know that the money raised goes towards supporting good causes.

17. The Gay Movement

For years, people in governments have discriminated against homosexuals. In 2012, an author called Sister Margaret Farley has gone from 142,982 on the Amazon best seller list to number 16. Her book was written in 2006 and is called *Just Love*. She argues that "b ecause divorce in marriages are valid, masturbation can be a great good for women, and that same sex relationships and activities can be justified according to the same sexual ethics as homosexual relationships." These thoughts are discussed at length, but devout Christians and people of many other religions are concerned about her thoughts even though she is a member of a church.

18. Marketing Boards and Subsidies

In Europe and Canada, farmers are heavily subsidized with the consumers paying a much higher price for their food than in the United States. At present, the Canadian government is taking steps to destroy marketing boards while the United States is strongly for the right to grow whatever you want and sell it as you see fit even though they receive subsidies. Each side has a valid point.

19. Pensions

There is no doubt some areas of the Unites States, with the slowdown in the car industry and North Americans buying vehicles overseas which when they do so puts their fellow Americans out of world, do not think of this. At the same time, if there are only twenty thousand people working in the auto industry and forty thousand people on pension, the writing is on the wall. There will be no pensions, and this will happen throughout the world in a short period of time as more people keep drawing pensions and less people pay into them. Quite naturally, the system will go broke.

On the other hand, people seem to think that if they can get something for nothing, then it is a good deal. Not extrapolating the situation to the point where they should realize that pensions can only be paid out if there is a sufficient amount of people paying in.

20. Pets

An issue throughout the world is raising pets for sale in pet stores. In Mattie's opinion, these stores should be shut down immediately as the humane societies such as the Society for the Prevention of Cruelty to Animals (SPCA) have thousands of pets available across North America of all kinds, which could be adopted rather than being left in cages to suffer. On the other side, people think that you are taking away the freedom of businesses to sell pets even though it is not an entirely fair practice.

21. Privacy and Fairness

Privacy is probably the most important item in the world today as new technology allows governments and big businesses to invade the privacy of taxpayers and residents of any city or country. They are doing this at a very rapid rate. There are few places in the world you can go now where you are not being spied on. With the new drones, our airspace will be invaded by various government bodies and corporations allowing us no more individual freedom. We see this at the airports where we are molested in the name of security. If the individual were to molest an individual in the same manner as the government allows at the airports today, they would be charged. The government claims they need to spy on us, search us, molest us, and treat us as potential criminals. If the governments were not killing women and children in foreign lands, there would not need to be so many different ways of invading our privacy and taking away our rights.

The partner of Conrad Black, when charged by the United States government and served four to five months in jail, became a witness for the government and received a very minimal sentence even though he was just as guilty as Conrad Black who served six years, a stiffer sentence tan Canada.

The United States and Canadian skies are open to police and private drones. Will this be the end of privacy? Drones are coming to America, and are already here. The drone era is just beginning. Predator drones, which are remote-controlled aircrafts used to hunt terrorists, have been patrolling US borders since 2005. They are used to search for missing persons and to track forest fires. Police departments are testing drones for surveillance and search-and-rescue missions.

The question is why is the government allowing more drones?

Law enforcement officials love them. Police agencies shopping for drones that fit the new federal air regulations can now choose from 146 models manufactured from sixty-nine different companies in North America. The police states, "We see a huge potential market." What can these drones do? Snoop on people without their knowledge? In Texas, a drone called the Wasp was launched over a suspect's house before sending in a SWAT team. Last year, a North Dakota sheriff called in a drone from the Canadian border to locate a man and his sons suspected of cattle thieving. All members of an antigovernment group and all were unarmed.

If lobbyists get their way, police won't be the only people with this technology. Real-estate brokers have already used drones to photograph properties for sale; and in the future, these devices could be used to monitor oil pipelines, crops, or snap photos of celebrities.

What about privacy? The American Civil Liberties Union says that "drones will change the character of public life, ushering in an era in which Americans can be monitored every time they step outside. Important roads and public spaces may be constantly patrolled by hovering drones. Now you can't be sure you are not being watched." That prospect alarms many people. A recent poll found that more than 50 percent of Americans opposed drones used in domestic skies even though in 1986 and 1989, the Supreme Court ruled that police don't need a warrant to observe a private property from public airspace. The technology is here and isn't going away.

22. Privatization

Privatization is discussed widely throughout the world. The advantages of privatization are that various companies, big and small, will bid for work from various governments and corporations. Therefore, there should be competition between all, providing it is fair and no company or partnership will receive special privileges. Adversely, government does not have to make a profit, so if the works were completed by competent people, which includes manager and superintendents, the various forms of governmental bodies should be able to compete. The ideal scenario is for the government to do half the work themselves—be they municipal, federal, or provincial—and the other half to be done by other private companies.

23. Prostitution

Prostitution is another item that has been recently in the news and has been in the public eye for hundreds of years, yet we still have the do-gooders who want to do away with prostitution which will cause individuals who would normally use the services of a prostitute to rape and molest women and children as a last resort. In Canada, prostitution has been made legal in one province, but no doubt the do-gooders will have the government of the day wrongly approach the Supreme Court to hear the case at a later date.

On the other side of the coin, we have to remember that there are always people who say that there should be no prostitution, and if we were somehow able to eliminate it, the world would be a better place. This is hard to imagine as places such as Holland have tried legalizing prostitution and has worked out for the better.

24. The Senate

In Canada, there is a strong movement for a reformed senate, which is elected, efficient, and equal. In the United States, there are two senators from each state making for one hundred senators in total. In Canada, there are hundreds of senators, and some provinces may have dozens representing them and others only one, which is extremely unfair. Mattie drew up the charter for a Triple-E Senate back in the mid-1980s and was instrumental in getting a five-star general in the Canadian services who later was a corporate executive to run as the first elected in Canada. We felt that the Americans, who got their first elected senators in 1910, had a much better system. He later helped raise a large amount of money for Mr. Stan Waters who became the first elected senator in Canada. Mattie's friend of many decades who was the premier and another Irish friend who was the prime minister of the country agreed to allow Mr. Waters to become the first elected senator in Canada. Unfortunately, he died of a brain tumor after only one year in office.

25. Taxes

Taxes have become far too high, and secondly, the money that is taken in from taxes is being spent in a wasteful manner. As soon as possible, the people of North America should rise up and ask for a flat tax, which would require a considerable less amount of government people to administer the system. Mattie does not believe that anyone could debate that our tax system at present is a worthwhile system.

26. The Queen

In the United States, they have a republic which is also the case in many other countries. In Canada and Australia, the Queen rules over the British Commonwealth. This has caused unhappiness with many people who, for over one hundred years, suffered under the British Empire. The British killed many of the citizens of various countries, but at the same time, they immigrate to places such as Canada and are forced to take an oath on the Bible to the Queen. On the other side, Ireland and the United States are now republics with presidents, the right won with lengthy battles over the years.

27. Roads

Roads are much better in places such as Germany and in the United States than in other parts of the world. No doubt these roads cost considerable amounts of money, but they also pay for themselves. In countries such as Canada where the infrastructure is very poor, the roads are very unsafe and time-consuming to travel throughout the nation.

28. Unemployment Insurance

Government is trying to change the rules, stating that a lot of people work for a few months a year and then draw unemployment for the majority of the time. Unemployment insurance is a big issue in Canada because some state it is simply subsidized welfare. On the other side, if you pay for insurance and become unemployed, should you not be able to draw insurance? Imagine if you insured your car or house and you got into an accident or your house burned down and an insurance company said they did not feel that you are entitled to insurance after paying all those years, you would be a very unhappy client.

29. War

Wars have been fought for thousands of years. There is never an ultimate winner. In the '40s, the last major war fought against two European countries and one Far East country was won by the Allies, but what different would it make if we were governed by the Germans and the Japanese, two of the most successful nations on Earth. As we can see now with the War on Terror, which was totally needless because there were no weapons of mass destruction and Sadam Hussein was a friend of America and was supported by the American government with all of the weapons he required to fight the neighboring nation of Iran. As long as we keep harassing and declaring war on the women and children of foreign nations on their soil, we will be never free of terror. Hopefully in the near future, Americans will rise up and say, "We do not want any more war, we want jobs and a decent economy because if we kill others they will try to kill us."

Mattie grew up in an area where a large percentage of the population were conscripted and were forced to fight in a war. Many were killed, and the ones that came back were without limbs and were mentally disturbed. It is quite common for people who have been in a war to never discuss it upon their return. Naturally, these people perhaps have hunted animals, but when they get to killing human beings, they realize after they have done the deed that it is a stain on their manhood which remains for the rest of their life.

I hope that I have outlined in these reasons that it is time that people start to speak up and start to salvage this great country of ours. If they do not, we will lose it, and we will be ruled more than likely by countries from the Far East.

In conclusion, I must touch on a few subjects that one can never emphasize enough. In the *Calgary Herald* business section, there is an article written that was taken out of the *Financial Post*. This article states that reality hasn't stopped one in five from lying on their insurance policies. This is a falsity that is perpetuated by the insurance company. These insurance companies, banks, brokers, etc., have people who are not competent and who in some cases phone up and take information over the phone do not ask proper questions and then refuse to pay the claim. This had happened to Mattie on occasion, and he had sued a company, formerly AIG, which was bailed out by the president of the United States to the tune of $186 billion. Hopefully no small business tries to get money from the government like this because they would find it would be a lost cause.

Mattie is the first Canadian to ever sue the sitting president of the United States for payment of an insurance claim. It will be interesting to see the outcome of this claim. Now AIG is now operating under the alias of Chartis Insurance in Canada and Travel Guard Insurance in the United States. The article states that you would lie on your insurance claim to keep your premium down. Can you imagine lying on your claim to save a couple hundred dollars when you could be out of pocket thousands of dollars? This does not stand the smell test. Big business seems to feel that with the backing of big government, you can say anything.

The main problem between Canadians and Americans is that Canadians are willing to compromise their life away. In actuality, when a person gets to live in Canada, they will come to realize that they are weak and wimpy and are willing to accept anything no matter how wrong it is from big business to big government. Mattie reads a dozen magazines per week as well as three newspapers. He is continually disturbed by the daily listing of big business being convicted on bribery charges. A company in July of 2012 will pay $5.2

million in charges after being convicted for bribing government officials in order to obtain sales contracts with hospitals. The company, which makes spinal and orthopedic products, spent hundreds of thousands of dollars to the Mexican officials from 2003–2010.

Mattie has stated in previous chapters that employees of General Electric often boast about making big money off of the government in Alberta. Another case where the American securities in the exchange commission has filed fraud charges against a man, who made his name against betting against mortgages. He is accused of attempting to manipulate bond prices; another example of Wall Street destroying the standards of over 40 percent of Americans in the past four years, resulting in the average American family's net worth declining by 40 percent between 2007–2010. This translates into the loss of eighteen years of savings and investment as a result of the financial crisis created by the Wall Street billionaires.

A prime example of big business and big government destroying the privacy of Canadians and Unites States citizens is unwanted phone calls to people who have their name on the do-not-call list, which at present nears eleven million people. Nevertheless, political parties, newspapers, charities, etc., still continue to call. A nuisance is still a nuisance regardless of where it originates. In Canada at present, we are putting in more laws which take away the rights of the individual. Mattie has driven across Germany in perfect safety, driving at top speeds. In Canada, this would land you in jail. Why?

Why is it that you rarely see any accidents in Europe whereas in Alberta there are multiple accidents per day? Is it better trained drivers? Likely it is better road design. Is it neurotic enforcement of low speeds by an obsessed police force and politicians?

To touch again on excess taxes, which are unethical and wrong, taxes make up about 29 percent of pump prices for gasoline and 22.5 percent of diesel fuel according to recent reports. Albertans pay the lowest portion of taxes, 21.7 percent. This indicates that Canadian prices are totally out of control. With the unstable economy throughout a large part of the world that is causing considerable concern to Mattie and has caused him to invest into gold. It is very important for one to realize that success depends on trying things that may fail, no matter whether it is in church, charity, business, politics, or community. No one wants to fail, but some failure is inevitable, at least if you hope to succeed. Virtually all success depends on trying things that fail. Great entrepreneurs have usually failed before they became successful.

Small business owners do not have the luxury of failure that other do. Small companies do not have extra resources, so whatever investment of time and money they have put into a project, it means a lot—failure takes a bigger toll. Small business owners and high-growth entrepreneurs need to embrace and learn from failures. Failure does come in many different ways. In order to succeed, the best ways to fail are fail fast, get over your failure as quickly as possible, and move on to something else. If you are going to fail, you should fail in the way that moves your company, products, and services into a new direction. Always remember innovation does not require perfection. Consumers have a great tolerance for new products and services that are not always perfect at first.

Fail smart. You don't learn if you fail because you are doing something stupid and avoidable. Learn from the mistakes of others. Fail cheap. Try to keep your financial losses from a failure as minimal as possible. Try new things with the least amount of investment to test a concept. Also, fail with integrity. Character matters, even if you fail, people who have worked with you before may be willing to team with you in the future. Mattie was able to prove this by paying back the money he lost; it had taken him six years to when he finally had enough money to pay everyone off all at once. They gave him a million dollar line of credit with no personal guarantees.

Be prepared. Big business is cutting back on hiring and laying off people, even though the senior corporate managers are sitting on cash and are able to borrow at the lowest rates in history. If you are in business or have investments, it is always wise to keep money ahead and be prepared for these low points in the economy, just like playing defense in sports. Otherwise, you will find yourself out of business due to decisions made by others which are beyond your control.

The governments will keep interest rates low in order to help out big businesses that support them strongly at election time. Be prepared for high oil prices as Shell and ExxonMobil top the Fortune 500 ranking. These companies saw a 35 percent boost in profits. Unfortunately, nothing will change as big companies are the main source of income for politicians when they are run in elections. Oil prices are jumping even though there is a considerable surplus of oil throughout the world on the premise that Norway's workers may go on strike. Also, Iran may shut down the Strait of Hormuz. Nothing really has to happen, just the threat of anything and prices immediately skyrocket.

An example of inefficient politicians and bureaucrats is in Alberta, there is only $15 billion in a rainy day fund over the last third of a century; whereas in Norway, they have been able to stock away vast sums of oil wealth while having a very high standard of living. At present, Norway boasts of over $600 billion in a savings account as well as the world's highest living standards. This is a price that most Albertans in Canada would be happy to pay. In 2011, only 9 percent of the revenue from oil, gas, and bitumen resources was delivered back to Albertans. As this province rapidly burns through its natural wealth, Albertans can only look on with envy as Norwegians enjoy the benefits of high living standards and wise financial planning. David Campanella, a public policy research manager at the Parkland Institute, outlines this in an article he wrote.

It is time for penalties for illegal political donations in Canada, according to an individual named Shayne Saskiw, who believes there are many cases of improper donations that election officials are making no effort to find. Information from Elections Alberta shows twenty-six cases where donations have been ruled illegal. Another article in the *Edmonton Journal* by Karen Kleiss states that an individual named executive director of the main political party has been the subject of controversy for many years. This high-ranking individual served as executive assistant to a governing cabinet minister for nearly eight years before, leaving the legislature in 2001 to start a government relations business dealing with the government. He made headlines in 2004 when the auditor general reported that one of the government ministers had given this individual more than $400,000 in untendered consulting contracts, with scant records of what taxpayers got in exchange. This cabinet minister had the nerve to run for the leader of the party and has a cushy job in the Orient while his friends who got the ill-gotten $400,000 have one of the highest paying and cushiest jobs in the province.

A recent article in the *Calgary Herald* states that one of the fastest-growing areas in Calgary, Alberta, which has very poor street infrastructure, will receive in twenty-seven years a rapid transit system. By this time, people who retire here if they are fifty years old will be eighty years old. The mayor states, "When you think about the fact that it is almost a $3 billion project and the city's operating budget is $3 billion, you get the sense of what the scale here is." It is time it was brought to the attention of the mayor and council and that they were informed by a hired city auditor that the city has wasted three-fourths of a billion dollars through mismanagement, waste, and corruption. Should they have listened to this auditor instead of firing her and saved three-fourths of a billion dollars per year, then in four years' time they would have enough extra money to pay for this rapid transit. Instead of doing so, they fired the auditor instead of the high-up individuals who are responsible for all of the problems.

To touch again on several recent fraudulent individuals and companies, the head of Peregrine, a US brokerage firm, has been charged with theft of $100 million. This chap who tried to commit suicide and is now being charged by the FBI says that his Iowa financial company is now in bankruptcy, where the firm listed assets of a few million and liabilities of hundreds of billions. The firm says that it had at least ten thousand creditors when it filed under chapter 7, and only has about seventy employees left—another example of greed among the richest people in America.

A further example of greed and corruption is an article in the nationwide *Globe and Mail*, where in a report from Reuters, Hong Kong condominium kings face corruption charges. Brothers Raymond and Thomas Kwok are accused of paying millions of dollars to city officials for land-sale information. These billionaires played a major role in transforming Vancouver's skyline with a series of luxury condominiums. As devout Christians, they are the coheads of a family-owned business empire that is among the most powerful in Asia. The brothers made a brief court appearance on July 13, 2012, to face allegations from Hong Kong's Independent Commission Against Corruption. They were accused of paying $4.5 million in bribes to the city's former chief secretary in exchange for information on pending land sales. The chief secretary, who was Hong Kong's second most senior official between 2005 and 2007, has also been charged.

The two brothers are also in a fight with their oldest brother who they want to kick out of the company, claiming that he is mentally unstable and unfit for the job after he was kidnapped by bandits who were later captured by the Chinese police and executed. What a sad state of affairs to see billionaires, who have no idea what to do with their money, continue to be charged with corrupt practices. It is absolutely unbelievable how corrupt senior officials in the world are now becoming.

In Arizona, several robbers who tried to steal from a jewelry store owner were shot by the proprietor rather than being charged by the police. The proprietor was honored by the city, which is the way it should be and results in considerably less crime. In Canada, it is the direct opposite. An owner of a food store in Alberta was initially charged with kidnapping and assault for tying up a thief who robbed his store. Police even got the thief to testify against the owner, even though the owner is a folk hero in the city. In Ontario, a man was charged for firing a shotgun on the pavement that ricocheted and wounded a guy who was robbing a neighbor's garage. Despite what seemed an obvious act of good citizenship, the guy who fired the shotgun was deemed irresponsible, at fault, and a bad example for the community.

Another horrible example of how the police and justice system turns into injustice occurred one night in 2009, when a man who owned a all terrain vehicle spotted three guys invading his property. Two ran away, but the third stole his vehicle and sped off. When the thieves ran away, the owner fired a shotgun loaded with light birdshot that didn't do any harm to the thief. Nevertheless, when the cops arrived, both the thief and the property owner were taken into custody. The thief received thirty days in jail, and the property owner received ninety days in jail for defending and recovering his property. He was also convicted of criminal negligence causing bodily harm, three times the sentence the thief got. Unfortunately, that sentence still stands, and the owner is burdened with a criminal record for catching a thief, all the while defending his property. When will the police and judges exercise common sense in such cases?

It was mentioned before that a very rich family that takes $60 million in salaries, including a $5.9 million pension for a fifty-four-year-old, who have a contract with the government of Alberta, had a fire in one of their properties resulting in all the registry offices, health care records, etc., being unavailable to the health care professionals and the general public. A total disaster, yet nothing will happen, and they will continue on with their contract even though they should have had fire suppression systems that have been available for the past forty years. Maybe the highly paid family should hire nonfamily members to run the business or should be fired from doing work for the government.

Canadians are tired of waiting for medical care. Individuals in Alberta are waiting for eight to twelve hours in the city's emergency rooms. In British Columbia, a hospital is often packed with patients and stretchers. In Nova Scotia, one community resorted to a lottery to determine who would have the opportunity to join a physician's practice. According to the Fraser Institute, Canada has the longest waitlist in the developed world. It now takes an average of nineteen weeks for Canadians to go from a general practitioner visit to treatment (a 60 percent increase since 1997). It is an average wait of 9.5 weeks from the time of a GP referral to a visit with a specialist, up from 5.1 weeks in 1997. An estimated seventy-five thousand British Columbians are waiting for nonemergency surgery. Federal and provincials governments have thrown plenty of cash at the waitlist problem, yet the situation is only getting worse. In Alberta, the government spent $16 billion on health care with $10 billion of it being totally wasted on overpaying for equipment for the hospitals, waste, etc.

Mattie went into the hospitals for treatment for a stomach virus and catching *C. difficile*, a very serious problems which kills 99 percent of seniors who came in contact with it caused by dirty conditions in the hospital. Fortunately, as mentioned beforehand, Mattie was able to meet a doctor from the Far East who saved his life after spending ninety-two days in the hospital, losing over sixty pounds and taking a month to walk again—an absolute disgrace. The aforementioned is what Canadians get for their money-eating system that is fed by 66 percent of Canadians income tax and 40 percent of government budgets. Don't let words like *Medicare* or *universality* confuse you. There is no such thing as free healthcare in Canada. You may or may not have to pay the private sector but you will always have to pay the government.

No wonder two Alberta men are now challenging the province's ban on private medical insurance for essential health care. These two men were debilitated by back paying and waiting for years on the province's surgical waitlist. They finally gave up and travelled to the Unites States and paid tens of thousands of dollars to regain their lives. The government then refused to reimburse them because the surgical procedures were available in Alberta, providing you lived long enough to receive them. Mattie has paid millions of dollars in taxes to the governments in Canada, and when he was hospitalized in the United States for two days for a total of $30,000, the government offered to pay $400 towards his bill. This added insult to injury.

A May 2012 analyst for Healthcare Canada looked at the attitude of Canadians towards their health care system. Contrary to what most people believe, they say it is "overburdened," "unreliable," "wasteful," "needs leadership," and "can't be fixed with just money." Health care has been changed over the last decade; medical technology and drug costs are high. Imagine, Olympus selling a $2,000 endoscope for $40,000. No wonder ten billion dollars in one province alone is wasted. The number and availability of doctors is low. Waiting lists are unreasonably long. Those who use the system know it, and those who have been lucky enough to have been healthy and not have any serious illnesses are still in denial. Health care delivery in Canada will change, and it is just a matter of time. This is an article from the *Calgary Herald* written by a reporter Susan Martinuk.

Newfoundland, bordering the Atlantic Ocean, is in a fight with ExxonMobil over $100 million dollar. The oil company wants to build in another part of the world instead of in Newfoundland where the people could use the jobs. The province and the oil company have drawn a line in the sand, and hopefully the oil company will realize that the proper thing to do is build a module where they get their profits and do not to go to some other parts of the world. With 82 percent of the oil in the world being owned by the governments, oil companies are finding it very difficult to drive hard bargains and rip off countries throughout the world. Furthermore, a lot has been said about bitumen that flows through the pipelines of North America. Mattie, who has worked in the industry from bottom to top over the past fifty-seven years, feels that as long as there are pipelines growing older day by day, there will always be spills. But one cannot solely blame the oil company as that is part of the risk that companies and people take in order to be provided access to these resources.

Mattie has been critical of big business, including four oil companies; but on the positive side, both have contributed to charities, provided thousands of jobs, and have been the backbone of the economy in many areas in the world. When problems are reported in the media, they are only caused by a few corrupt companies or individuals who put money before anything else. We must bear in mind that if you rise to the top in a major corporations, local or foreign, if you do not make money, the shareholders will fire you on short notice. Therefore, some people feel they have no choice but to make money at any cost, as that is what business is all about.

The day Mattie sold out his nationwide businesses that were competing against some of the biggest foreign and local companies in the world was the happiest day of his life. He now works for community, church, charity, politics, and the general good of the community and the country. He can, at the end of the day, relax and feel happy that he made the right decision twenty years ago to get out of the big league and do something that he could be proud of and enjoy the rest of his life.

A prime example of a man who lived to the fullest would be a man named Ron Cahill. Mattie and Ron met over half a century ago in the oil field where they had worked together. Ron got a degree in both engineering and geophysics. It was then that he married his wife of nearly fifty years. The couple was transferred to Louisiana while Mattie was transferred to Texas. Within a few years, they were both transferred back to Alberta. Both spent many years in the construction industry building various types of buildings. Both were engaged in farming throughout their life, and Ron started a gravel pit on his farm. In the Calgary, Alberta area, Mattie brought gravel from his friend. Ron had what was called in the Orient an ideal family, a boy and a girl, including four grandsons. Ron had only one brother, as did Mattie. Both their fathers died before they were out of their teens, and both loved sports and travelled the world during their lifetime.

Ron also had planes, was a cattleman, farmer, sportsman, loved the water, golfer, and was a loyal friend and a great model to his family and all Albertans. Alberta and Canada will be worse off now that Ron has passed away. Ron died a very rich man, yet throughout his life, he lived a very low-key lifestyle that even his memorial service will be held in a garden chapel which without a doubt will be filled at a capacity with many people standing outside the doors. This is an example of what you can do with your life if you wish to succeed, get an education, and use it as a backup; but using the money from your salary, start investing it into land, buildings, etc., allowing you a lot of free time with your wife, family, grandchildren, and friends. If Mattie were to list one individual who impressed him the most in North America, it would have to be Ron Cahill, who enjoyed one of the greatest lives in the world and became one of the most successful individuals in Canada. If you wish to model yourself after an individual as a male or female, this sort of success with luck and friends is available to anyone in North America.

Mattie hopes that this book will cover all parts of your life in order that you may live a happy and healthful life and become successful at whatever you decide to work at. Bearing in mind that if you enter the big league, climbing higher and higher on the ladder of success, you not only take the chance of falling, which is far greater the higher up you are on the ladder. But if you pick the middle of the road such as Ron Cahill, you can be very successful, happy, and a success story in your own right.

Two Canadian corporate giants, the Potash Corporation of Saskatchewan and Calgary based Agrium Inc. are among the list of potash producers who face a revised United States lawsuit that accused them of acting like a tight-knit global cartel, similar to the OPEC heyday. The US Court of Appeals for the seventh circuit in Chicago last month revived a multibillion-dollar antitrust case by potash buyers. The lawsuit targets the two Canadian companies as well as the Mosaic Company, which is based in Plymouth, Minnesota, and four Russian and eastern European companies. The governments state the companies controlled 71 percent of the world's potash in 2008 and allegedly coordinated cuts in production to keep prices rising. Basically, to the extent that a cartel operates outside the United States and the effect is felt in the United States, especially in a commodity product like potash. "Companies are going to have to live by US antitrust laws," said the San Francisco lawyer Bruce Simon, who argues the case for the plaintiffs. The case has not gone to trial, and the allegations against the company are unproven—the defendants deny the allegations.

Even though the case is a long way from trial, the plaintiffs have yet to get their hands on the documents that would show they are colluding to drive up the prices. The government states, "We do know that there were meetings and cuts in production that caused the price to go up but do not have their internal emails. We just have the tip of the iceberg at this time period." Articles in the media have indicated that the price of potash has skyrocketed from a few hundred dollars a ton to over a thousand per ton, with share prices going from a few dollars in Potash Corporation in Saskatchewan to over $200. This is from an article in the *Globe and Mail* in Canada.

Mattie has been critical in this book of the various government politicians and bureaucrats. It is only fair to say that the majority of politicians and bureaucrats are excellent people and do their jobs to the best of their ability. In regard to politicians, when they are elected if they are not with the party in power, they have literally no say in the government of any city, state, province, or country. Even if they are with the government, as one prime minister came to say in Canada, "When they are a mile away from parliament they are nobody, with zero power." As for bureaucrats and civil servants, they have to work with thousands of others; even though they may want to help out the taxpayer or consumer, they may find their hands tied resulting in them being unable to do anything to help. And by far the vast majority of civil servants are excellent people who sometimes can be just as exhausted with the system as the taxpayers or consumers.

A major problem in the world today is that the people who have built the countries throughout most of the world, and who used to get anywhere from 10 percent to 20 percent interest on their money, now are getting 1 percent while the big corporations and the very rich are borrowing money as low as 1 percent. An example is Mark Zuckerberg, a kid who operates Facebook which does nothing for the economy of any country, has built himself a luxurious mansion and has borrowed $5.95 million, almost $6 million, for his California home with an interest rate of 1.05 percent according to public records. This is an absolute disgrace while seniors throughout America have seen their standard of living drop tremendously caused by little or no interest on their hard-earned money.

An article in the *Calgary Herald* in Alberta, Canada, has stated that a new highway is opening in the capital of Alberta, and a contract has been awarded to a foreign company for a thirty-year period for the maintenance. The contract for building the road, and no doubt operating it as well, is being done with what they call a P3 model, which means that foreigners will control the roads. This foreign company was on the verge of going out of business when it hired a senior official in Calgary, Alberta, and within a short time they started to turn a profit. When Rudy Klinker privatized all the highway work in Alberta, they got the southern third of the province as well as all the equipment and buildings that were owned by the government and the people of Alberta for next to nothing. Now this company is one of the most prosperous in the world, thanks to Rudy Klinker and his friends who ended up costing this one particular province over $200 billion; yet that political party still gets elected even though they are wasting money on health care, etc. up to $30 billion per year.

As Alberta, Canada, is one of the richest pieces of ground in the world in primary resources, one day these resources will be sold off and the inhabitants of this province will be left with scars on the landscape due to mismanagement. When we see contracts being awarded to foreigners for thirty years, one wonders how long before they will be awarding them for three hundred years, which is causing the window of opportunity to be slammed shut for any and all entrepreneurs in an area that is being sold out to foreign capital.

In real estate and business, it is so often stated that location, location, location is most important in setting up your business. This is where the wise individual does their due diligence before they move to a particular area, making sure the cost of living is reasonable, there is an opportunity to business, and the area has an efficient and intelligent government rather than mismanagement, waste, and corruption.

Thousands of books have been written by thousands of authors on how to make money and be a success while living the good life. Most of these books are written by people who relate to stories of individuals who have made money; these stories in real life have no connection to the ordinary individual. Most of the books state that common sense is the road to success. Mattie met a successful farmer back in his teenage years who stated quite often that common sense, good judgment, friendship, and luck were the keys to success. This gentleman, if he were still living, would be 120 years old. Therefore, if you are going to read a book and model yourself after someone who has been extremely successful and who has gone from misfortune to millionaire, then it is wise to read about an individual who has been there, done that, and describes in detail what it takes to make you successful and happy.

Mattie noticed over the years working for various companies and individuals that a large number had no idea how to run an efficient organization, resulting in poor wages, operating inferior equipment, and in general going downhill rather than building a good organization.

A prime example of this is the city of Calgary in Alberta, who brings people in from all over the world to work in top management and contract to provide goods and services. An example is hiring two individuals with military experience to run their streets and roads department—a very important division in any city, state, or province. These two individuals were trained in blowing up roads and bridges in the military; and when Mattie asked several superintendents why they did not hire these long-term Calgary employees, he was told, "We know too much about what we are doing after decades on the job; therefore, in order to protect their butt, the city mayor and council, including the top management who have run this city for years with mismanagement and waste to the tune of three quarters of a billion dollars as outlined by a hired auditor, the last thing in the world they would want is individuals who could jeopardize their jobs."

A prime example is when the tenders come out for hourly rate for equipment, if we were to take on example street sweeping, the city could hire sweepers for $125 an hour; instead they operate some of their own which they charge out at $200 an hour. At the very minimum, they should hire 50 percent contractors and 50 percent city owned and operated and compare who does the best work at the lowest price. This is already proven on paper and done by other cities across the country, but no doubt the unions have a large say on how the city is operated. At present, they lease sweepers for $10,000 a month, and when they factor in the added cost of operators, maintenance had doubled the cost of what they could do to work for themselves. The cost now increases to double the rate for what they could hire contractors, yet the taxpayers do not seem to care that it is costing the city double to do their work while providing half the service at double the cost. This results in taxes being triple what they need to be on both residential and industrial property.

At present, in mid-July of 2012, there is an excess of property available to rent. While the city is raising taxes, the rental rates are going down except for big business, which can raise rates as they see fit and raise the cost of living and causing undue suffering to seniors, small business, and working individuals with large families. But as long as Calgarians continue to vote in a council who mismanages the city budget and does not control waste, then coupled with terrible health care, poor education, and bad infrastructure, then the city will remain a poor place to do business or live in.

People wonder why cities across Canada, especially Calgary, Alberta, are so unsafe at any hour. It is because the Canadian government imports criminals from countries where crime is rampant and drugs are legal. If they are going to continue to allow immigrants to come into Canada who use and sell drugs, then they should make drugs legal and tax the profits.

At least when speaking to Jason Kenny, the Canadian Immigration Minister, at a meeting at the University of Calgary in mid-July, he stated to Mattie as well as on TV that now if you are a qualified tradesman and ready to put your tools to use, then in sixty seconds you can immigrate to Canada. This policy is long overdue as they have been stopping people from the UK and the continent from coming to Canada, while at the same time, bringing people in from other parts of the world that have large families and are a burden on the education system and parents and grandparents who overload the health care system, resulting in Canadians who have worked long days, seven days a week, in business on the land, for themselves or for others, unable to get health care due to the way the system is mismanaged, overloaded, waste, and corruption.

If the Canadian government had any guts, they would regulate foreign big business as they come into Canada and buy up all the resources; and as they ship the products out of Canada, they also move out the profits, resulting in a country that lacks services and is overtaxed. Even the third world countries that used to be controlled by European countries and the UK now have kicked out these foreigners and taken over their own resources, resulting in 82 percent of the primary resources of the world being owned by the governments and the people of those particular nations.

Nevertheless, unless Canadians in general and a few outspoken individuals stand up for their country, they will continue to remain in a recession and depression as one cannot believe what he or she reads or sees in the media. These people live on advertising and gain their revenue from big business, and therefore spread the propaganda to the people for these foreign-owned businesses.

In conclusion, I would hope that this book has given some insight and helps the reader understand the severe problems that are forcing people throughout the world at present, which are destroying the livelihood of so many people and causing great inconvenience and suffering. Bear in mind that you must stand up for your rights, even though you will be told it is a privilege to live in your country and that society and the economy is great when in reality we are facing insurmountable problems. Bear in mind the motto of the US Air force, "The difficult only takes time, the impossible only takes longer." It is time for North Americans and people throughout the world to be like Mattie—keep fighting until the day you die. It is not whether you win or lose, it is how you play the game. You always live with a dream of a better tomorrow for all involved.

Mattie would like to repeat again in a closing statement of the book how important it is to make sure you get an occupation that pays well in order that you may save a large amount of money very quickly, which will enable you to buy a house and start a business on the side if you are a professional or a government worker. It is also wise to remember how much and when. You need to know when you are doing business, when whatever you are buying is going to be delivered, and most important, how much it is going to cost. If it is not on sale at half price or discount, then you don't need it. Always remember to think it through. If you enter into any contract, whether it is marriage, big or small business, or government, you have to make sure. If you are not positive, you have to ask others and do your homework and due diligence to make sure that the deal is going to make money and work for you and your company or partnership. You have to make sure whatever you are buying, be it travel, a vehicle, a house, or food, that you buy it at a discount with at least a third off, or hopefully 50 percent off as Mattie has done all of his life.

When buying property, make sure you get it with at least a 20 percent to a 30 percent discount. There are always deals available if you search hard enough. If you do not have enough money to start a business or buy real estate, always take in a partner or a number of partners if you need them. Eventually over the years you will end up selling to them and making money or buying them and owning the property yourself while waiting for it to go up in value over the years. When investing, rather than putting your money in the banks, it is wise to invest it in property and mortgages, allowing you to make a fortune and someone else will pay off your mortgages. If you are lending money, you can always charge double what the banks do as that is the way they make their money—taking your hard-earned money and giving you half of what they lend out to others.

Always remember, if you work hard when you are young and are physically able to put in the extra hours, the additional money that you make will be the icing on the cake; and as you grow older, that money will be yours to invest, live a terrific lifestyle, travel the world, and retire in the place of your dreams.

Always remember when investing in the stock market to only buy in the service industries and make sure that they are old blue chip, such as utilities, banks, etc., as the very large companies go up in price over the years and always pay a good dividend. Speculative stocks are usually not a good investment in the long run.

One of the most important parts of life is making friends who will help you in your journey through life. Most friends are a detriment to you; whereas intelligent, well-off, real friends will contribute to your lifestyle and success in many different ways. Bear in mind that you must always drive a new vehicle, or less than three or four years old, and live in a nice house as you will spend your years enjoying the comforts of a good house and a good neighborhood while it goes up in value. Always remember when you buy your vehicle that you must buy it with at least a 25 percent discount in order to ensure that when you sell it, it costs you very little to drive it over the years. Under no circumstances do you ever lease a vehicle, as it is just money down the drain. If you have a company, buy the vehicles in your own name and lease them to your company so that you are the one that makes money in the leasing business rather than a stranger.

It is a good idea when buying stocks to think of companies like iOS, which was founded by Bernie Cornfeld. Forty years ago, his shares went sky-high and then dropped to nothing. Many companies have had a similar situation happen to it:

- Bre-X: shares went from 20 cents to over $200 and then went to nothing.
- The Yellow Pages: shares went from 75 cents to $75 dollars then to nothing
- Gauntlet Resources: shares went from 20 cents to $7 then to nothing

Mattie could name one hundred companies that he participated in and more than a thousand companies that he has read about where people invested hard-earned money in the stock market and wound up with nothing. It is a "buyer beware" market. However, in real estate, if you do due diligence, over time it will always go up in price as well as providing you with a source of revenue. Bear in mind three examples in residential housing that Mattie invested in.

1. A place a few miles outside Calgary, Alberta, on a lake where Mattie paid a thousand dollars originally and a few years later the lot sold for a million dollars
2. A residential lot where he built a house cost $200,000 and fifteen years later sold for $1 million.
3. A lot overlooking the river in Calgary, Alberta, with one of the best views in the world where the lot and house cost a total of $394,000,

which Mattie built.. Now the property next door sold for $4 million even though it was smaller with half the view.

Three property acquisitions in forty years have resulted in a tax-free gain of $3 million for Mattie. The media now is full of articles on the banks and the stock brokers throughout the world being charged by courts for devious works and manipulation of the stock markets and losing investor's money. Therefore, it is very important that you be extremely careful as we are in a four-year recession and depression, from 2008 to 2012. Now that the financial situation in the Western world is getting worse (like in the thirties), we may have an additional five years of recession and depression. Jobs in America have been shipped all over the world, started by companies like Wal-Mart, and the price of food and fuel has skyrocketed which was caused by major oil companies. Wall Street and the big banks throughout the world are engaging in scandals to the amount of billions and trillions of dollars.

Countries such as Canada that have sold off their primary resources to foreign companies will soon slow down, as there are only so many resources to sell. When the resources are sold, the country will be in terrible shape. An example was on July the 24, 2012, a Chinese oil company invested $16 billion to buy one company, and in the same week, there was another deal for $8 billion more. That is more than $25 billion invested in one week. There will probably be over $100 billion worth of Canadian resources sold in one year alone. These major corporations in 2008 laid off over one hundred thousand people. Now they state that there is a shortage of labor. Naturally, when people lose their jobs, they have to go somewhere else if they wish to continue eating.

There are a lot of workers in Mexico who are looking for work to do the low-paying labor jobs, and it is time that Canada and the United States bring in professional people such as doctors and give them courses in the English language. Within a year, we would have a surplus of doctors just like Scandinavia. They should have all patients phone the specialists directly rather than having to go to a doctor first, and people should be able to get prescriptions directly from the pharmacists which would, within one month, enable patients to get what they require instead of having to wait for several extra weeks.

It is extremely important to remember that with globalization, privatization, unionization, and giant companies amalgamating to control the markets throughout the Western world that we will be faced with difficult times and unemployment for many years to come. It is doubtful that we will ever recover to our former greatness, at least in the next generation. With the Far East, China, Japan, India, South America, etc., becoming the leading powers in the world, it is time to prepare yourself for a secure and financial future which is not that difficult to do if you follow Mattie's advice in this book, as well as gaining information that will allow you to travel and happily retire for the rest of your life and possibly leave millions to your heirs.

Now that you have finished the book and have got a number of causes to work for the good of your country, you may want to take a holiday. During the summer, Prince Edward Island is one of the prettiest places on Earth, with very reasonable accommodations and food. A second great place to visit in the summertime is Ireland, a beautiful country full of friendly people. In the winter, a great place to visit that is relatively expensive but well worth it is Hawaii, which has perfect weather and great scenery. New Zealand is also a great place to visit during the winter months because the island is beautiful, full of friendly people, and has great sights to see. For year-round enjoyment, Alberta and Western Canada are home of the Calgary Stampede—the greatest outdoor show on Earth—and contains the Rocky Mountains which are beautiful for summer events and winter skiing.

In the United States, J and J are fined $1.1 billion by a judge after an Arkansas jury found the company's officials mislead doctors and patients about the risks of the drug Risperdal. The judge found that J & J committed more than 238,000 violations of the state's Medicaid by illegally marketing Risperdal over an almost four-year period, starting in 2002. It's very important to check for drugs before you buy as, in the United States, a 400 mg vial of Avastin cost $2,400, but a Canadian drug company was selling foreign versions to doctors for $1,995, invoices have shown. Such low prices attracted a wave of new doctors/customers, one person who formerly sold non-FDA-approved cancer drugs to the doctors said.

An article in the *Canadian Press* states that a Canadian RCMP officer who was involved in the death of a Polish tourist has voluntarily left the force. The deputy commissioner of the Mounties of the RCMP stated, "While I have been clear that I was seeking his voluntary dismissal, the opportunity to discharge him from the organization this morning was one of which was eliminated for the delays and costs of uncertainty." The forty-two-year-old RCMP officer was convicted earlier in the year for obstruction of justice after his vehicle struck and killed a twenty-one-year-old in Delta, south of Vancouver, in October 2008. Imagine a senior police officer that has been involved in two deaths, and he cannot be fired from the force—they have to wait until he resigns.

An article on government affairs indicates that a senior aide to the prime minister of Canada is taking a government affairs job with Air Canada, raising pointed questions about the strength of ethical rules that are supposed to guide the post-political actions of Parliament Hill staffers. This is just another individual in the long line of politicians and senior bureaucrats who jumped ship to go to work for a big business.

An article in the *Calgary Herald* states that the country's worst drivers are found in Alberta. Results of an Ipsos survey revealed that Alberta motorists lead the country when it comes to bad driving habits, such as running red lights, and are most likely to lose their cool when they encounter a bad driver. This is mostly caused by very poorly designed roads which frustrate drivers and are unsafe at any hour. In a letter to the editor, a Calgarian writes regarding the taxi rate hike, stating that there is a monopoly at the airport and across the city by several companies. There is crippled, slow, and ill-responding service, horrible rates that are going even higher. This is caused by a premier in the '80s who gave hundreds of tax licenses to several individual companies for a few thousand dollars. Now these companies have hundreds of licenses that are worth $80,000 each, and in total, each company's licenses are worth multimillions of dollars.

Now that there is a three-hour wait at night for a taxicab, the city council is reluctant to give out more licenses as this would lower the value of these two outfits who manage to secure the majority of the licenses in the city. The proper thing to do would be to give out hundreds of more licenses to small one-owner operators in order that better service could be provided, taxi rates could be kept reasonable, and it would open a window of opportunity for private owners and new immigrants to the city. This is probably wishful thinking because when you are in the driver's seat in big business, city council seldom ever challenges the status quo.

Another prime example is that due to a drought, the price of corn has doubled. This has resulted in an increased food cost to many people throughout the world and will probably cause people to go hungry. While at the same time, 40 percent of the corn crop is being used to create ethanol to put in gasoline, which is totally unnecessary as North America has a surplus of oil and gasoline.

In America, a judge gave MGM the go-ahead to raise a hotel tower that never opened in Las Vegas, Nevada, that was to cost $8.5 billion to build. There are presently lawsuits to try and keep the hotel from being demolished, but inspectors have found flaws in the steel reinforcements built into the lower floors. Therefore, one of the most expensive buildings in the world may have to be torn down.

A major city in Canada is in need of recreational and cultural facilities, and tremendous amounts of money are needed to fund these new projects. If people want recreational and cultural facilities, they should have to pay an admission for using these buildings. Seniors, widows and widowers, and single mothers should not have to pay for something that they do not use. In the same Canadian city, services are provided to new subdivisions for new homeowners by existing taxpayers. In Eastern Canada, these services are paid for by a $25,000 to a $30,000 levy against the developers. This results in the people who want additional new housing paying for the services that they require. Hopefully the taxpayers will get up in arms and will force the developers to pay for the services that they require.

In a US publication, a New York casino man has pledged at least $60 million for political purposes. His checks may even buy his way out of a federal corruption investigation. The publication states, "As long as we have ⊠no legal or moral limits to the purchase of influence', the super rich will buy politicians the same way they buy fancy vehicles or ocean-front mansions." Another example of the power of big business was in an article in *Bloomberg Businessweek*, an excellent US magazine. The reporter stated that once a big oil and gas company gets into your area, they own you; they own commissioners, your property, and they will do what they want.

The examples listed beforehand are indicative of why people and countries will self-destruct in the future. It is a pity that there were not more good politicians like the one who stated, "In the States, one returned serviceman from the war in the Middle East commits suicide daily. Money corrupts in both politics and in business." He stated this in an interview with Piers Morgan on CNN.

To continue on in regard to war, Mattie and his friend a short while ago were speaking of the Second World War. The Allies were composed of the Americans and the English, together with the Russians, and fought the Germans and the Japanese. It was a rare combination with the communistic Russians under Stalin, who had killed up to nine million Ukrainians; the capitalistic English, who had killed millions of Gaelic people; and the American capitalists who had killed millions of colored people and American natives. The Germans had killed up to six million people of Jewish heritage, and the Japanese had killed millions of Chinese. Mattie's friend wondered who was in the right when all parties involved killed millions of innocent soldiers, men, women, and children. How could anyone look up to a nation who would do such terrible deeds? He asked Mattie for his opinion, and Mattie was unable to give a satisfactory explanation despite reading five thousand pages of literature a month, resulting in a total of five hundred thousand pages over the past fifty years.

When Mattie was young, soldiers in Eastern Canada who had returned from the war were reluctant to talk about their experiences overseas. Occasionally, when they got a few drinks, they would describe the horrors of war and how they hated every minute of it. They broke into tears as they told the stories of their exploits overseas, leading Mattie to be against war from a very young age.

On the financial side, it is wise to bear in mind to never get into a business where there is a very good possibility of losing money, as no matter how little money you make, if you keep saving and investing it, eventually you will be able to retire in comfort in a part of the world where you can enjoy a decent lifestyle and a reasonable cost of living. That is why Mattie explained in the aforementioned paragraphs why you have to be careful in the path you choose originally to work or to do business, and secondly, to ensure it has a growing economy where even the basic real estate goes up in price. Thirdly, that the area where you decide to live or where you decide to retire has a good government system which will provide you with a cost of living that is economical and the services, health, infrastructure, etc., that you need to enjoy life.

It is very important to remember some simple ways that anybody can save money and double their salary in a matter of one year. Mattie was paying on his extra cars $1000 per year on insurance. He cut his costs back by 50% by just insuring for collision and upset, and he also reduced his costs by buying cars over 25 years old. These cars were like new and the insurance for an antique classic is less than $200. Cut your insurance cost by 75% by only insuring the minimum of what you require on your car. The majority of people are over insured. Since the return on invested capital to insurance companies has gone down considerably, which results in costs going up, look for ways to save a dollar any way you can. He also cut his gas costs in half by buying vehicles that have double the mileage and cut his driving by 50%, therefore reducing his overall costs. When buying cars, it is wise to buy a two year old vehicle that is on sale, which will cut your cost by at least a third.

Mattie cut back on electricity and heat by putting electric air conditioning and heaters in each individual room, therefore cutting his utility bill by 75%. Instead of going to sports events at $100 to $200 per game, Mattie watches the games on TV. This cuts his cost completely. Mattie was able to cut his food costs in half by reducing the amount of unnecessary food he eats by a large amount, and when he goes to a restaurant, he usually gets his meals at half price. If he does not get his meals at half price, he takes half of his meal home and that saves cooking the following day as well as purchasing another meal. By eliminating tobacco and alcohol, he was further able to reduce costs. It is wise to buy your movies on sale and then resell them; this will cut your cost of entertainment by a significant amount. By going to Mexico for your dental work, a person can cut their dental costs by 90%.

If you can live in southern United States, either as a retiree or running your business – which is possible now with electronic communications, you can live for approximately a third of the cost as you would in Canada or northern United States. When buying travel, you can easily save 50% as there is always sales on if you book early and occasionally there are last minute specials. When renting property, make sure you get at least one tenant in every building who will look after cutting the grass and removing snow.

When it comes to rental property you should do it yourself, which will allow you to gain better knowledge about your tenants. A big company will always rent space to corporations who own a lot of property while small business individuals get left out in the cold. In order to make more money, Mattie worked from 5am to 9pm for nearly forty years. He then changed his hours from 9 am to 5 pm, only working four days a week for the following twenty years. Even when he was working long hours and wanted to take time off for vacation, he was always free to because he had the money to spend on whatever he and his wife desired.

When you put your money in banks, they take 50% of your money by lending it out. It is quite easy for any individual to lend money, thereby doubling the return on their investments. Always bear in mind that money invested over the years will provide a far greater return in real-estate than it will in the stock market and you will have much better control over your investment. Remember when investing in the stock market, you should invest in utilities. In Canada, banks are always a good investment as these stocks will not only pay dividends but will hold their value over the years.

Alberta Energy, which changed its name to Encana, is a company that a group bought for $2 billion, and within a couple years had tripled in value. Encana Corp has just showed a $1.5 billion U.S second quarter loss. This would equal $6 billion of a loss per year, while the same company is building a multi-billion dollar building in Calgary, Alberta; one of the highest in North America. Deciding on such a building during such a large quarterly loss is an example of poor leadership and bad business.

Another major incident that is mind-boggling is the former Citigroup chief, stating, "Big banks should be broken up, causing jaws to drop all across the financial industry and throughout the world." The former chairman and chief executive of Citigroup appeared on CNBC on July the 25th, 2012, and announced on no uncertain terms that he thought big banks should be broken up. The gentlemen in question once was the head of one of the biggest banks in the world. This is a man who led a single-minded quest to turn what was once a large but normal bank into a giant, going from acquisition to acquisition until its reach stretched into every conceivable financial product on the planet.

"Times have changed", he said, and he has had a change of heart. "What we should probably do is split up investment banking from general banking, and make some banks be deposit takers and have other banks make commercial loans and real-estate loans. Banks should do something that does not risk the taxpayers' dollars and that is not too big to fail. I'm suggesting that they be broken up so that the taxpayer will never be at risk, the depositors won't be at risk, and the leverage of the banks will be something reasonable."

This gentleman said he has been thinking hard about this for the past year.

He maintains that breaking up the banks would help the United States reclaim its leadership of the global financial industry, and resurrect bank's reputations more broadly. "I want us to be a leader, and what we are doing now is not going to make us a leader," he said. Many important and prominent people in the world are also stating that it is time to impose more regulation on banks and remove the deregulation that was put in place several years ago by various presidents who allow big banks and big corporations to do what they want.

As this book is being written, politicians are facing heat over 'sweetheart pensions'. The average politician in Canada gets a monthly pension of almost $6,000, while the average Canadian taxpayer who pays for these pensions gets an average check for $538 for their pension, with the numbers being less for women. A massive billboard campaign has been launched by the Taxpayers Federation urging Canadians to sign a petition as taxpayers are fed up footing the bill for pensions that are among the most lavish in the world.

Another problem is security cameras now being urged in all taxis at a time when no matter where we go, whether it be on the streets, in stores, government building etc. we are being spied upon. We even have Google taking pictures from the air and spying on people walking their dogs or going to their job. It is time that citizens in general stop being so complacent and start asking for their rights to stop being trampled upon.

Politicians travel and pay thousands of dollars per night for lodging, and $16 for a glass of orange juice. This is an absolute waste of money, particularly when we see what it costs to hold the Olympics with various federal, provincial, or state and municipal governments all chipping in order that the very rich, including the heads of big business and government, can travel and waste the taxpayers money, while a large number of seats are empty.

With interest rates in general being very low, and stock markets down at least a fifth of their value in less than a year, it is time to review your portfolio and consider the advice that Mattie has outlined in this book should you wish to enjoy a high standard of living and a good retirement.

Articles are constantly being writing by newspapers throughout North America on the selling off of our country to the highest foreign bidder. Always ask the question, if we continue to sell off our non-renewable resources, what will be left for the next generation? An example is Western Canada being sold off; $25 billion of assets being sold in one week. Many people are also questioning why the goods that we buy are made offshore. Third world countries are kicking out foreign companies with 82% of primary resources owned by locals.

In Canada, the Alberta government wants to build a gas line pipe across British Columbia so Alberta's natural resources can be sold overseas. Should this pipeline go ahead? It will result in Albertans having to pay increased costs for their own resources, and depleting a non-renewable resource. This gas should be used for vehicles and power plants, reducing pollution, and saving the taxpayers in Western Canada money. The government of Alberta wants to take all of the profit from the pipeline, while giving the neighboring province 8%. Alberta would get an immediate short term gain, while the neighboring province would get the pollution and environment problems. The Keystone pipeline from western Canada to the Southern states fortunately was stopped in its tracks by the President due to the large amount of environmental spills in North America.

This pipeline should be run from western Canada to the provinces of Ontario, Quebec, and the Maritimes, along the existing trans-Canada pipeline as there are a large number of big refineries in eastern Canada, with the biggest being located in the Maritimes. This would result in eastern Canada no longer having to bring crude oil from off shore, mainly Venezuela. A sign of the recession/depression is the world's largest equipment maker's shares are down; signaling one of the worst slowdowns in history when a large company such as this is suffering depressed share prices.

Mattie has discussed one city, Calgary, Alberta in more detail than anywhere else. To give credit where it is due, the latest council has discontinued putting fluoride in the water which was a waste of money, cut back on bike paths that were slowing traffic, built a tunnel to a major airport in conjunction with several billion dollars worth of construction done at the airport. The new mayor, who is considerably more intelligent than the three previous mayors, has advocated permitting basement suites in order that Calgarians can have low cost rental fees. It is very difficult for a mayor of any city to get things done as he only has one vote out of many and has to convince the others on council to go along with his thoughts and ideas to make the city a better place to live.

When the Irish came in the mid-1880's, there were signs up all over the Eastern Seaboard where they landed in America saying "No Irish need apply", yet one chap who had just enough money to get a pick and shovel found his way west to Virginia City where he struck it rich in gold. He then moved to Montana, where he found a giant mine which later became the Aluminum Company of America (Alcoa), proving that you can start with nothing and become very rich. There are many stories of the same nature, especially in mining and oil, but it is hard for the ordinary individual to relate to people who have become rich beyond belief.

It is easier to believe the real-life story of Mark Walsh, who worked for Mattie in the 1970's and was an engineer by profession. Mattie soon realized that Mark was intelligent, hard-working, and was very shrewd in saving the dollar. At that time Mattie owned three engineering firms, so Mark became interested in buying one which operated five survey crews in the oil exploration industry during the winter, and in the summer did road engineering in Alberta,

Canada. Mark bought one engineering company for very little as he drove a hard deal and Mattie wanted to see him do good. In a few years, he started out with nothing: no house, driving a company vehicle, etc. Nevertheless, he parlayed the oil field and engineering company into an excellent living. He then asked Mattie if street sweepers and maintenance would be a good investment, which Mattie believed it would not be because maintenance was seasonal, sweepers were nights and weekends and were a high-maintenance piece of equipment.

Mattie mentioned to Mark that a person he knew owned cranes and Mattie had watched him grow from a standing start to a very rich man. Mark immediately looked for a company to buy in the crane business involved with oil companies. Soon finding a company where one partner wanted out, Mark bought its shares on time and paid him out of the next few years while gaining two partners who knew the business inside and out. To this day, Mark is a very wealthy man worth many millions, living on a ranch south of Calgary, Alberta. He is semi-retired but still involved in his business, playing golf and hockey, travelling the world, and enjoying the life of a wealthy rancher. This is an example of how a young person can make their stake in a few decades and then retire in their early 50's to enjoy the last half of their life doing what they prefer with their wife or husband and family.

Mattie was going to hire Mark's brother Hank, but instead hired Mark. Hank went back to college for a master's degree and joined an oil company. When the oil company sold out, Hank started up his own oil company with next to nothing, just options on leases. He went on in a decade to make a small fortune, while buying real-estate on the edge of the city of Calgary and selling it for ten times what he paid for it. That land is now developed into a subdivision. Hank has semi-retired and is travelling the world with his wife and family in his mid-50's, with many decades of a retirement to enjoy in the years to come.

The third brother, Theo, decided to join the federal government and marry a nurse, resulting in living the good life for decades and retiring in his mid-50's with an excellent pension and full benefits. He is now living on a farm on the East Coast and enjoying life like an English country squire. Their sister, Jean, became a teacher, making good money during her lifetime while raising a family and retired in her 50's along with her husband, who was an accountant with the federal government making hundreds of thousands per year. They are now drawing three pensions each, travelling the world, and enjoying the good life. Should Jean decide to go back to work, she can make hundreds of dollars a day as a teacher working a short day and working when she feels like it.

This shows how a family of four, three boys and a girl, can start out with nothing and become extremely successful in business or as professionals. It is something that can be accomplished by the vast majority of Americans. It is something that any American can relate to as they know people in every walk of life who has done something very similar, working for decades and hopefully living the rest of their decades retiring rich. Particularly in the case of the three brothers, they were intelligent enough to realize when they had made millions of dollars, it was time not to jeopardize their future and instead semi-retire and enjoy life.

We see so many articles in the media of people who get in the banking and insurance business and lose tens of millions of dollars, sometimes billions. A young man called Todd Tannas, who was in his 20's working in the travel business putting together bus tours, was barely making enough money to eat at a time when he had just had a young child and his wife was a stay at home mother. Todd Tannas' father, Ron, was a high school principal who owned a travel agency and whose wife was a nurse and a business person who owned a retail clothing store. Ron, who was involved in politics, asked Mattie what his son could get into where he could make good money. Mattie reminded Ron that he was in the travel business and had a wife in retail, and all his son had to do was the same thing that Mattie did when he was told by Reverend Olsen: put together a half dozen different businesses into one.

Mattie suggested to Ron that he and his son, with a few others, get together and expand the travel agency into insurance, selling financial certificates, as well as banking investments. He wisely imitated Wal-Mart and bought up small businesses in these various lines of work in small towns across western Canada where there was little to no competition. It very quickly became the largest company of its kind in Western Canada.

Mattie knew this would be a success because in town of a few hundred people, a business man had many employees selling insurance and financial investments. In a decade Tannas' company, which he called the Western Financial Group, started its own bank called Bank West, and in April of 2012, he sold Western Financial Group to a large company in Canada for $440 million. This resulted in him becoming a very rich man with little or no investment before he was 50. He too has now decided to retire, having run for an elected senator in Western Canada and hopes to be appointed a senator in 2014. This is something that was offered to Mattie on two occasions by Prime Ministers who were picking senators at large but Mattie had no interest in moving to the eastern part of Canada and becoming a politician.

Another example that anyone can relate to is Ron Bardahl, who was engaged in big-time farming with a very large investment in land and equipment. This was at a time when there was little money in farming. Ron was a brother-in-law of Mattie, and Mattie realized the difficult times that Ron and his family were going through. Mattie bid on all the hunting licenses in the province of Alberta when the various guides throughout the province decided that they did not like the way the province operated its hunting licensing business. They refused to bid, resulting in Mattie getting 100% of the licenses in the whole province.

Since Mattie had never shot a gun, nor did any of his ancestors in America, he was only interested in passing on this lucrative business to his chemist Dr. Lerbscher PhD, who was a chemist for one of Mattie's companies and was an avid hunter. Dr. Lerbscher decided he was not interested because Mattie had told him about an opening at one of the largest chemical companies in the world who were paying a third of a million dollars for a chemist with a doctorate, so Dr. Lerbscher took the job with the big company. Mattie sold at cost all the hunting licenses in the province back to the guys who had previously refused to bid on them, making them extremely happy. Without Mattie's help, they would have all been out of business and Mattie could have kept the licenses and sold them to rich American hunters.

Mattie informed his brother-in-law that a First Nation's individual in northern Saskatchewan had a several hundred head cattle operation, and in the fall he ran a hunting camp making hundreds of thousands of dollars in a month or two. Ron immediately jumped on the idea, leasing a bunch of land in the north with several houses on it and with no money down advertising in the American hunting magazines and had booths at the American hunting shows. This resulted in dozens of hunters coming to Saskatchewan to hunt, as a hunter in the northern part of that province had just shot a deer with the biggest antlers in history. This kill set a new record in the Boone and Crockett's book of records. Within a couple of years, another hunter in central Alberta shot an even bigger buck deer setting a new record, and Ron increased his hunters from a few dozen to over fifty and the price from $2000 for a week's hunting to $5000. This caused him to take in a quarter million in one month.

Within a few more years, he sold the business to a wealthy American hunter who had just sold several hundred restaurants in the eastern United States. Ron immediately invested in land in a small town at the crossroads of the main east-west and north-south highways in Canada. The land was low lying, but suited growing vegetables which he was doing during the summer months as a hobby. In a few years, he sold the land with highway frontage to two of the largest companies in Canada, making millions of dollars more. He did this while staying on for five years at $50,000 for one month in a year instead of working eleven months with one month off. In his mid 50's, he retired to Texas for the winter to golf and fish, and now spends his time fishing in the spring, golfing in the summer, and hunting in the fall: the life of a Baron in Germany or a Lord in England. Something that few people can do is quit when they have made their millions of dollars and instead of investing and losing it, retire and enjoy it for many decades.

In life, it is not how rich you are or where you have lived, but what you do with your life. Few people realize that this is the most important part of being on earth. One must remember even though the Chinese are success stories at present, their shares trading in the United States have lost 50% of their value in one year on the stock exchange. Now these Chinese companies are going private, realizing that the stock market is not all what it is said to be.

The one area in North America that you can never get ahead of or get fair treatment (pardon the pun) is in healthcare. In Canada, you pay healthcare all of your life, and when it comes time for medical treatment, you may have to wait months or perhaps years for something that you will already paid for in advance; a very sad state of affairs. In the United States, they have private health centers where doctors are making a million dollars on their investments and buying houses for four or five million dollars. These are the very same doctors that have had their education paid for by the taxpayer, and when the time comes for that same taxpayer whose health has failed and who needs treatment is charged ten times what it should be. Mattie has met a lot of good doctors in his life as he has had several serious health problems.

An article in Bloomberg Business magazine has stated that publishers and authors crank out as many as eleven thousand new business books each year, and that doesn't account for the untold number of self-published e-Books. Most authors who write business books have never been in business; they write about someone else who has been successful with no knowledge about making money, investing, and what living the good life is all about. You have to have been there and done that if you really want to write in detail, which Mattie has done throughout his life. The article stated that you could hire a ghost writer to write the book for you, with an average fee being around $40,000 with some asking for $250,000. In Mattie's opinion this is a waste of time.

The reason that Mattie writes is to leave a legacy about real-life small business as well as dealing with big business and big government. He has outlined in detail how one can get through the ups and downs, and still live a good life. A large number of people write books in order that their name will be recognized and this will enable them to speak to groups for a fee per session, which is one way to make a living and cannot be criticized. Nevertheless, Mattie is not interested in making money out of his books or in public speaking engagements. Should he speak on occasion in public, then he would donate whatever profits were raised to people with disabilities, as there are so many people in the world who could use extra money and facilities to make their lifestyle more enjoyable.

The most important thing in life is what you want personally. Do you want freedom, or is it security? If you want to live your life like a dog with a chain tethered to a post, then you can always work for big business and take the chance that you might get laid off. If you work for big government you will always have a job but have no freedom to do what you want. If you are fortunate enough to marry a partner who has a job in big business or big government, you will be able to retire with six pensions, and benefits to boot. This will allow you to live an excellent life with hundreds of thousands of dollars of income during your working years, and over one to two hundred thousand dollars in pensions jointly for the rest of your life.

You also have to decide if you want to be receiving the pay check or signing it. Mattie informed his father that he wanted to sign the pay check and have the freedom to do what he wishes to do with his life when and where he wanted. This resulted in Mattie entering the small business world and working hard in hopes of becoming successful.

As Mattie completes this book, he reads about a young person who is in their 20's and has written two best selling finance books called *Rich by Thirty* and *Rich by Forty*. She has a financial planner to assist her. Can anyone in their right mind visualize themselves reading something written by someone in their twenties who tells them how to be rich by thirty or forty when they have not even reached that age? Mattie has heard thousands of speakers over the past sixty years. Mattie has never been a fan of public speakers. Many decades ago, Mattie's friend went to hear Dale Carnegie speak. When he asked Mattie to join him and to pay money to go see Carnegie, Mattie just said buy his book and hope to get something worthwhile out of it. In the book, Mr. Carnegie stated, "Put the monkey on someone else's back." That was one of the dozens of things Mattie did in his life. If you had hundreds of people doing various jobs for you and creating a profit, you could wind up being extremely successful enjoying free time, learning this from Dale Carnegie's book.

An article in the Calgary Herald states that the life of one lady who was born extremely poor but had the dedication and work ethic to become the first in her family to graduate from college took a drastic turn in June of 2011. She was followed home by another lady leading a pack of women who viciously beat the young college graduate. This resulted in the young college graduate shooting the leader of the pack of girls. When it came to court, the justice system in Arkansas gave the lady who was defending herself 30 years in jail. This is an example of Southern justice and something to be wary of when you are travelling or retiring in the Southern United States.

In another article in the Canadian Press, hundreds joined a RCMP harassment lawsuit. The RCMP force is being accused of harassing women who have now banded together to fight in a class action lawsuit, making one concerned about the justice system. In another article in a British Columbia newspaper, it was stated that no jail time was handed to a disgraced RCMP officer who should have received jail time. This officer gained notoriety for being one of four Mounties involved in the taser-related death of Robert Dziekanski, a Polish tourist who was killed upon arriving at the Vancouver, BC airport.

The same police officer was also driving a vehicle that struck and killed a young man in an intersection in a Vancouver suburb four years ago, after he had consumed five beers early in the night. After the crash, the off-duty officer left the scene to bring his two children home. While at home he gulped two shots of vodka that he later claimed was simply to calm his nerves. The officer is also facing perjury charges in connection with his testimony and the public inquiry into Mr. Dziekanski's death at the Vancouver, BC airport in 2007. The judge said that the officer's conduct causes one to lose faith in the Protect and Serve Police Mantra, particularly because he has shown no remorse for the offense or acknowledged any guilt. Despite all of this, the judge refused to send the officer to jail. This is an example of how there is one law for the rich and the government individuals, and another for the ordinary people.

An article in the Globe and Mail stated that a person in the Prime Minister's office in Canada has been charged with influence peddling, a crime that is punishable by up to five years in jail. When Mr. Abraham, a United States lobbyist, was caught doing the same and went to jail for years. It will be interesting to see what happens in a case where a government official is charged with a similar offense in Canada.

An article in a Canadian national newspaper states the now one of the big Wall Street firms in the United States is going to fund a jail program. Their new social impact bond will see the bank invest nearly ten million dollars in a four year program aimed at helping inmates. Evidently the message has finally gotten through to them that the United States government is going to act on their shoddy practices which have caused nearly 50 percent of the American families to lower their standards of living, some losing their jobs and houses, all caused by the greedy individuals in these large Wall Street firms. The time has come for the United Stated government to start laying criminal charges and locking up the people responsible before it totally destroys America.

An article on the Queen of Versailles and her husband, a former self-made billionaire in his senior years, had a starter mansion with 17 bathrooms. At a time of collapsed stock markets and general depression in the United States, they are now building a new mansion designed in nuveau rich style. Unfortunately now with the extreme slow down in the world economy they have to put this new mansion up for sale as the money he made selling time share villas is rapidly disappearing down the drain. There is no doubt that the time share business is long past its prime. Mattie always believes that anyone who buys a condo should do a lot of research as condo fees can amount up to $1,000 a month.

In Alberta in the health department an employee who squandered hundreds of thousands of dollars was employed by the provincial government was awarded a salary of $425,000 per year. He racked up $350,000 in expenses on top of his salary, and even though he has only worked for three months, he still is walking away with a severance package. This often occurs in the health system with approximately $10 billion of waste per year due to mismanagement and corruption. This all goes on while seniors are eating reheated frozen dinners and thousands are dying from neglect in the hospital system. This is the same system where we have seen a former health minister pay almost $400,000 on a contract to his executive assistant. The health minister has now moved on to a lucrative job overseas costing the government approximately a million dollars per year, and that same assistant is now a director of the governing political party of the province. One wonders what it will take other than a rebellion to get the government to take notice as well as attract attention of the voters of that province who keep electing people who waste their money while health, education, and infrastructure suffer,

In the United States, a city in Georgia is experiencing with outsourcing government work to an engineering company owned by Saudi Arabia. It is no wonder why the United States is in a state of depression. In Calgary, Alberta, a city of a million with a 2.5 billion dollar budget was presented by their auditor a statement indicating that the city was wasting $750 million. Instead of firing the people responsible, the city fired the auditor. What will it take to get the voters to turn out in force and throw out the dysfunctional council in that city? In that same city, the taxpayers pay tens of thousands of dollars on each new house being built for families moving to that area. When will the city wake up and start charging the people who purchase these new homes for the services that they require?

One only has to turn to the quotations of Milton Friedman, who was an economist and noted critic of the over-mighty state, which has gotten a lot mightier. According to the Economist, several of his one-liners remain memorable. "If you put the federal government in charge of the Sahara Desert, in five years there would be a shortage of sand," and, "Nothing is so permanent as a temporary government program," are two of the most noted quotes from Milton Friedman. He had a lot of good ideas such as giving parents vouchers which they could spend at a school of their choice.

In a book Milton Friedman co wrote titled *A Monetary History of the United States,* he stated that the federal government was an accomplice in the depression thanks to its failure to reverse a stunning fall in the money supply. He also stated that efforts by the government to push employment above economies limits raised inflation.

The good thing about China investing in Canada's primary resources will be before the end of the present recession/depression, which will likely last another five years; China will no doubt decide to take over the world economy. The good part is that Canada, which in five years will have a large Chinese investment in its primary resources, will be safe from takeover, as China will already own Canada therefore providing a safe haven for Canadians. We have watched historically the rise and fall of powerful nations over the last several thousand years, and in our generation we have watched the decline of the British Empire and the fall of America as a world power since the Second World War. Now with the world in a recession/depression, it is only a matter of time until China becomes the new world power.

The rise of Chinese companies is beginning to cause concern throughout the world. Huawei, a leading global information and communications technology (ICT) solutions provider, has overtaken Sweden's Ericsson becoming the world's largest telecom-equipment maker. Now Lenovo is challenging the United States Hewlett Packard as the world's biggest PC maker. Geely, from China, is the world's largest manufacturer of cars.

China also controls a large part of the United States debt, as well as manufacturing most of the products that the citizens of the United States use on a day-to-day basis. China has no debt and a much larger population, compared with the United States who has sixteen trillion dollars in debt with a much less dense population, and has now the capabilities to take over the world economy in the near future.

Canada would be wise to encourage Chinese investment in the primary resources in the country, as most of our oil, gas, and minerals are already foreign owned. Canada would need to encourage the Chinese to invest in Canadian industry, as well as supply a cheap labor force in order to make Canada competitive in the world markets again. This would ensure that when China goes to war against the Western World, Canada will be safe and on the right side.

A crisis in higher education has been brewing for years. Universities have been spending like students in a bar who think that a Rockefeller will pick up the tab. Long-term debt at not-for-profit Universities in America has been growing at 12% a year, estimated by BAIN, a consulting company. A new report that looked at the balance sheets and cash flow statements of 1,692 universities and colleges between 2006 and 2010 found that one-third of universities are weaker than they had been several years ago. Universities hope that vast investments will help them attract the best staff and students, drawing in research grants and donation, ultimately boosting their rankings and drawing in more talent and money.

To pay for all of this, universities have been enrolling more students and jacking up their fees. The average cost of college per student has risen by three times the rate of inflation since 1983. The cost of tuition alone has soared from 23 percent of the median annual earnings in 2001 to 38 percent in 2010. Such increases cannot continue. Student debt has reportedly reached a record of one trillion dollars.

In an article in The Economist, Glenn Reynolds, the author of *The Higher Education Bubble,* predicts that the bubble will burst "messily". A BAIN consultant puts it cautiously, "Higher education has not delivered extra value to match the extra cost." He says, "Indeed the average student is studying for a few hours and learning less than in the past. Grade inflation only masks these trends. Still, the doomsayers may be on to something. Four year residential colleges cannot keep on forever raising their fees faster than the public's capacity to pay for them, especially when online degrees are so much cheaper. Universities that fail to prepare for the hurricane ahead are likely to be flattened by it."

Debt takes years to build up. In the United States, debt was around seventy percent of GDP in the year 2000 and grew at about four percent points a year to reach close to one hundred percent of GDP by 2007. The same was true of European banks and governments; debts rose hugely but steadily. It was hard to stop debt from forming. Now that the crisis has erupted with the realization that some prime exposures were wide-spread. Many assets are worth less in the market than they had been bought for. Falling asset prices mean that many banks and firms have debts that outweighed their assets, leaving only three options: Renegotiate debt, raise equity, or go bankrupt.

After two hundred and eighty two years at sea, a shipper was sunk by today's recession/depression. Britain's oldest shipping company survived two world wars and weathered the Great Depression before finally sinking under the weight of a global trade slump Stephenson Clarke Shipping Limited (SCS) in operation since the year 1730 has sold its last vessel in July and slipped into liquidation in early August. The company said it could no longer hold out against the massive downturn in the moving of dry goods such as iron ore and coal, commodities that once propelled the shipper to Britain's Industrial Revolution. Simon Benet, the director of external relations of International Chamber of Shipping said, "The effects of the depression, which started in 2008, followed the bank crisis and have been severe, causing the worst shipping market internationally in history." It is now being reported by the end of 2008 that companies are doing business for no profit just to keep customers. You can't do that for very long and stay in business.

The situation has gotten so bad in one city in western Canada that now the ordinary fireman want to censure the fire chief. The union seems to forget who the boss is and who the worker is. This is happening all across North America, and it will not be too far in the future before the unions will face a severe reprimand themselves. In that same western area, the government spends sixteen billion dollars on the Alberta Health system, and approximately ten billion dollars of that is sheer waste. Mattie witnessed this first hand when he was in a number of hospitals for three months and saw the dirty conditions that were allowed to exist along with slop for food.

While at the same time a former Health Region CEO received four million dollars in pensions. Another CFO got 1.6 million dollars in pensions, while putting $336,000 on his expense account, up to $2,000 for one meal. Other health CEO's and VP's received 1.2 million dollars, and 1.4 million. A medical officer receives $763,000, and another VP receives $171,000. All of this occurs while hundreds of thousands of people are suffering in the health care system and waiting years for operations while the health care system is thrown into chaos. This is the Canadian Health Care system that has been held up as a model.

The Americans don't have it any better and the cost of their healthcare system skyrockets through the roof making it unaffordable for anyone but those who have their healthcare covered by the government or the business they work for. The Canadian government has lots of money to buy planes and bullets to fight wars in foreign countries, killing women and children, yet complain that they have no money to stop the suffering and unnecessary deaths in hospitals across Canada; an absolute disgrace.

Mattie upon reading the Globe and Mail was very concerned to read that in Saskatoon, Saskatchewan they are building a new police station with a special architectural design for 101 million dollars in a run-down part of the city. This goes to prove that it does not do any good to be sitting in a province loaded with resources and billions of dollars coming in thanks to Mother Nature, and it is wasted when a $20 million building would do just as well. This is at a time when one of Mattie's key employees moved to Saskatchewan because it had a hospital and was close to a federally funded lake, only to find out that the Saskatchewan government had no money for healthcare and there was no doctor in the hospital. This man had to sell his house and move back to Alberta, even though Alberta has terrible healthcare as well.

A retired Dr. Levant states that twenty years ago he discovered that an immigrant had defrauded healthcare insurance. When he presented proof to the most senior bureaucrat in the health industry, the bureaucrat said that he was the first physician to ever expose fraud by a patient since 2000 and it was only a "drop in the bucket" of a $4 billion budget and was going to do nothing about it. Due to ministers in the cabinet and bureaucrats such as this, the budget now has grown to $16 billion. The doctor then left in disgust stating that other patients would learn of his attitude and thousands of other may copy this criminal.

Upon making suggestions to improve delivery, quality, and efficiency of healthcare, the doctor was told, "Your suggestions may make good medical sense, but do not make good political sense." The doctor stated that the spending of $10 million to investigate queue jumping (which has existed for a long time and will continue to occur) is an obscene waste. The moral of those practitioners on the front line is as high as a snail's belly." The doctor said he took early retirement because of financial abuse that impedes the practice of good medicine. It is unfortunate that waste throughout North America and particularly in Canada continues while patients are without healthcare, he stated in his address to the Canadian Medical Association annual general meeting,

Doctor John Haggie said, "A movement of self examination for the healing profession is in order." He states, "I am not suggesting that we turn back the clock, we could not practice the way we do without the use of modern technology. Today we are relying on ever bigger, better, and more expensive gizmos. He states, "Instead, the tendency now is to order more and more tests to rule out every possible diagnosis. We have to remember that we were taught in medical school about how to talk to our patients and how to listen to them, as well as the power of touch. The strength of the physician lies in the relationship they have with their patients."

He said that witnessing the impact of impoverishment and remoteness on patients was a stark reminder that Canada sometimes falls short on living up to its reputation as a highly developed, fair, and compassionate nation.

When we need to look at waste, we have only to read about the Pentagon's foreign suppliers in the United Sates. Russia was paid $378 million for helicopters to arm the Afghan military, Australia received almost $2 billion for a combat ship, Britain received $7 billion for fighting vehicles, Italy received nearly $2 billion for electronics, aircraft parts, and planes, and the Netherlands received $2 billion for meals ready to eat and other food.

This is at a time when the US military trainers in Afghanistan handed an AK-47's to a soldier to defend his village, which he used to kill two United States military members. An Afghan soldier wounded two more coalition servicemen hours later. A political science professor in Massachusetts states, "I have never heard of anything in Vietnam comparable to what we have recently experienced in Afghanistan." The war in Afghanistan has been for nothing as the British fought there for years, followed by Russia, and now the Americans. This goes to prove that wars do not solve anything. They kill innocent people as well as their own soldiers, who are committing suicide at the rate of one per day.

It has become very evident that the communistic system has failed in Russia and Cuba because it provides benefits for everyone with no incentives to work. The capitalistic system has grown to the point where a large number of very rich billionaires control the economy and the window of opportunity for small businesses that create over 60% of new jobs is gradually closing.

The future will be decided not by eastern Canada or in the Eastern Seaboard in the United States and Midwest where industries now are moving to the Southern United States because of lower labor costs. The cost of production is what decides the price of what is sold; resulting if the price is too high there is nothing being sold. China is taking over the production of goods throughout the world. Another problem is as raises increase throughout North America, Europe, and England, the goods produced in these countries become too expensive. This results in production being moved offshore. Any individual wishing to do business in the years to come would be wise to learn one of the Chinese languages and be prepared not only to sell to China but to import goods from China.

A high-ranking health services CEO created a stir when he suggested there was a backdoor system for politicians, police, and their friends to get people moved up on waiting lists. He said he put a stop to it, and the federal police declined a request to investigate. The CEO was fired for issuing public statements outlining the corruption in the system.

The irony of preferential access in a public healthcare system is all of us pay for the system, but if only some of us get a leg-up, those who do (probably the most connected) get this benefit without the need to pay their way to the front of the line as in the United States. Overall, the problems with the Western health system have their roots in previous government administrations, including the culture of entitlement that the past governments have been known for.

Mattie was asked for the second time by a Canadian Prime Minister if he would become a senator. When he declined, they picked a lady who was an environmentalist, human rights advocate, and former western Canada provincial cabinet minister. She is now one of the remaining federal conservative parliamentarians in Canada. The senator now sits as an independent and she is a classic example of the middle of the road conservative, another label that has been effectively wiped off the federal political map in Canada. With no official party caucus, she is a political lone-ranger in the upper cabinet chamber. She believes she brings "desperately needed independence of thought" to the institution of senate, which goes to show the radical changes in Canada over the past decade.

Two of Mattie's business acquaintances were debating why such large severance checks were being given to ex-employees in government and big business in general. One individual stated, "These higher up employees know a lot about what is going on in government and big business and these outrageously high severance checks are paid in order to keep these former employees from going public with what they know."

In northern Canada where a two-lane highway stretches for hundreds of miles from the capital of Edmonton, Alberta, to one of the largest oil sand developments in the world. It has been a regular occurrence for dozens of people to be killed. We should also wonder why they would not have to build a proper four-lane road to carry the heavy trucks and the constant flow of cars carrying individuals to and from their work in the oil sands. This is yet another example of big business being allowed to do what they wish by various governments at the expense of other people's safety.

While wineries in Canada live in fear of liquor control boards, there is absolutely no reason why these small wineries – which are owned by families and small business people – should not be allowed to sell their product direct from coast to coast. For the time being they have to live in fear of the various governments.

The opposition party in Alberta, Canada states that seniors are being treated like dogs that are being served warmed up, crappy food and scraps both in hospitals and in senior citizen homes. There are nearly fifteen thousand seniors waiting for continuing care, thousands of sick and disabled seniors waiting in hospitals taking up beds that are badly needed to serve the sick, and yet nothing is being done about it. A Mr. Donovan, who is a member of the opposition, states "Let's remember who built this province. These are the people who made the province what it is today. And to treat them like they are a dog in a kennel is absolutely deplorable in my eyes." Naturally a spokesperson for the Alberta Health service did not reply to a request for an interview.

Recently, two thirds of a page at approximately $15,000 per day, an advertisement has been running and paid for by the Alberta Union stating "Let's Stop the Rip-off," in large words. The advertisement is also making the statement "We all pay taxes for senior's health care, but a few private companies take millions of the senior's money and pocket it. That's not right and we need to stop them. Please support the seniors." This is a cause that young, working individuals and retired people should devote their time to. Unless one joins protest movements, signs petitions, and turn out at the polling stations to vote out the politicians and governments who are destroying the standard of living and quality of care in any province, state, or government, will see deterioration in services in the years to come. This would result in chaos throughout the country.

Advertisements such as the one mentioned above are appearing in many parts of North America, Europe, and the United Kingdom. There are many newspaper publications which have articles that inform people about what is going on in their country, for example, the Wall Street Journal and the Arizona Republic, published in the United States. There are also many excellent magazines such as Bloomberg Business Week, The Week, and National

Geographic. In Canada, one of the better magazines published twice yearly is The Taxpayer, which is put out by the Canadian Taxpayers Association and outlines waste and mismanagement throughout Canada.

In Bloomberg's magazine, a recent article stated that Expedia Inc, Starwood and Marriott hotels are among a group of online travel sites that are accused of conspiring to fix prices for hotel rooms. The travel sites sought agreements to prevent the hotels from selling large blocks of hotel rooms at discounted prices at the last minute.

As the recession/depression depends, very large companies have put major project decisions on hold as big companies reign in production costs. This is a regular occurrence in the media throughout North America. Very large companies are cutting back as after five years, the recession/depression is not improving but is slowing down further throughout the world. A further article in the Calgary Herald states, "Fiscal cliff" looms in United States. Spending cuts plus tax raises add to economic woe. Massive spending cuts and tax raises due next year will cause even worse economic damage than previously thought if Washington fails to come up with a solution. It is ironic that the governments that caused the problems over the past five years are now expected to get the country on the upswing. I doubt whether or not they will effectively be able to do anything about the slowdown.

An article in the Calgary business section of the Calgary Herald states, "Alberta baby boomers are to toil during retirement. Workers have to keep meaningful jobs. In a poll conducted by a marketing firm, it was found that 57% of Albertans plan to work during retirement and plan to retire at the age of 64." It is unfortunate that in one of the richest places on Earth, that people are going through hardship during retirement as well as having to contend with horrible health conditions and poor infrastructure, with a budget of 39 billion dollars per year and a population of less than four million people.

It is always wise to remember the four D's when you are purchasing any item, and these four D's are purchasing from people who have encountered debt, divorce, death, or diversion where they have gone on to something else and lost money, therefore having to sell at low prices.

Many books have been written on how to have money in your old age by simply saving, not spending, etc. There are few people in life who would want to live out their existence while not enjoying life and spending a few of their hard earned dollars, so it is wise to save and not spend foolishly, yet you must enjoy life.

A lot has been made about investing in index funds. There are a number of large companies where you can invest in funds that are spread out over a number of companies. Many companies are good to invest in as long as you invest in utilities to ensure that you are receiving good dividend checks while you're money grows over time.

The most often quoted success story is that of Warren Buffett, a chairman who invests in simple things such as McDonalds, pipelines, and utilities. Investments that earn money day and night throughout the year for an investor if done well. A lot of financial writers talk about real-estate, but it is wise never to forget that lands investments typically double in their worth after several years. Real-estate is one of the best investments a person could make.

Financial planners are not necessary to some people, but Mattie always believe that a financial planner is good to use when starting up making investments so you get the idea of what you should and should not be doing. Companies that sell products which continually rise in price are good to invest in. The stock market is a gamble to invest in, and there is no one who can predict what any company will due in the future and in the long run. Companies have to contend with weather, different management, the ups and downs of the market place, etc. When you factor in that the heads of the companies make extremely large salaries with bonus' and options as well as flying jets, living in large luxury towers as well as working in them, and charging large expenses to their share holders, in a lot of cases it leaves little for the ordinary investor. Should one want to gamble, you would be better of going to Vegas because you know the odds before you gamble. If you have a good memory and you are able to know the odds, Las Vegas proves to be a better investment than the stock market as the stockbrokers and company people on the inside know what is going to happen before anyone else. This results in the insiders making the money before the ordinary individual has a chance to. This is why Wall Street, when it was deregulated by a President of the United States, threw the whole world in chaos. Without regulation, greedy people will have a tendency to destroy the market place.

There are all kinds of newsletters put out by people who make their money publishing various letters on what to do in the market place. Mattie has never subscribes to or bothered to read any as he realizes the money is made in distributing the letters and not the advice contained within. Mattie learned early in life from a gentlemen farmer that he used to work with that it was always good to buy when prices are low at an auction sale. This man would buy pigs that were young and worth next to nothing, and sold when they were worth much more; buying low and selling high. This is what you want to do when investing.

It is fine to buy bonds if you are buying strong government bonds issued by a high income industrial company or blue chip bonds such as Coca-Cola or Wal-Mart. It is wise to remember when you are investing that you should always make sure that you are not signing a contract where you have to invest money continually. Mattie has known people who have invested in second mortgages who have made a lot of money over the years and are usually senior employees of big business companies.

An article in a book Mattie recently read stated that the investment business is a giant scam. You should simply hold good utilities and strong general stocks over the years. There is no doubt about it. This statement was evidently attributed to a Harvard University fund manager, when interviewed in 2004. It is extremely interesting to read people who are producing statistics for the last 100 years are failing to take into consideration the depressions and recessions over the years where a lot of money was lost, mainly by people selling when the stock market went down. Also, nobody seems to mention big companies and individuals who have lost billions of dollars for their investors.

A lot has been written about hedge-funds, which are fine for wealthy investors, but the chances for the ordinary individual to become wealthy like these people is about one in a million. Those who invest in these funds pay several percentage points upfront and usually the funds will take a commission. This forces them to make large amounts of money or else the investor will lose money. There are millions of crooks doing business in the world who never get apprehended, because you are never labeled a crook until you get caught.

Money Sense and The Canadian Geographic are two more examples of excellent sources of information. Probably the best worldwide publication is The Economist, which is available throughout North America and the United Kingdom, and has commercial offices in Dubai, Paris, and Singapore. Mattie has subscribed to these magazines for decades and much of what he has written in this book is knowledge he has gained from reading these magazine articles over the past half-century.

When moving to a new city, it is wise to check out what conditions are like when starting up a small business or profession. You must also consider where you would want to live for a number of years and perhaps the rest of your life. Mattie finds now in Calgary, Alberta that the media states that there is a shortage of labour, but after running an advertisement for employees, there was an abundance of replies. This indicates that there is not a shortage of those who are looking for employment, but perhaps a shortage of experienced trades people. Mattie, in one of his retail buildings, wanted to install new doors. It took several weeks before he could get a quote. Even though there were twelve companies listed in the phone book, there were only four companies that were interested in quoting the job. Mattie estimates that it will probably take months for the new doors to be installed due to a lack of productivity.

Another item of major concern is Mattie has advertised his rental spaces on Kijiji, with all of the real-estate agents in Calgary, and has sent out four thousand fliers which outlined that he has the cheapest rent in Calgary, the best buildings. Mattie also offered that if you or one of your friends rents his properties, he will give you a free two week trip for two to Alaska or a trip by plane for two to Vancouver, a two day cruise for two to San Francisco, plus airfare and three nights of free accommodation to Las Vegas, and free airfare back to Calgary. Even with a tremendous offer like this, there are very few replies from interested individuals. This indicates that the economy is in a recession/depression, even though Calgary, Alberta sits on more primary resources than anywhere else in the world.

Two neighbors in Calgary had an argument over a dog. The argument resulted in one of the neighbors, who was at the time in his forties, going to the other neighbor's house where a handicapped gentleman in his mid seventies resided and punched him several times in the face. The handicapped old man pushed the young fellow out the door, resulting in the young man's wife calling the police. She told the police that the old man had a gun, even though the elderly chap had never shot a gun in his life.

Three police cars arrived with lights flashing over such a small matter, and they charged the old man with assault for pushing the aggressor off his doorstep. Of the three cops, one was colored, the other was a skinhead, and the third was a nice looking and neat young man. The elderly man ordered them out of the house as the fuss caused him to have a heart attack. The end result was when the judge heard of this travesty of justice, he threw the colored policeman out of the court and dismissed the charges. This indicated how the police department can become detrimental to the justice system.

Mattie has had rental space for forty years and during that time he has never had one solved by the police. Mattie and his tenants have had over one hundred break-ins and has never had one solved by the Calgary police. This has resulted in Mattie having to put bars on his doors, put up security lights, fence all of his yards, create compounds enclosed with fences and barbed wire, and put alarms in all of his rental spaces, including 'beware of dog' signs and safety patrols. In fact, Mattie's rental areas are more secure than a maximum penitentiary due to a lack of services by the city police.

Mattie emphasizes so often that the city of Calgary can hire street sweepers for $125 per hour, yet continue to operate their own sweepers and now have gone to renting sweepers. This has resulted in large additional costs to the taxpayer of nearly $300 per hour, as well as giving very poor service.

An article in The Week Magazine by Phillip K. Howard, states, "The American government is a deviant subculture. Its leaders stand on soapboxes and polarize the public by pointing fingers while secretly doing the bidding of special interest groups. Many public employees plod through life with their noses in rule books, indifferent of the actual needs of the public and unaccountable to anyone. The professionals who interact with government – lawyers and lobbyists – make sure every issue is viewed through the blinders of a particular interest, not through the broader lens of the common good. Who is in charge? It is hard to say. The most powerful source in this subculture is inertia. Things happen a certain way because they happened that way yesterday. Nothing can get taken a way, because that would offend a special interest. "

A prime example of how big business wastes money is AMTRAK, which has managed to lose $834 million on its food and beverage services over the past decade. "This is largely because of waste, poor management, and employee theft," government auditors have told congress.

Record setting performance by woman athletes in running and swimming events have steadily gotten closer to men and their times about 90% as fast in all events. This was proven when a fifteen year old girl from China set a record at the Olympics in London, England.

An article in The Week Magazine's business section states, "Markets: The End of Stocks? The bond king says that stocks are dead." Bill Gross, the Co-founder of PIMCO, the world's largest bond fund, says, "There is no longer any benefit to buying and holding stocks for the long run." Gross says, "The cult of equity is dying." This just goes to back up Mattie's point that it is no longer wise to invest in stocks unless you are going to buy electric, pipeline, telephone, utilities, and banks.

Another article in the business section in the same magazine stated, "As every frustrated American knows, no major banking executive has gone to prison or has been fined any significant amount in the aftermath of the financial crisis. What is astonishing is that the Wall Street bankers seem not to have paid any social cost either. They sit on corporate and non-profit boards, and attend functions and galas. They remain top Wall Street executives, or even serve as regulators, and travel back and forth between government and big business. The nation's prominent talk shows and conferences seek their opinions. If you are rich, you must therefore be intelligent; your views must be worthwhile. Never mind the track record."

A few rich and top government politicians live in a very different world and do what they want, when and where they want, to the detriment of the public in general throughout the world.

It is becoming a serious issue in North America with the unions on the far left becoming extremely powerful, owning controlling interest in shopping centers, large corporations, and controlling a large part of the economy of the nation. On the other hand, we have the billionaires and the super rich who are controlling big business, the various governments, and the politicians throughout North America. This no doubt will continue for a few years until China becomes a world power, and then only time will tell what will happen to North America and the world.

Mattie runs his business from Arizona six months of the year and travels two to three months on business and pleasure during the summer months. However lately, due to the problems in Calgary, Alberta he is interested in locating elsewhere in the summer months. Mattie does not deal with General Electric because of what he has been told and how they have dealt with Alberta healthcare. Mattie does not do business with Esso or Husky Oil because of past experiences.

Mattie needed to hire an electronics technician for technical work, and when he phoned two companies – Satellite Services and Ascot Services – the satellite people were a day late in coming, whereas Ascot were Services were very prompt. Mattie had them both work simultaneously. Ascot charged half the rate of the company, clearly indicating that you must be very careful when purchasing either goods or services as there is a tremendous discrepancy between individuals and companies.

Remember as a young individual to:

1. stand up for your rights
2. Start getting in the habit of saving your money
3. Whether you operate a lemonade stand, babysit, or have a paper-route, develop a work ethic which will stick with you throughout life.
4. If you feel that you want security you should get an education. The more education you receive the better as it will get you into big government and big business where you will have a certain amount of security, benefits, and a life-long pension
5. Should you wish freedom to travel when you feel like it throughout the world, go skiing, fishing, or whatever other pursuit of happiness you so desire, nothing beats a small business for personal freedom
6. Bear in mind that when you are doing business with anyone in any walk of life, always be concerned that they make take advantage of you. A large number of people will always strive for a better deal at your expense.
7. Always try to develop a way to help out in the community, politics, church, and charity. This will give you a sense of fulfillment throughout your life and at the end of the day you will be able tor retire and think back on all the wonderful memories and friends you have made.

It is essential when you are starting a new business to make sure that you have a, such as a franchise or an invention, that you feel will work. If you take in partners to get a business started – as some people do – it is wise to prepare at the very start a shot-gun clause that allows you to buy them out. Your partners may be your friends, family, etc, but they can decide not to stay in the business and this can happen at any moment. If this does happen you will be forced to buy them out or sell the company immediately, so it is extremely important to have an agreement in place should your partners decide they do not want to be in business anymore or in the case of death, sickness, or divorce.

Mattie has outline examples of individuals who have started up their own business such as the Walsh brothers or examples of people who have went to college and received a profession, then marrying a professional where they had two incomes and excellent benefits and pensions. An example of a company that was started from scratch is when Mr. Kelleher in the United States started Southwest Airlines. This airline went on to become one of the most successful airlines in the world; never losing money and starting from scratch with no money. A Canadian example is WestJet, which was started by a number of partners by leasing property and airplanes, and hiring non-union staff. This enabled them to do business at a lower cost. WestJet gave its staff shares in the company which created an interest in the company for their employees, enabling them to provide better service than other airlines. One specific individual gradually bought out most of his partners and now this airline is now one of the fastest growing and most profitable airlines in North America.

Mattie invests:

1. Fifty percent of his money in real-estate. It has gained at least fifty to a hundred percent over the years as well as providing substantial rental income.
2. Twenty percent in blue-chip stocks, which has shown a ten percent gain over the years while paying a five percent dividend. These stocks are banks, pipelines, telephone, electrical utilities, and railroads.
3. Ten percent in equipment. Mattie has invested in rental equipment, he buys, rebuilds, rents for a couple of years – which pays for the equipment several times – then sells it for more than he originally paid for it, buying at a time when there's usually debt, divorce, or death, causing a quick sale.
4. Ten percent in gold which has doubled in price in the last few years which is very saleable should he need money for a business deal.
5. In GIC's for one year, this brings in several percent per year in interest and can be cashed at any time.
6. Five percent in cash which he invests in the various currencies in different countries which is readily available for living expenses, travelling, and donations to charity, community, church, and political parties.

The author was responsible for increasing revenue for doctors per patient from $21.80 to $39.00 because he feels it is so important to have good medical care in any part of North America. Canada and the United States are fortune to have excellent general practitioners and some of the best specialists in the world.

Mattie has outlined that in small business, you must be very careful of big business and big government. Good guys do not always win. Mattie could go on to list hundreds of companies he dealt with over the years who enabled his companies to be successful, also the hundreds of employees who went beyond their call of duty to work in Mattie's companies and who he could never pay enough for all of their hard work and dedication. They were exceptional employees. This also includes all the people who work for the various governments and big business that go out of their way to help small business owners to succeed. Should he name the people in this book that helped, it would be 1000 pages. All that can be said is a heartfelt thanks to each and every one and hope that the people who read this book will have the good fortune of meeting such wonderful people and become lifelong friends whose company you enjoy as you get old.

Mattie has outlined the problems with big foreign business, all governments and politicians in general.

It is now time to mention that small business who create 60 percent of the new jobs in Canada are operated for one main reason, to make a profit therefore a lot of them will scam a customer at the drop of a hat, so it is buyer beware.

The following are three articles out of "The Week", one of the best publications in the world, that outline the problems with one – the super rich, two – the stock brokers and stock market, and three – our bloated banking sector.

Some people may consider part of this book as a general rant against certain corporations and people in particular. If so, it's a long overdue rant and time for Canadians and Americans to start standing up for their countries which are in chaos and will fade into obscurity if people in general do not take immediate action.

The Splendid Isolation of the Super-Rich

Mike Lofgren

The super-rich "have seceded from America," said Mike Lofgren. "Our plutocracy now lives like the British in colonial India: in the place and ruling it, but not of it." Since the rich can afford their own security, "public safety is of no concern." From the windows of a Gulf-stream jet, crumbling bridges matter little. And with private doctors on call, they don't need to worry about the future of Medicare. This disconnect is why the super-rich so often sound "abstracted and clueless," and why "Mitt Romney's regular-guy anecdotes always seem a bit strained." Of course, the rich "have always secluded themselves." But over the past several decades, their "palpable animosity" toward the rest of America and its public institutions has become overt, even as their grip on power has tightened. Hedge fund billionaires with 15 percent tax rates complain that the poor lack "skin in the game." The rich decry social safety nets even as they stiff the system, and dismiss the military as a place "for suckers from the laboring classes." A century ago, we at least "got some attractive public libraries out of Andrew Carnegie." Today, our super-rich offer up little more than contempt.

It's Foolish to Focus on Stock Prices

Lynn Stout

The relentless pursuit of higher share prices has done investors no favors, said Lynn Stout. Maximizing "shareholder value" has been corporate America's religion for over three decades now. To crank up share prices, companies sell key assets, outsource jobs, shower CEOs with stock options, and drain cash reserves by paying out dividends. These tactics often produce short-term market bumps, but they also hurt a company's "long-term ability to grow and prosper." Investors have borne the brunt of this trade-off, suffering "more than a decade of the worst investor returns since the Great Depression." So why does the charade continue? Because investors continue to believe that companies are legally required to maximize returns in the short term, even though that's just a "pure myth." In reality, corporate directors have no such obligation. Only with the rise of the "Chicago School" of free-market economics in the 1980s did share price become the default gauge of corporate performance. It's time to step back from misguided short-term thinking so that companies can finally "do a better job for shareholders – and the rest of us too."

OUR BLOATED BANKING SECTOR

DAVID FUTRELLE

Do we really need so many bankers? asked David Futrelle. Though the financial sector is "as necessary for the economy as blood is for our bodies," it's grown far larger than it needs to be. In the 1950s, an era of growth and prosperity, the financial sector accounted for 3 percent of GDP. Today, it accounts for more than 8 percent, and "our economy is a mess." A new paper by several International Monetary Fund economists says large economics can have "too much finance," and that banking in the U.S. has almost certainly reached the point where it adds nothing to economic growth. But even if we reduce the number of our bankers, don't we still need to pay them top dollar? The research says no. A recent New York University study suggests that we're currently paying people in finance "anywhere from 30 to 50 percent more than they're worth." At those inflated rates, "bankers aren't adding value to the economy; they're extracting a 'rent' paid for by the rest of us." Until we better align our economic interests, "our financial sector will keep costing us more than it's worth."

For information on bulk purchases of
"MISFORTUNE TO MILLIONAIRE"
Please phone 1-866-279-1001 or write to
Marton Murphy & Associates
Suite F, 4415 – 58 Avenue S.E.
Calgary, Alberta T2C 1Y3

Any reader who wishes to submit their **travel experiences,**
we will publish in our travel book and give you credit.

Similarly, any person who wishes to **submit recipes** I
will publish in my recipe book and give you credit.

If you are an inspiring **experienced writer who wants to be an** author
please contact me through email: marton.murphy@hotmail.com

CPSIA information can be obtained at www.ICGtesting.com
Printed in the USA
BVOW030906061212

307414BV00001B/1/P